a wonderful adventure

TOTO!

1

Yuko Osada

Translated and adapted by Elina Ishikawa

Lettered by Foltz Design

DEL REY

Ballantine Books · New York

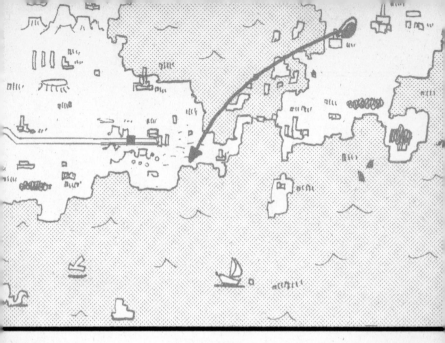

A Del Rey Manga/Kodansha Trade Paperback Original

Published in the United States by Del Rey Books, an imprint of The Random House Publishing Group, a division of Random House, Inc., New York.

DEL REY is a registered trademark and the Del Rey colophon is a trademark of Random House, Inc.

Publication rights arranged through Kodansha Ltd.

First published in Japan in 2005 by Kodansha Ltd., Tokyo

ISBN 978-0-345-50147-9

Printed in the United States of America

www.delreymanga.com

1 2 3 4 5 6 7 8 9

Translator/Adapter: Elina Ishikawa
Lettering: Foltz Design

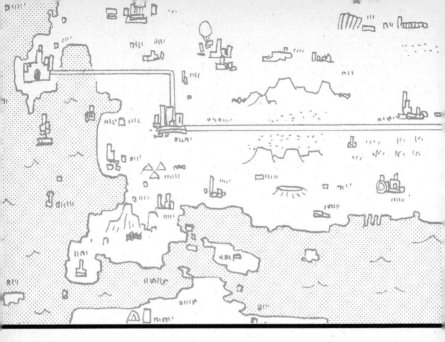

Contents

ToTo! the wonderful adventure

By Yuko Osada

CHILDREN'S
WORLD MAP

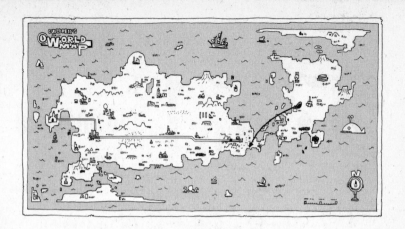

Contents

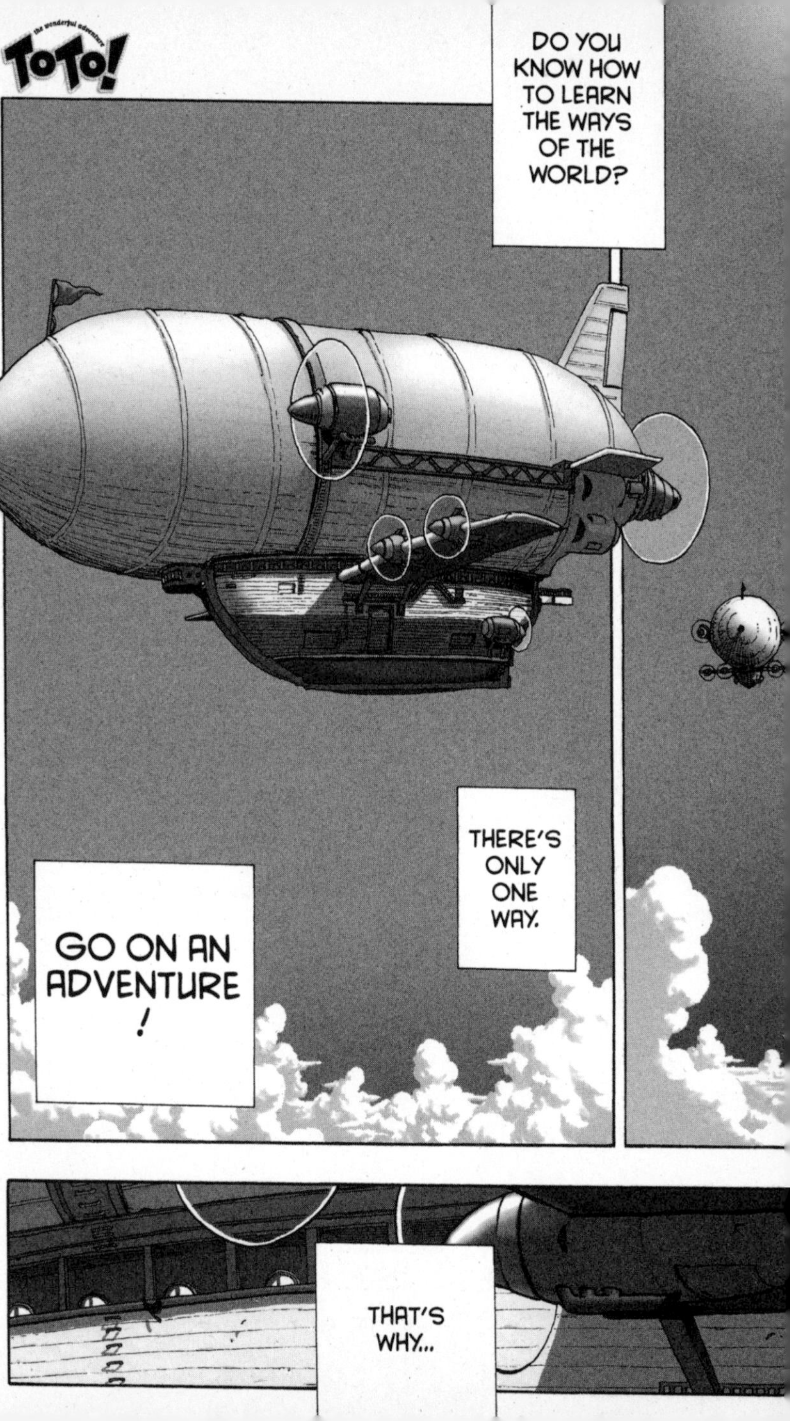
DO YOU KNOW HOW TO LEARN THE WAYS OF THE WORLD?
THERE'S ONLY ONE WAY.
GO ON AN ADVENTURE!
THAT'S WHY...

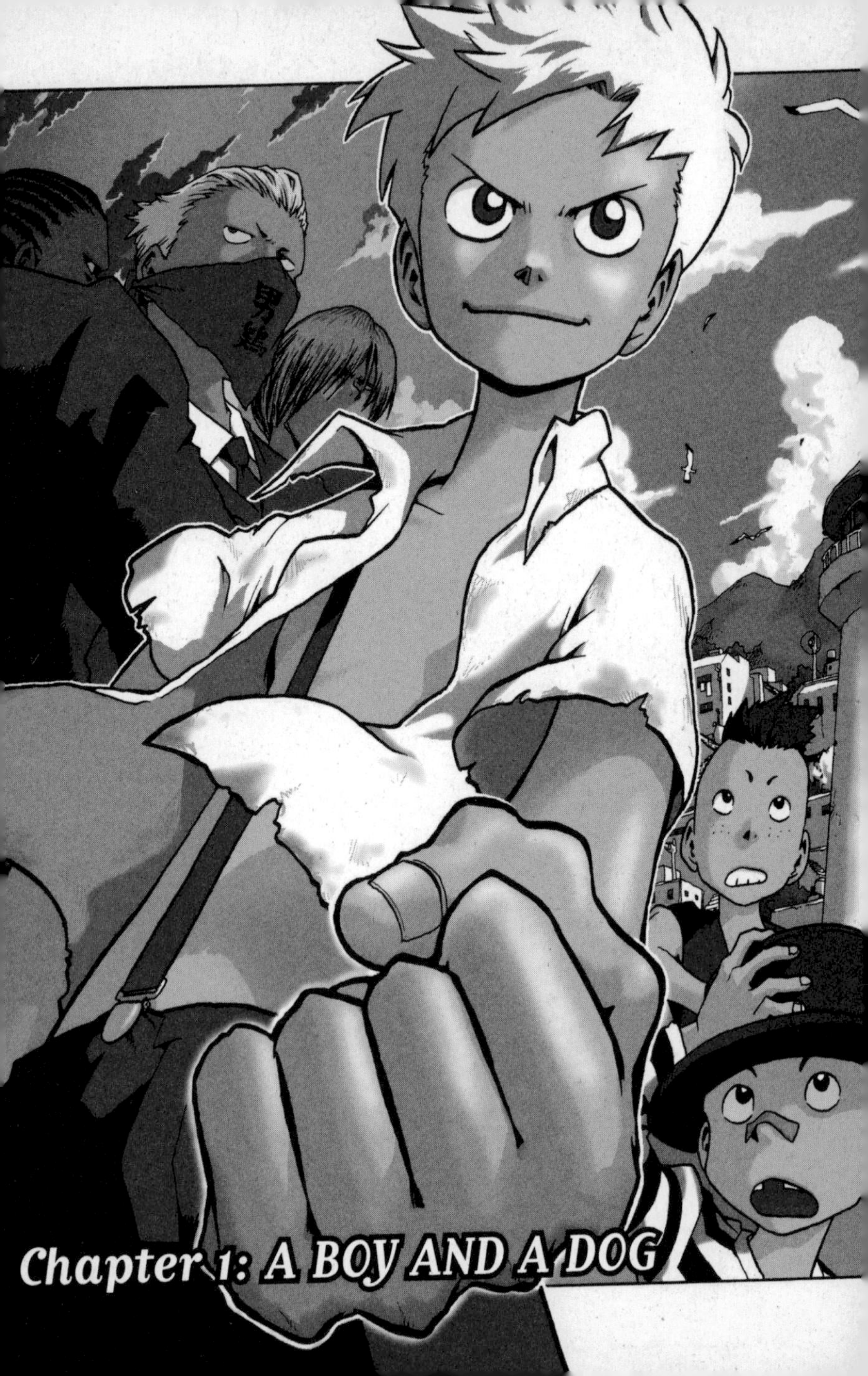

Chapter 1: A BOY AND A DOG

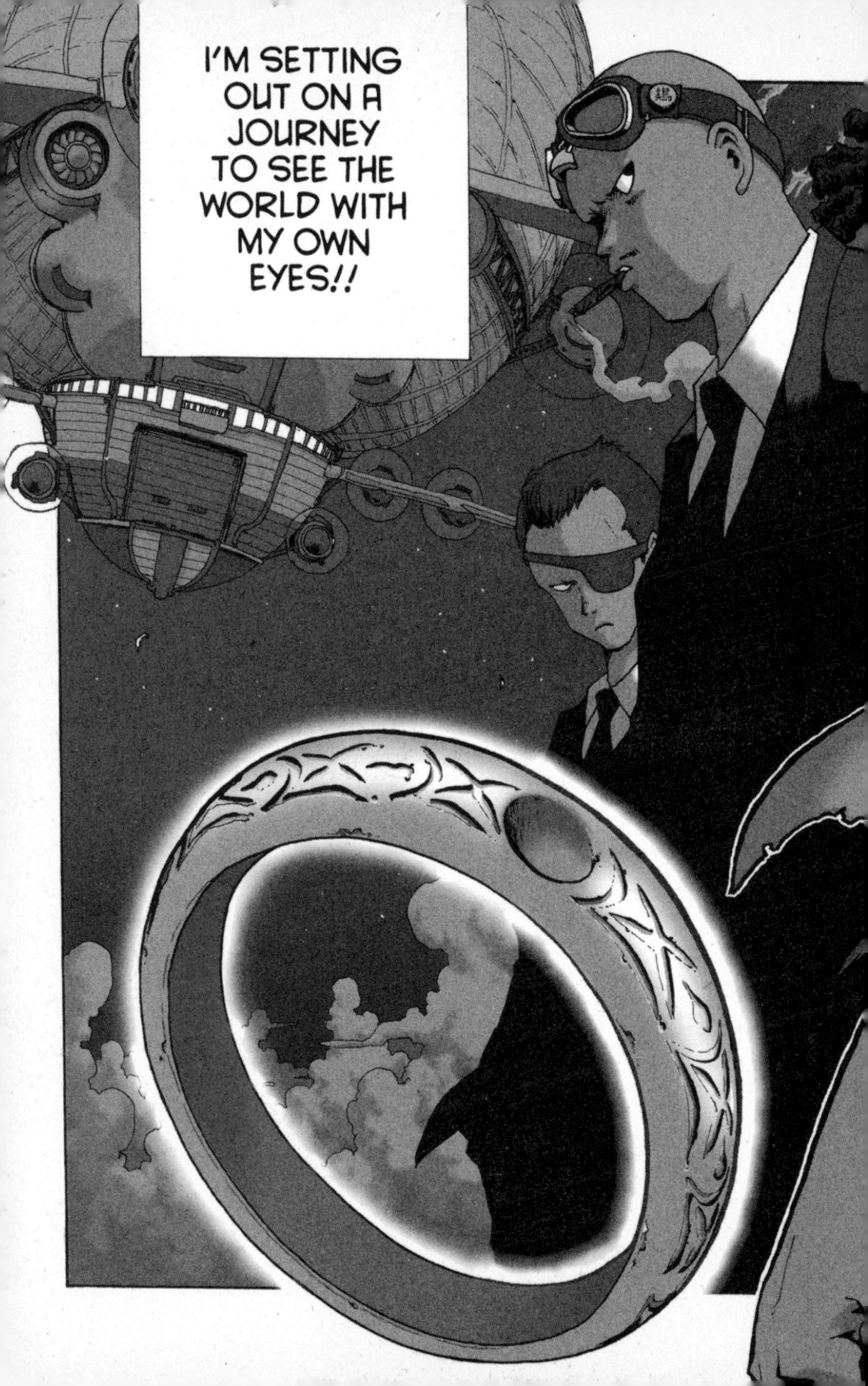
I'M SETTING OUT ON A JOURNEY TO SEE THE WORLD WITH MY OWN EYES!!

the wonderful adventure

TOTO!

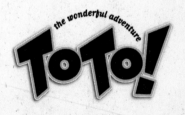

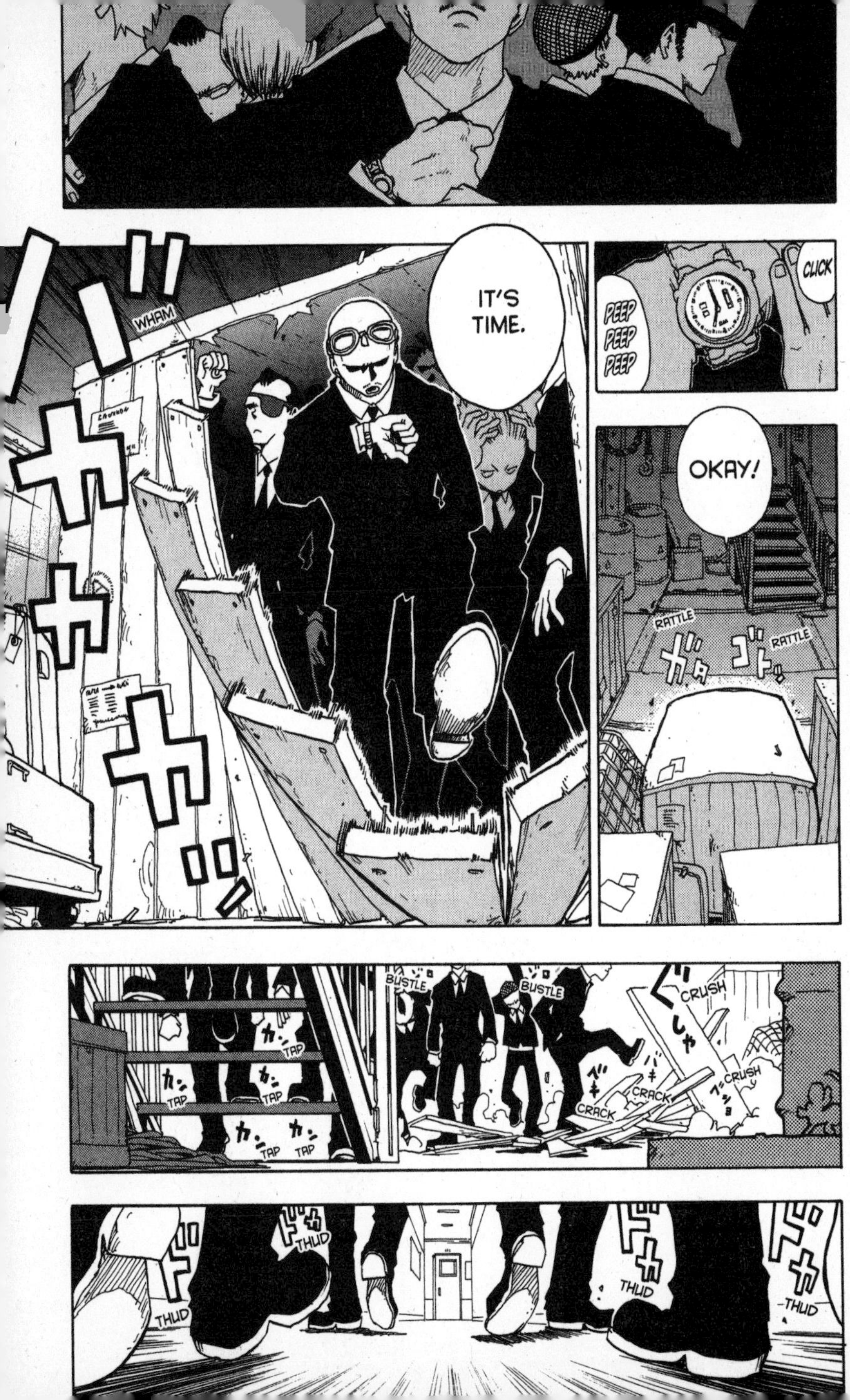
CLICK
PEEP PEEP PEEP
OKAY!
RATTLE
RATTLE
IT'S TIME.
WHAM
CRUSH
CRUSH
CRACK
CRACK
BUSTLE
BUSTLE
TAP
TAP
TAP
TAP
TAP
THUD
THUD
THUD
THUD

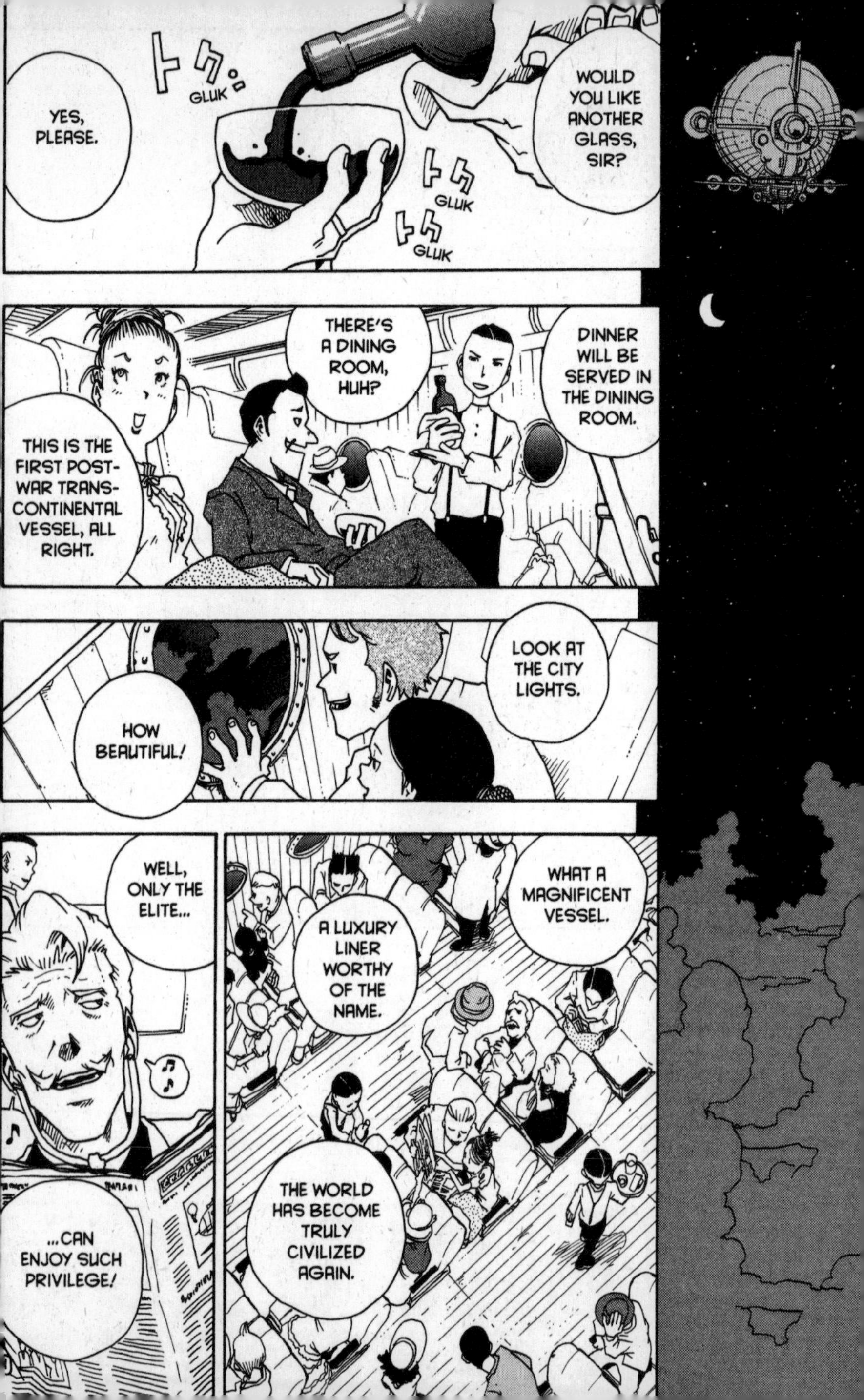
WOULD YOU LIKE ANOTHER GLASS, SIR?
トク GLUK
トク GLUK
トク GLUK
YES, PLEASE.
DINNER WILL BE SERVED IN THE DINING ROOM.
THERE'S A DINING ROOM, HUH?
THIS IS THE FIRST POST-WAR TRANS-CONTINENTAL VESSEL, ALL RIGHT.
LOOK AT THE CITY LIGHTS.
HOW BEAUTIFUL!
WHAT A MAGNIFICENT VESSEL.
A LUXURY LINER WORTHY OF THE NAME.
THE WORLD HAS BECOME TRULY CIVILIZED AGAIN.
WELL, ONLY THE ELITE...
...CAN ENJOY SUCH PRIVILEGE!

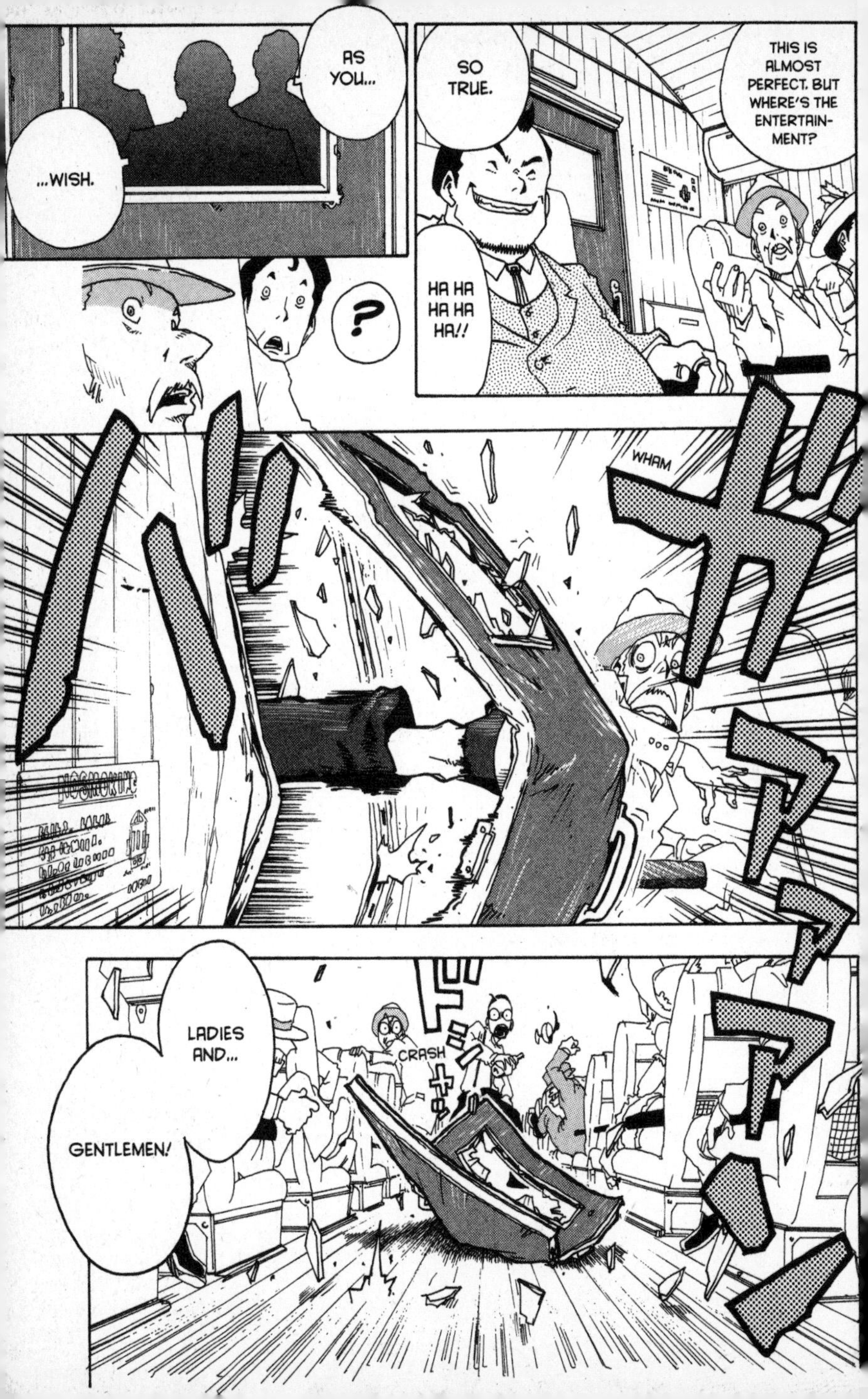
THIS IS ALMOST PERFECT. BUT WHERE'S THE ENTERTAINMENT?
SO TRUE.
HA HA HA HA HA!!
AS YOU...
...WISH.
?
WHAM
CRASH
LADIES AND...
GENTLEMEN!

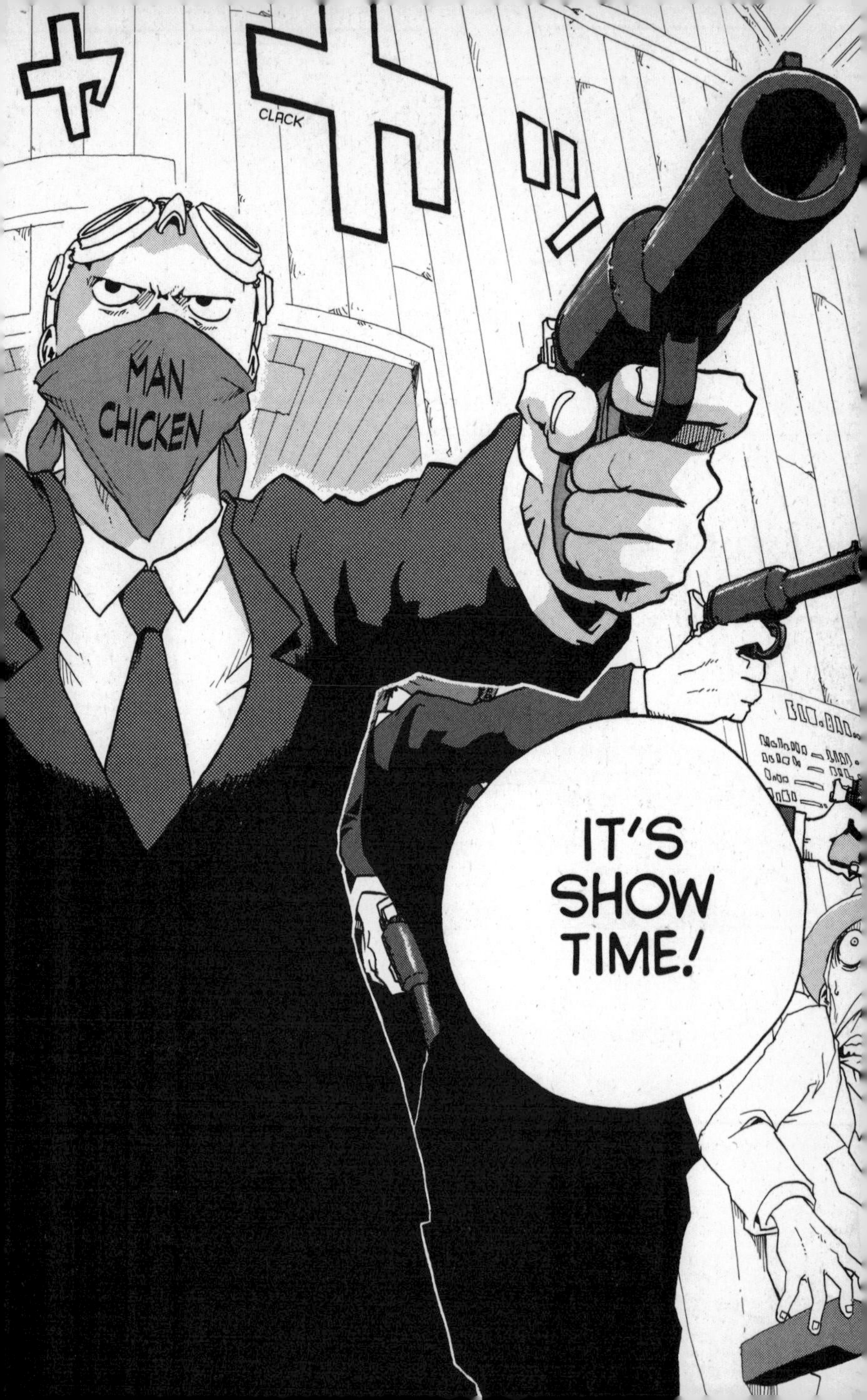
CLACK
MAN CHICKEN
IT'S SHOW TIME!

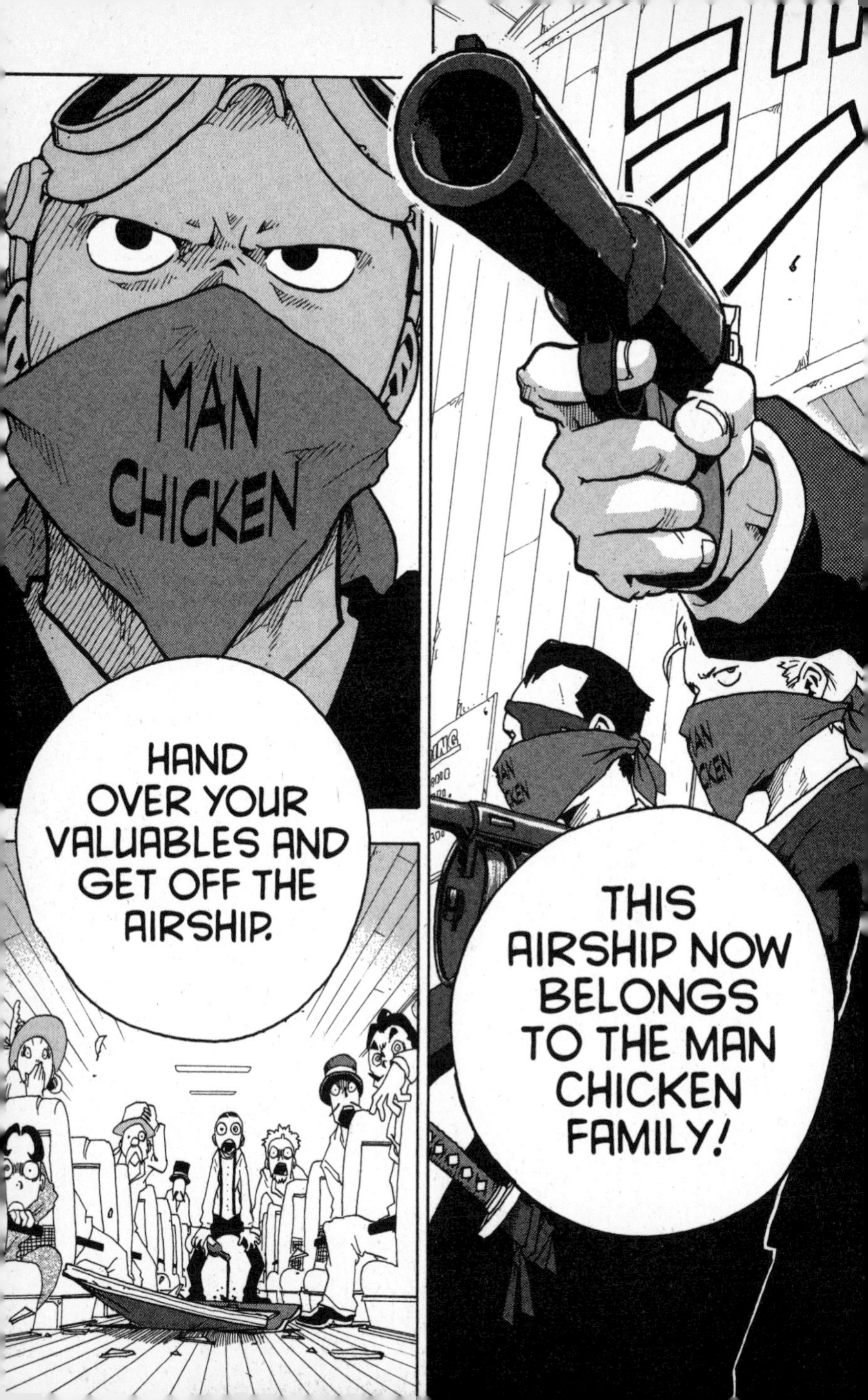
THIS AIRSHIP NOW BELONGS TO THE MAN CHICKEN FAMILY!
MAN CHICKEN
HAND OVER YOUR VALUABLES AND GET OFF THE AIRSHIP.

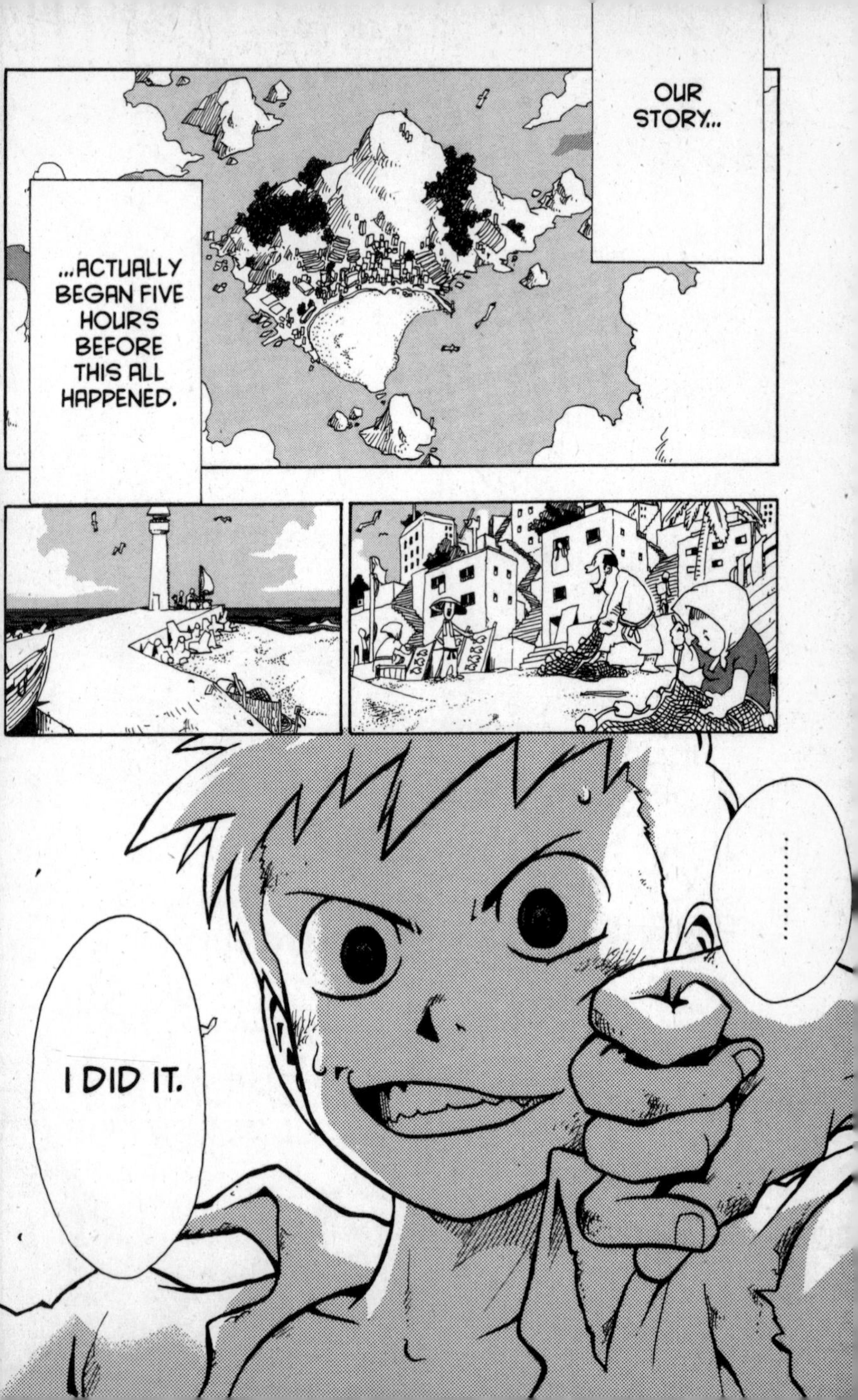
OUR STORY...
...ACTUALLY BEGAN FIVE HOURS BEFORE THIS ALL HAPPENED.
....
I DID IT.

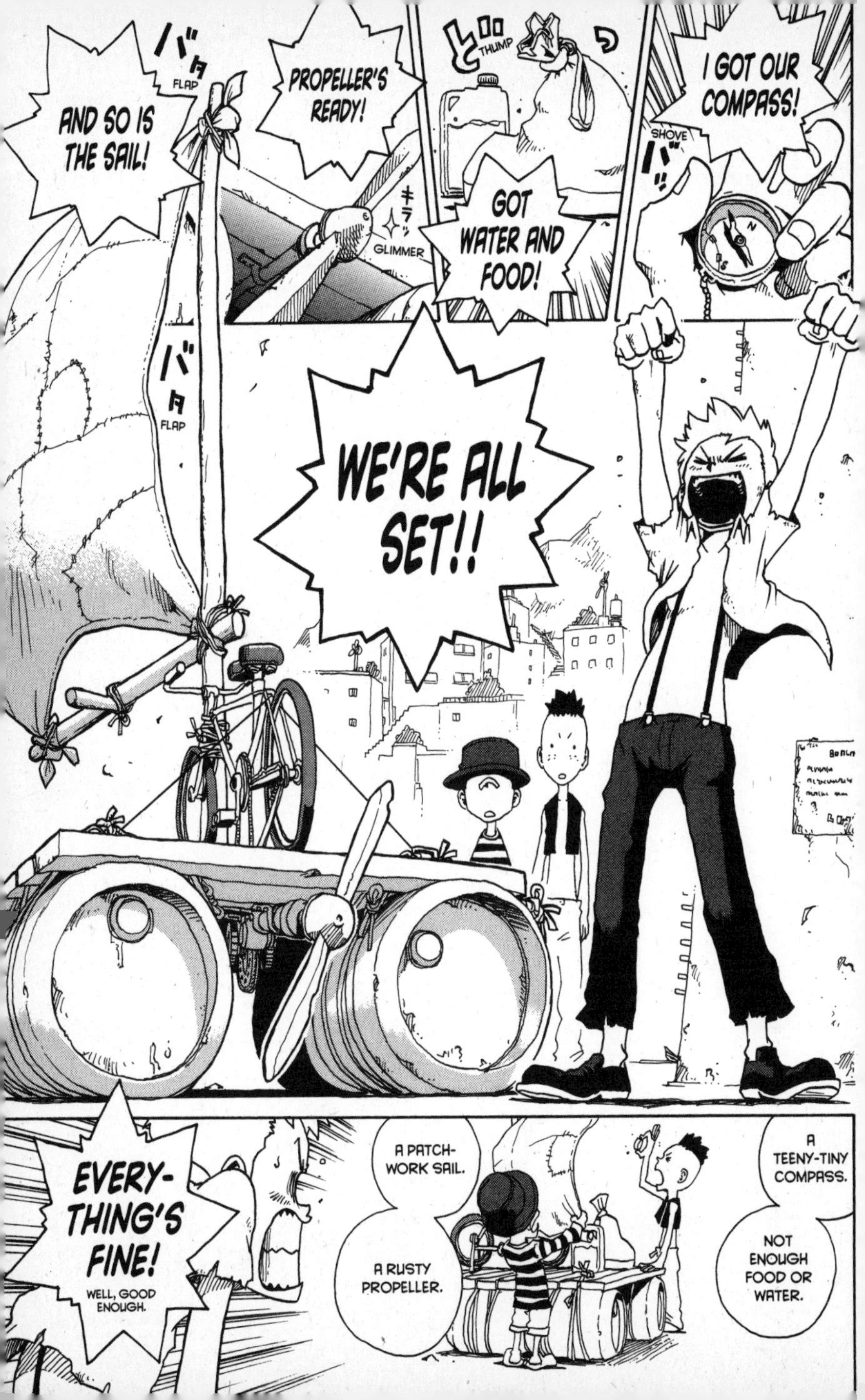

I GOT OUR COMPASS!
バッ
SHOVE
THUMP
GOT WATER AND FOOD!
PROPELLER'S READY!
キラッ
GLIMMER
AND SO IS THE SAIL!
バタ
FLAP
WE'RE ALL SET!!
バタ
FLAP
A TEENY-TINY COMPASS.
NOT ENOUGH FOOD OR WATER.
A PATCH-WORK SAIL.
A RUSTY PROPELLER.
EVERY-THING'S FINE!
WELL, GOOD ENOUGH.

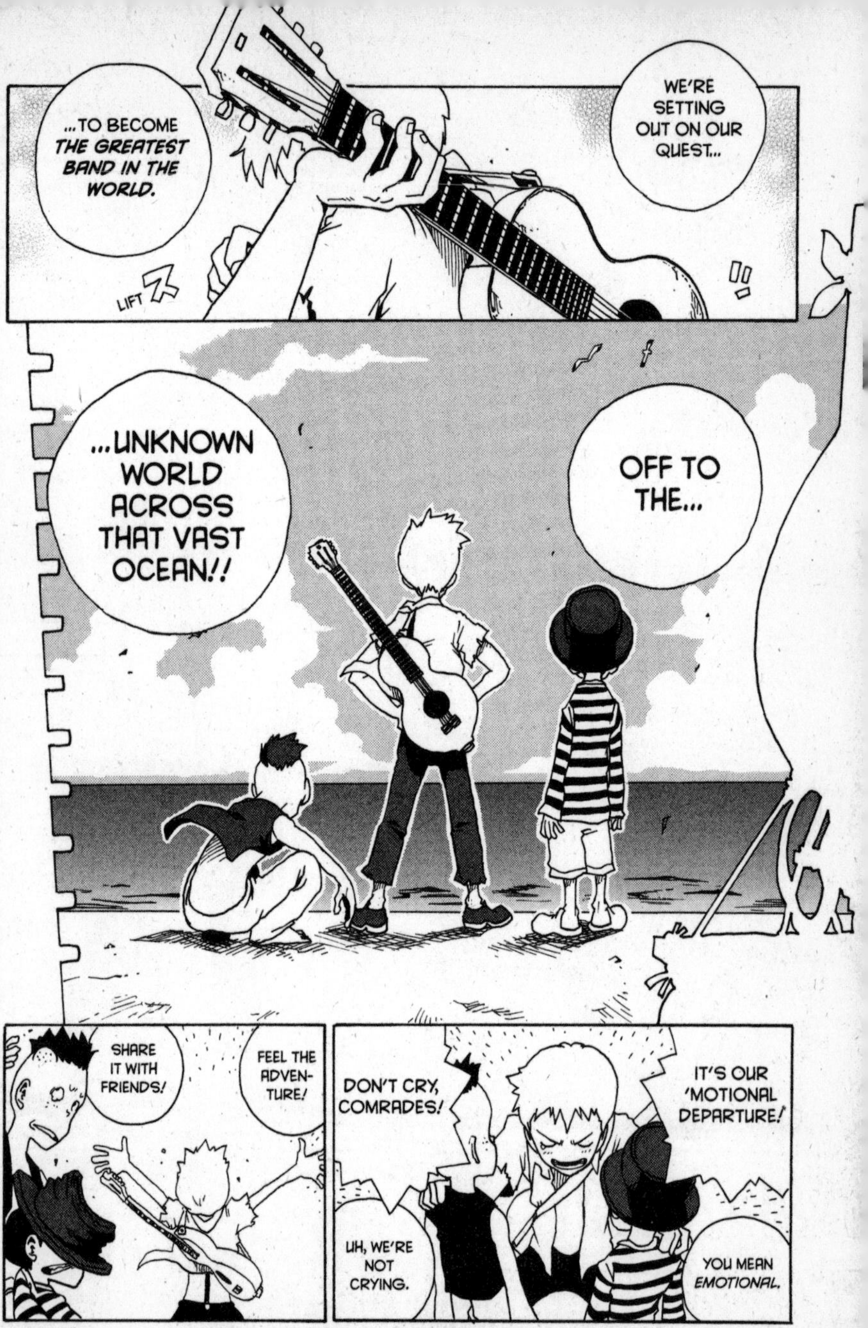
WE'RE SETTING OUT ON OUR QUEST...
...TO BECOME *THE GREATEST BAND IN THE WORLD.*
LIFT
OFF TO THE...
...UNKNOWN WORLD ACROSS THAT VAST OCEAN!!
IT'S OUR 'MOTIONAL DEPARTURE!
DON'T CRY, COMRADES!
YOU MEAN *EMOTIONAL.*
UH, WE'RE NOT CRYING.
FEEL THE ADVEN-TURE!
SHARE IT WITH FRIENDS!

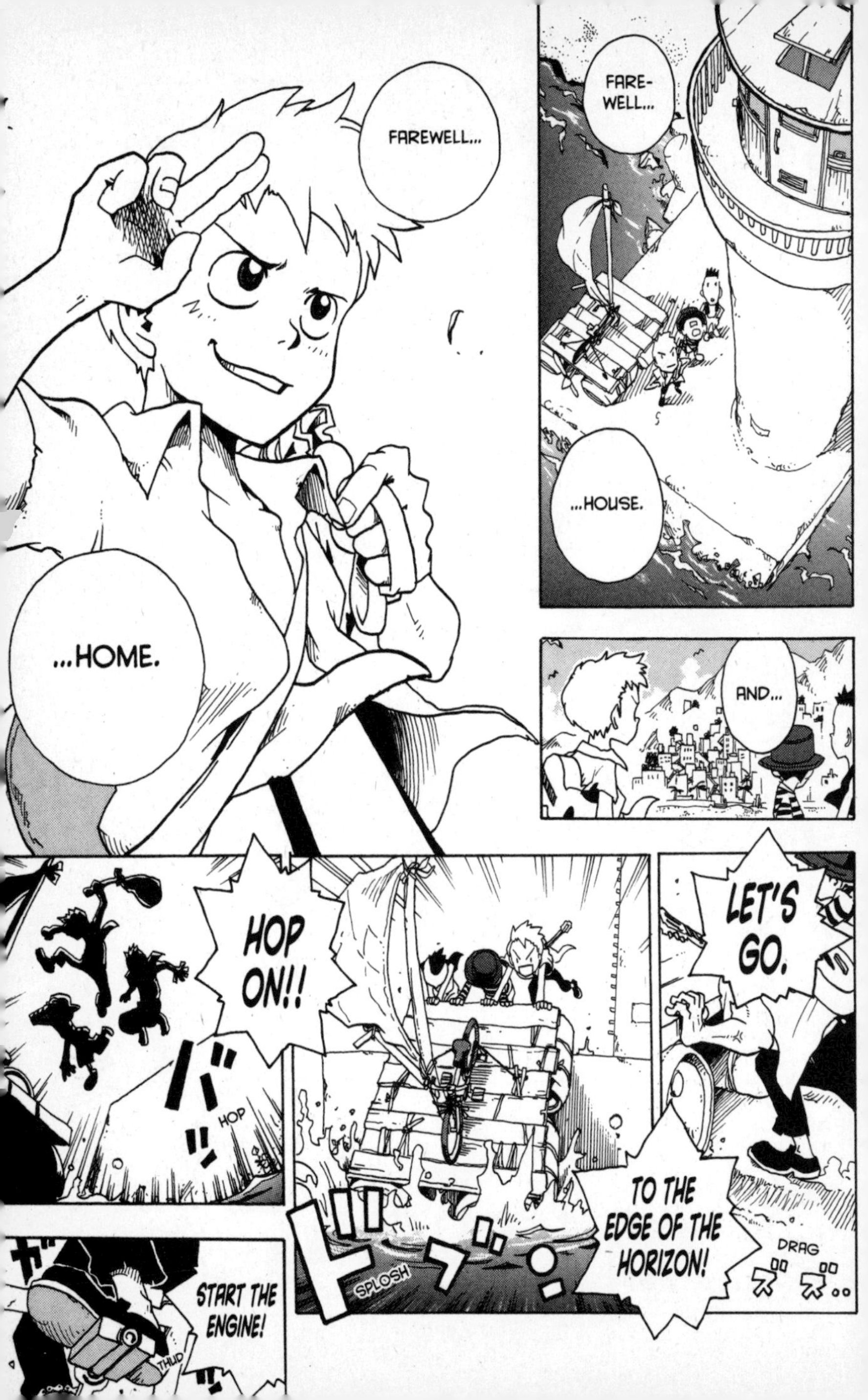
FARE-
WELL...
...HOUSE.
AND...
FAREWELL...
...HOME.
LET'S GO.
DRAG
TO THE EDGE OF THE HORIZON!
SPLOSH
HOP ON!!
HOP
START THE ENGINE!
THUD

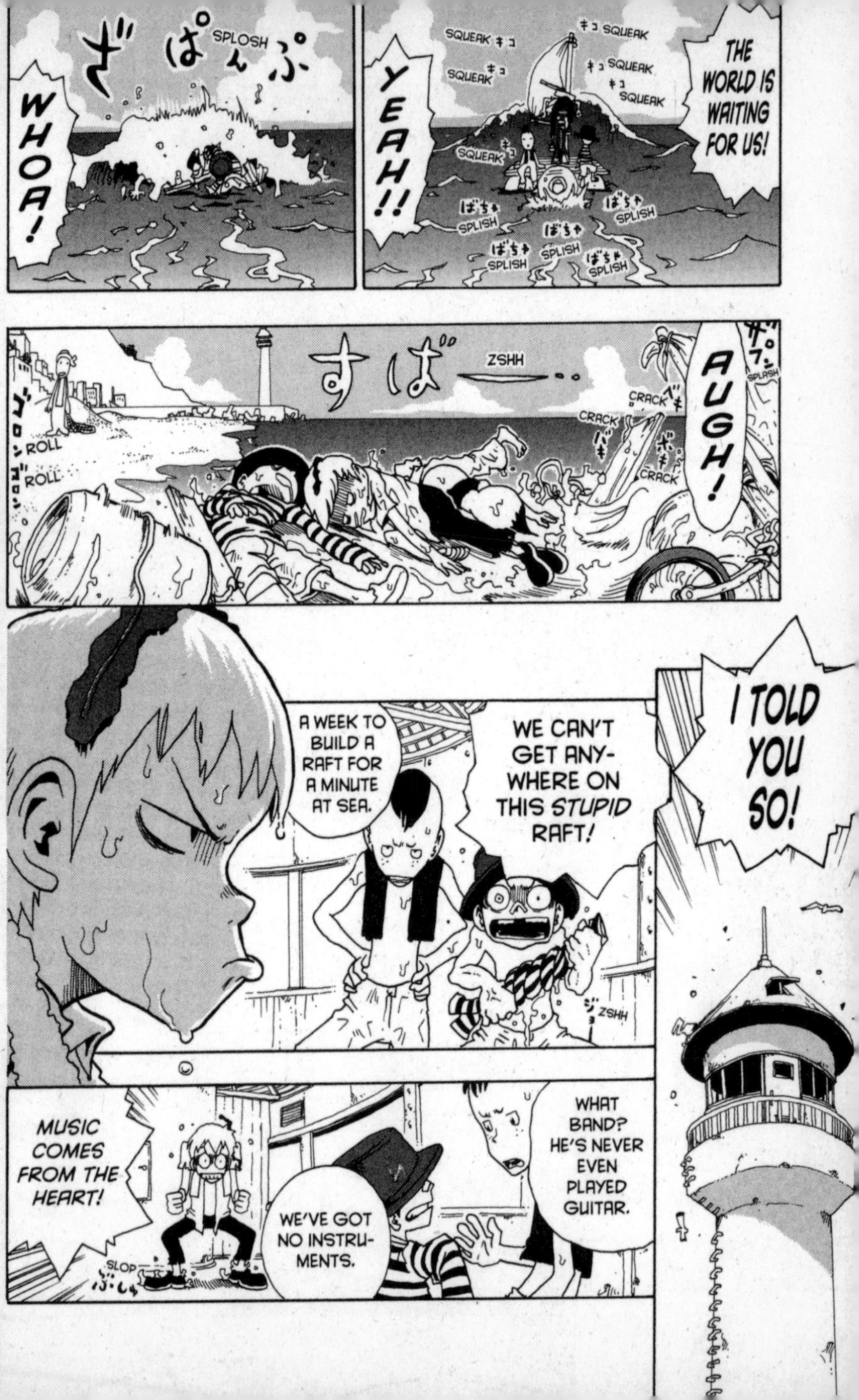
THE WORLD IS WAITING FOR US!
YEAH!!
キコ SQUEAK
キコ SQUEAK
キコ SQUEAK
SQUEAK キコ
SQUEAK キコ
SQUEAK キコ
ばちゃ SPLISH
ばちゃ SPLISH
ばちゃ SPLISH
ばちゃ SPLISH
ばちゃ SPLISH
ざぱんぷ SPLOSH
WHOA!
AUGH!
ザプン SPLASH
CRACK ベキ
CRACK バキ
ボキ CRACK
すばー ZSHH
ゴロン ROLL
ゴロン ROLL
I TOLD YOU SO!
WE CAN'T GET ANY-WHERE ON THIS STUPID RAFT!
A WEEK TO BUILD A RAFT FOR A MINUTE AT SEA.
ジョ ZSHH
WHAT BAND? HE'S NEVER EVEN PLAYED GUITAR.
WE'VE GOT NO INSTRU-MENTS.
MUSIC COMES FROM THE HEART!
SLOP ぶしゅ

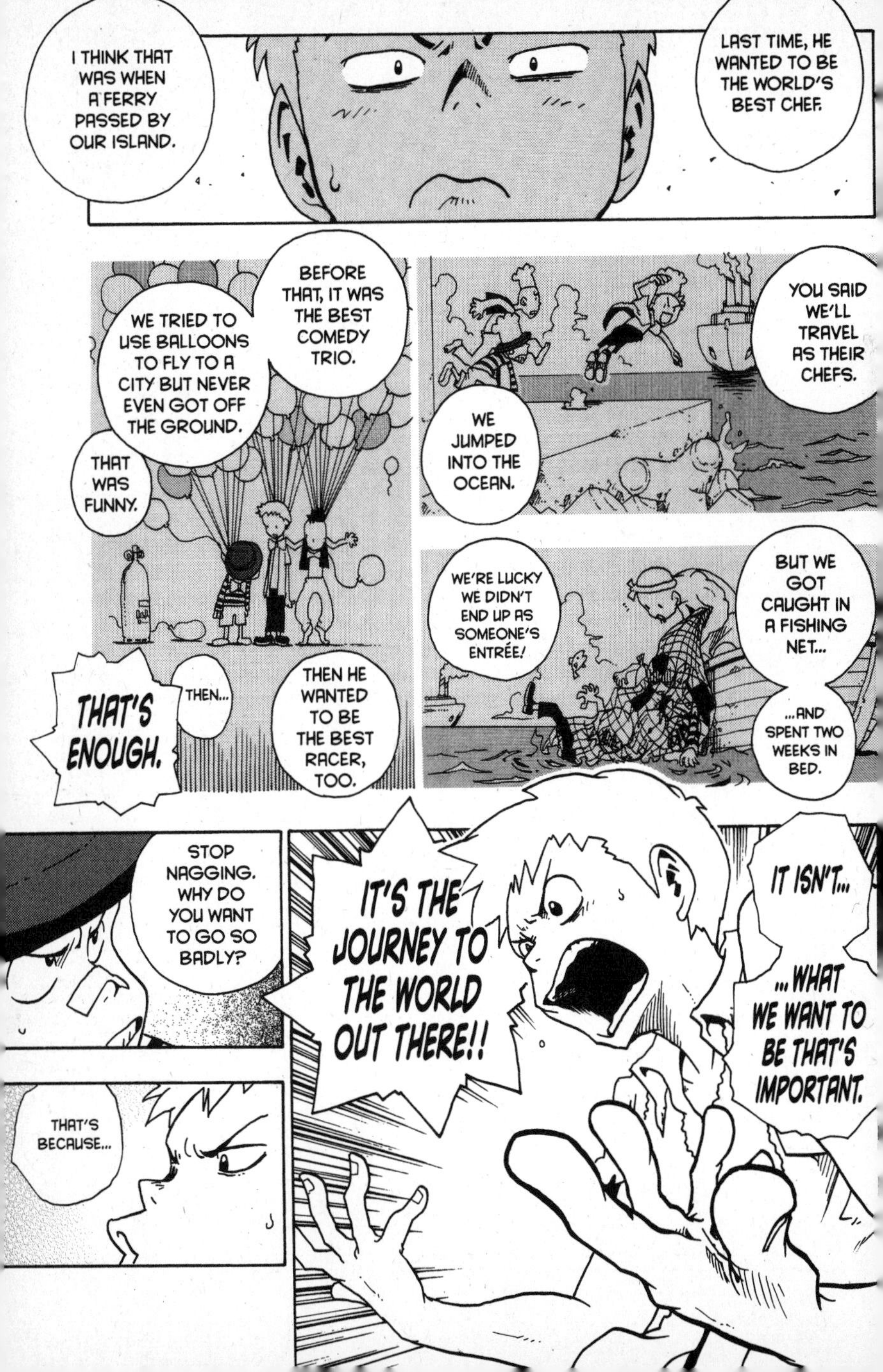
LAST TIME, HE WANTED TO BE THE WORLD'S BEST CHEF.
I THINK THAT WAS WHEN A FERRY PASSED BY OUR ISLAND.
YOU SAID WE'LL TRAVEL AS THEIR CHEFS.
WE JUMPED INTO THE OCEAN.
BUT WE GOT CAUGHT IN A FISHING NET...
...AND SPENT TWO WEEKS IN BED.
WE'RE LUCKY WE DIDN'T END UP AS SOMEONE'S ENTRÉE!
BEFORE THAT, IT WAS THE BEST COMEDY TRIO.
WE TRIED TO USE BALLOONS TO FLY TO A CITY BUT NEVER EVEN GOT OFF THE GROUND.
THAT WAS FUNNY.
THEN HE WANTED TO BE THE BEST RACER, TOO.
THEN...
THAT'S ENOUGH.
IT ISN'T...
...WHAT WE WANT TO BE THAT'S IMPORTANT.
IT'S THE JOURNEY TO THE WORLD OUT THERE!!
STOP NAGGING. WHY DO YOU WANT TO GO SO BADLY?
THAT'S BECAUSE...

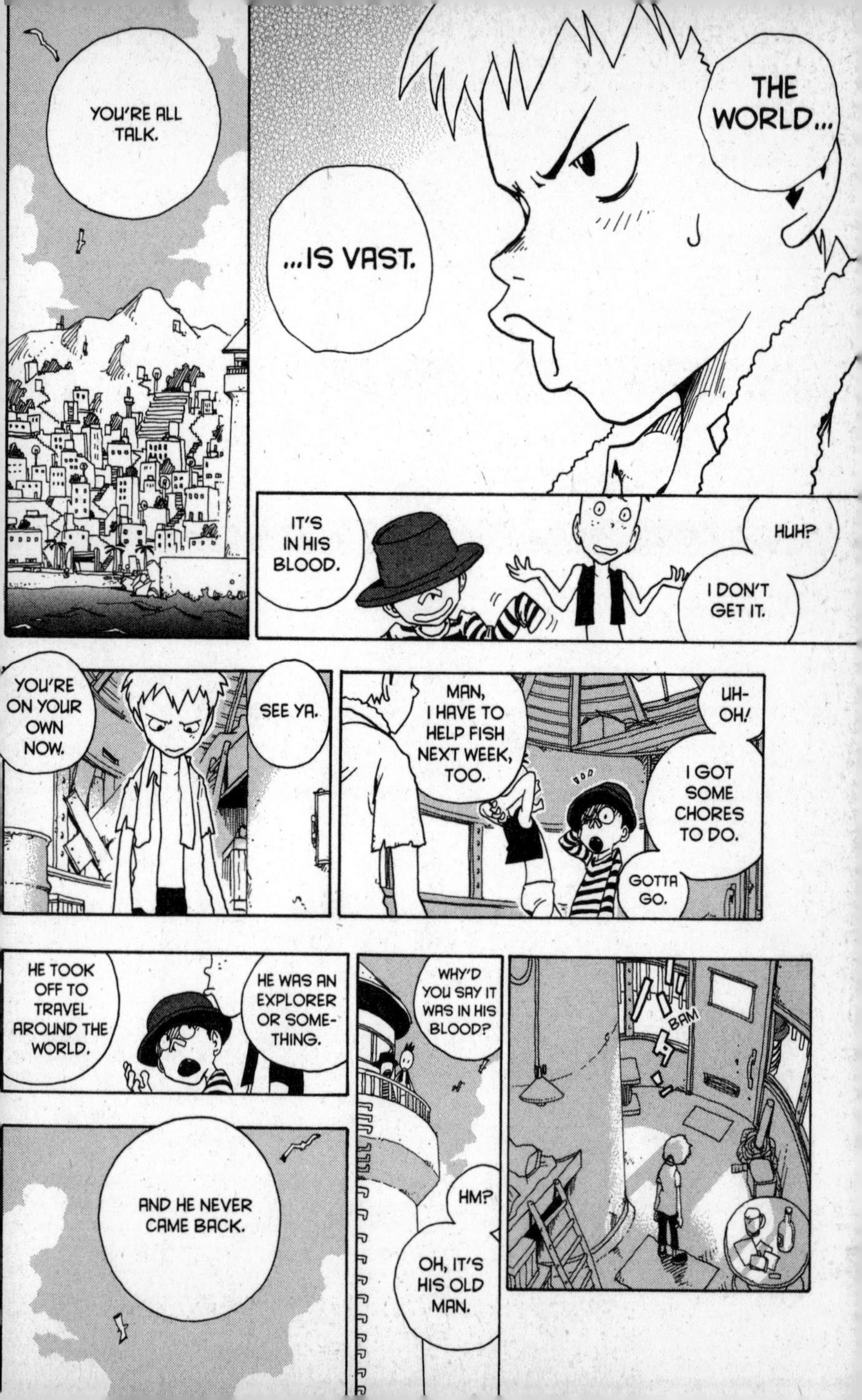
THE WORLD...
...IS VAST.
HUH?
I DON'T GET IT.
IT'S IN HIS BLOOD.
YOU'RE ALL TALK.
UH-OH!
I GOT SOME CHORES TO DO.
MAN, I HAVE TO HELP FISH NEXT WEEK, TOO.
GOTTA GO.
SEE YA.
YOU'RE ON YOUR OWN NOW.
BAM
WHY'D YOU SAY IT WAS IN HIS BLOOD?
HM?
OH, IT'S HIS OLD MAN.
HE WAS AN EXPLORER OR SOME-THING.
HE TOOK OFF TO TRAVEL AROUND THE WORLD.
AND HE NEVER CAME BACK.

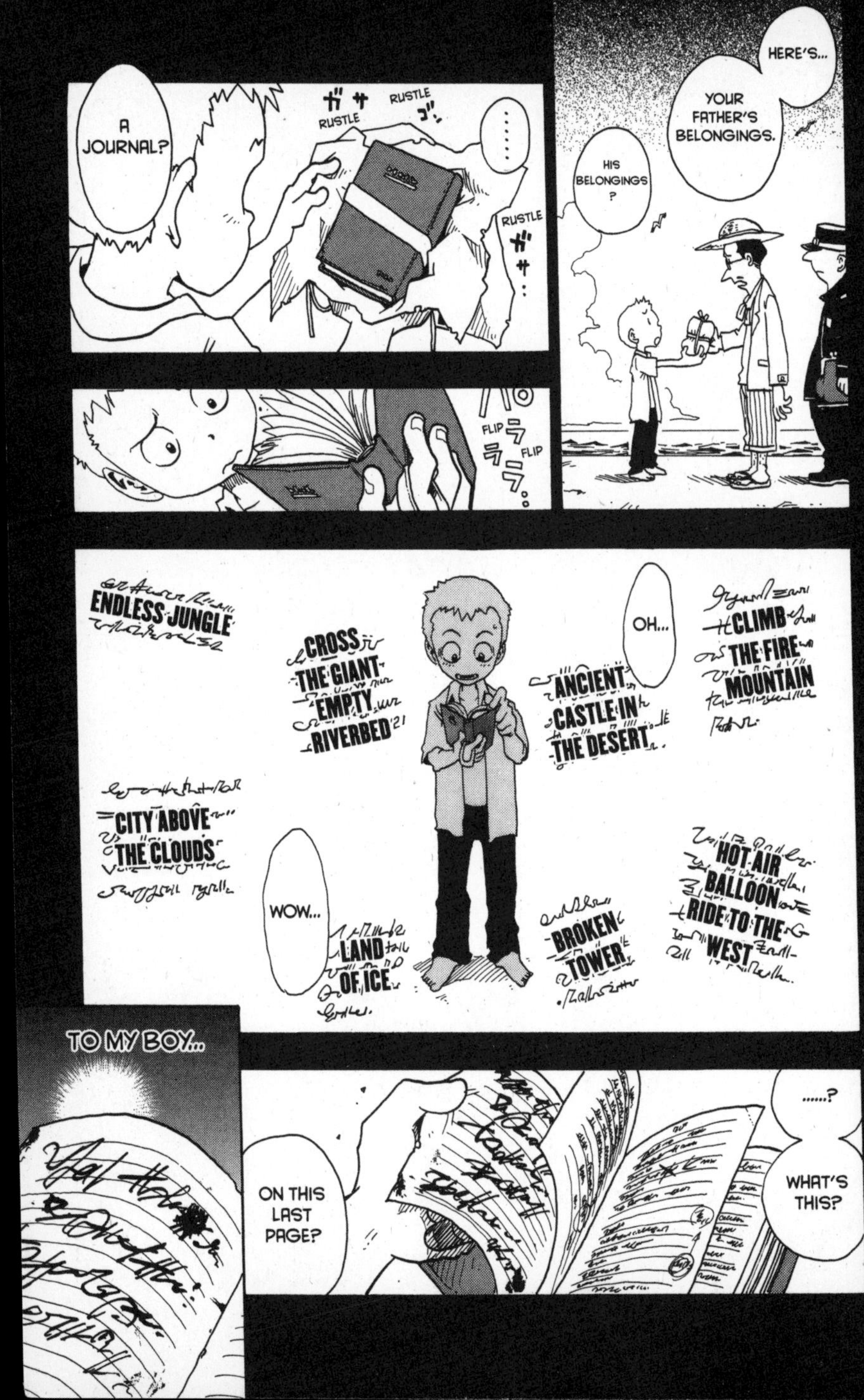
HERE'S...
YOUR FATHER'S BELONGINGS.
HIS BELONGINGS?
RUSTLE
RUSTLE
......
A JOURNAL?
RUSTLE
FLIP
FLIP
OH...
CLIMB THE FIRE MOUNTAIN
ANCIENT CASTLE IN THE DESERT
CROSS THE GIANT EMPTY RIVERBED
ENDLESS JUNGLE
HOT AIR BALLOON RIDE TO THE WEST
BROKEN TOWER
LAND OF ICE
WOW...
CITY ABOVE THE CLOUDS
......?
WHAT'S THIS?
ON THIS LAST PAGE?
TO MY BOY...

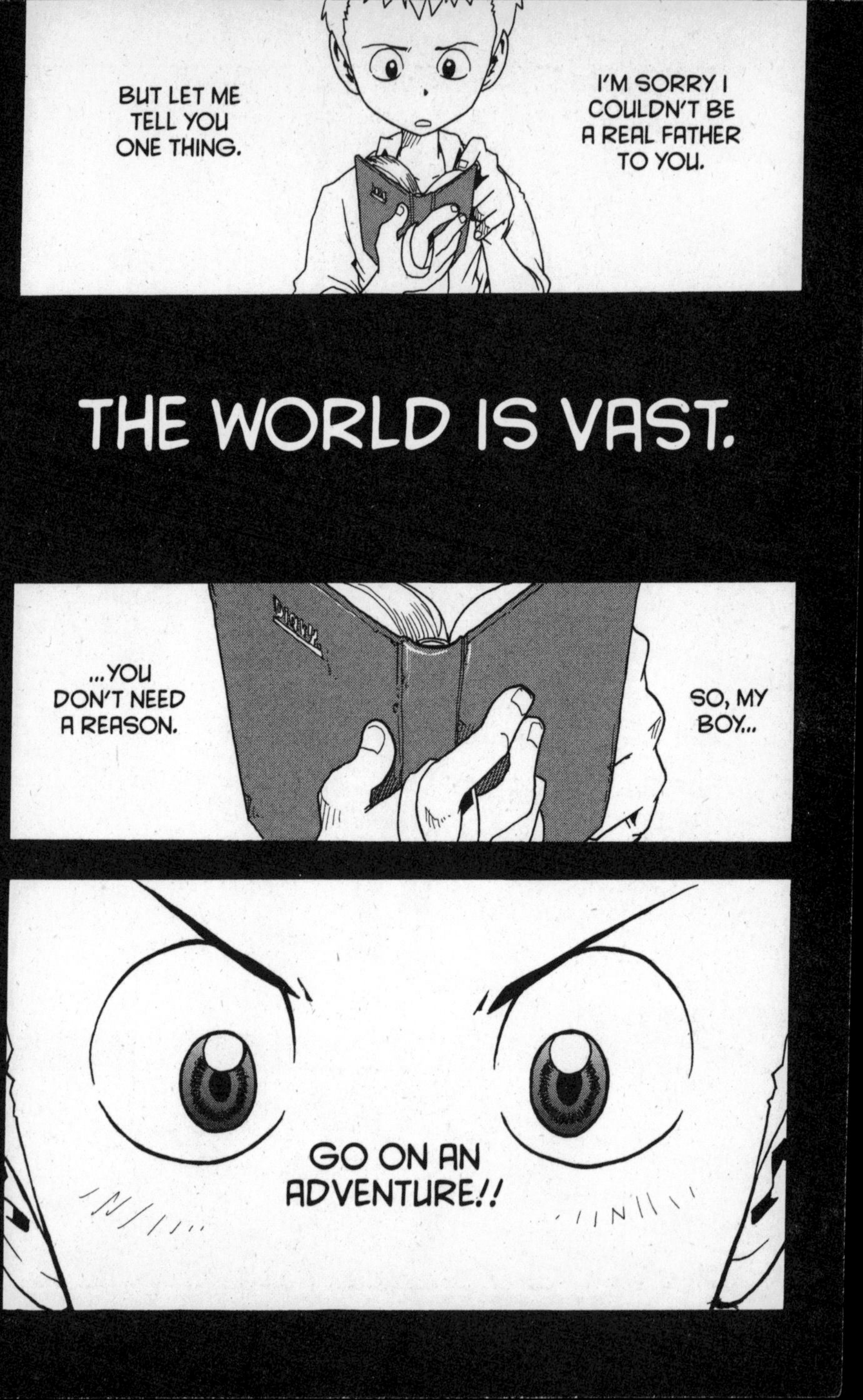
I'M SORRY I COULDN'T BE A REAL FATHER TO YOU.
BUT LET ME TELL YOU ONE THING.
THE WORLD IS VAST.
SO, MY BOY...
...YOU DON'T NEED A REASON.
GO ON AN ADVENTURE!!

……
FLOP
SHFF
スッ
ギィ
CREAK

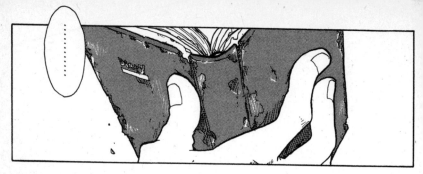

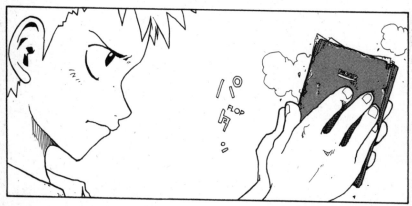

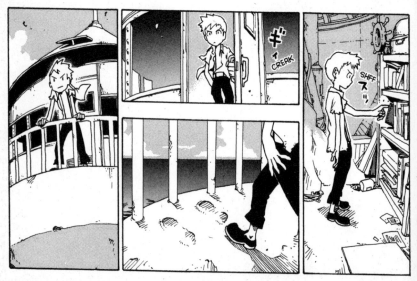

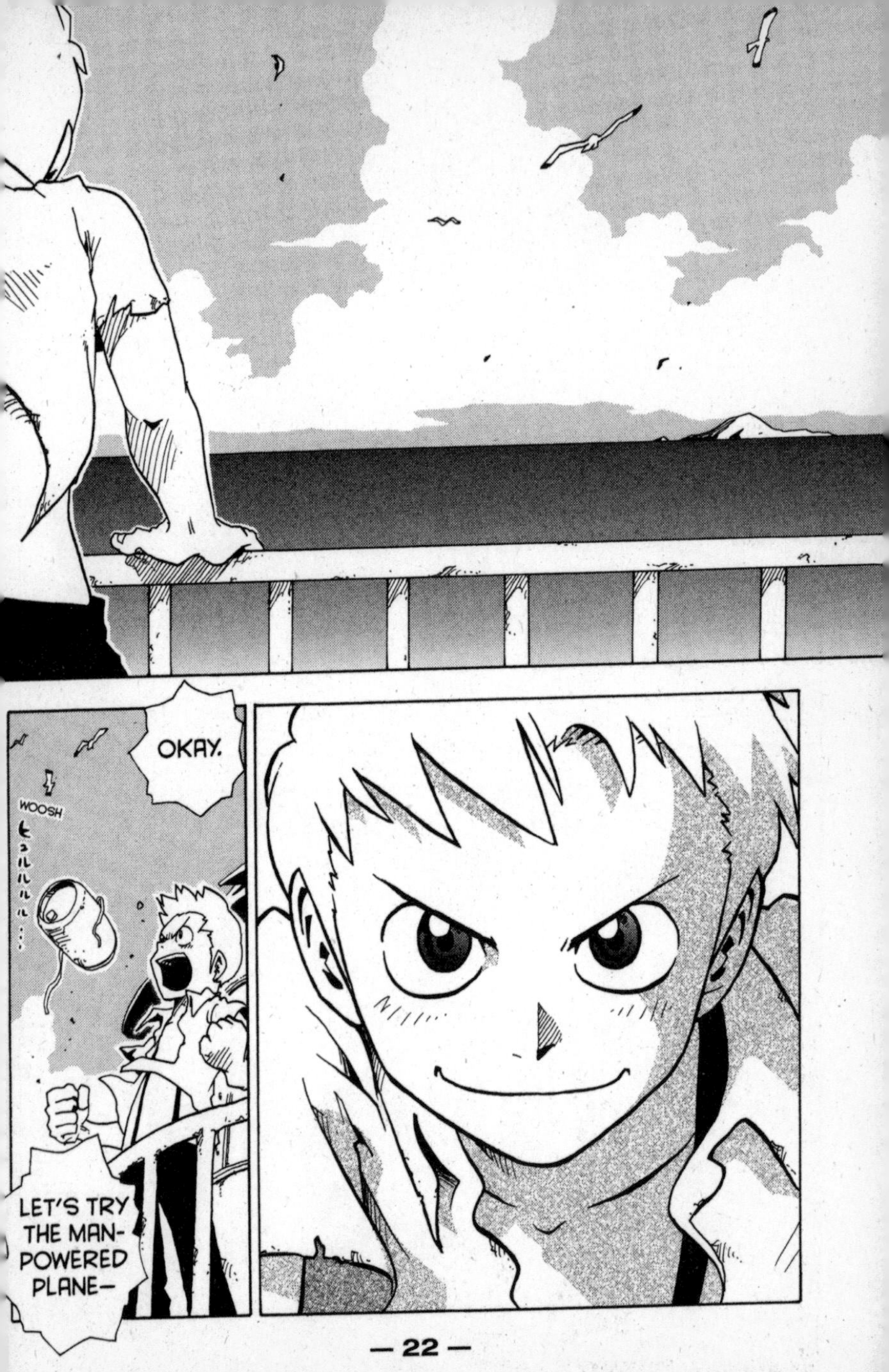
OKAY.
WOOSH
ヒュルルル…
LET'S TRY THE MAN-POWERED PLANE—

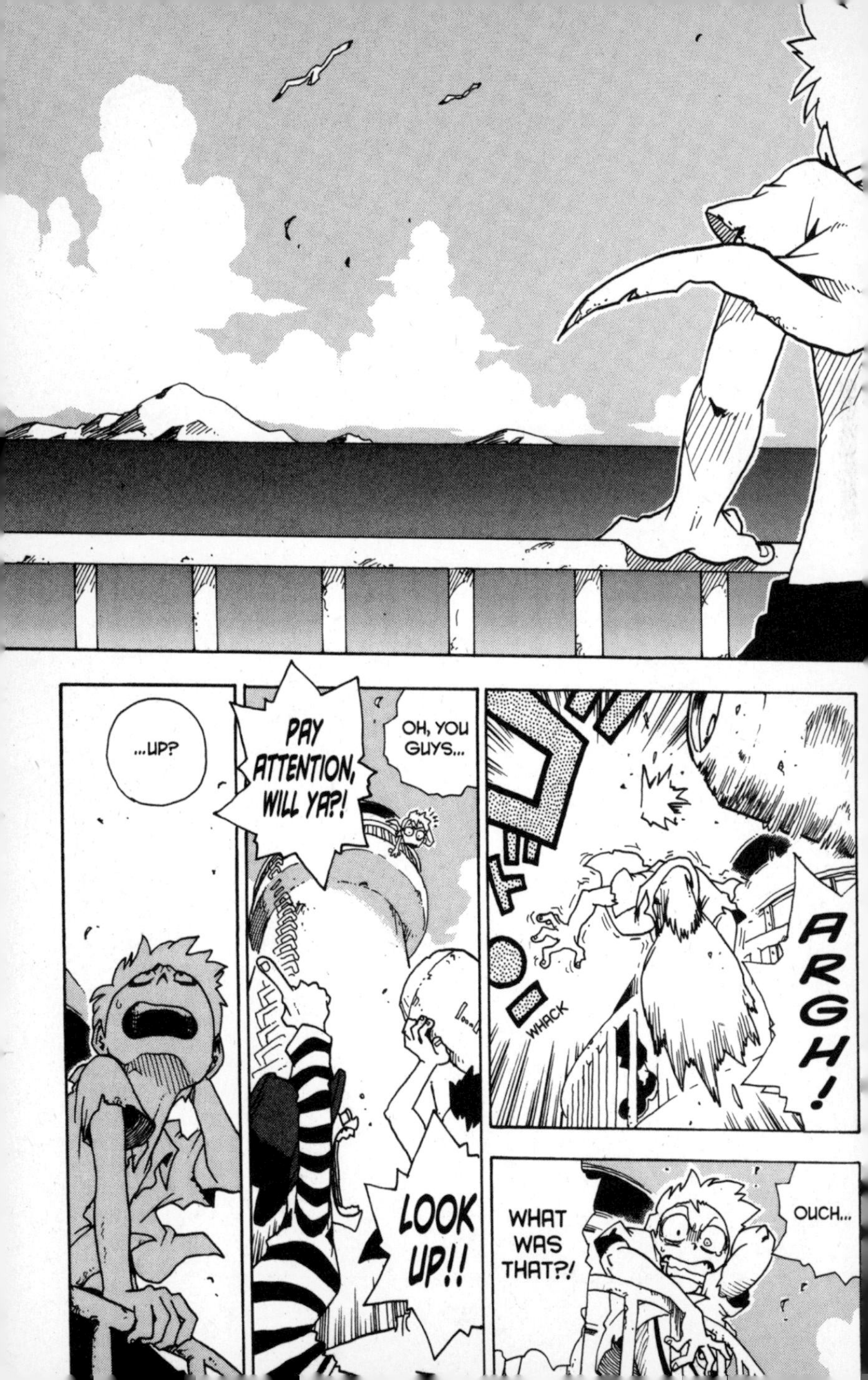
ARGH!
WHACK
OUCH...
WHAT WAS THAT?!
OH, YOU GUYS...
PAY ATTENTION, WILL YA?!
LOOK UP!!
...UP?

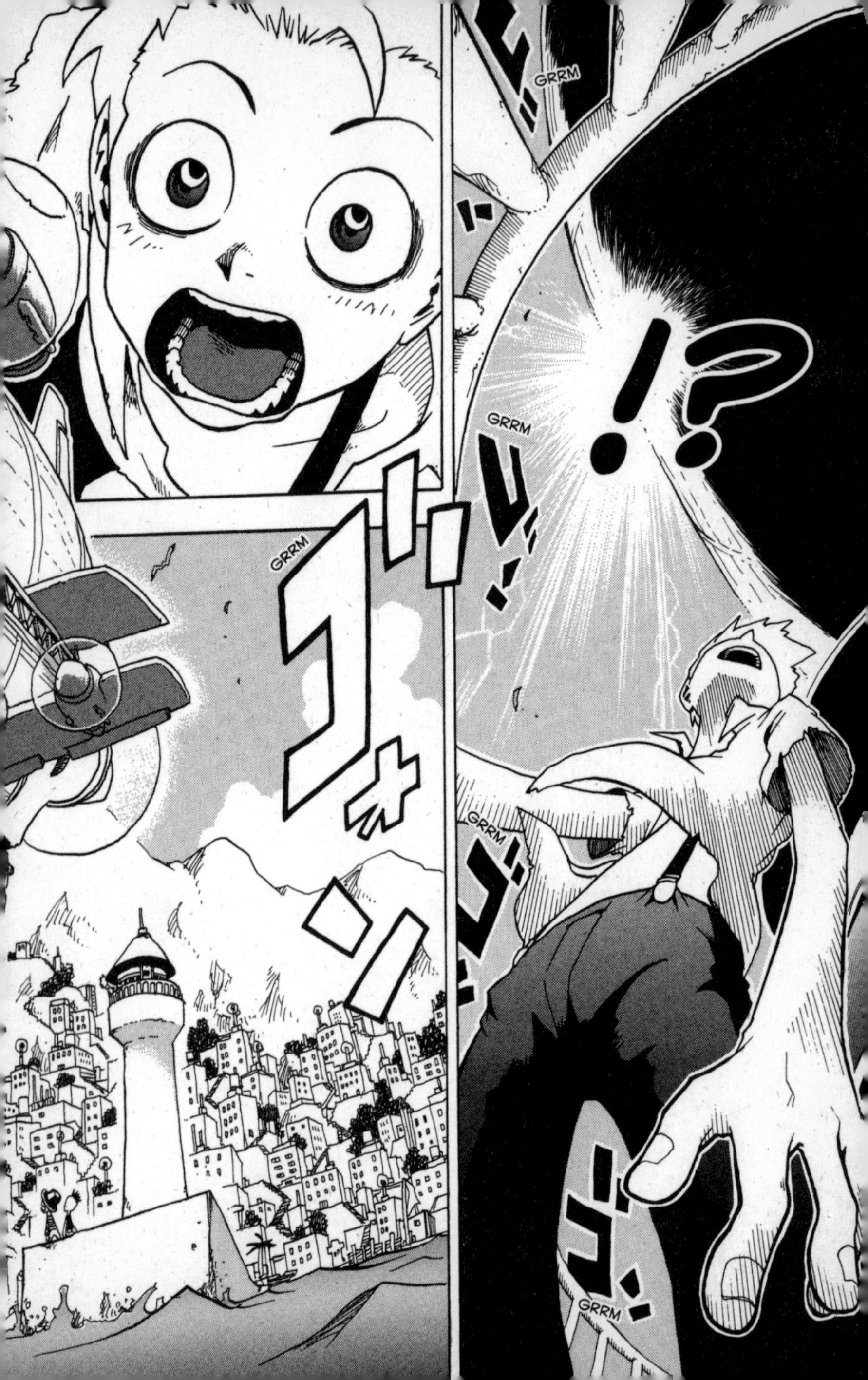

GRRM
!?
GRRM
GRRM
GRRM
GRRM

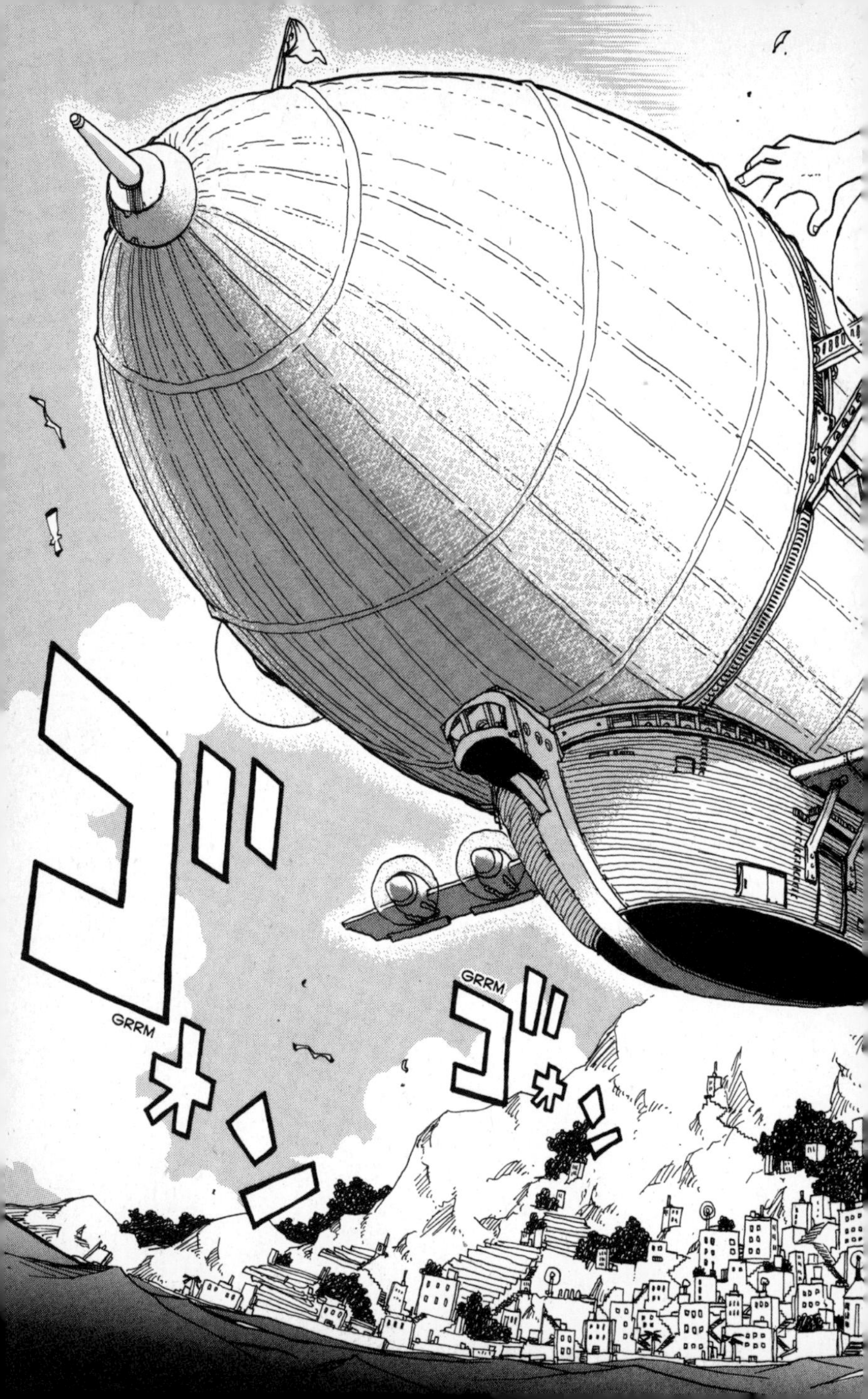
ゴォン
GRRM
ゴォン
GRRM

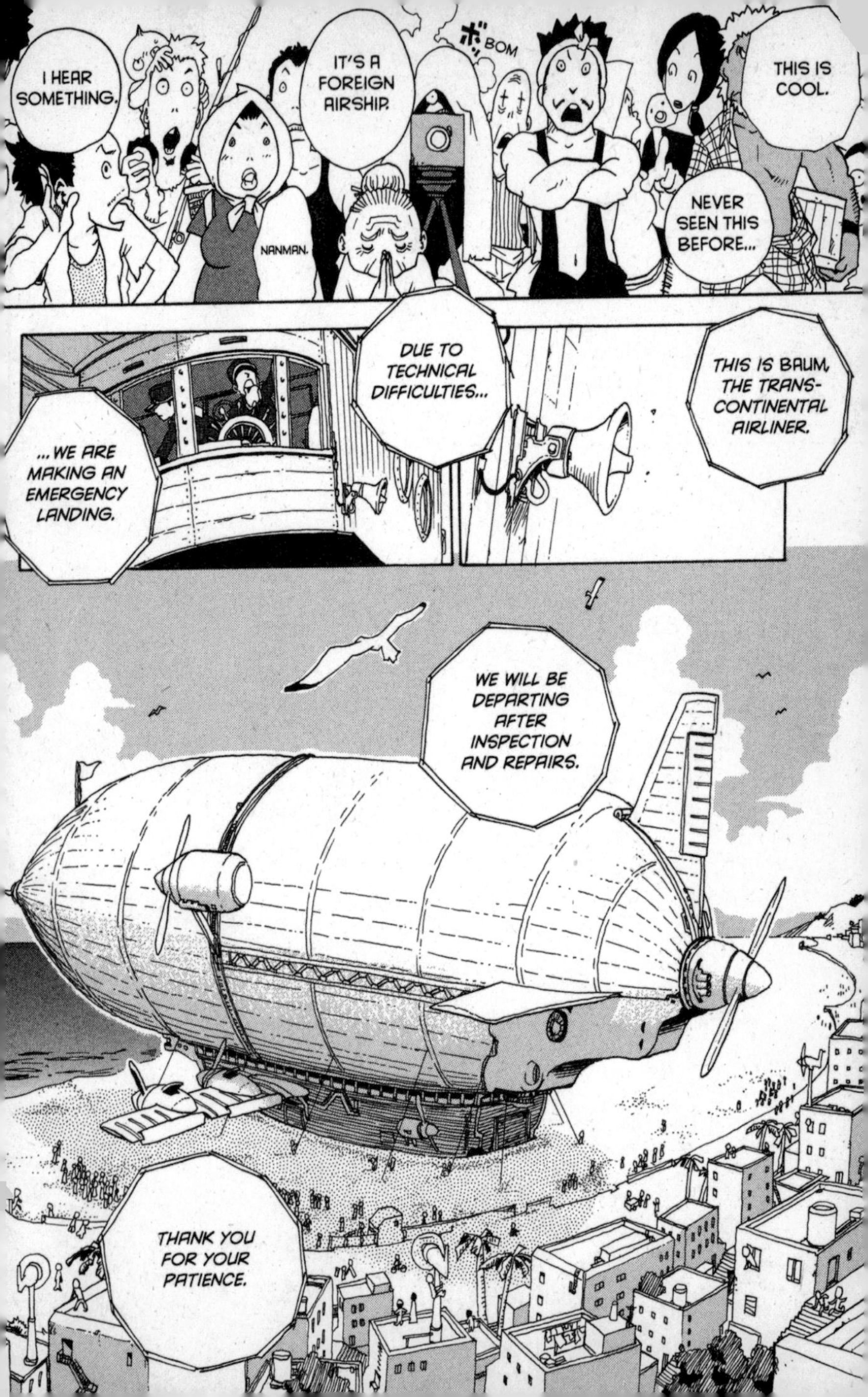
THIS IS COOL.
NEVER SEEN THIS BEFORE...
ボッ BOM
IT'S A FOREIGN AIRSHIP.
NANMAN.
I HEAR SOMETHING.
THIS IS BAUM, THE TRANS-CONTINENTAL AIRLINER.
DUE TO TECHNICAL DIFFICULTIES...
...WE ARE MAKING AN EMERGENCY LANDING.
WE WILL BE DEPARTING AFTER INSPECTION AND REPAIRS.
THANK YOU FOR YOUR PATIENCE.

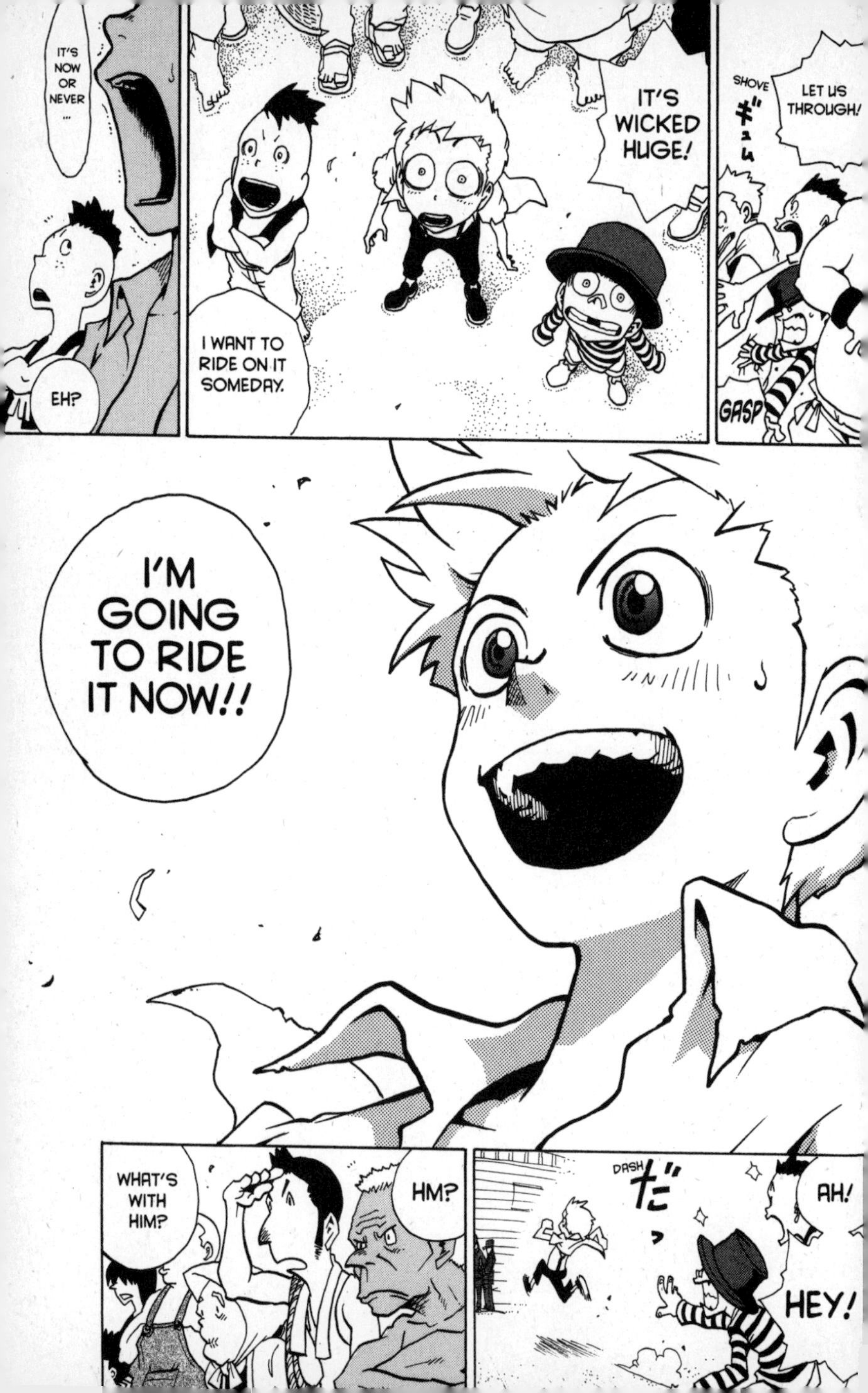
LET US THROUGH!
SHOVE
ギュム
GASP
IT'S WICKED HUGE!
I WANT TO RIDE ON IT SOMEDAY.
IT'S NOW OR NEVER ...
EH?
I'M GOING TO RIDE IT NOW!!
AH!
DASH
だっ
HEY!
HM?
WHAT'S WITH HIM?

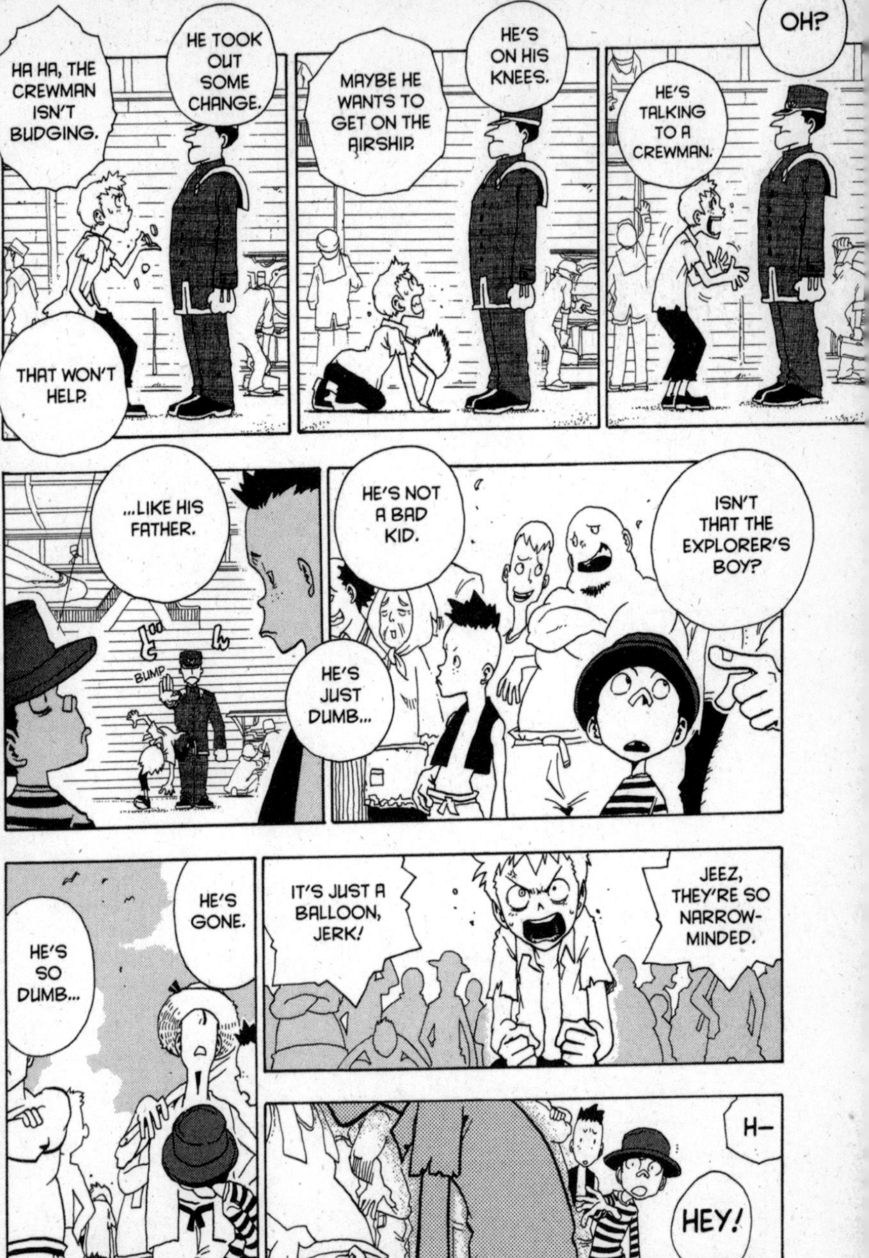
OH?
HE'S TALKING TO A CREWMAN.
HE'S ON HIS KNEES.
MAYBE HE WANTS TO GET ON THE AIRSHIP.
HE TOOK OUT SOME CHANGE.
HA HA, THE CREWMAN ISN'T BUDGING.
THAT WON'T HELP.
ISN'T THAT THE EXPLORER'S BOY?
HE'S NOT A BAD KID.
HE'S JUST DUMB...
...LIKE HIS FATHER.
BUMP
JEEZ, THEY'RE SO NARROW-MINDED.
IT'S JUST A BALLOON, JERK!
H—
HEY!
HE'S GONE.
HE'S SO DUMB...

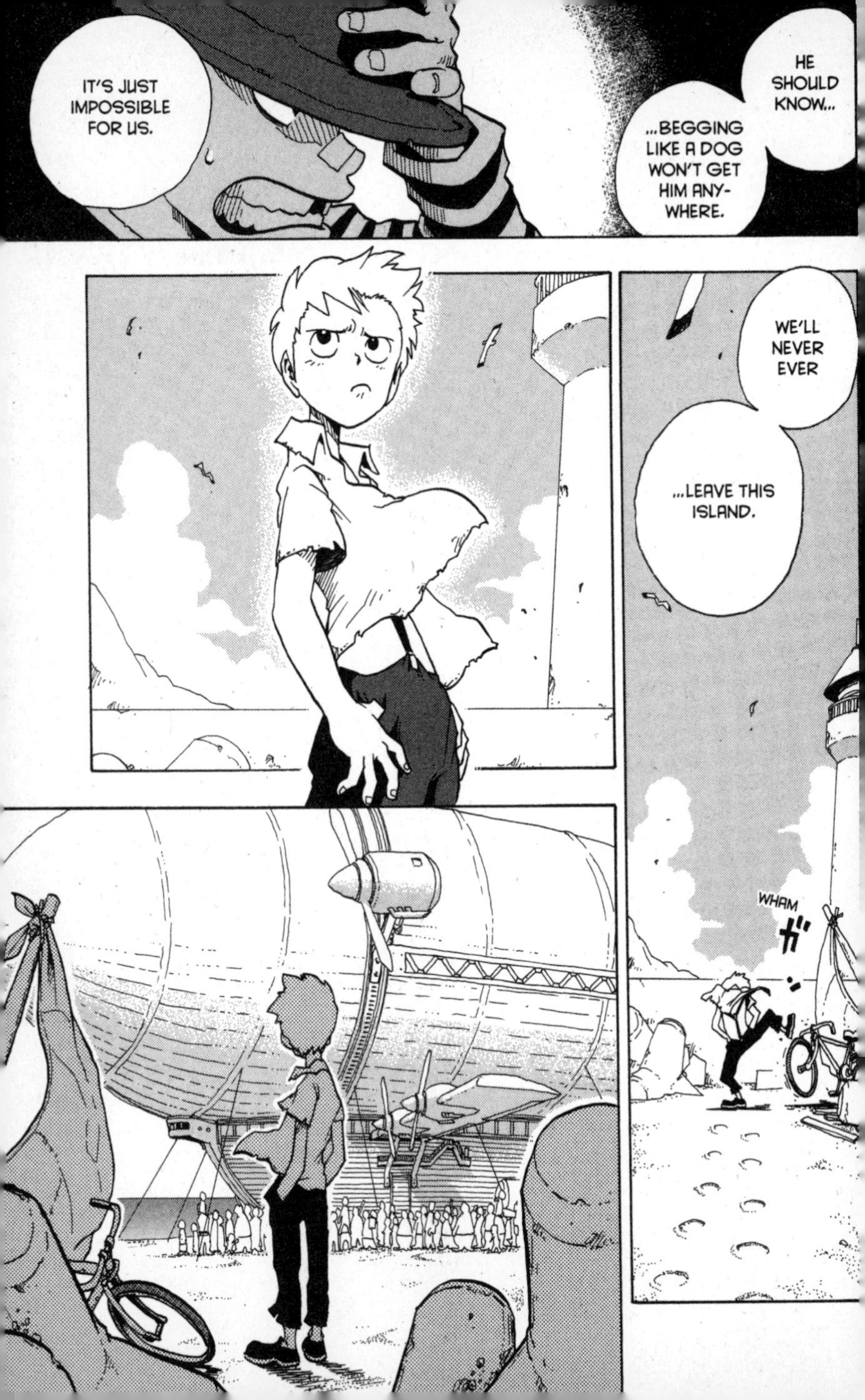
HE SHOULD KNOW...
...BEGGING LIKE A DOG WON'T GET HIM ANY-WHERE.
IT'S JUST IMPOSSIBLE FOR US.
WE'LL NEVER EVER
...LEAVE THIS ISLAND.
WHAM
ガ

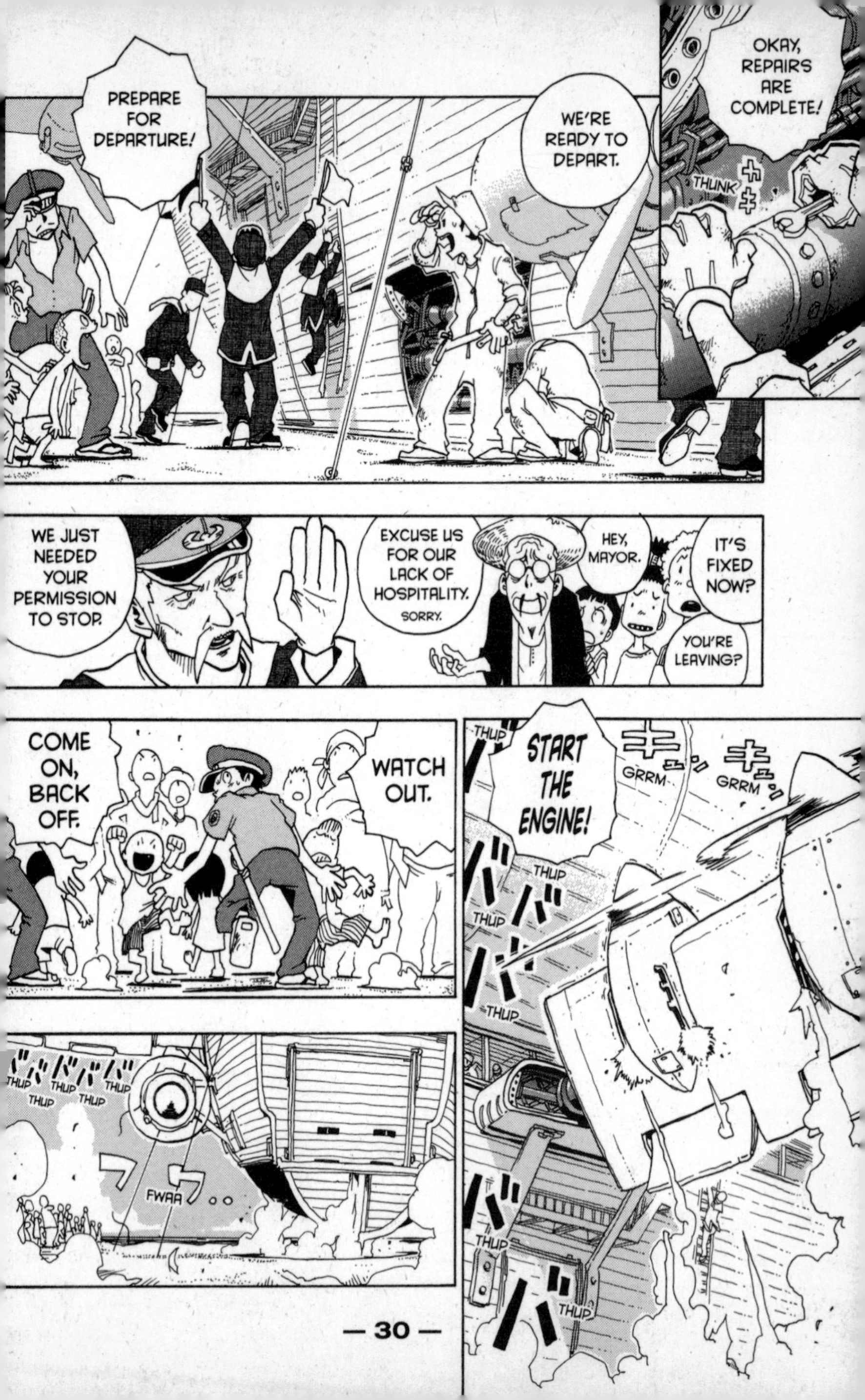
OKAY, REPAIRS ARE COMPLETE!
THUNK
WE'RE READY TO DEPART.
PREPARE FOR DEPARTURE!
IT'S FIXED NOW?
YOU'RE LEAVING?
HEY, MAYOR.
EXCUSE US FOR OUR LACK OF HOSPITALITY.
SORRY.
WE JUST NEEDED YOUR PERMISSION TO STOP.
THUP
START THE ENGINE!
GRRM
GRRM
THUP
THUP
THUP
THUP
THUP
WATCH OUT.
COME ON, BACK OFF.
THUP THUP THUP
THUP THUP
FWAA

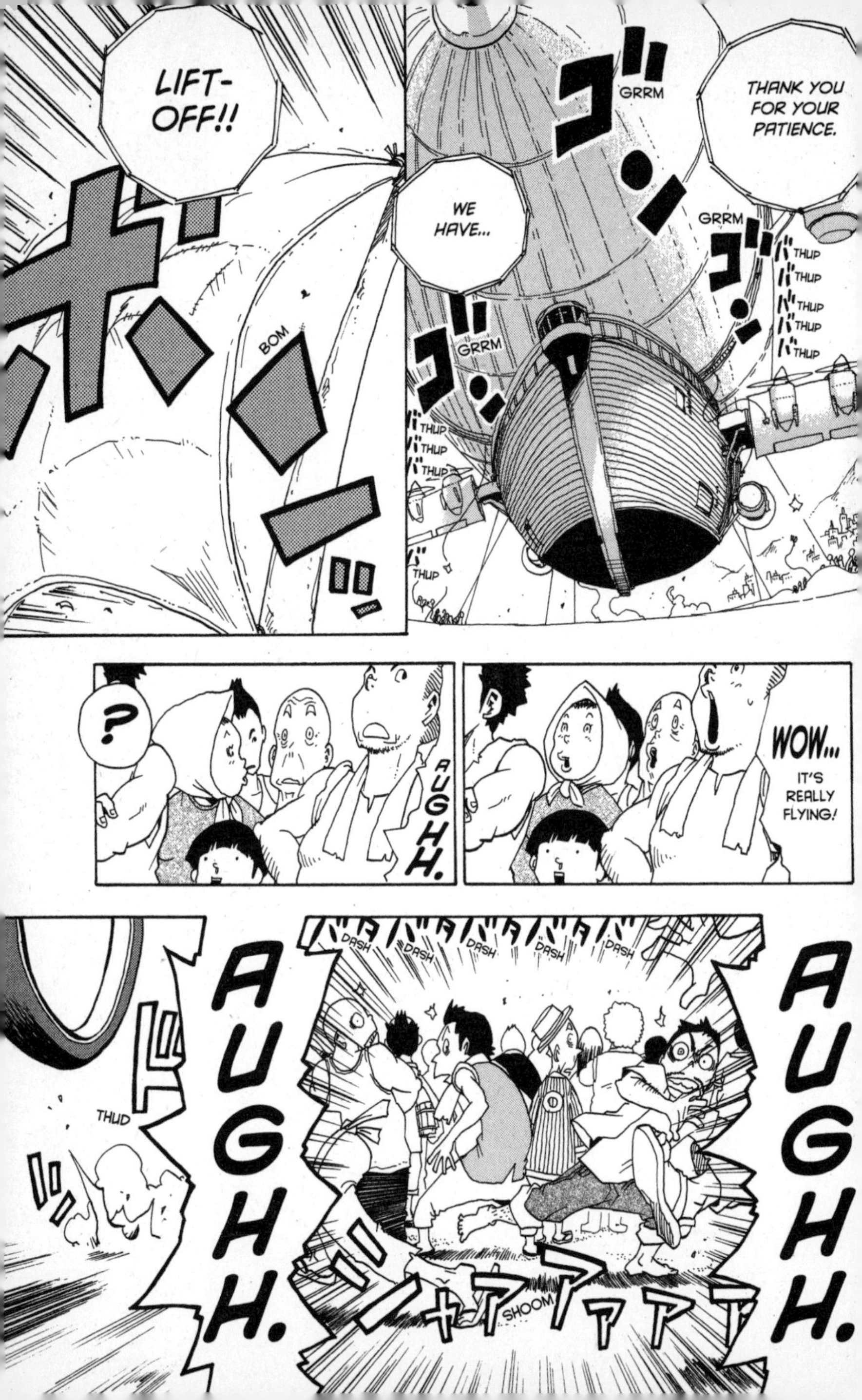

THANK YOU FOR YOUR PATIENCE.
GRRM
WE HAVE...
GRRM
GRRM
THUP THUP THUP THUP THUP
THUP THUP THUP
THUP
LIFT-OFF!!
BOM
WOW... IT'S REALLY FLYING!
?
AUGHH.
DASH DASH DASH DASH DASH
AUGHH.
SHOOM
AUGHH.
THUD

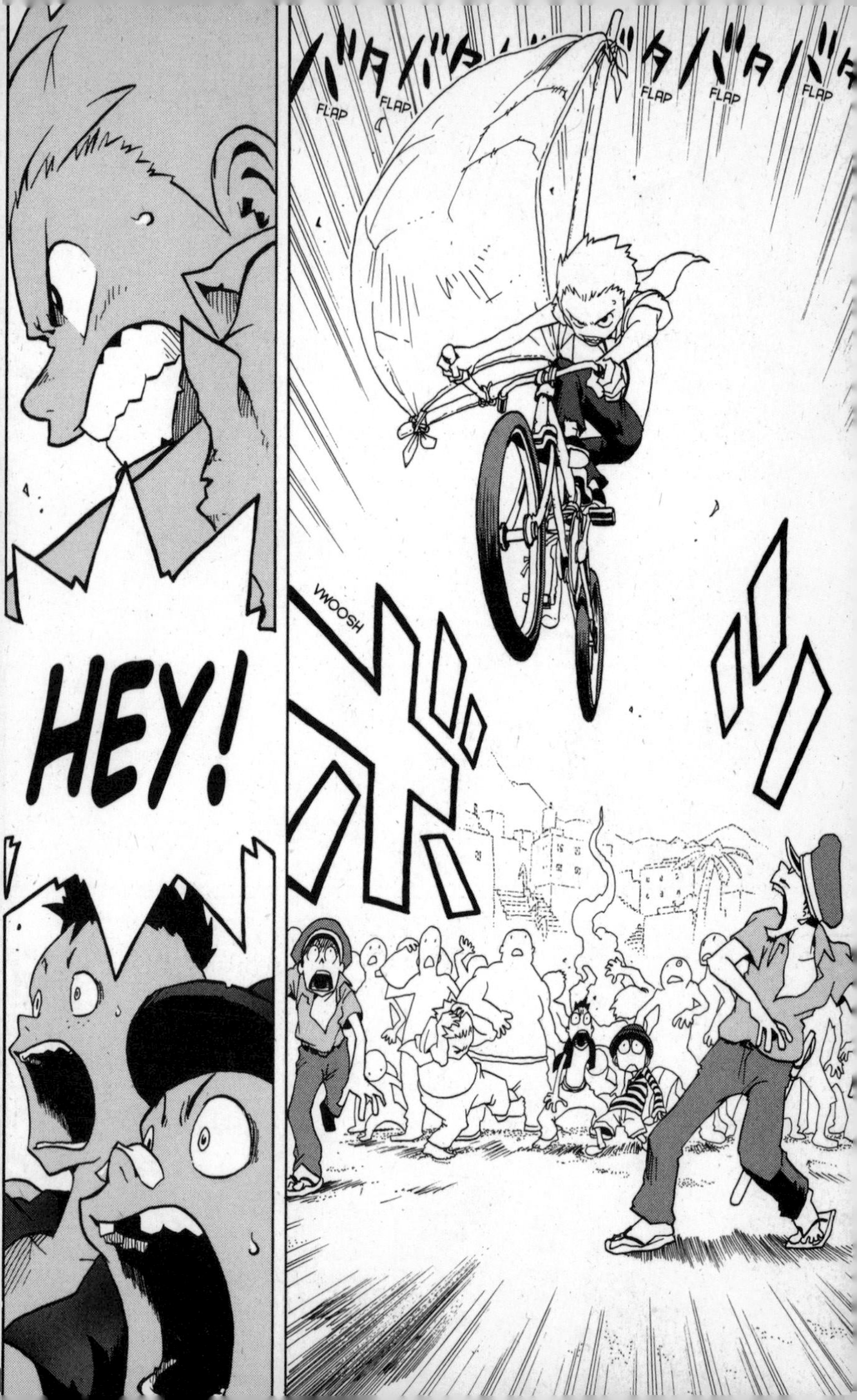
FLAP
FLAP
FLAP
FLAP
FLAP
VWOOSH
HEY!

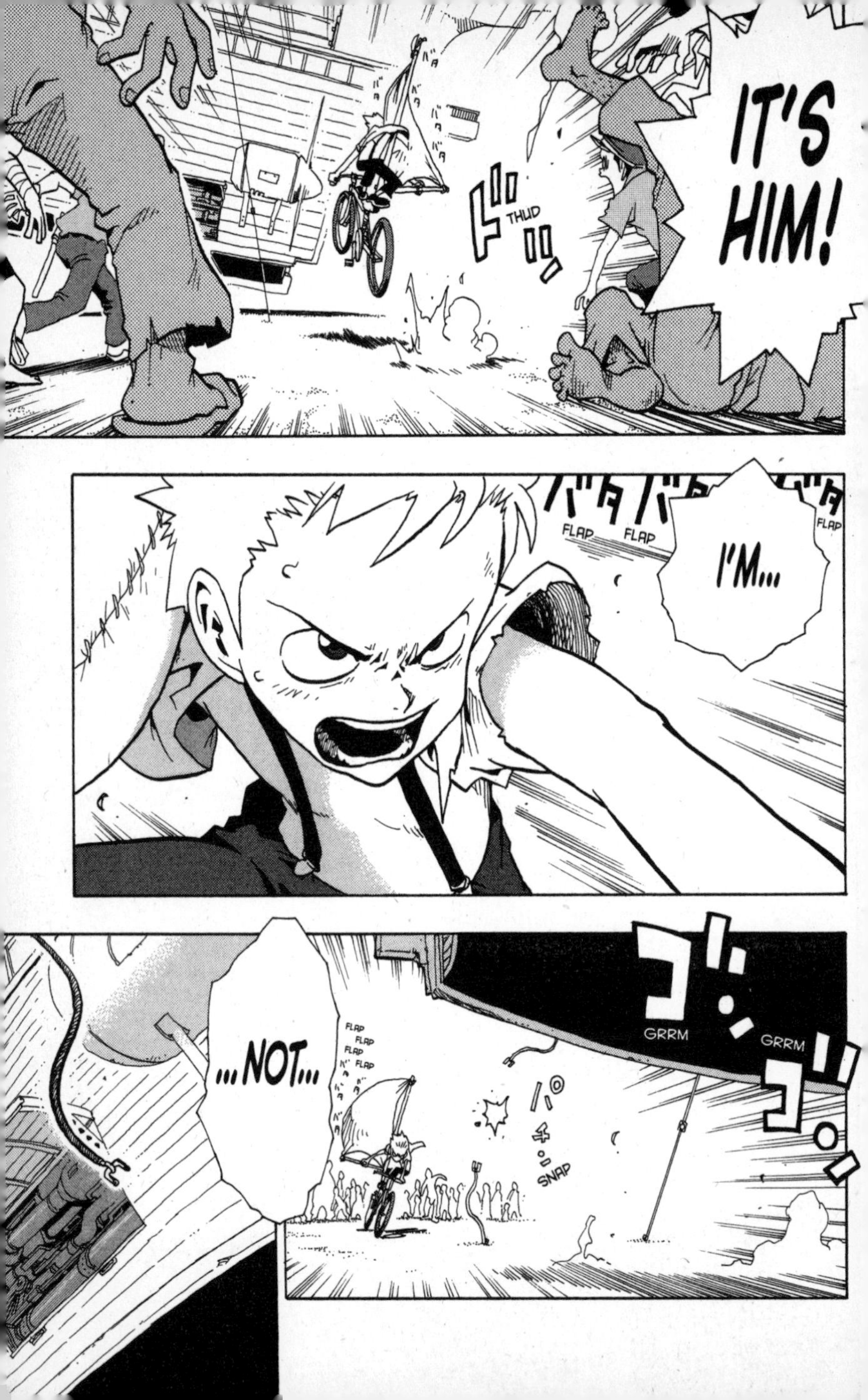
IT'S HIM!
THUD
FLAP FLAP FLAP
I'M...
GRRM GRRM
SNAP
FLAP FLAP FLAP FLAP
...NOT...

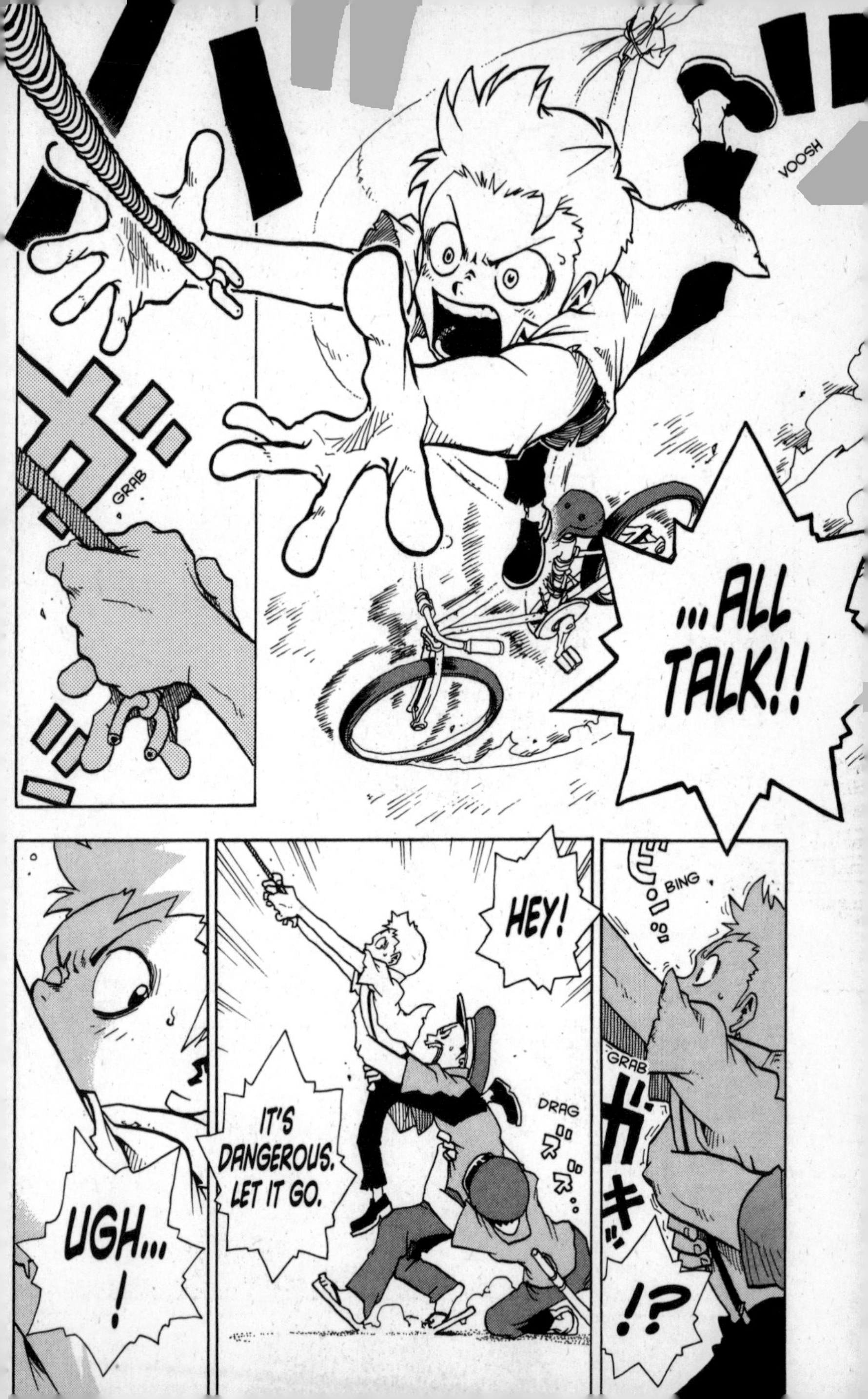
VOOSH
...ALL TALK!!
GRAB
BING
GRAB
!?
HEY!
DRAG
IT'S DANGEROUS. LET IT GO.
UGH...!

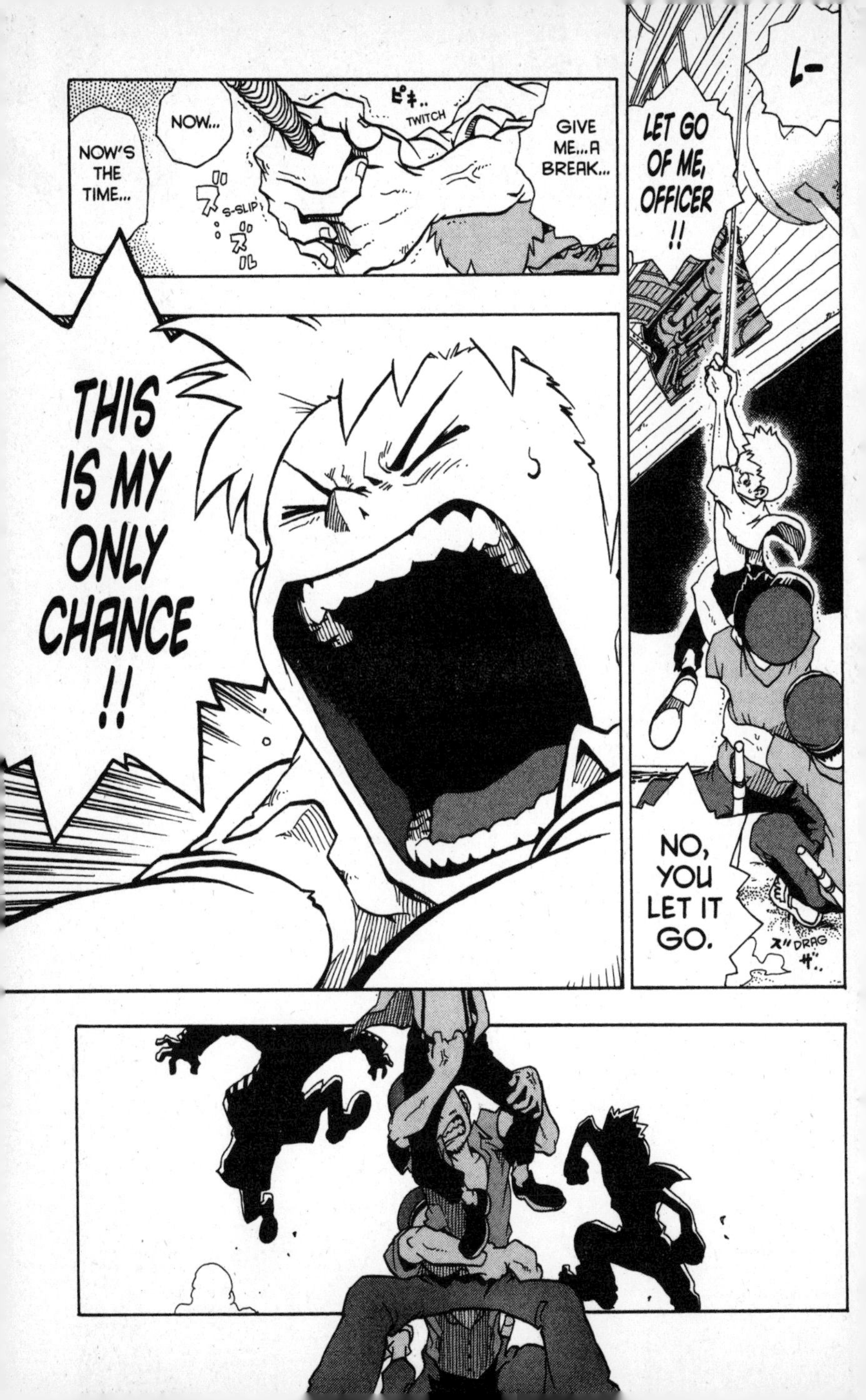
LET GO OF ME, OFFICER!!
NO, YOU LET IT GO.
DRAG
GIVE ME...A BREAK...
TWITCH
NOW...
NOW'S THE TIME...
S-SLIP
THIS IS MY ONLY CHANCE!!

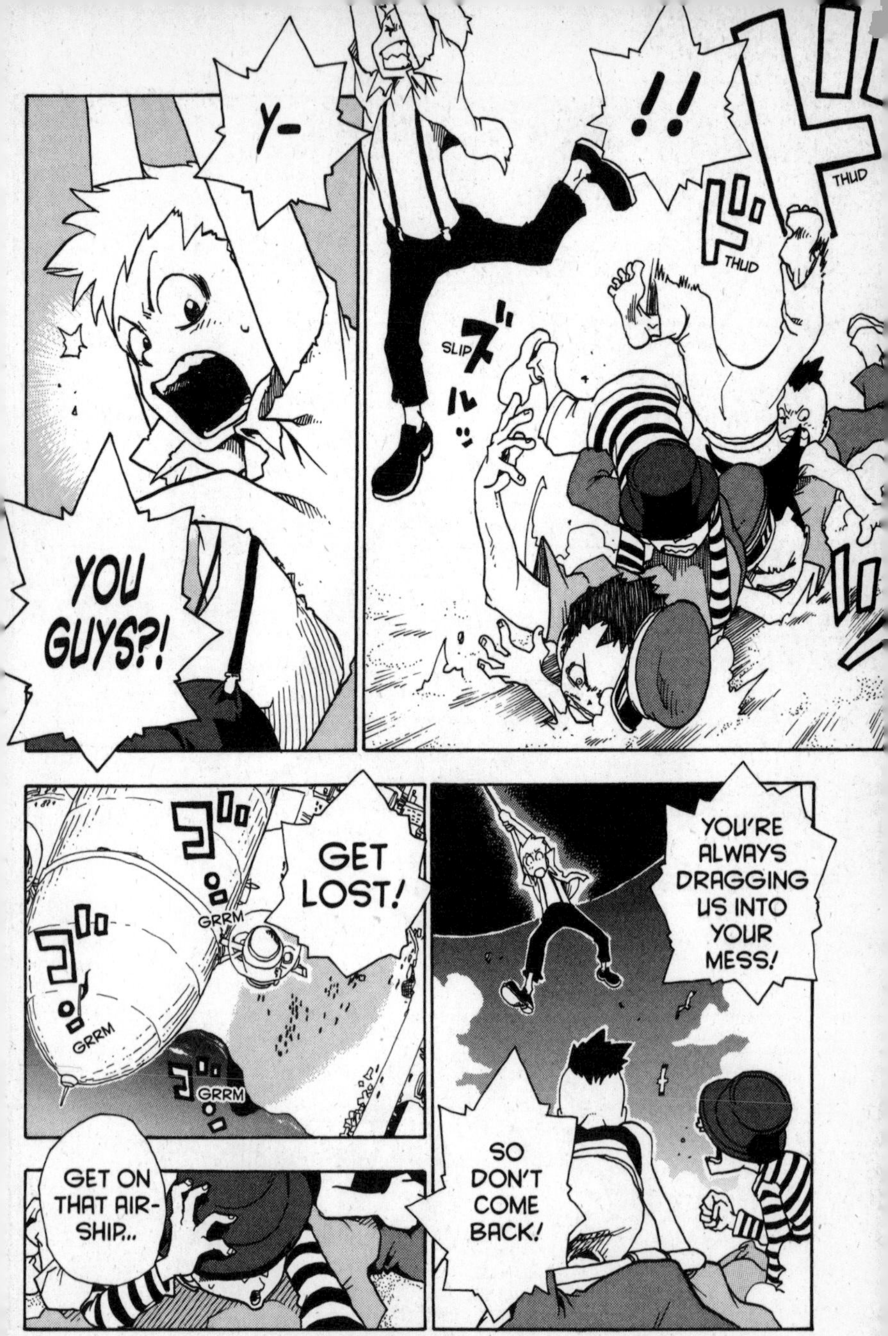
!!
THUD
THUD
SLIP
Y-
YOU GUYS?!
YOU'RE ALWAYS DRAGGING US INTO YOUR MESS!
SO DON'T COME BACK!
GET LOST!
GRRM
GRRM
GRRM
GET ON THAT AIR-SHIP...

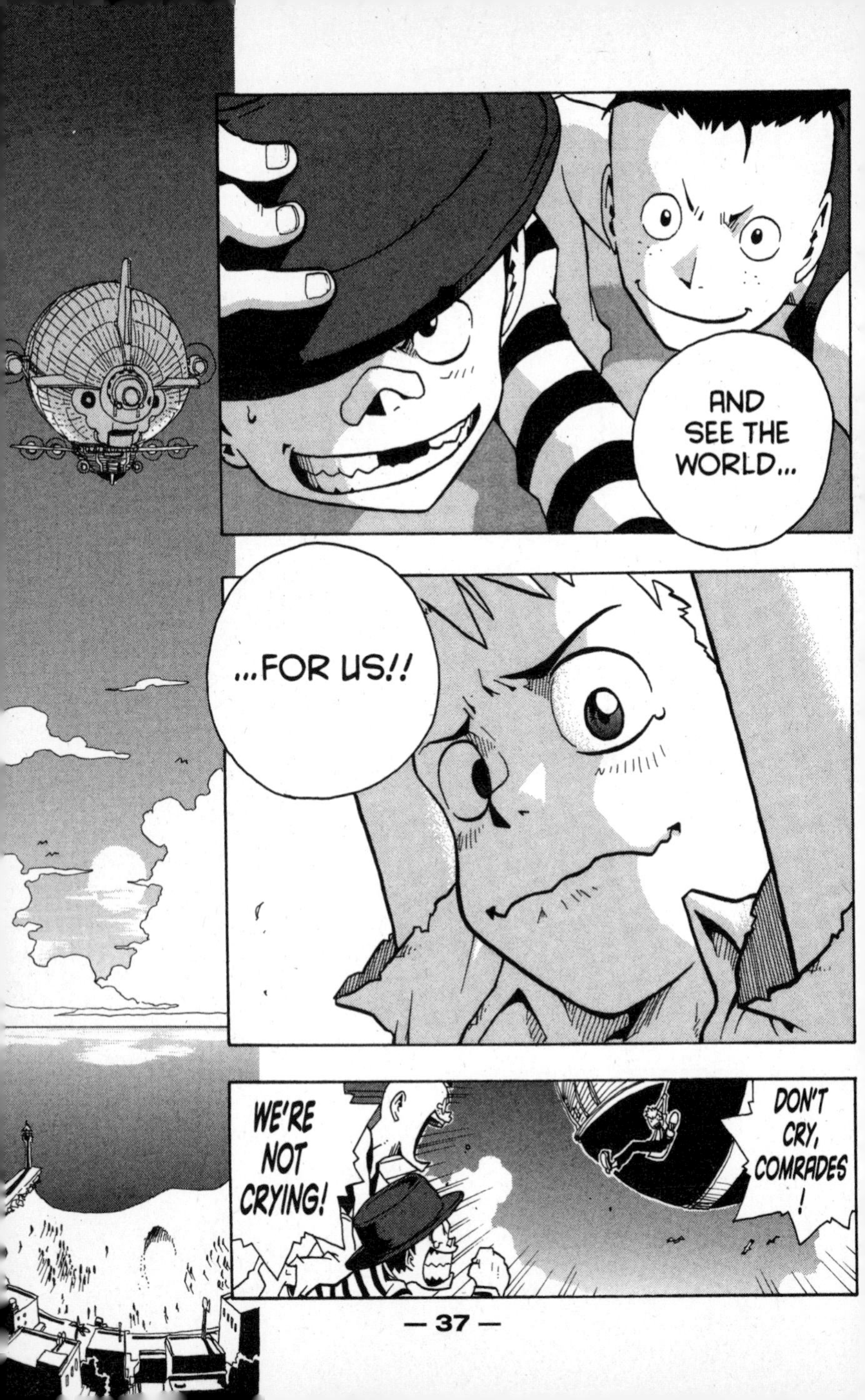
AND SEE THE WORLD...
...FOR US!!
DON'T CRY, COMRADES!
WE'RE NOT CRYING!

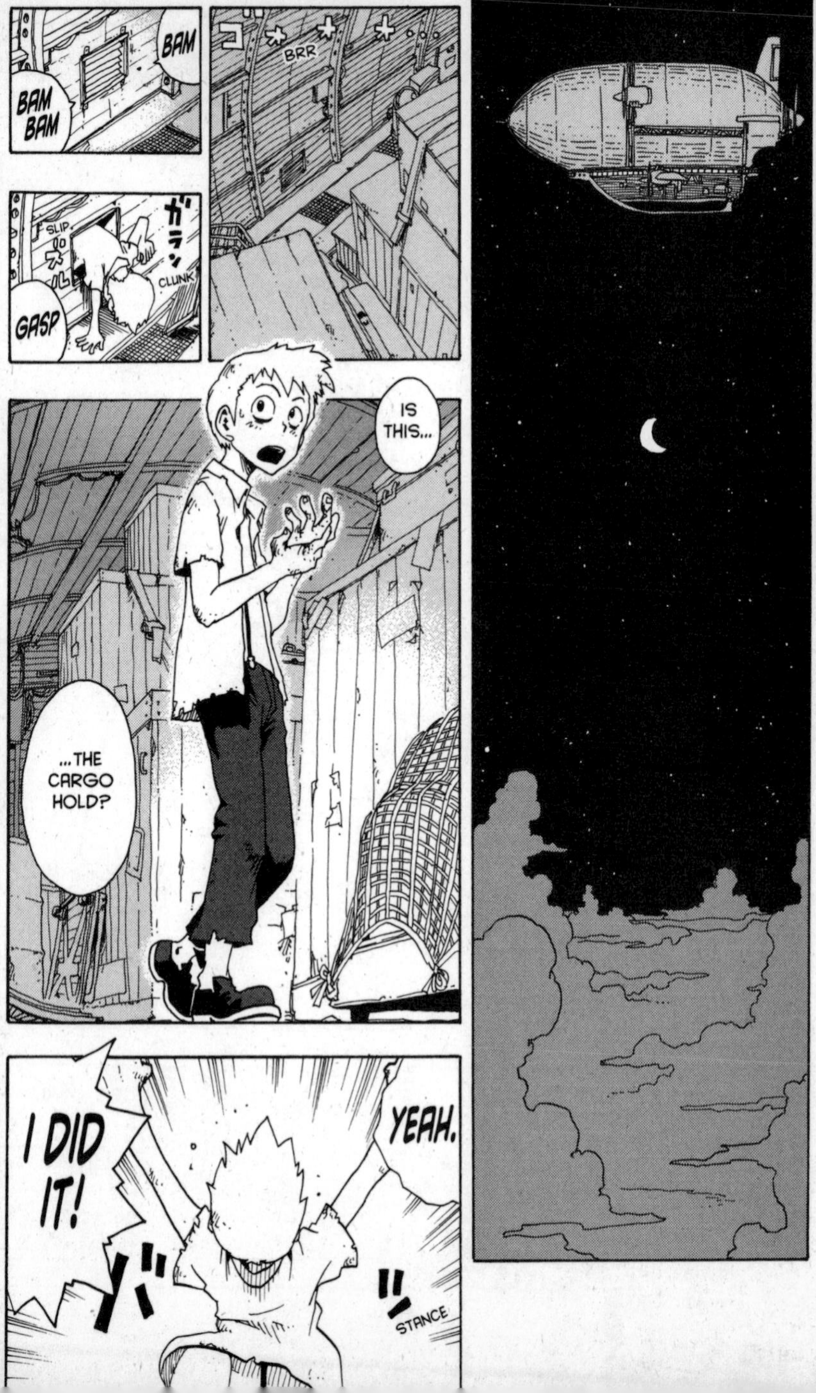
BRR
BAM
BAM BAM
SLIP
CLUNK
GASP
IS THIS...
...THE CARGO HOLD?
YEAH.
I DID IT!
STANCE

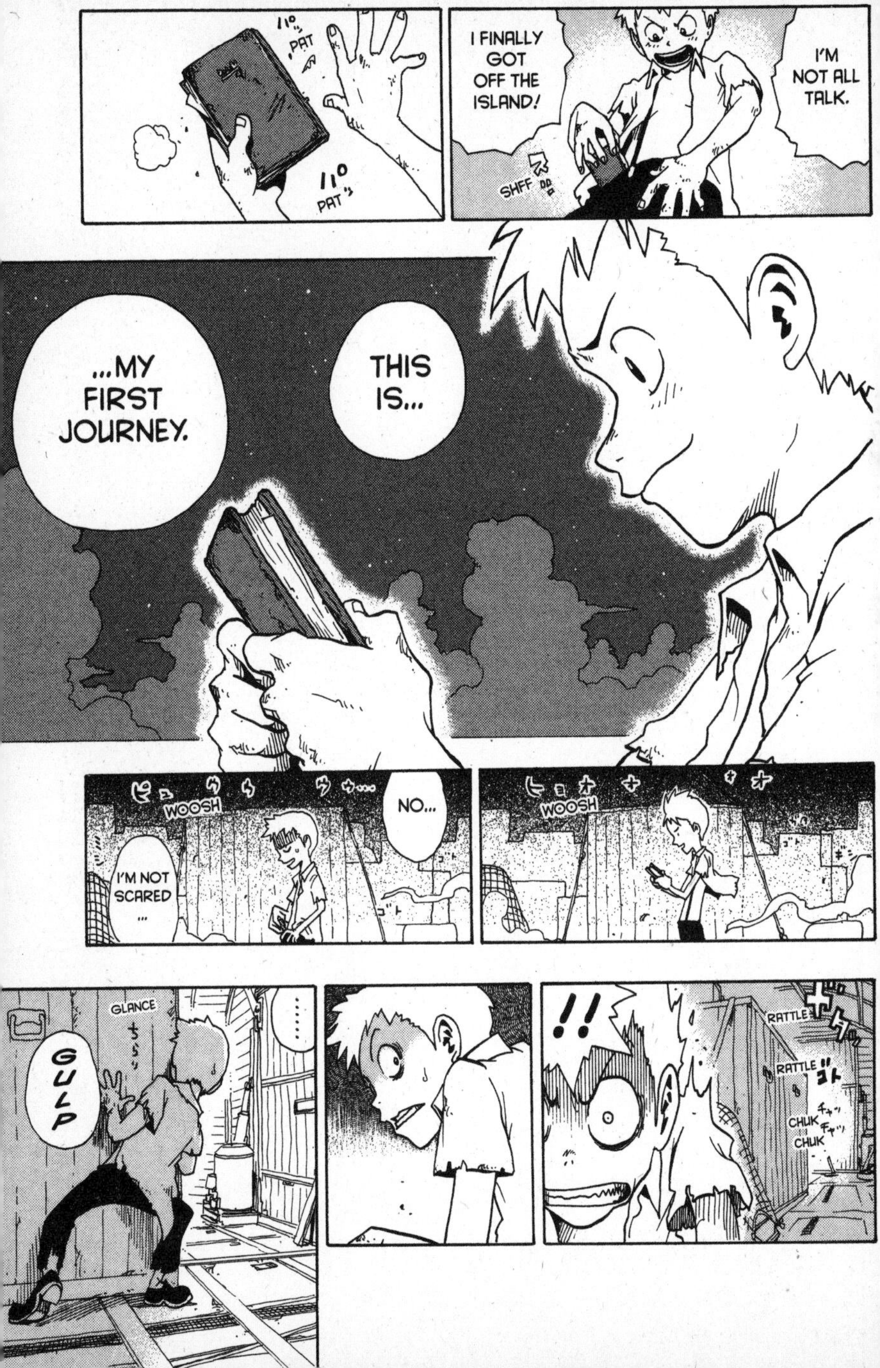
I'M NOT ALL TALK.
I FINALLY GOT OFF THE ISLAND!
SHFF
PAT
PAT
THIS IS...
...MY FIRST JOURNEY.
WOOSH
WOOSH
NO...
I'M NOT SCARED ...
!!
RATTLE
RATTLE
CHUK CHUK
......
GLANCE
GULP

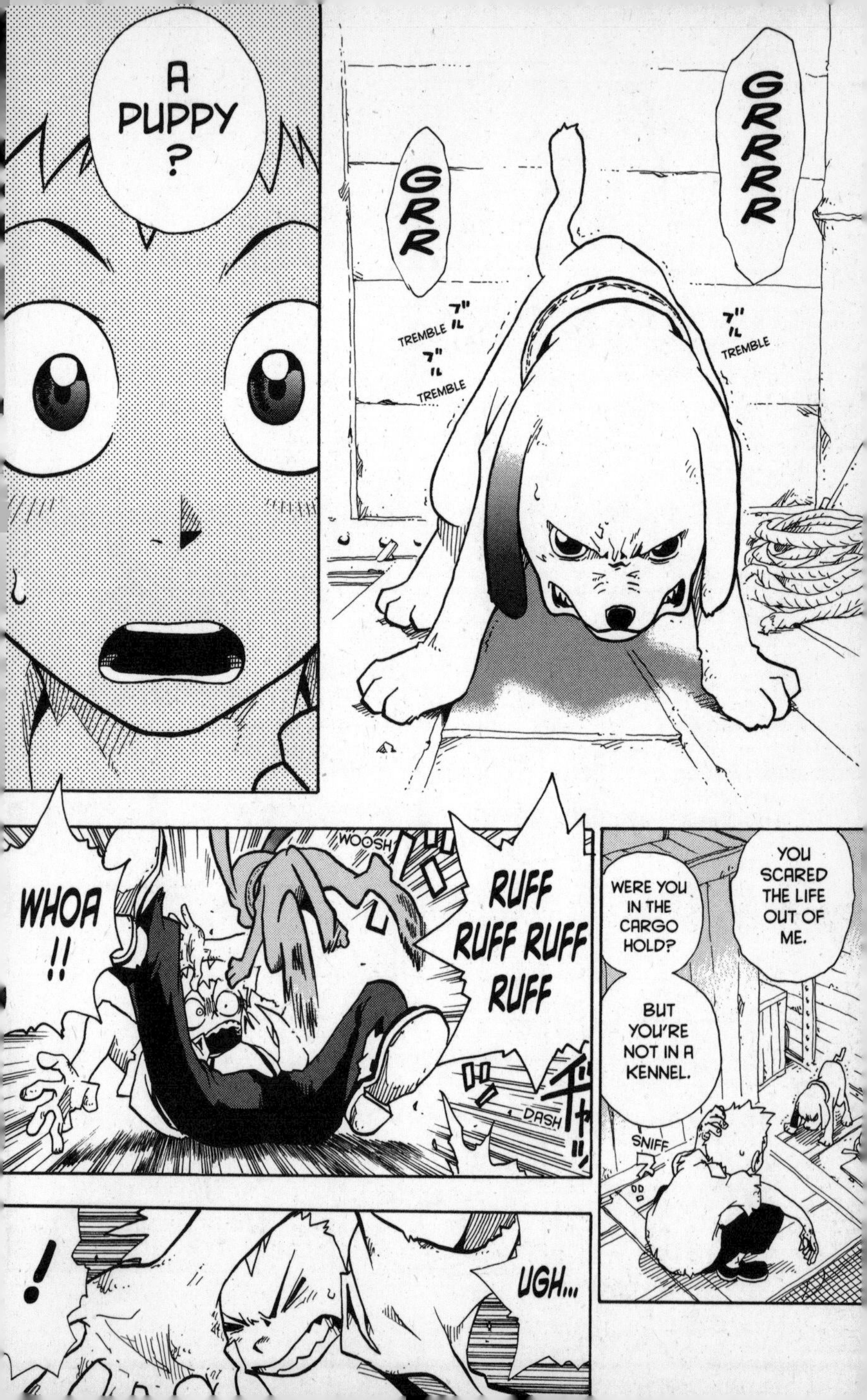
GRRRR
GRR
TREMBLE
TREMBLE
TREMBLE
A PUPPY?
YOU SCARED THE LIFE OUT OF ME.
WERE YOU IN THE CARGO HOLD?
BUT YOU'RE NOT IN A KENNEL.
SNIFF
WOOSH
RUFF RUFF RUFF RUFF
DASH
WHOA!!
UGH...
!

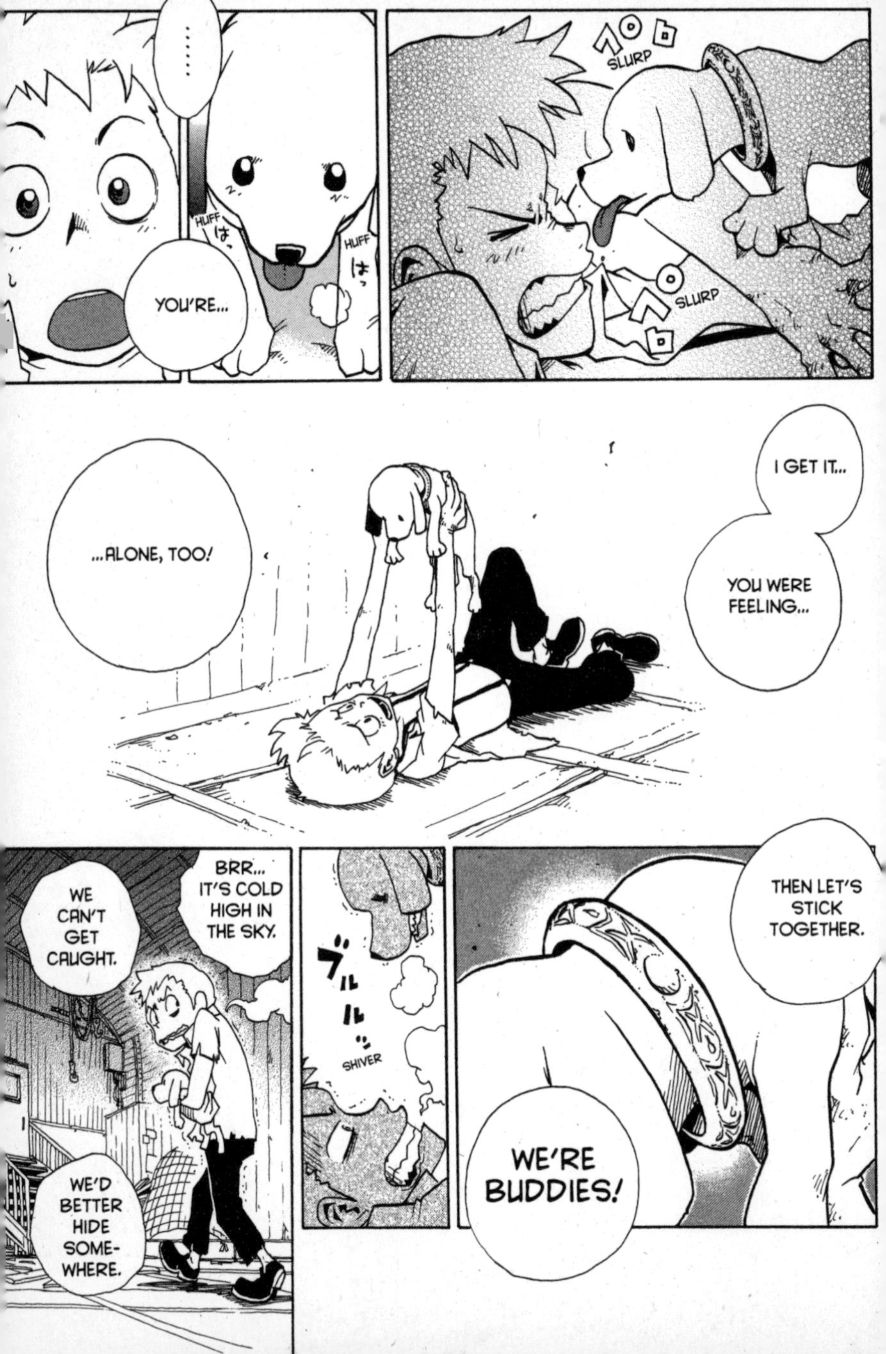
SLURP
SLURP
……
HUFF
HUFF
YOU'RE...
I GET IT...
YOU WERE FEELING...
...ALONE, TOO!
THEN LET'S STICK TOGETHER.
WE'RE BUDDIES!
ブルルッ
SHIVER
BRR... IT'S COLD HIGH IN THE SKY.
WE CAN'T GET CAUGHT.
WE'D BETTER HIDE SOME-WHERE.

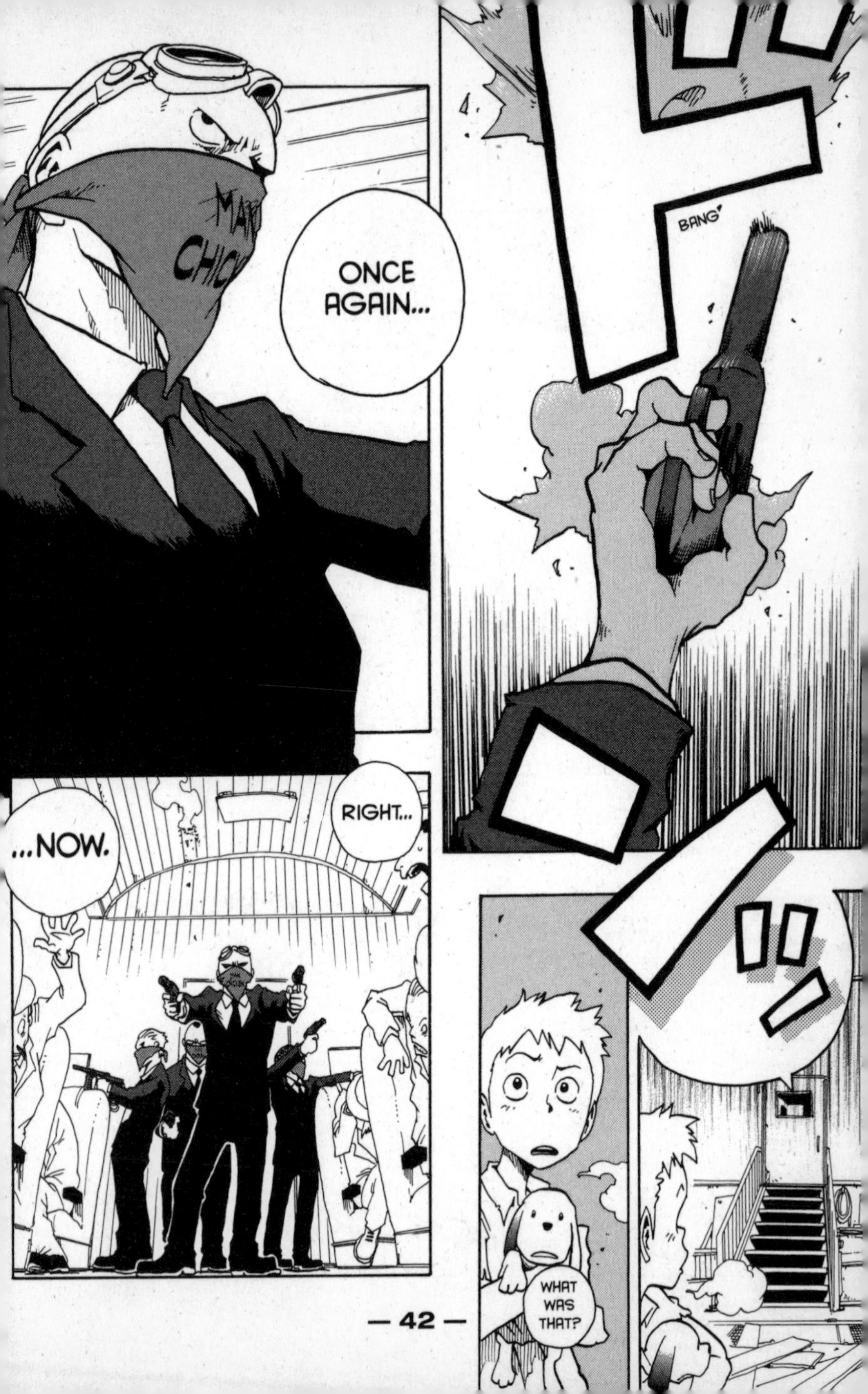
ONCE AGAIN...
RIGHT...
...NOW.
BANG
WHAT WAS THAT?

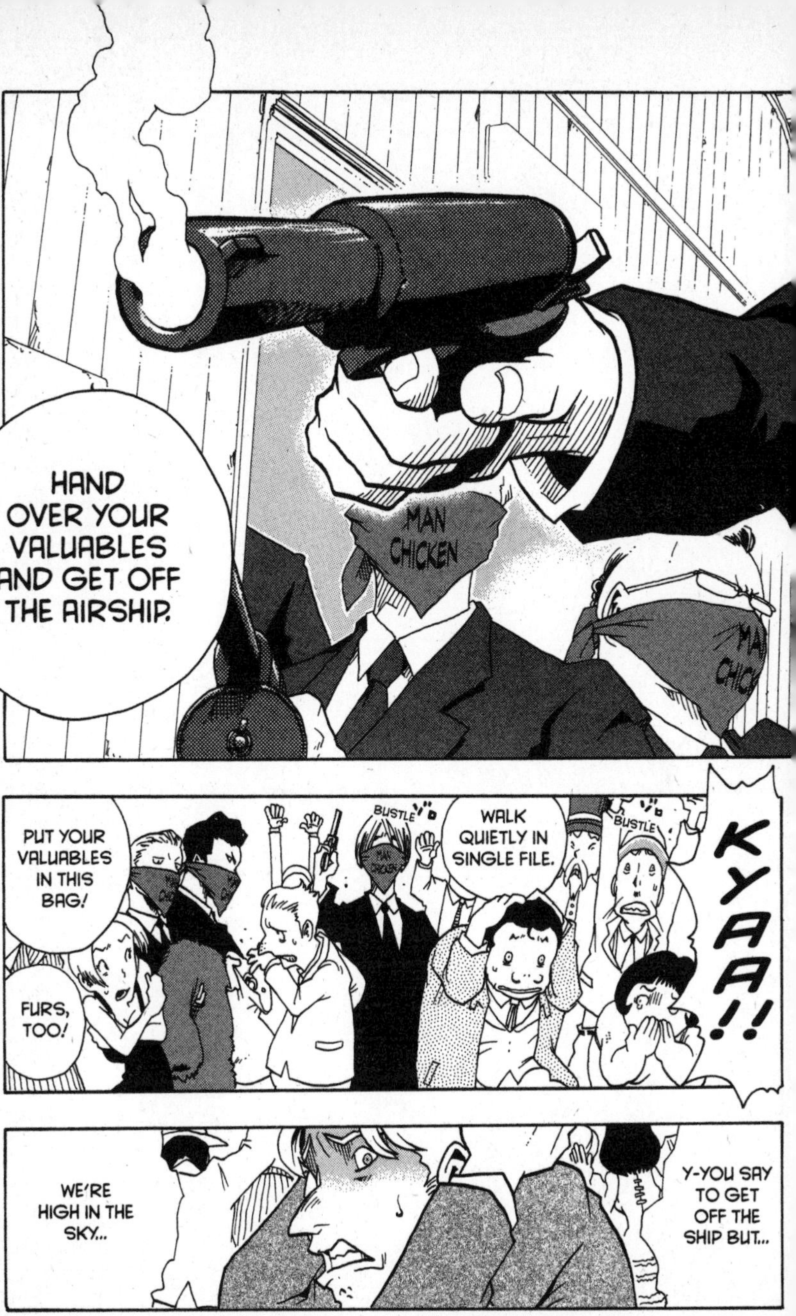
HAND OVER YOUR VALUABLES AND GET OFF THE AIRSHIP.
MAN CHICKEN
KYAAA!!
BUSTLE
WALK QUIETLY IN SINGLE FILE.
BUSTLE
PUT YOUR VALUABLES IN THIS BAG!
FURS, TOO!
Y-YOU SAY TO GET OFF THE SHIP BUT...
WE'RE HIGH IN THE SKY...

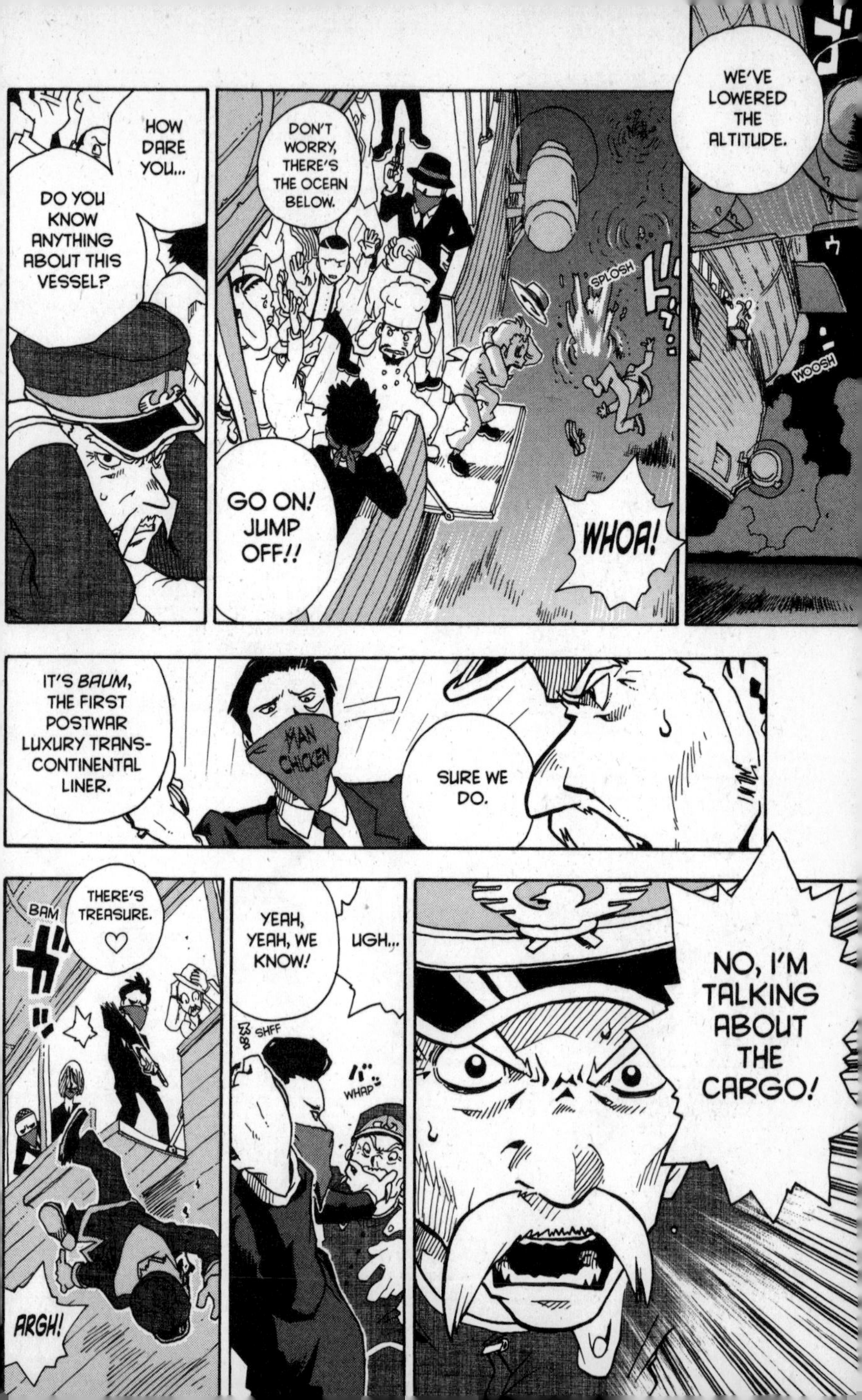
WE'VE LOWERED THE ALTITUDE.
WOOSH
DON'T WORRY, THERE'S THE OCEAN BELOW.
SPLOSH
WHOA!
GO ON! JUMP OFF!!
HOW DARE YOU...
DO YOU KNOW ANYTHING ABOUT THIS VESSEL?
SURE WE DO.
MAN CHICKEN
IT'S *BAUM*, THE FIRST POSTWAR LUXURY TRANS-CONTINENTAL LINER.
NO, I'M TALKING ABOUT THE CARGO!
UGH...
YEAH, YEAH, WE KNOW!
SHFF
WHAP
THERE'S TREASURE. ♡
BAM
ARGH!

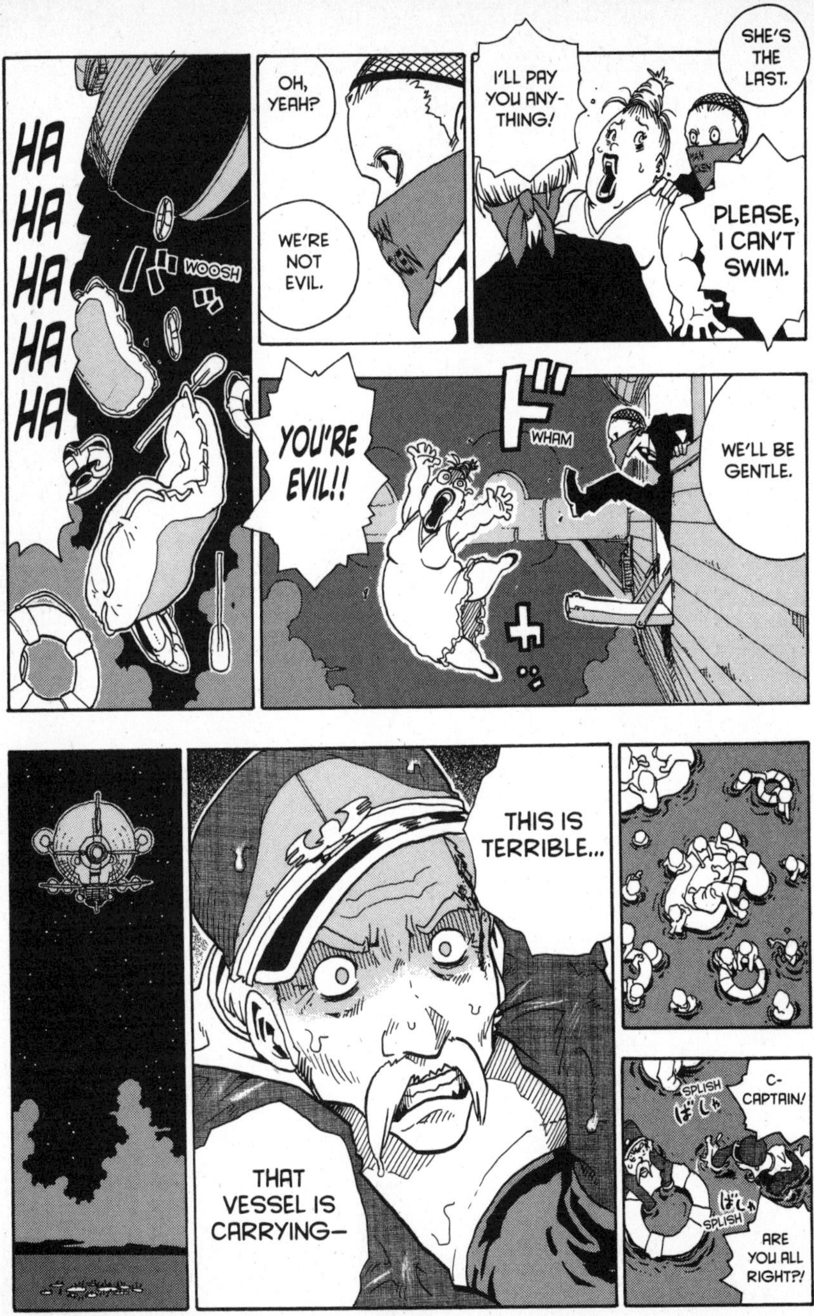
SHE'S THE LAST.
PLEASE, I CAN'T SWIM.
I'LL PAY YOU ANYTHING!
OH, YEAH?
WE'RE NOT EVIL.
WE'LL BE GENTLE.
WHAM
YOU'RE EVIL!!
HA HA HA HA HA
WOOSH
SPLISH
C-CAPTAIN!
SPLISH
ARE YOU ALL RIGHT?!
THIS IS TERRIBLE...
THAT VESSEL IS CARRYING—

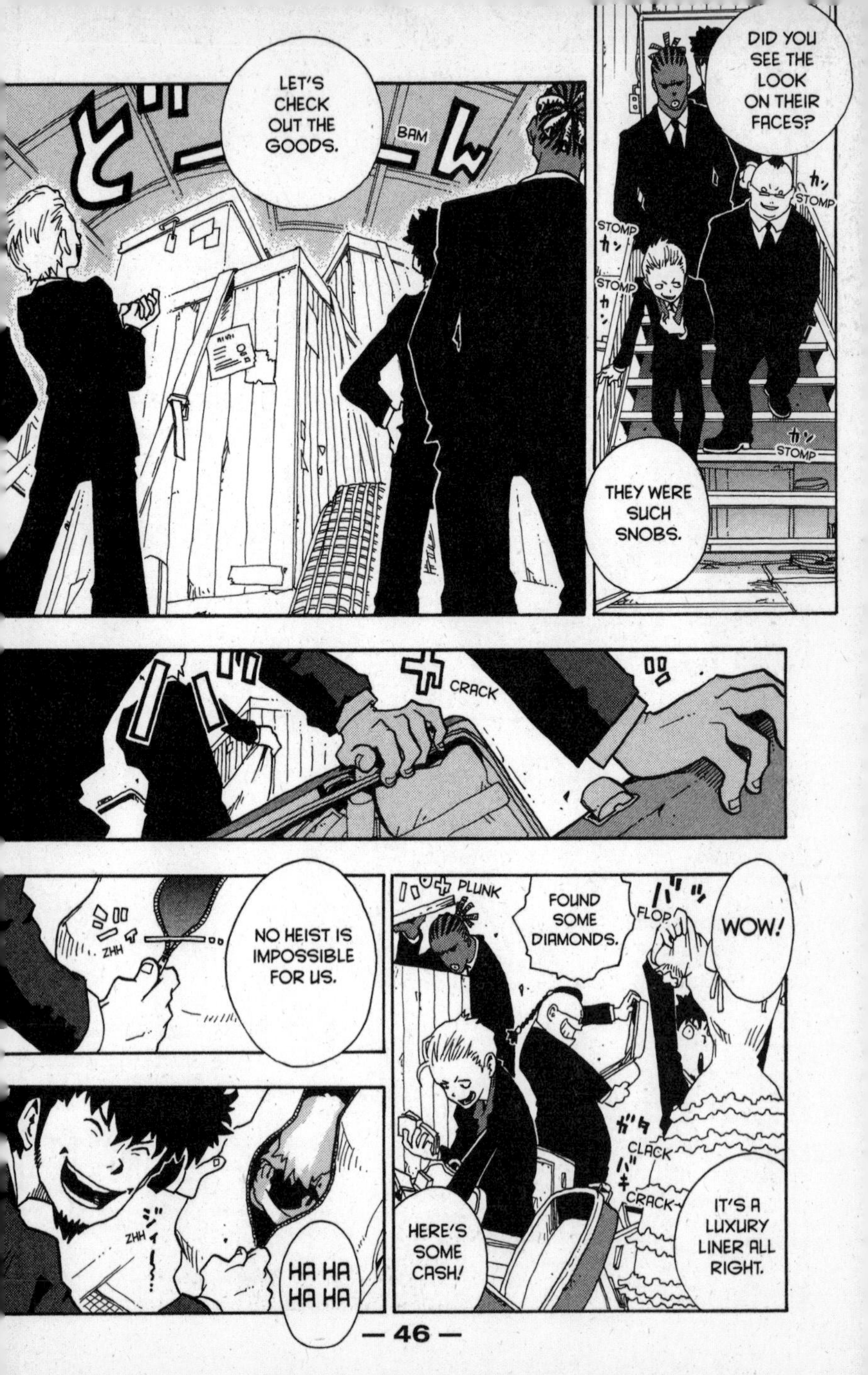
DID YOU SEE THE LOOK ON THEIR FACES?
カン
STOMP
STOMP
カン
STOMP
カン
カン
STOMP
THEY WERE SUCH SNOBS.
BAM
LET'S CHECK OUT THE GOODS.
CRACK
WOW!
FLOP
FOUND SOME DIAMONDS.
PLUNK
ガタ
CLACK
バキ
CRACK
IT'S A LUXURY LINER ALL RIGHT.
HERE'S SOME CASH!
ZHH
NO HEIST IS IMPOSSIBLE FOR US.
ジィー
ZHH
HA HA HA HA

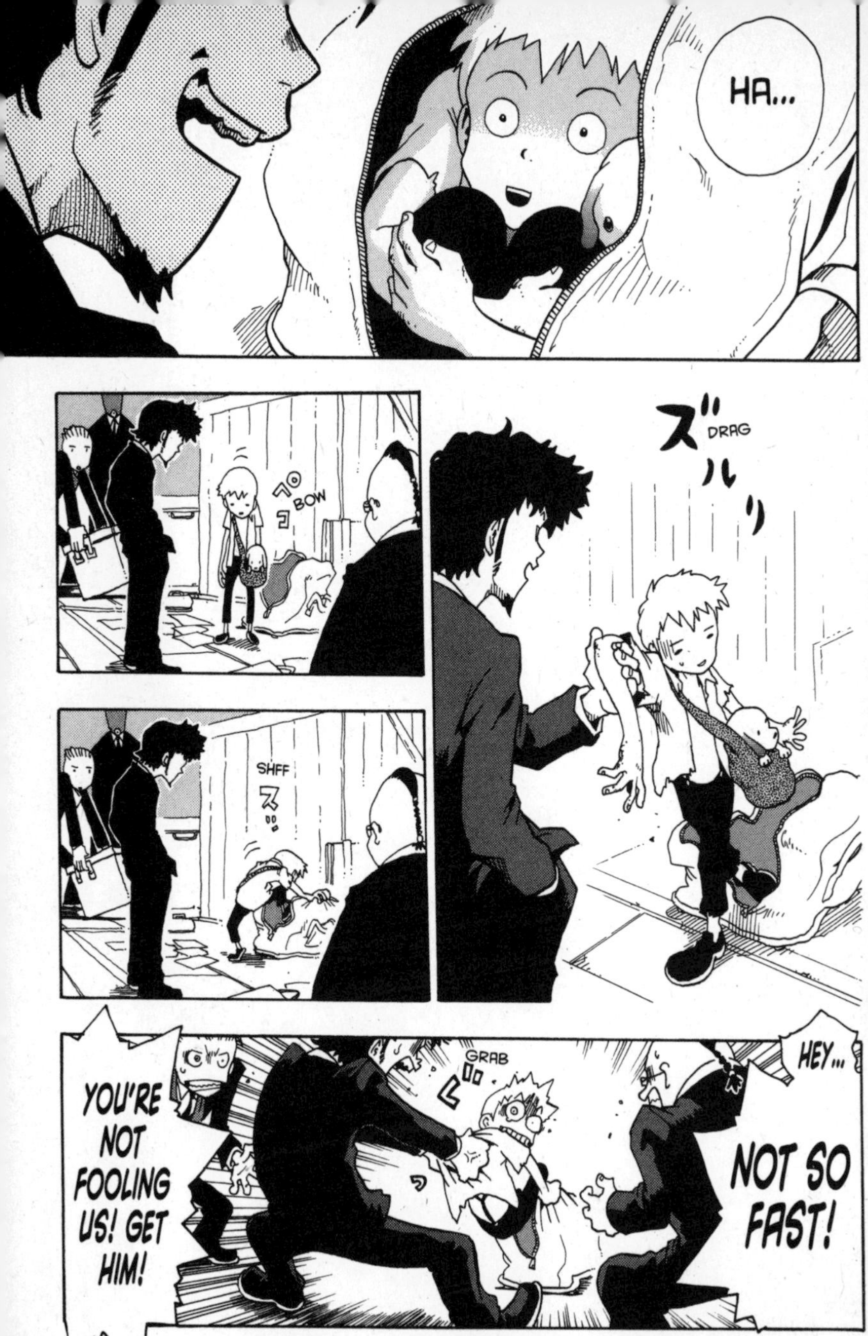
HA...
ズルリ
DRAG
ペコ
BOW
スッ
SHFF
HEY...
NOT SO FAST!
グッ
GRAB
YOU'RE NOT FOOLING US! GET HIM!

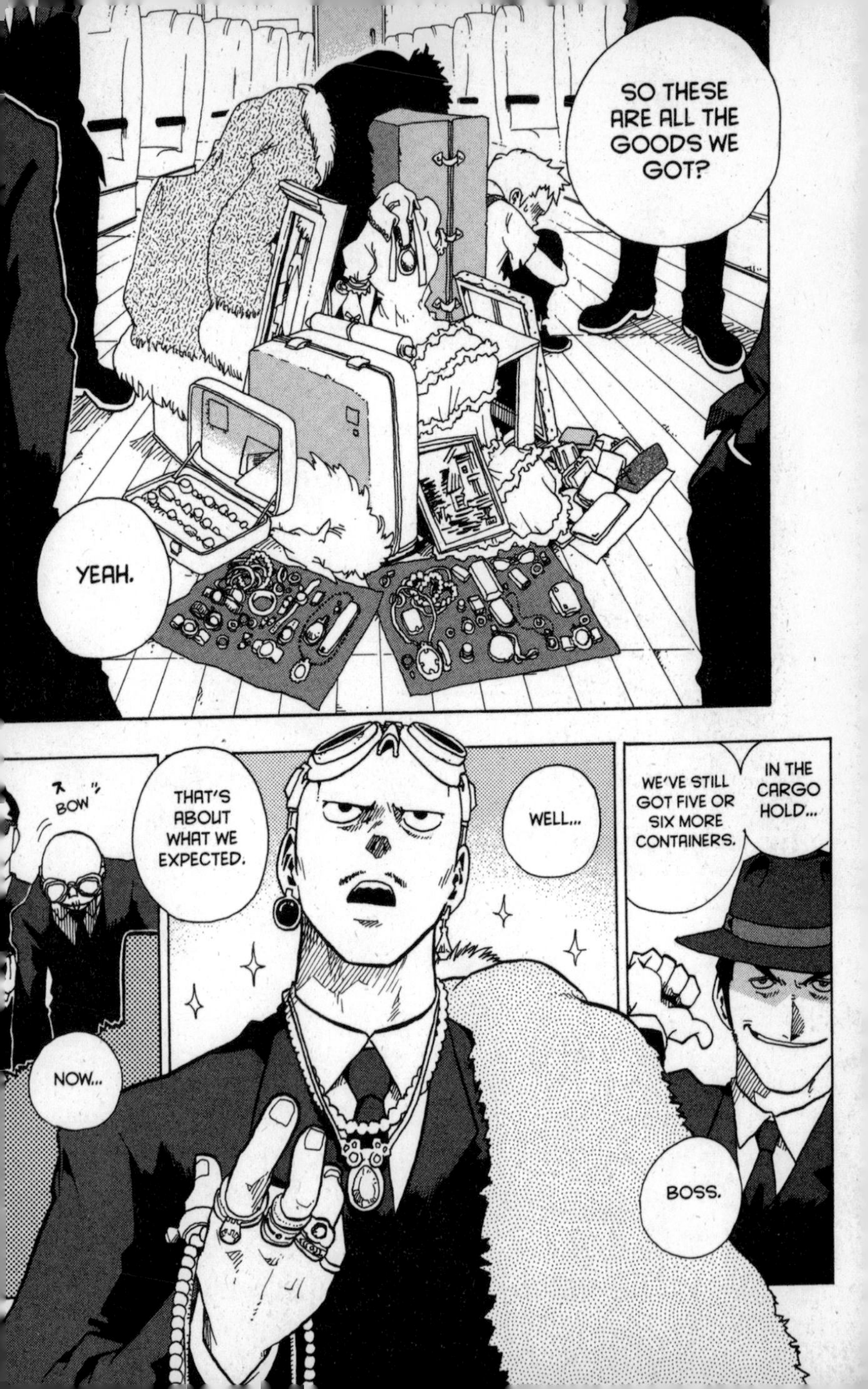
SO THESE ARE ALL THE GOODS WE GOT?
YEAH.
IN THE CARGO HOLD...
WE'VE STILL GOT FIVE OR SIX MORE CONTAINERS.
WELL...
THAT'S ABOUT WHAT WE EXPECTED.
BOW
NOW...
BOSS.

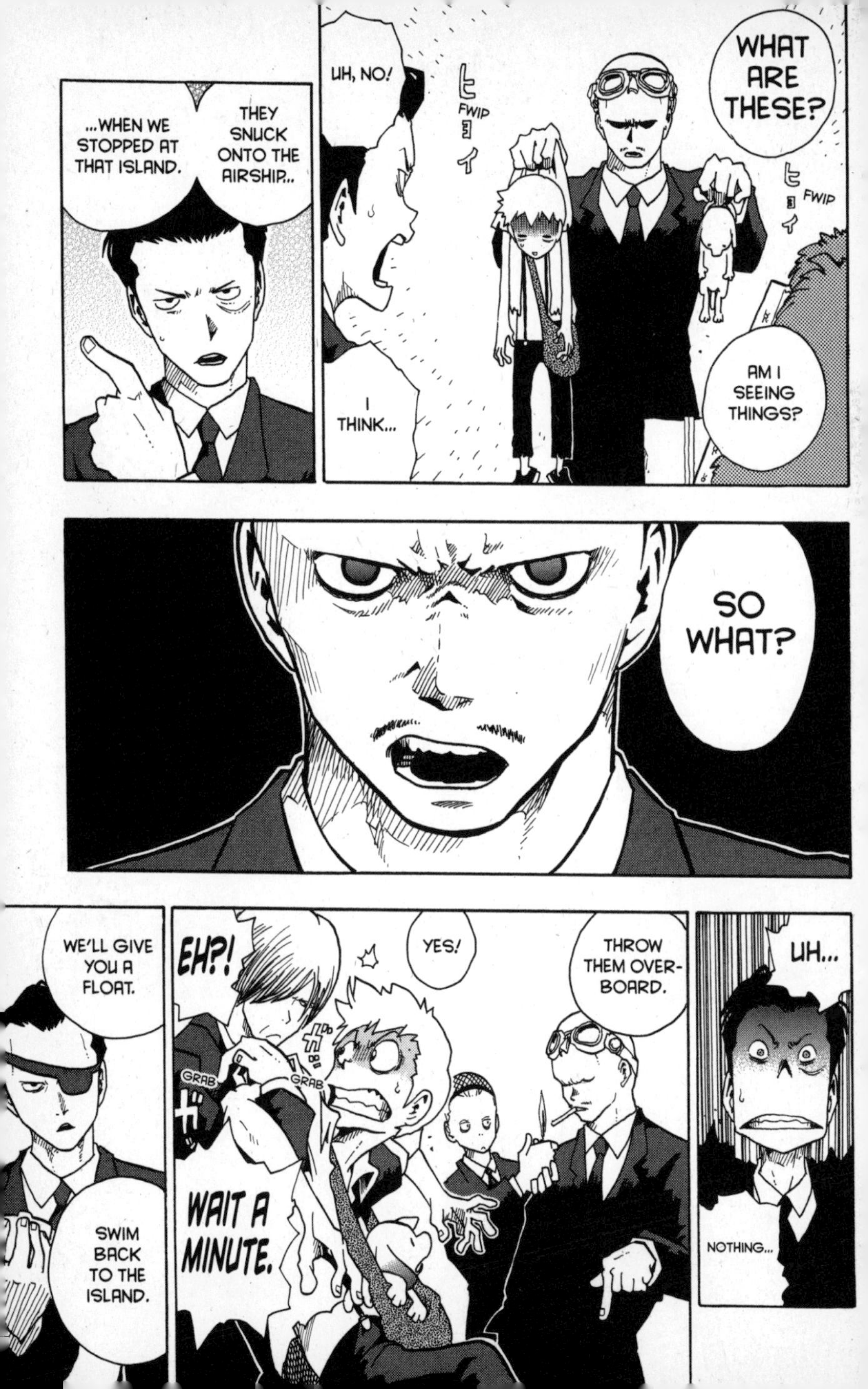
WHAT ARE THESE?
FWIP
FWIP
AM I SEEING THINGS?
UH, NO!
FWIP
I THINK...
THEY SNUCK ONTO THE AIRSHIP...
...WHEN WE STOPPED AT THAT ISLAND.
SO WHAT?
UH...
NOTHING...
THROW THEM OVER-BOARD.
YES!
EH?!
GRAB
GRAB
WAIT A MINUTE.
WE'LL GIVE YOU A FLOAT.
SWIM BACK TO THE ISLAND.

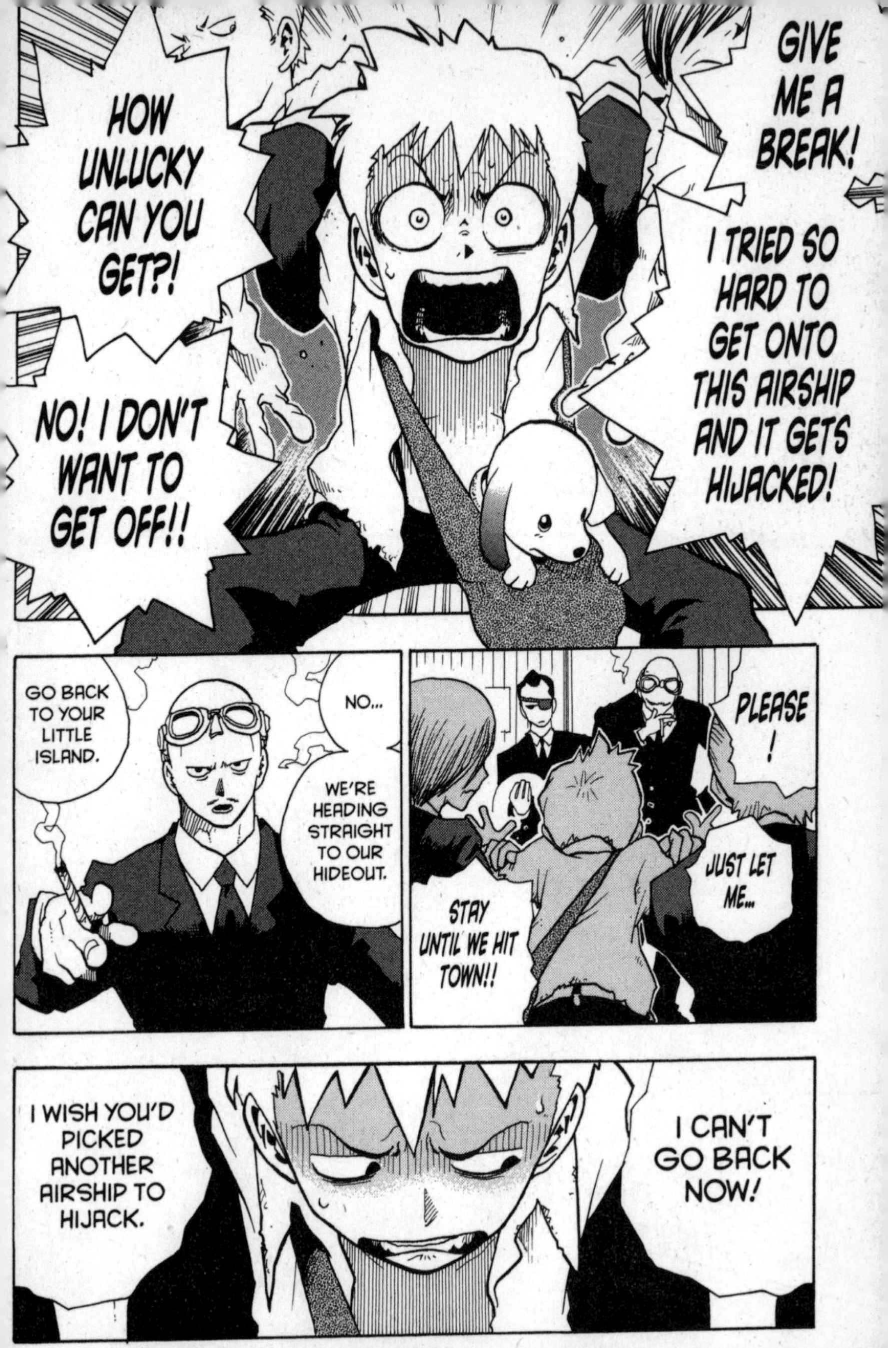
GIVE ME A BREAK!
I TRIED SO HARD TO GET ONTO THIS AIRSHIP AND IT GETS HIJACKED!
HOW UNLUCKY CAN YOU GET?!
NO! I DON'T WANT TO GET OFF!!
PLEASE!
JUST LET ME...
STAY UNTIL WE HIT TOWN!!
NO...
WE'RE HEADING STRAIGHT TO OUR HIDEOUT.
GO BACK TO YOUR LITTLE ISLAND.
I CAN'T GO BACK NOW!
I WISH YOU'D PICKED ANOTHER AIRSHIP TO HIJACK.

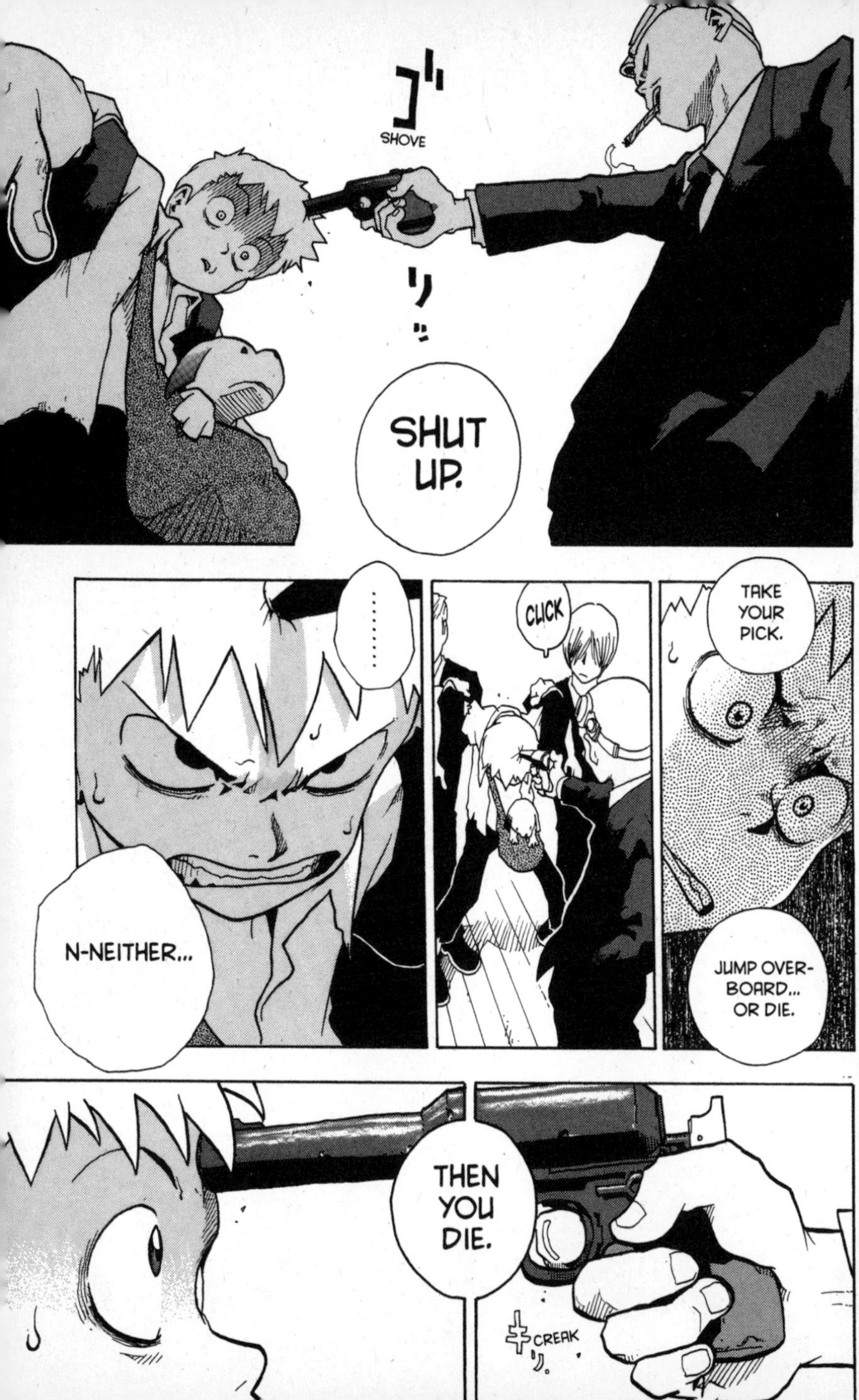
ゴッ
SHOVE
リッ
SHUT UP.
TAKE YOUR PICK.
JUMP OVER-BOARD... OR DIE.
CLICK
....
N-NEITHER...
THEN YOU DIE.
キリ
CREAK

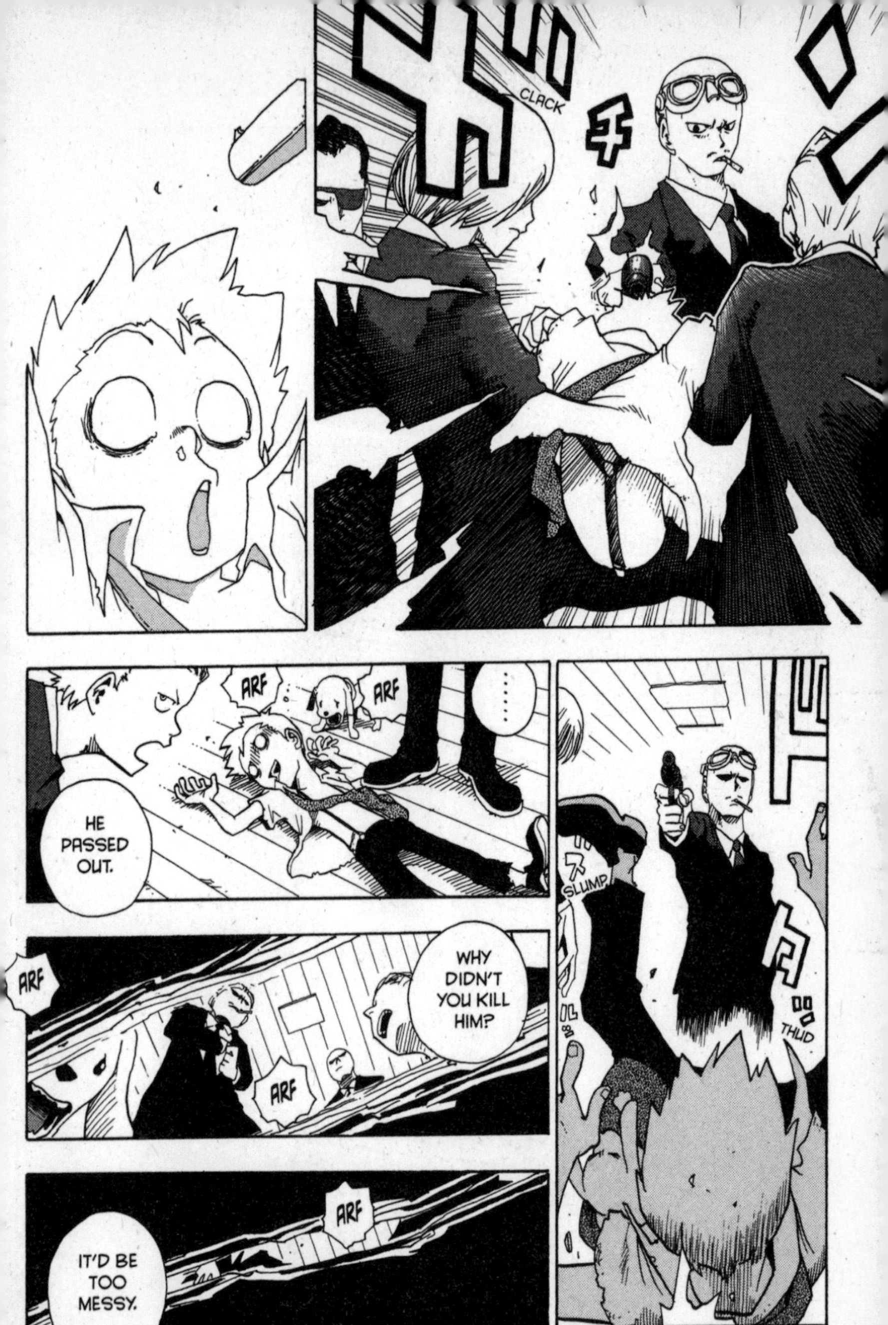

CLACK
SLUMP
THUD
......
ARF
ARF
HE PASSED OUT.
WHY DIDN'T YOU KILL HIM?
ARF
ARF
ARF
IT'D BE TOO MESSY.

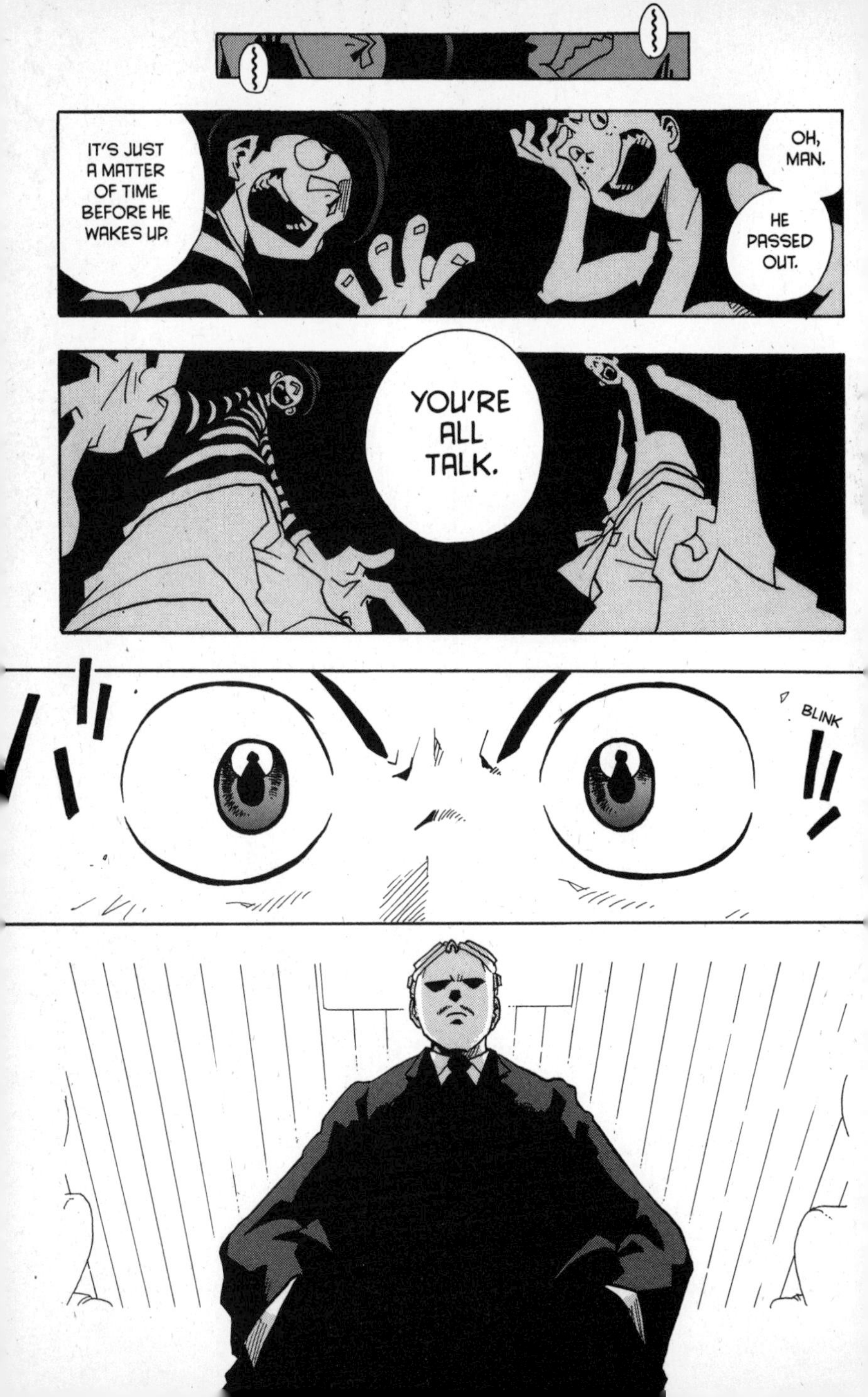
OH, MAN.
HE PASSED OUT.
IT'S JUST A MATTER OF TIME BEFORE HE WAKES UP.
YOU'RE ALL TALK.
BLINK

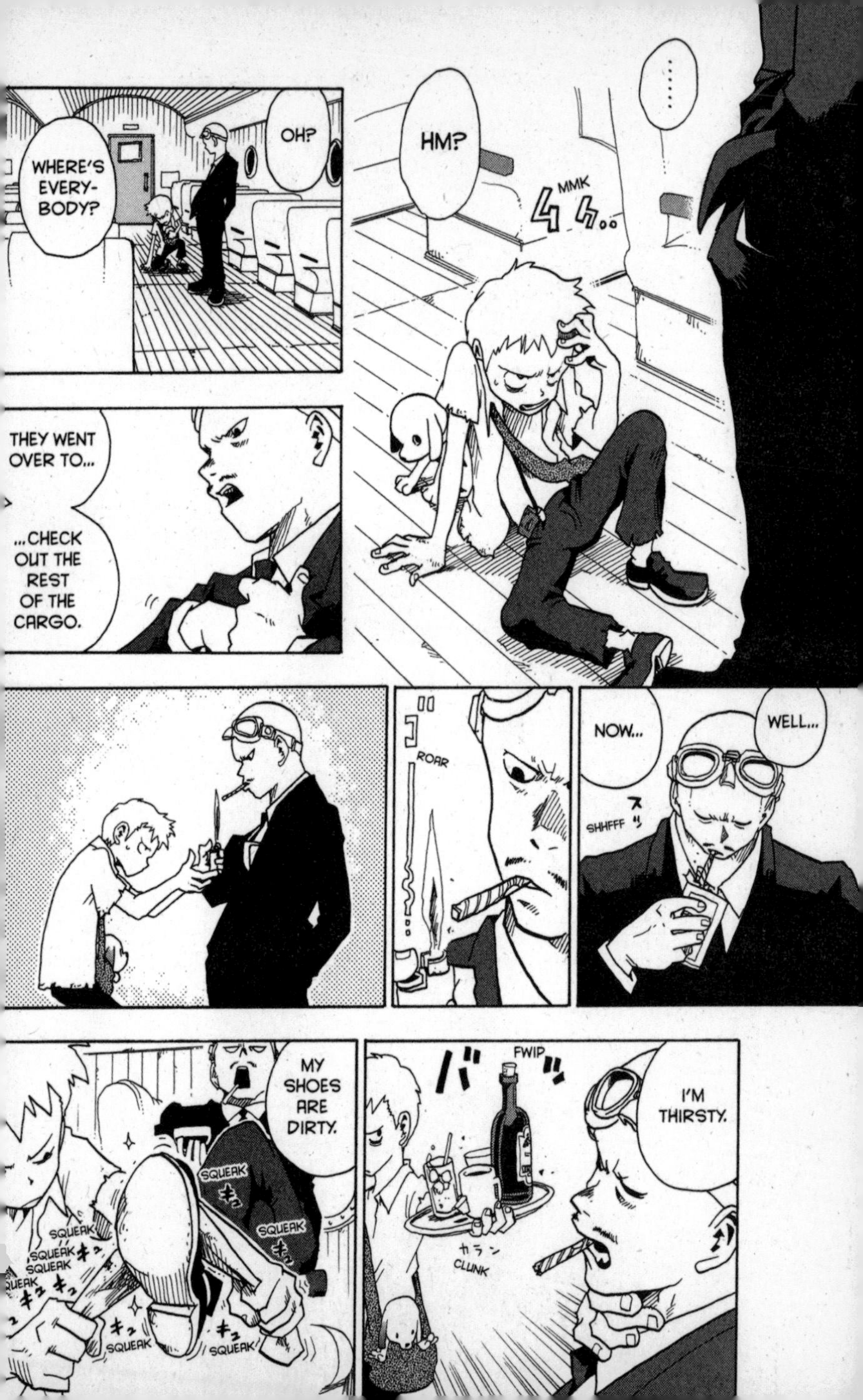
……
HM?
MMK
ムム..
OH?
WHERE'S EVERY-BODY?
THEY WENT OVER TO...
...CHECK OUT THE REST OF THE CARGO.
WELL...
NOW...
SHHFFF スッ
ゴ
ROAR
I'M THIRSTY.
FWIP
バッ
カラン
CLUNK
MY SHOES ARE DIRTY.
SQUEAK キュ
SQUEAK キュ
SQUEAK
SQUEAK
SQUEAK
SQUEAK キュ
SQUEAK キュ
SQUEAK キュ

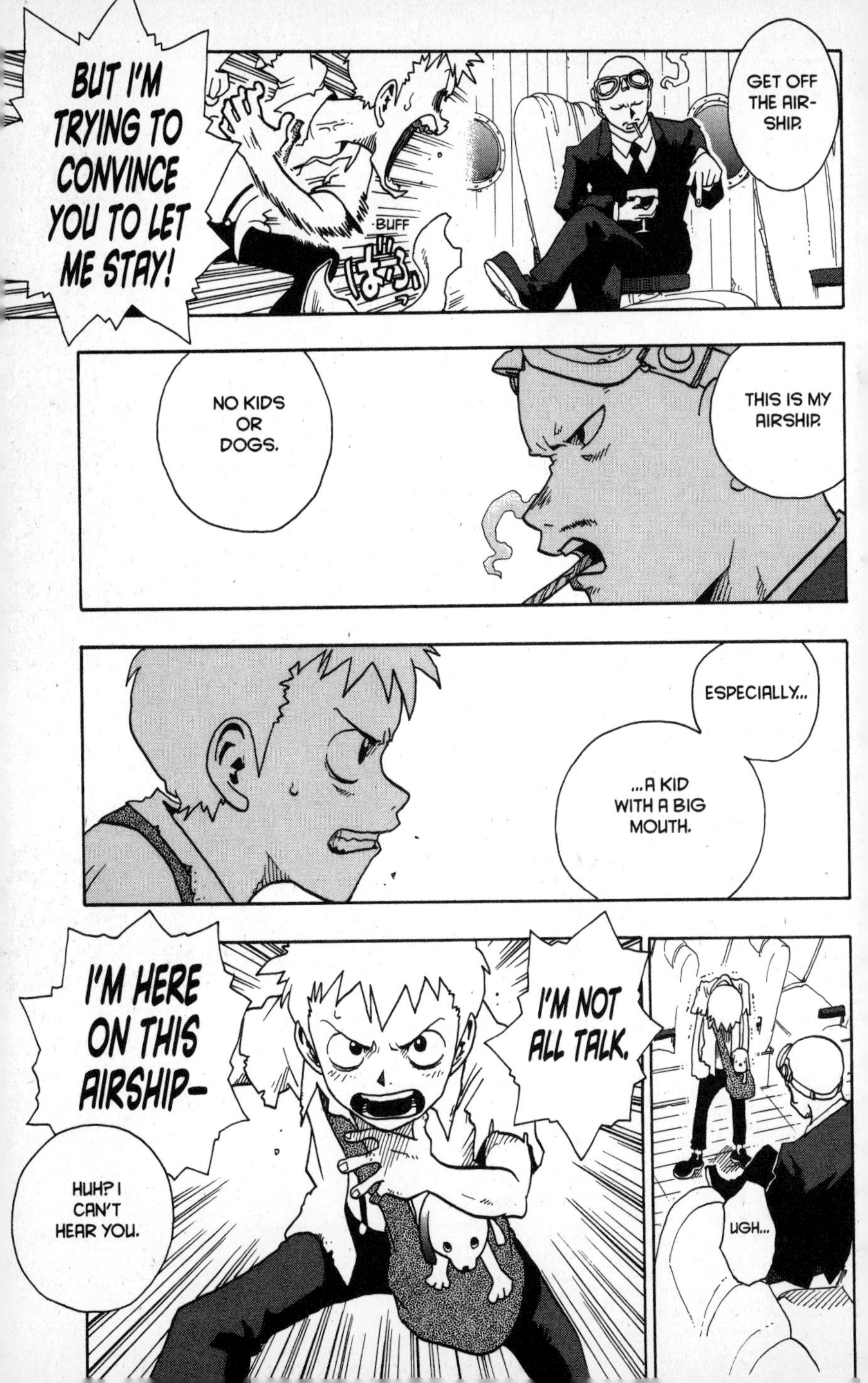
GET OFF THE AIR-SHIP.
BUFF
BUT I'M TRYING TO CONVINCE YOU TO LET ME STAY!
THIS IS MY AIRSHIP.
NO KIDS OR DOGS.
ESPECIALLY...
...A KID WITH A BIG MOUTH.
UGH...
I'M NOT ALL TALK.
I'M HERE ON THIS AIRSHIP-
HUH? I CAN'T HEAR YOU.

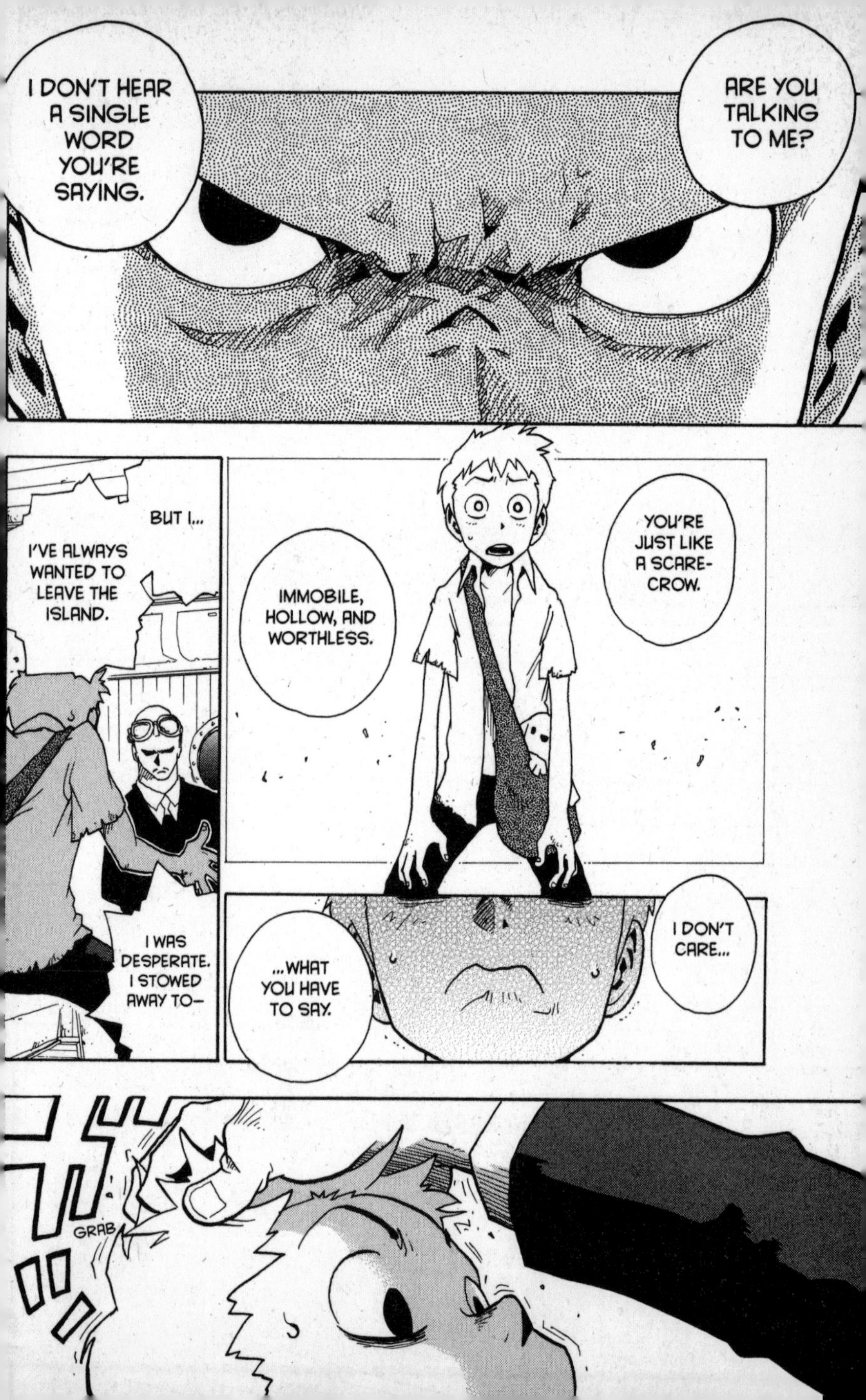
ARE YOU TALKING TO ME?
I DON'T HEAR A SINGLE WORD YOU'RE SAYING.
YOU'RE JUST LIKE A SCARE-CROW.
IMMOBILE, HOLLOW, AND WORTHLESS.
I DON'T CARE...
...WHAT YOU HAVE TO SAY.
BUT I...
I'VE ALWAYS WANTED TO LEAVE THE ISLAND.
I WAS DESPERATE. I STOWED AWAY TO—
GRAB

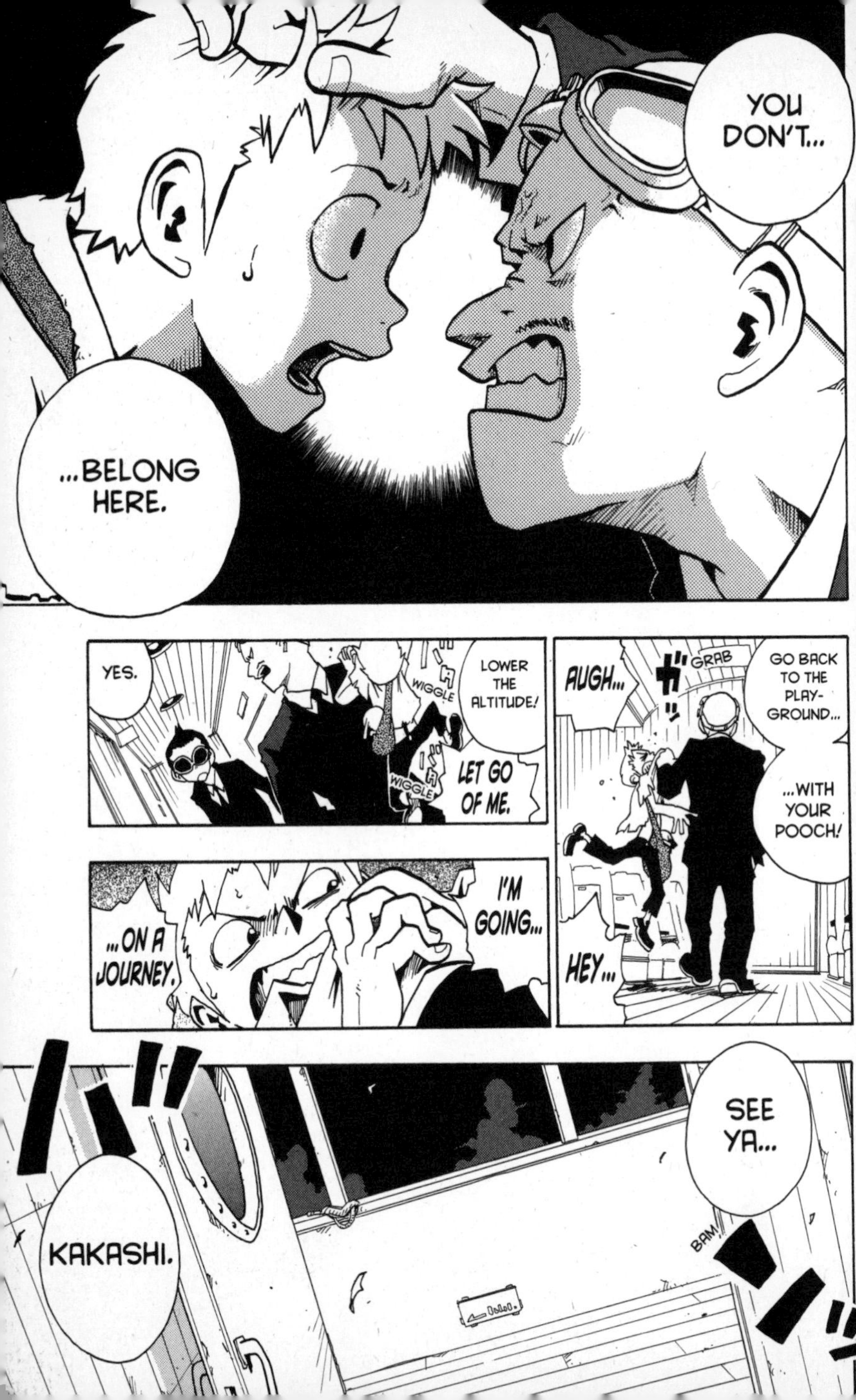
YOU DON'T...
...BELONG HERE.
GO BACK TO THE PLAY-GROUND...
GRAB
AUGH...
...WITH YOUR POOCH!
HEY...
LOWER THE ALTITUDE!
WIGGLE
WIGGLE
LET GO OF ME.
YES.
I'M GOING...
...ON A JOURNEY.
SEE YA...
BAM
KAKASHI.

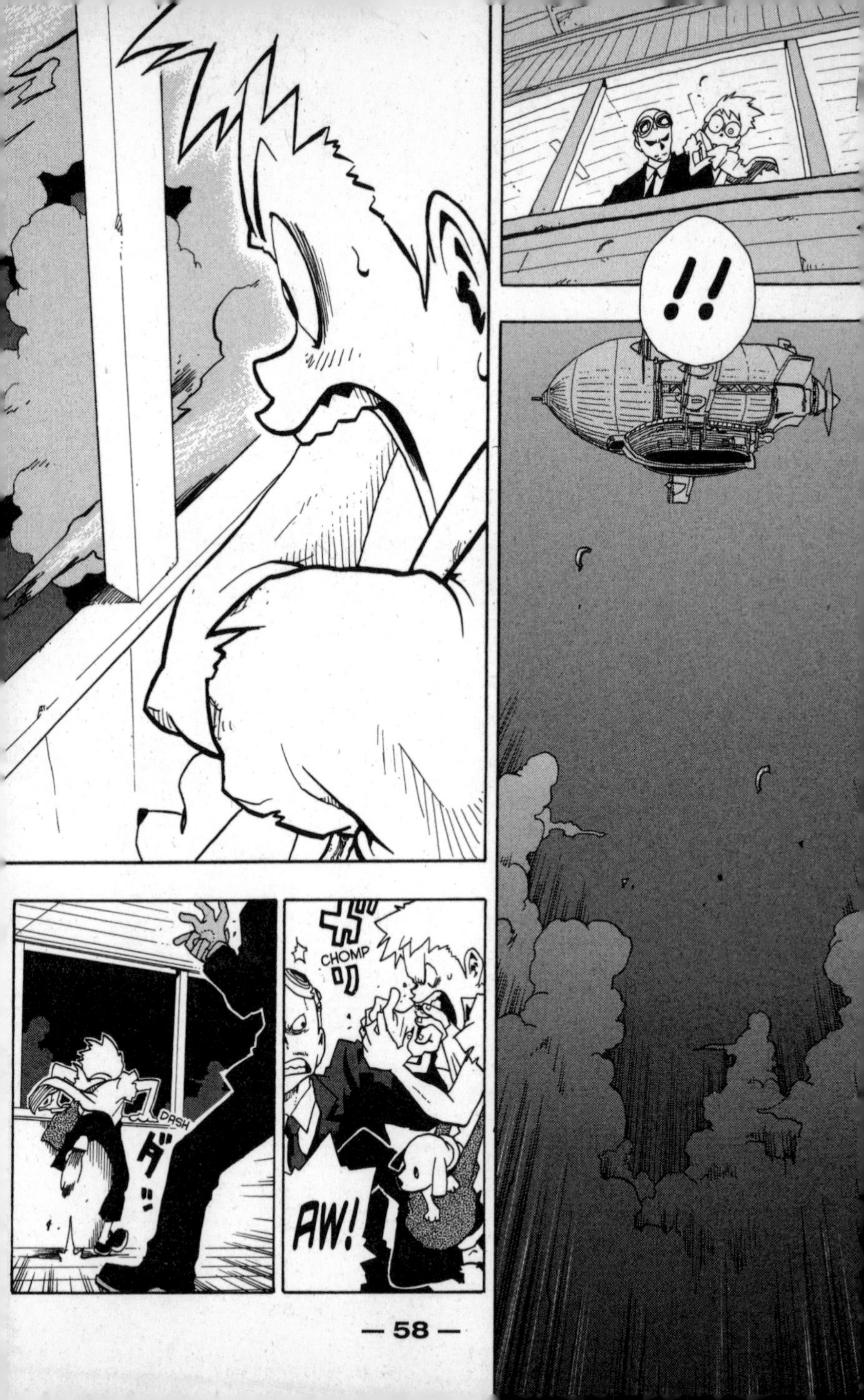
!!
CHOMP
AW!
DASH
ダ

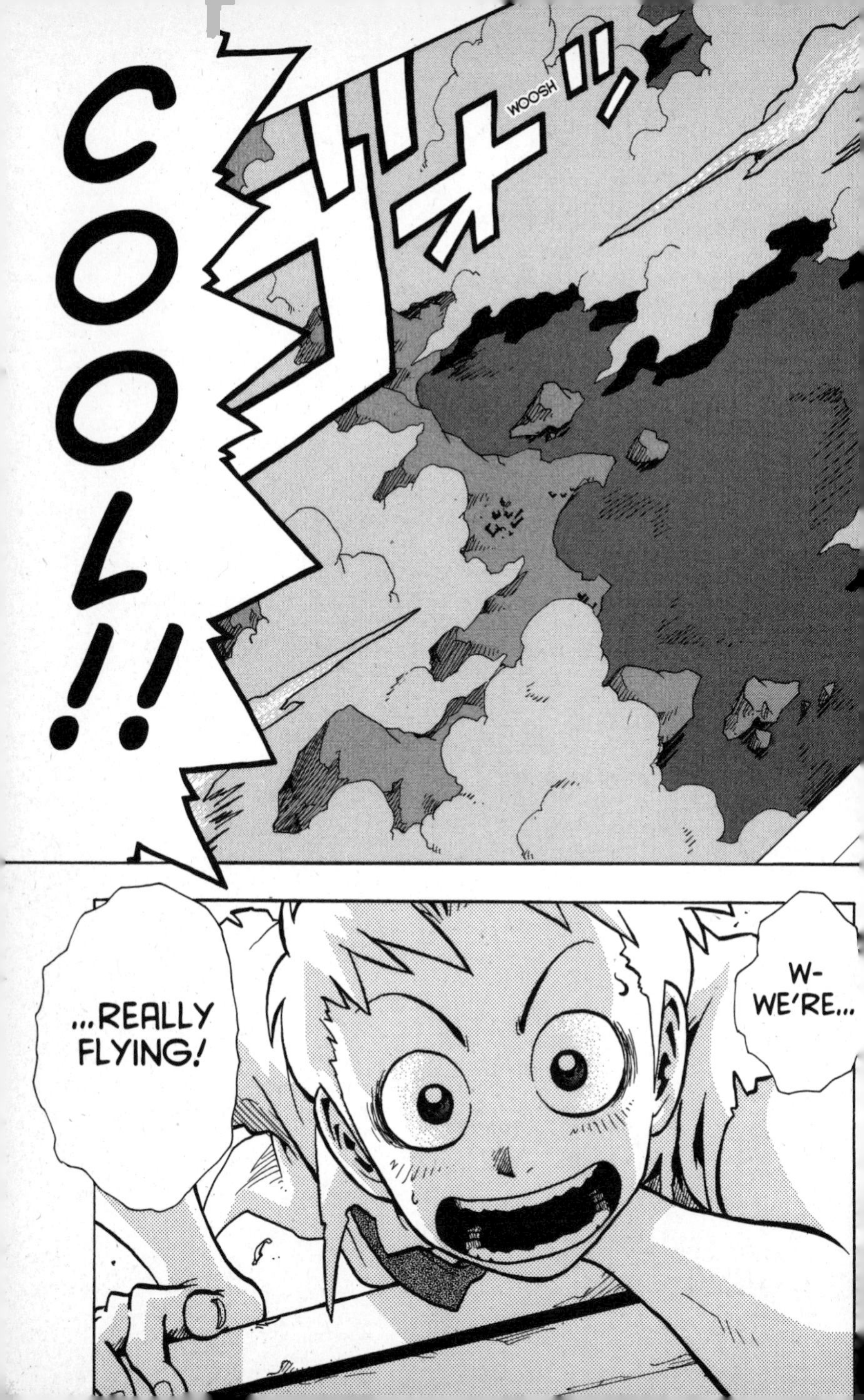
WOOSH
COOL!!
W- WE'RE...
...REALLY FLYING!

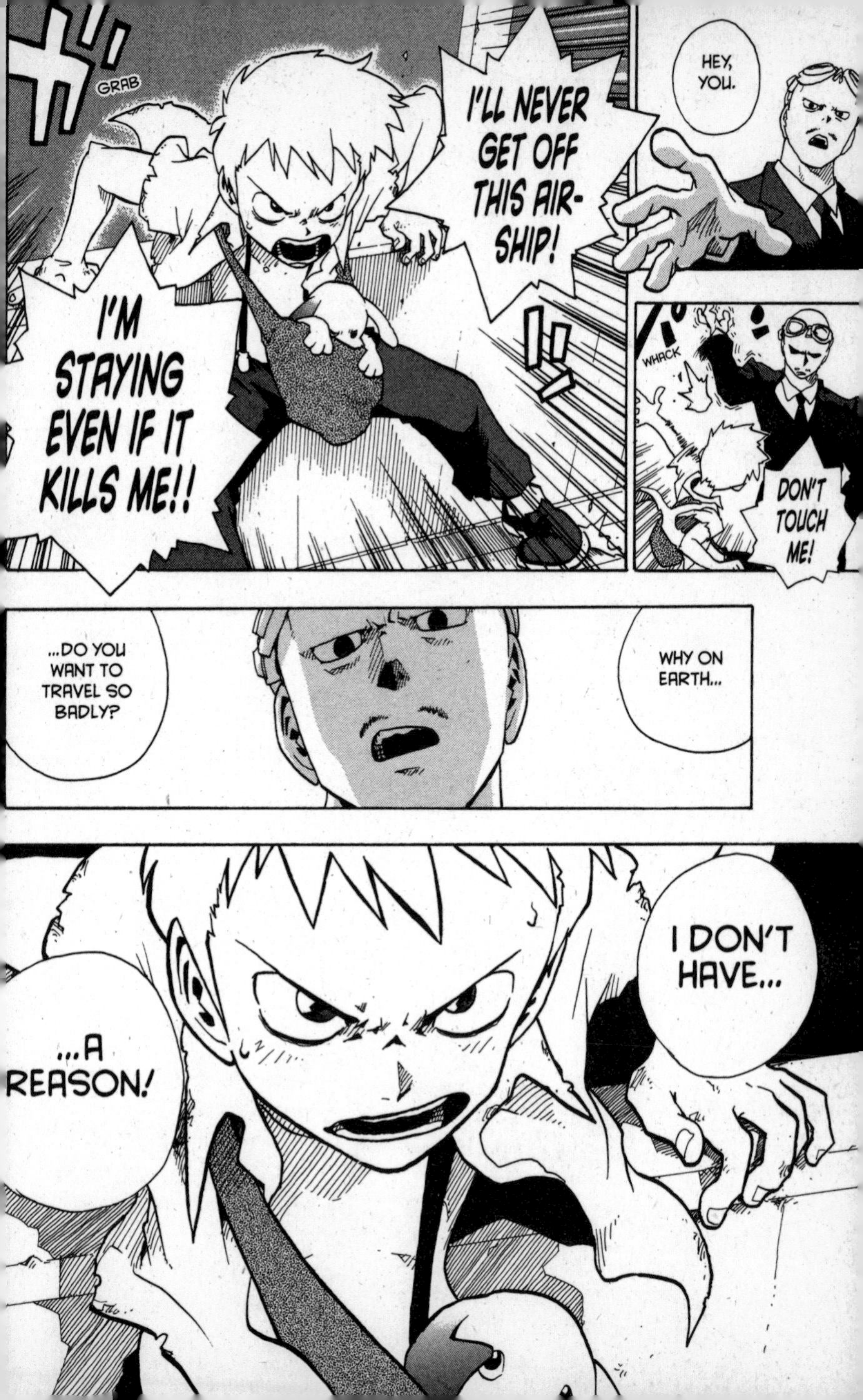
HEY, YOU.
WHACK
DON'T TOUCH ME!
GRAB
I'LL NEVER GET OFF THIS AIR-SHIP!
I'M STAYING EVEN IF IT KILLS ME!!
WHY ON EARTH...
...DO YOU WANT TO TRAVEL SO BADLY?
I DON'T HAVE...
...A REASON!

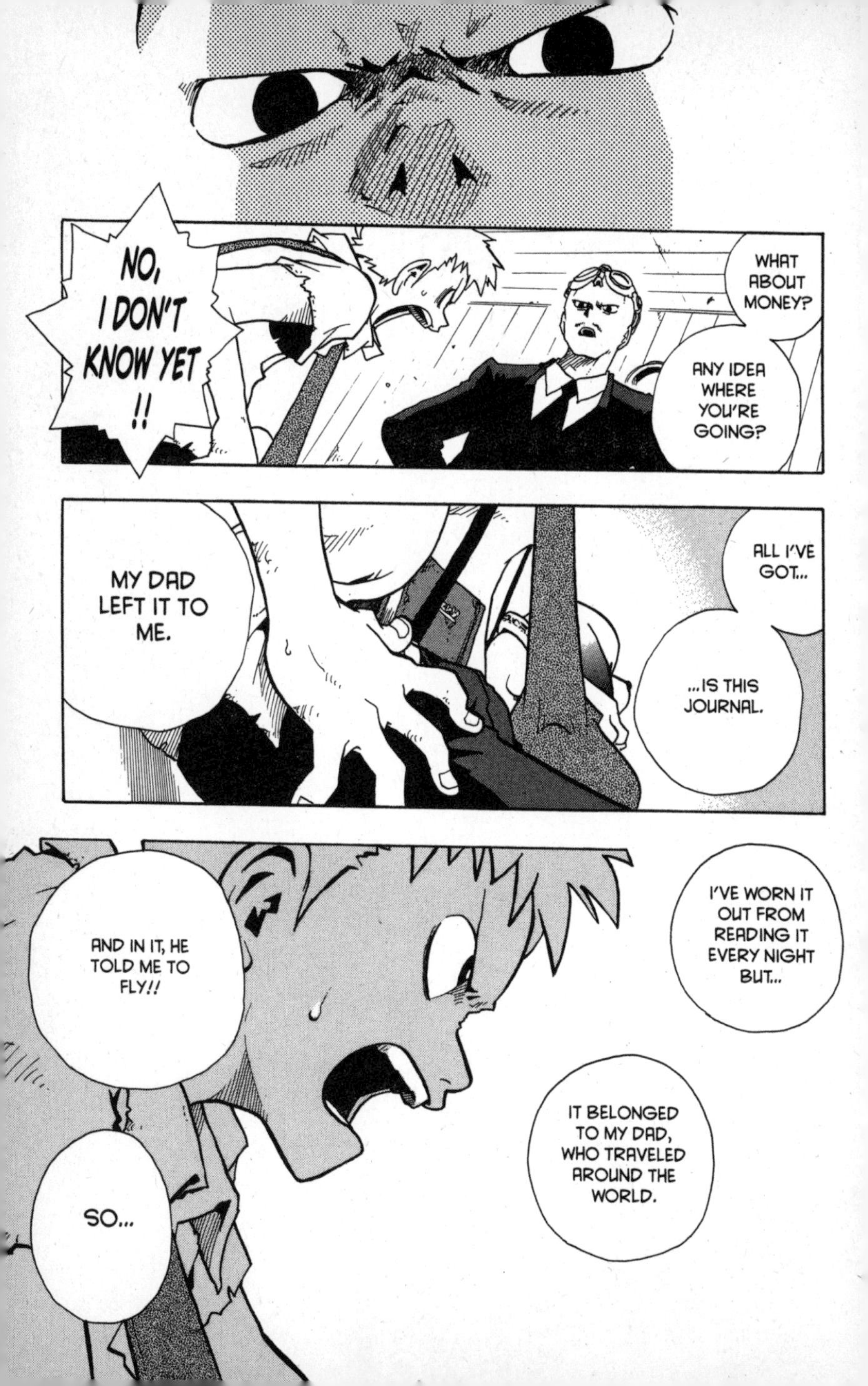
WHAT ABOUT MONEY?
ANY IDEA WHERE YOU'RE GOING?
NO, I DON'T KNOW YET!!
ALL I'VE GOT...
...IS THIS JOURNAL.
MY DAD LEFT IT TO ME.
I'VE WORN IT OUT FROM READING IT EVERY NIGHT BUT...
IT BELONGED TO MY DAD, WHO TRAVELED AROUND THE WORLD.
AND IN IT, HE TOLD ME TO FLY!!
SO...

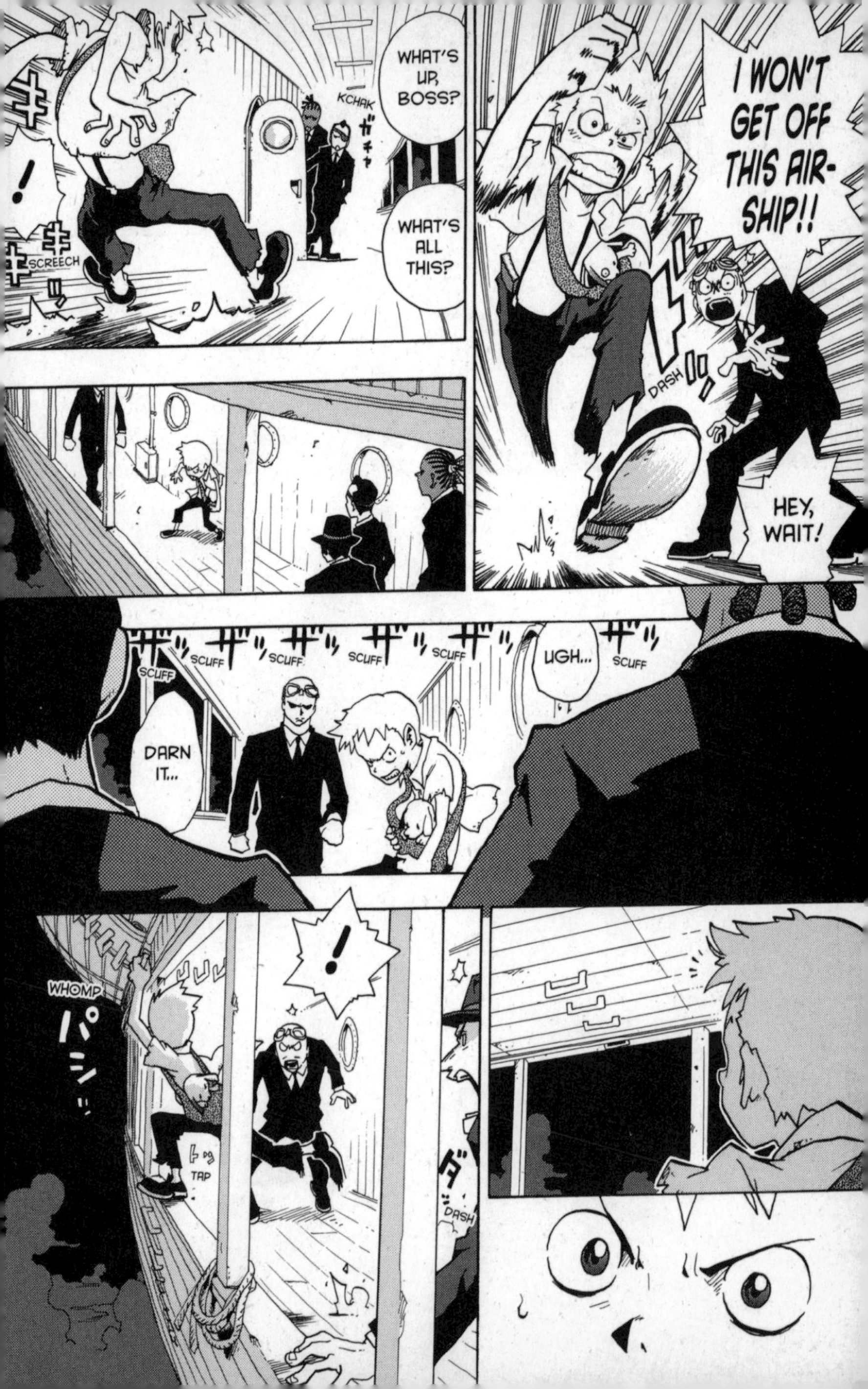

I WON'T GET OFF THIS AIR-SHIP!!
DASH
HEY, WAIT!
WHAT'S UP, BOSS?
KCHAK ガチャ
WHAT'S ALL THIS?
SCREECH
!
SCUFF
UGH...
SCUFF
SCUFF
SCUFF
SCUFF
SCUFF
DARN IT...
!
WHOMP
TAP
DASH

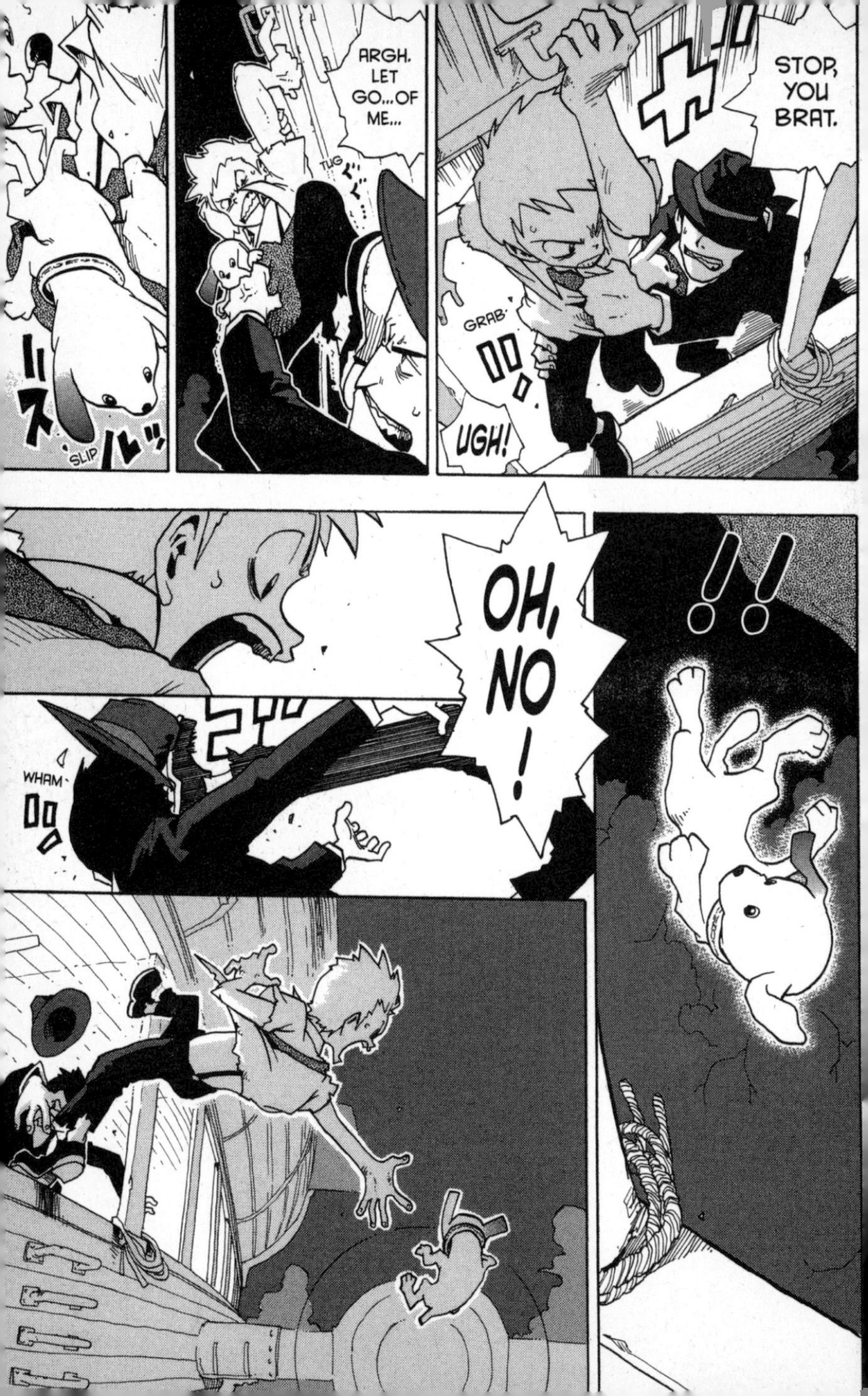
STOP, YOU BRAT.
GRAB
UGH!
ARGH. LET GO...OF ME...
TUG
SLIP
!!
OH, NO!
WHAM

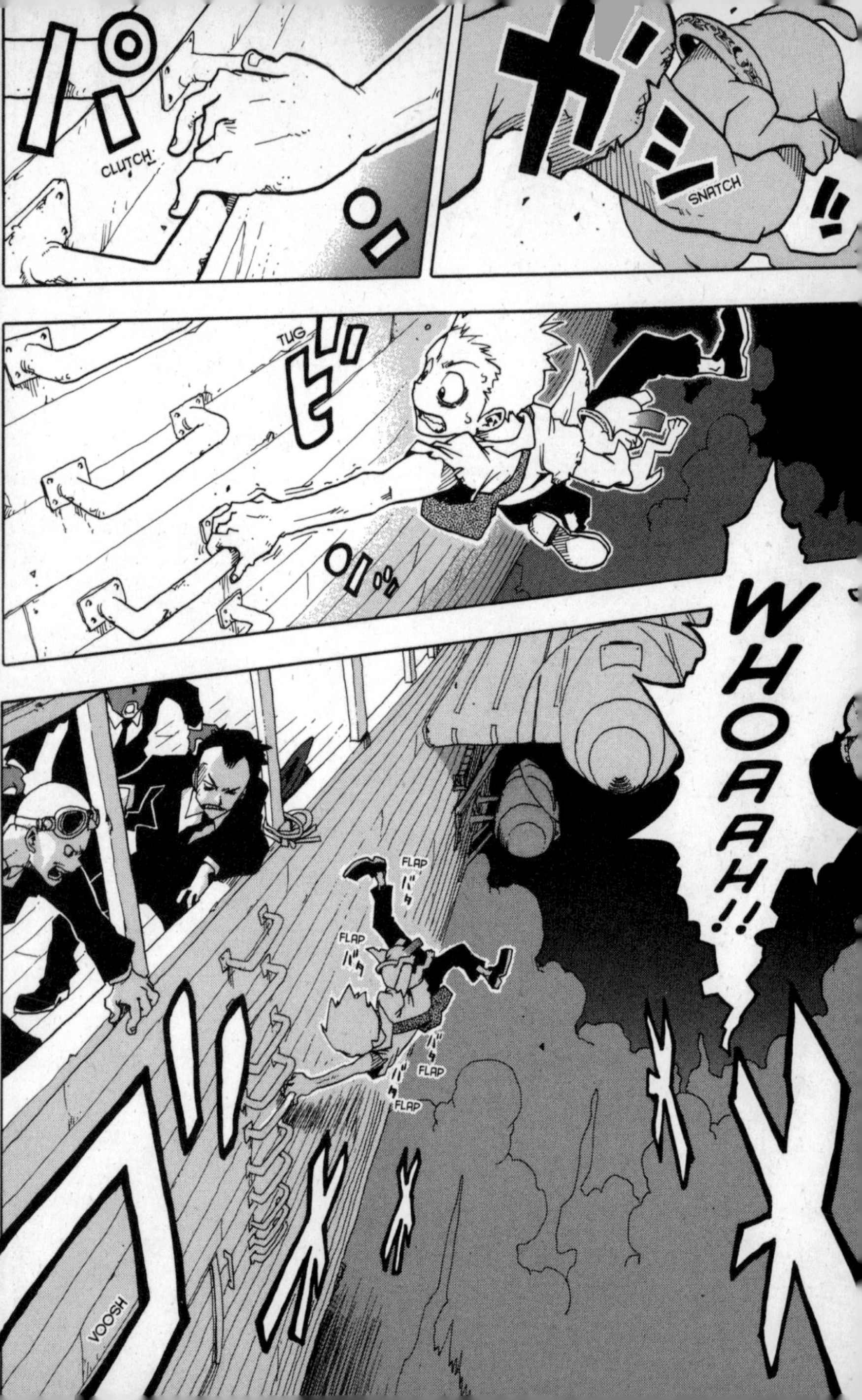
SNATCH
CLUTCH
TUG
WHOAAAH!!
FLAP
FLAP
FLAP
FLAP
VOOSH

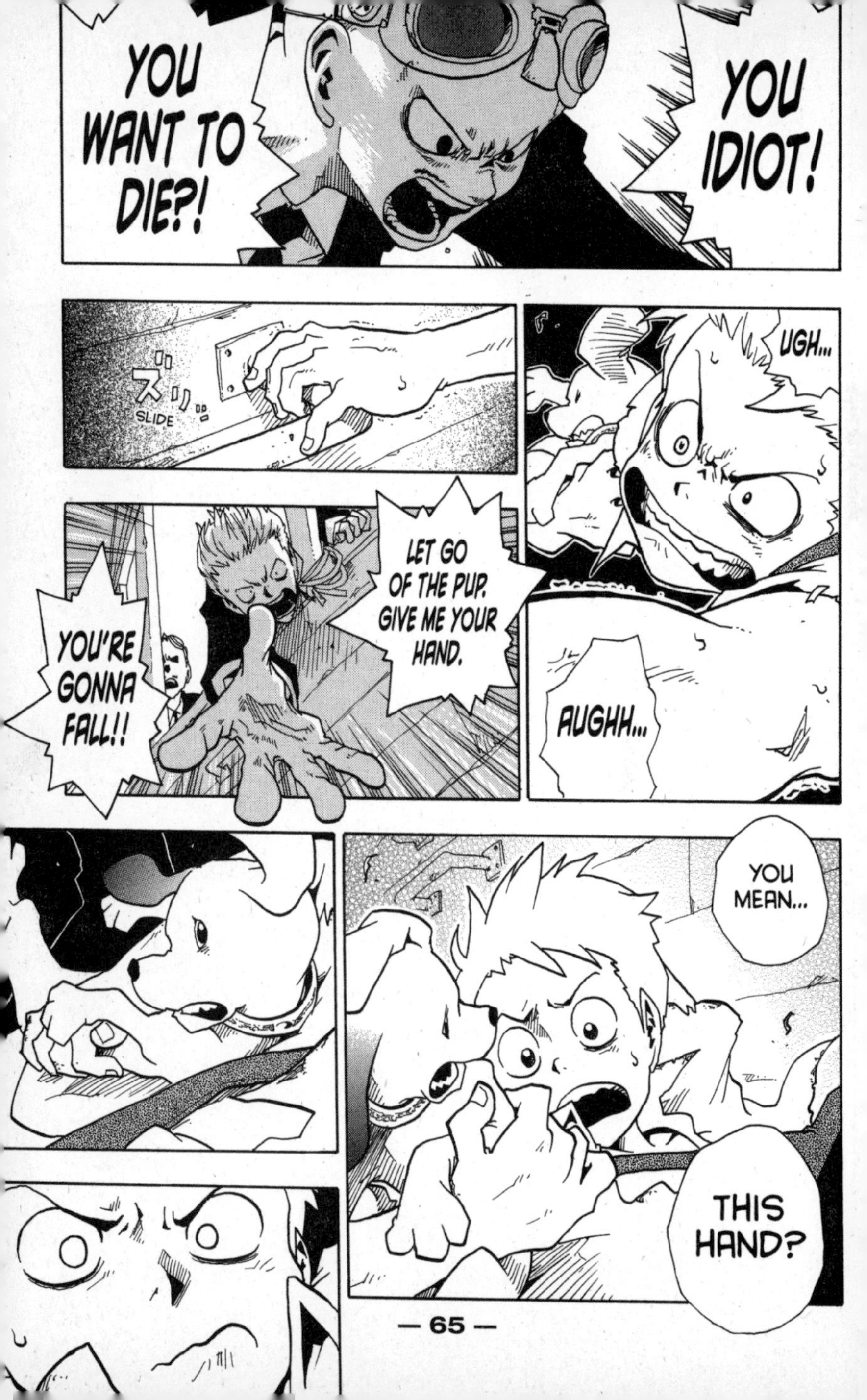
YOU IDIOT!
YOU WANT TO DIE?!
UGH...
AUGHH...
SLIDE
LET GO OF THE PUP. GIVE ME YOUR HAND.
YOU'RE GONNA FALL!!
YOU MEAN...
THIS HAND?

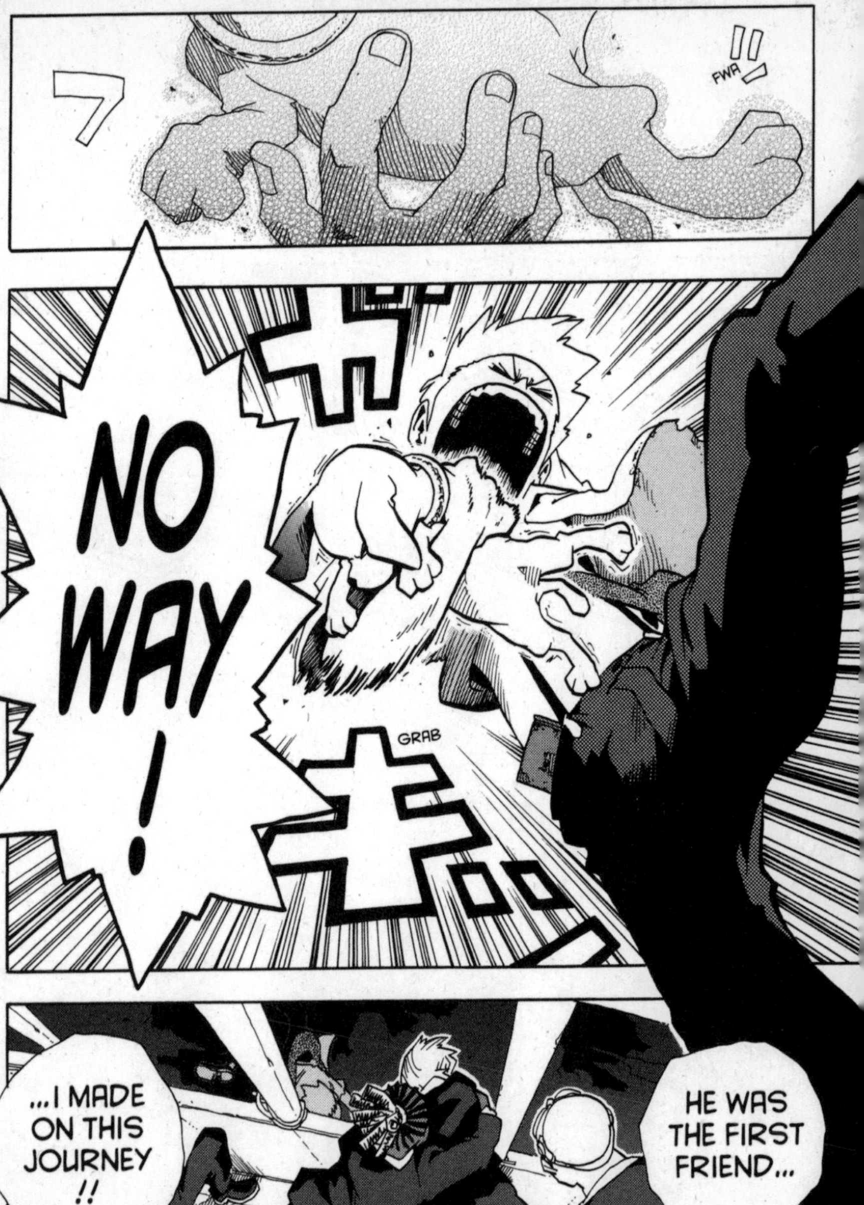
FWA
NO WAY !
GRAB
HE WAS THE FIRST FRIEND...
...I MADE ON THIS JOURNEY !!

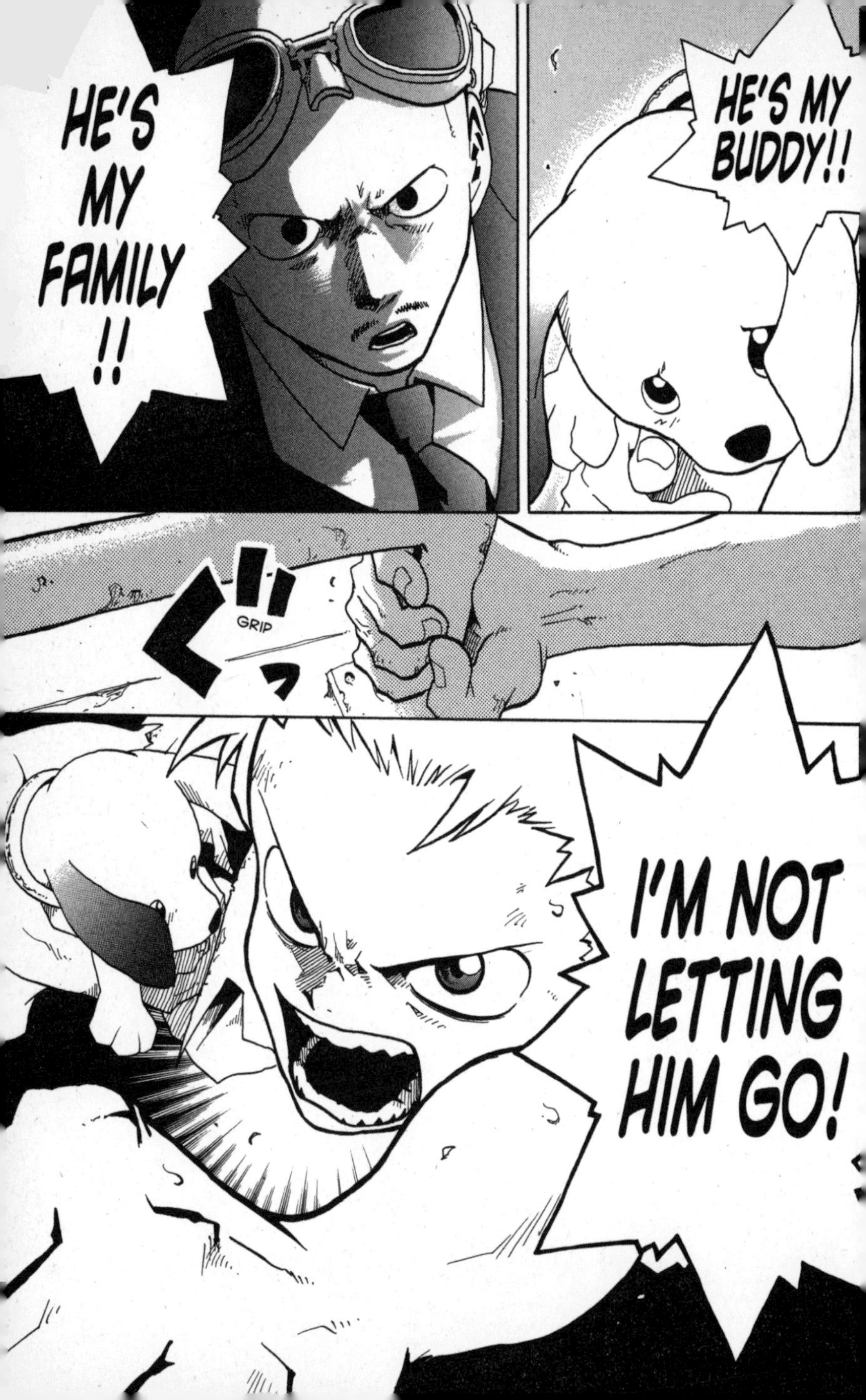
HE'S MY BUDDY!!
HE'S MY FAMILY!!
GRIP
I'M NOT LETTING HIM GO!

CRACK
UH-OH...
CRACK
SLIP

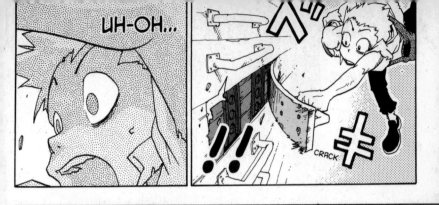

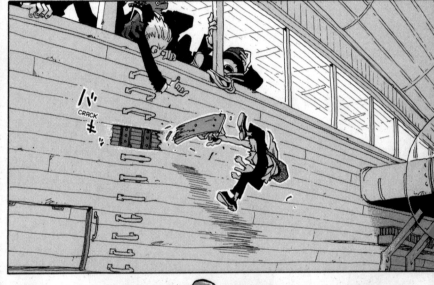

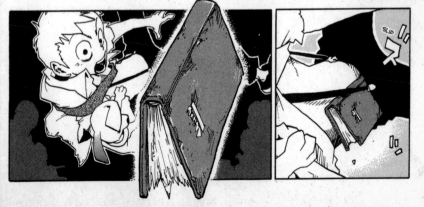

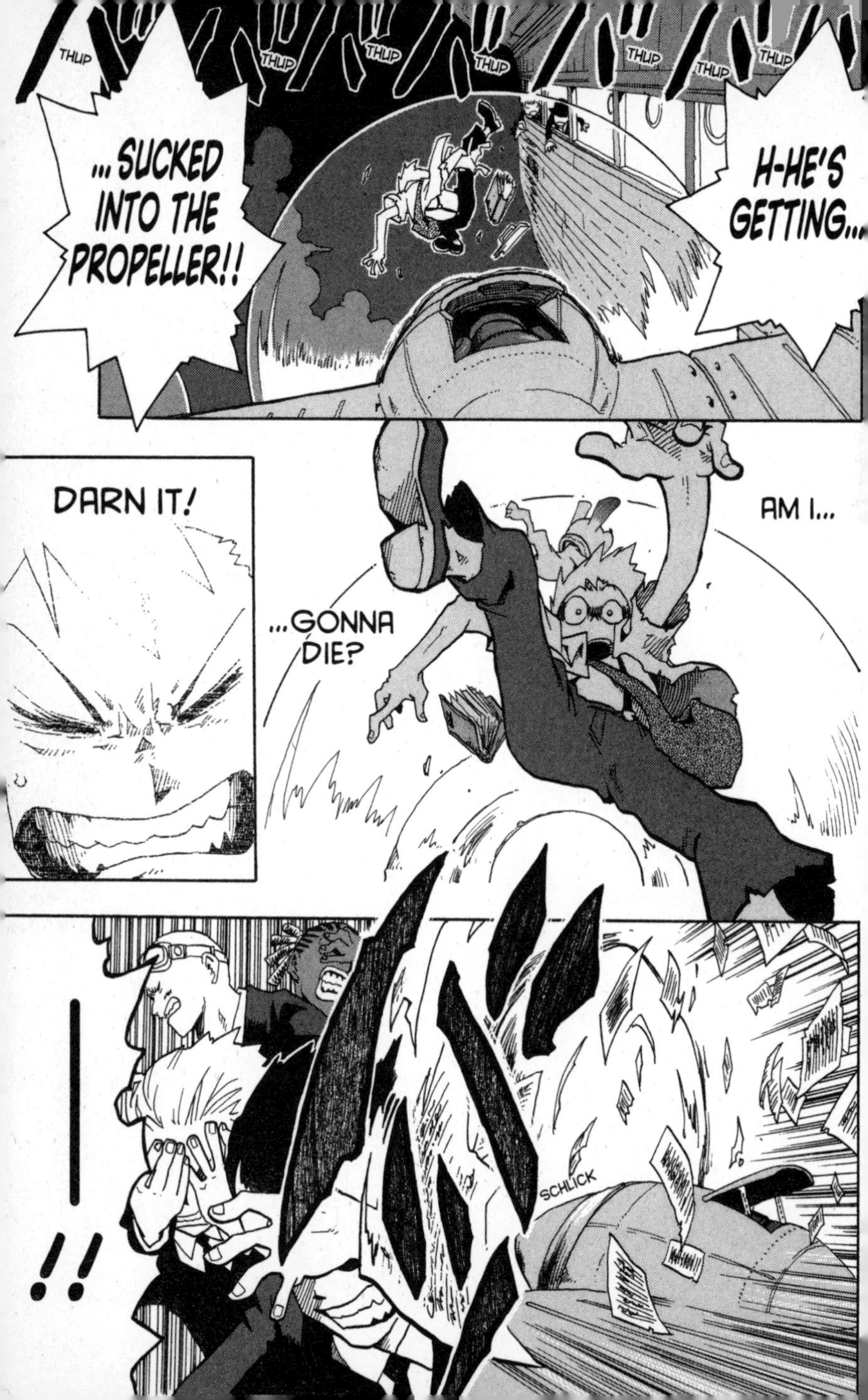
THUP
THUP
THUP
THUP
THUP
THUP
THUP
H-HE'S GETTING...
...SUCKED INTO THE PROPELLER!!
AM I...
...GONNA DIE?
DARN IT!
SCHLICK
—!!

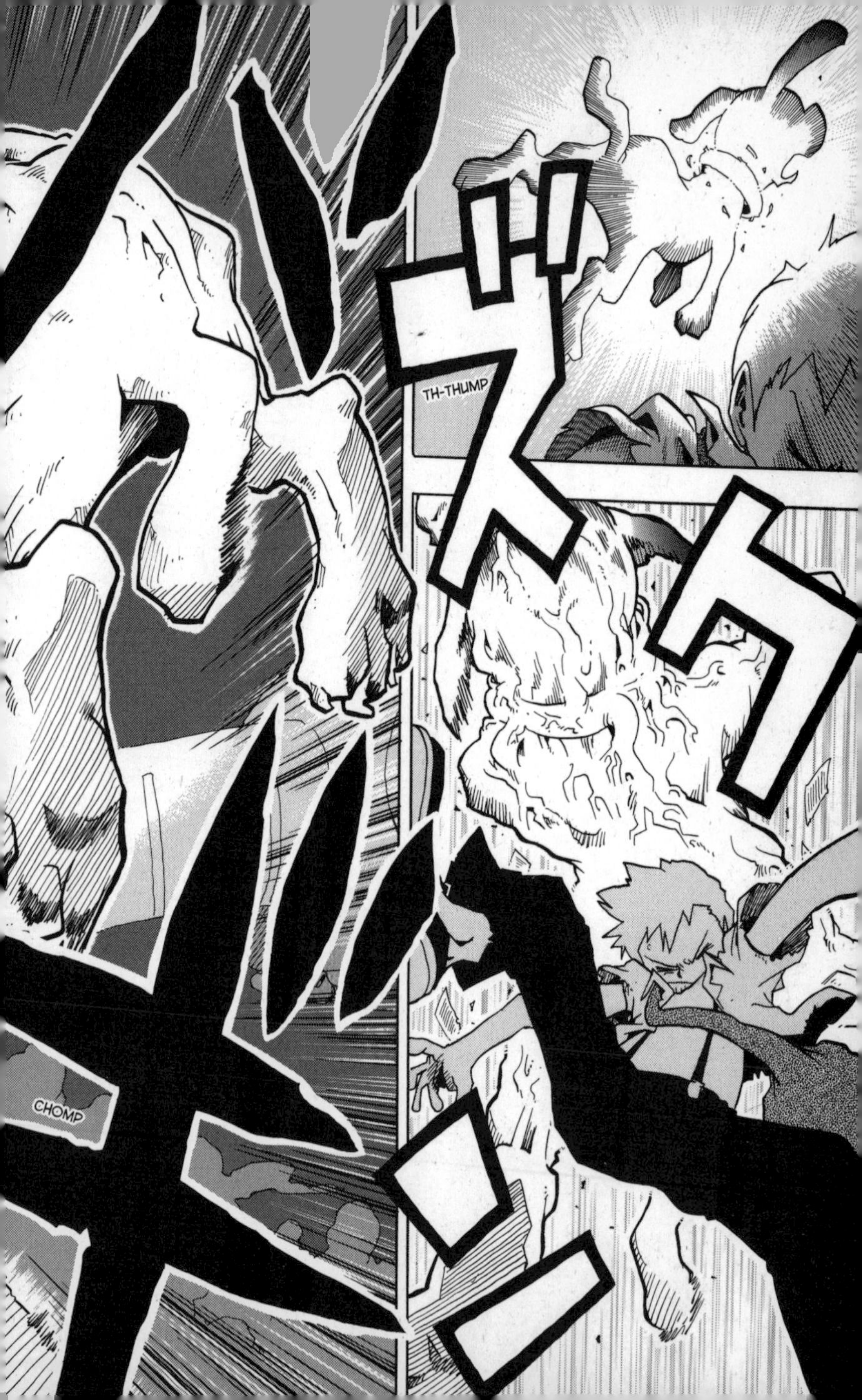
TH-THUMP
CHOMP

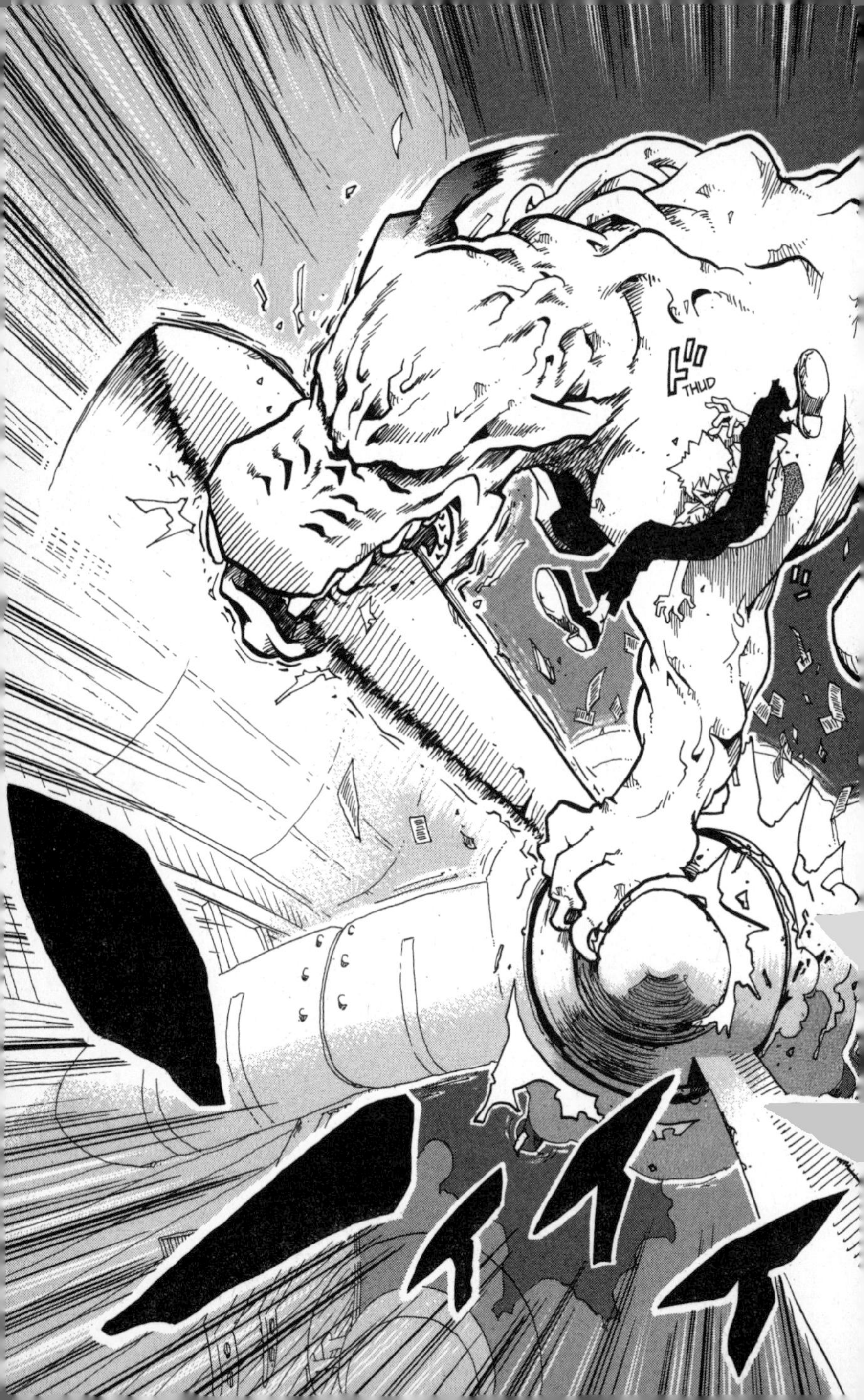
ドッ
THUD

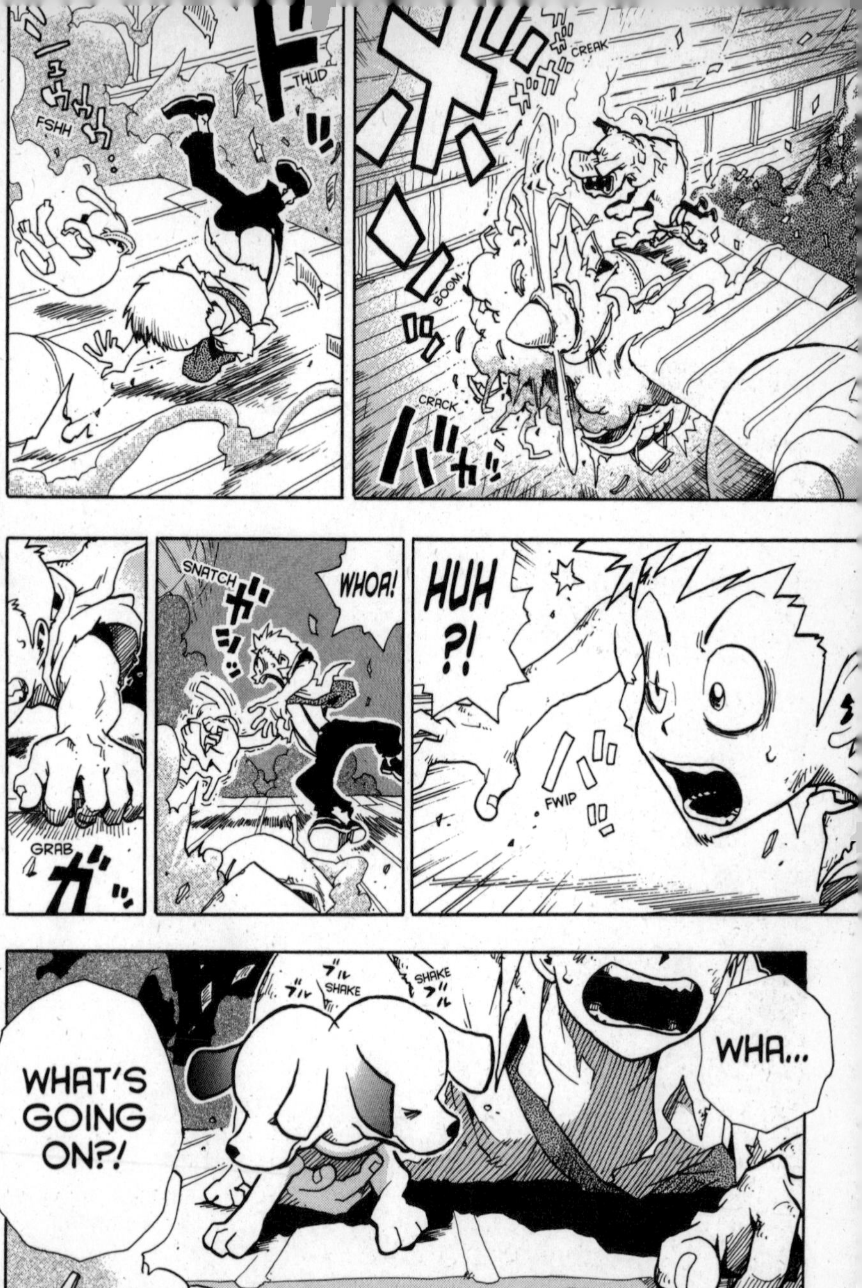
CREAK
BOOM
CRACK
THUD
FSHH
HUH ?!
FWIP
WHOA!
SNATCH
GRAB
WHA...
SHAKE
SHAKE
WHAT'S GOING ON?!

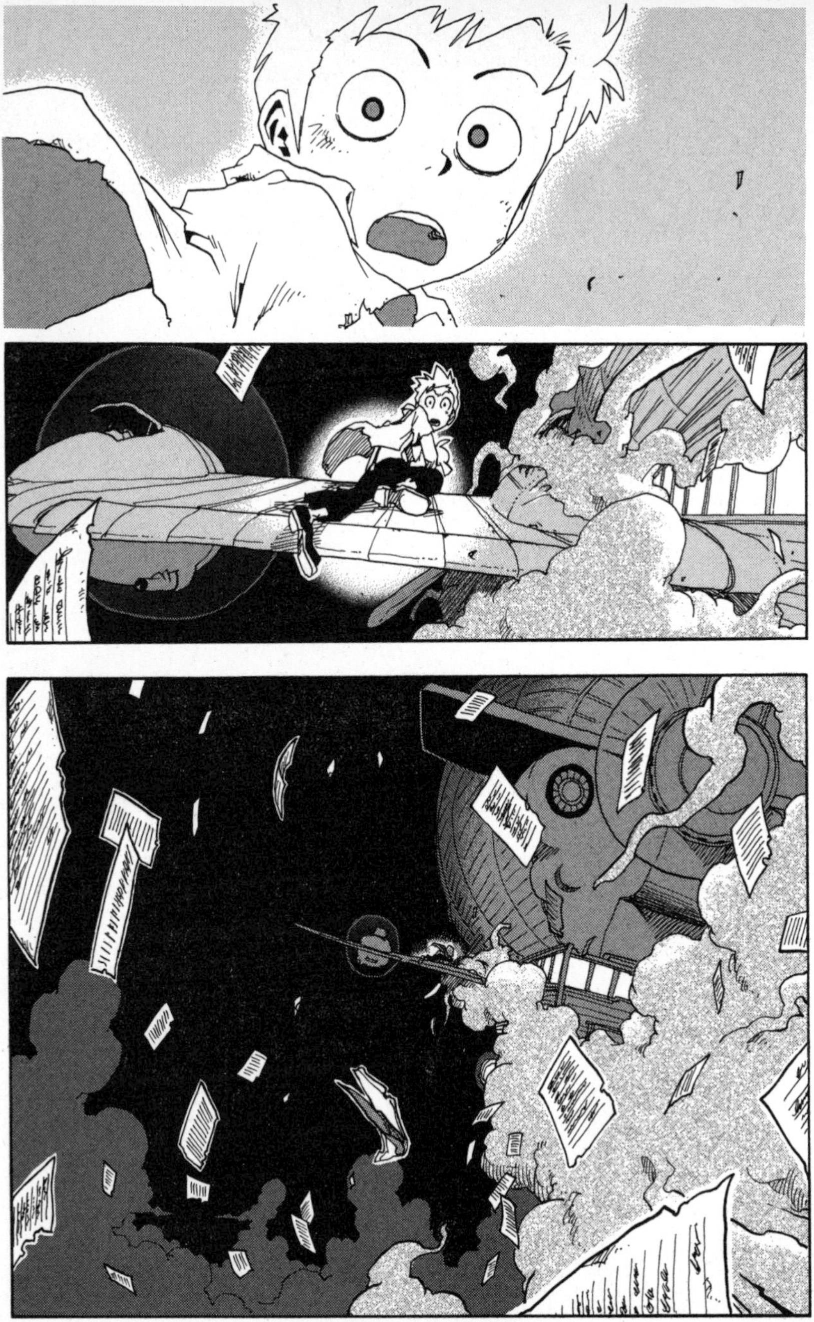

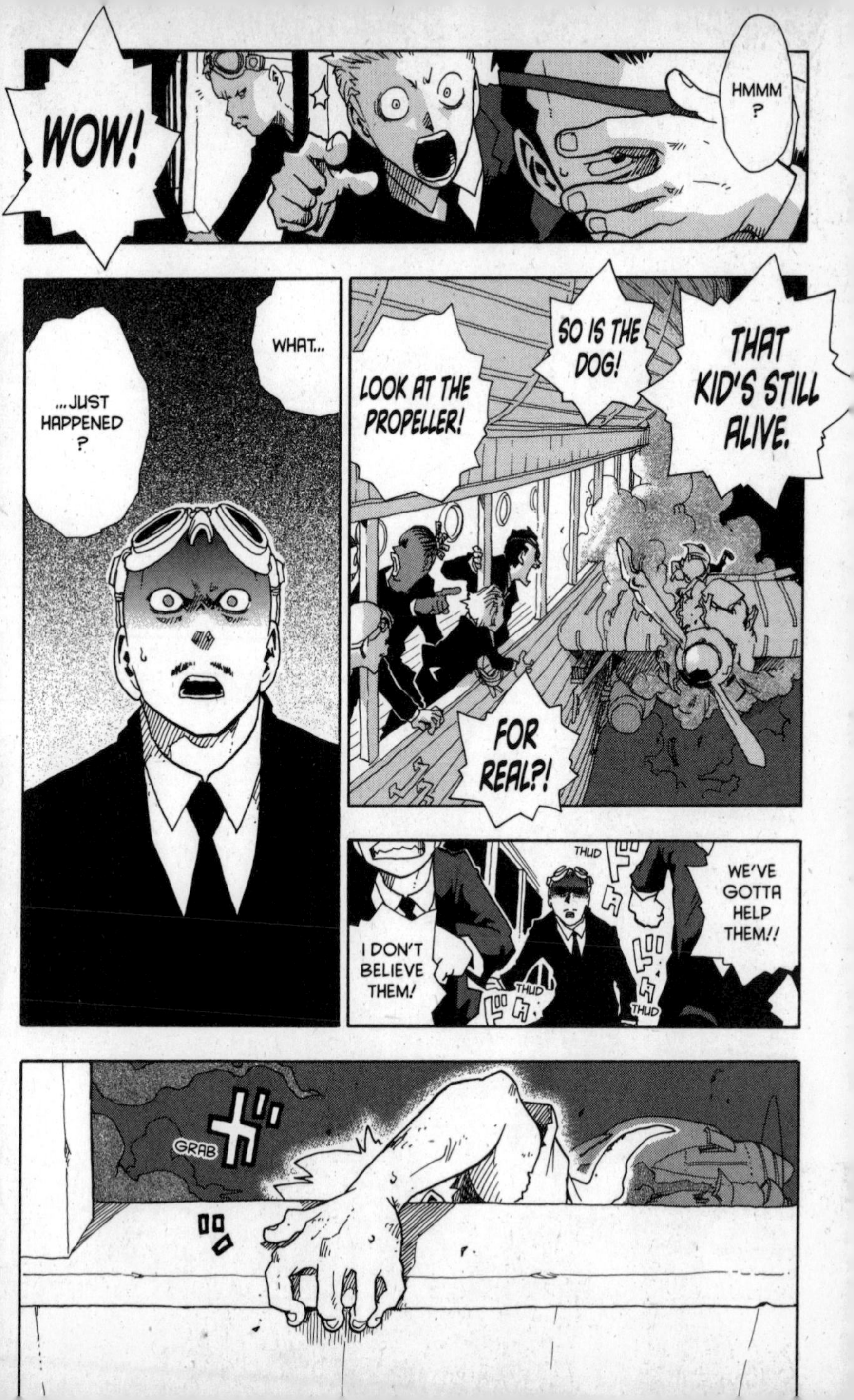
HMMM ?
WOW!
THAT KID'S STILL ALIVE.
SO IS THE DOG!
LOOK AT THE PROPELLER!
FOR REAL?!
THUD
WE'VE GOTTA HELP THEM!!
I DON'T BELIEVE THEM!
THUD
THUD
WHAT...
...JUST HAPPENED ?
GRAB

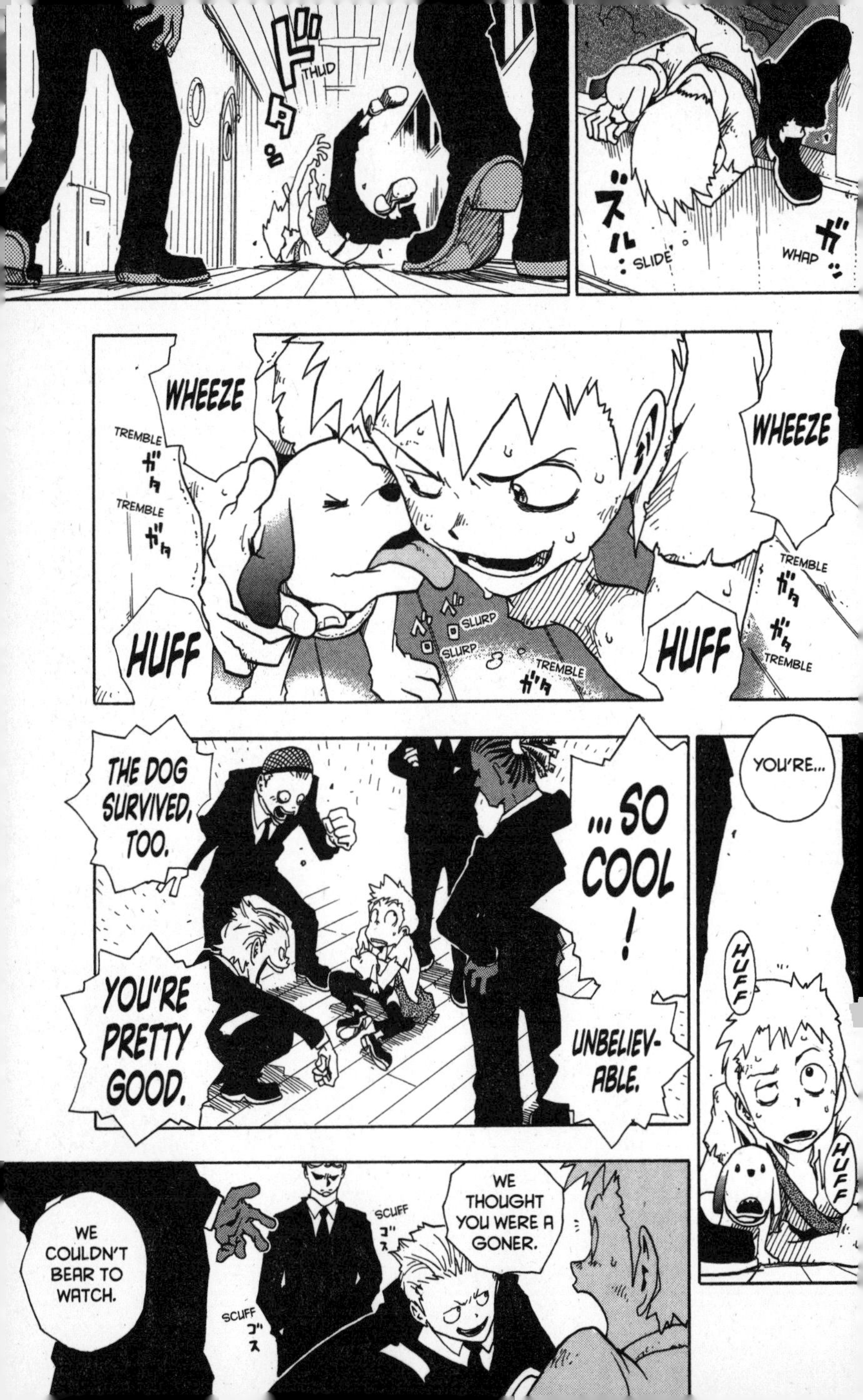
ガッ
WHAP
ズル
SLIDE
ドタッ
THUD
WHEEZE
WHEEZE
TREMBLE
ガタ
TREMBLE
ガタ
TREMBLE
ガタ
TREMBLE
ガタ
HUFF
SLURP
SLURP
TREMBLE
ガタ
HUFF
YOU'RE...
HUFF
HUFF
...SO COOL!
UNBELIEV-ABLE.
THE DOG SURVIVED, TOO.
YOU'RE PRETTY GOOD.
WE THOUGHT YOU WERE A GONER.
SCUFF
ゴス
SCUFF
ゴス
WE COULDN'T BEAR TO WATCH.

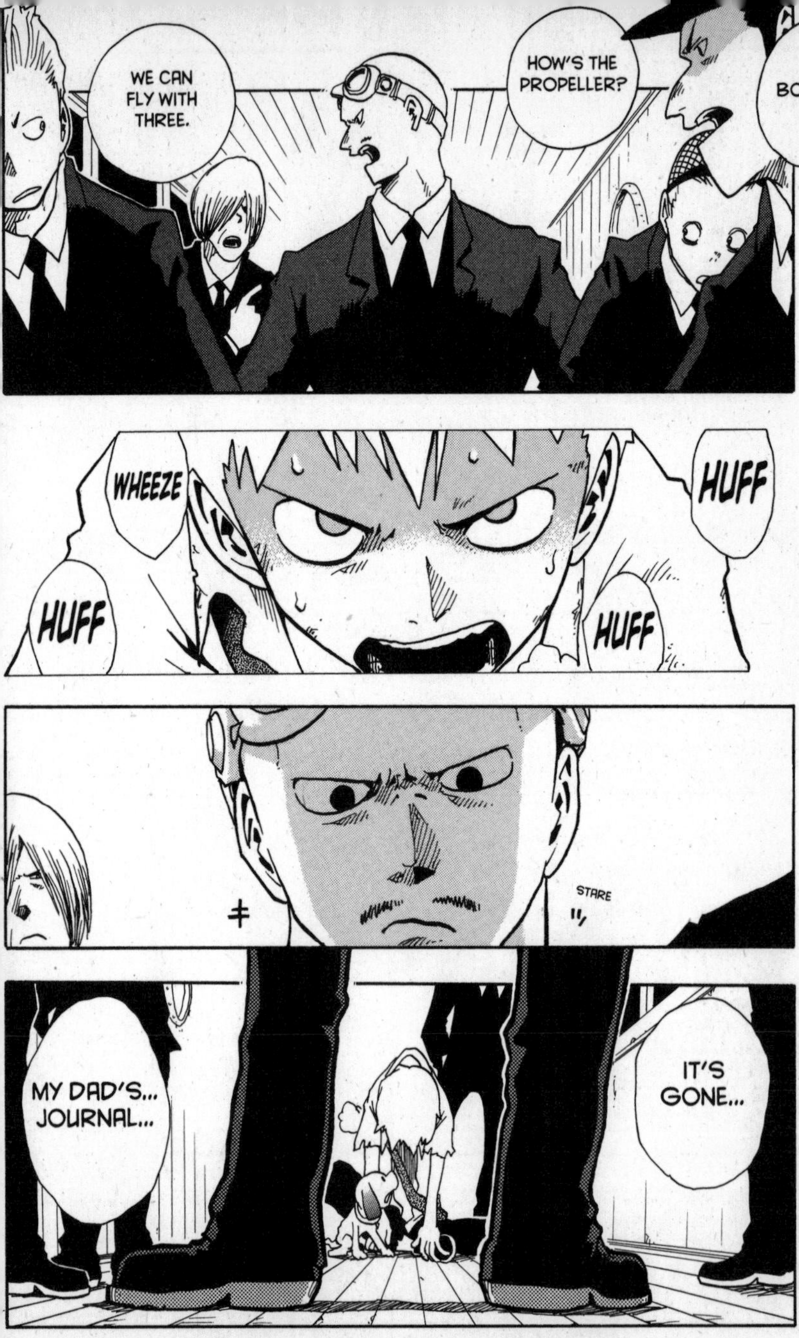
BOSS!
HOW'S THE PROPELLER?
WE CAN FLY WITH THREE.
HUFF
WHEEZE
HUFF
HUFF
STARE
IT'S GONE...
MY DAD'S... JOURNAL...

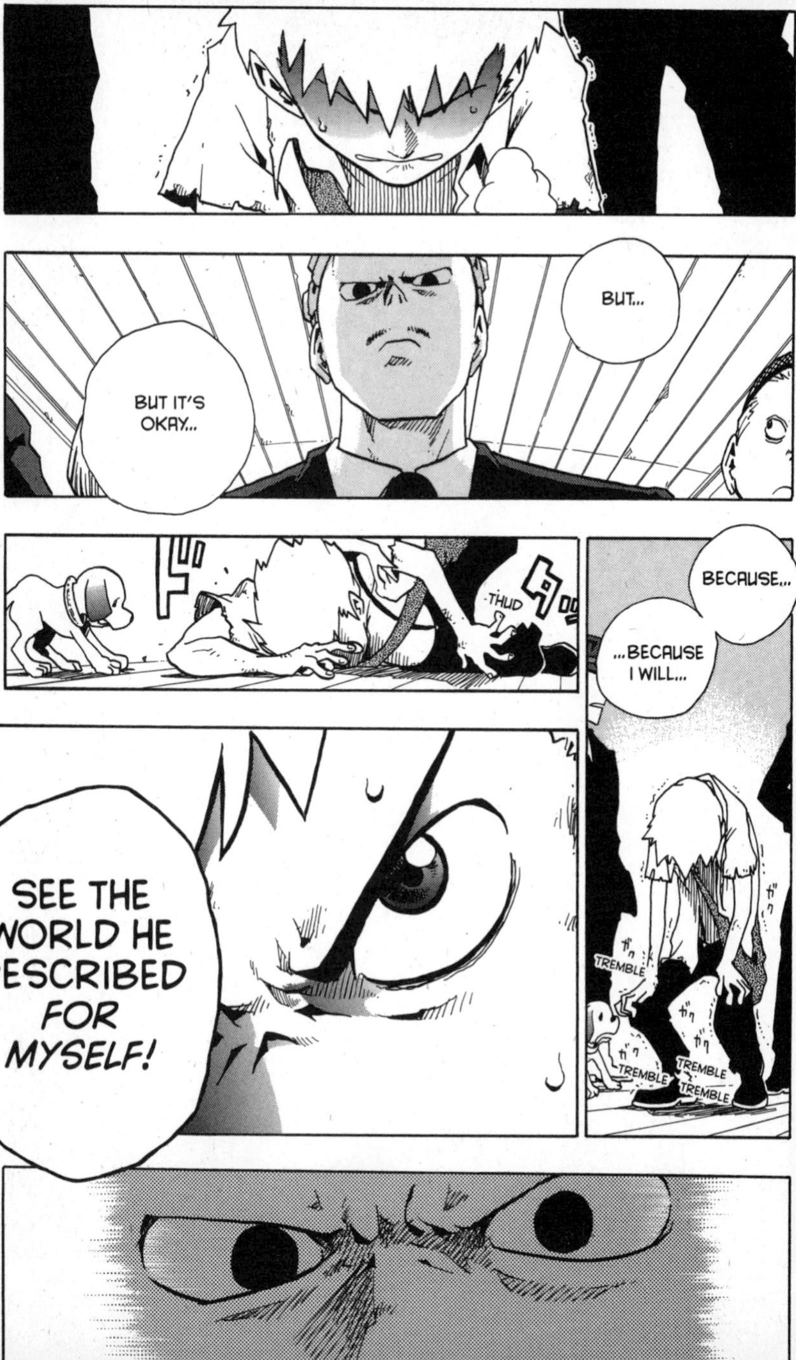

BUT...
BUT IT'S OKAY...
BECAUSE...
...BECAUSE I WILL...
TREMBLE
TREMBLE
TREMBLE
TREMBLE
THUD
SEE THE WORLD HE DESCRIBED FOR MYSELF!

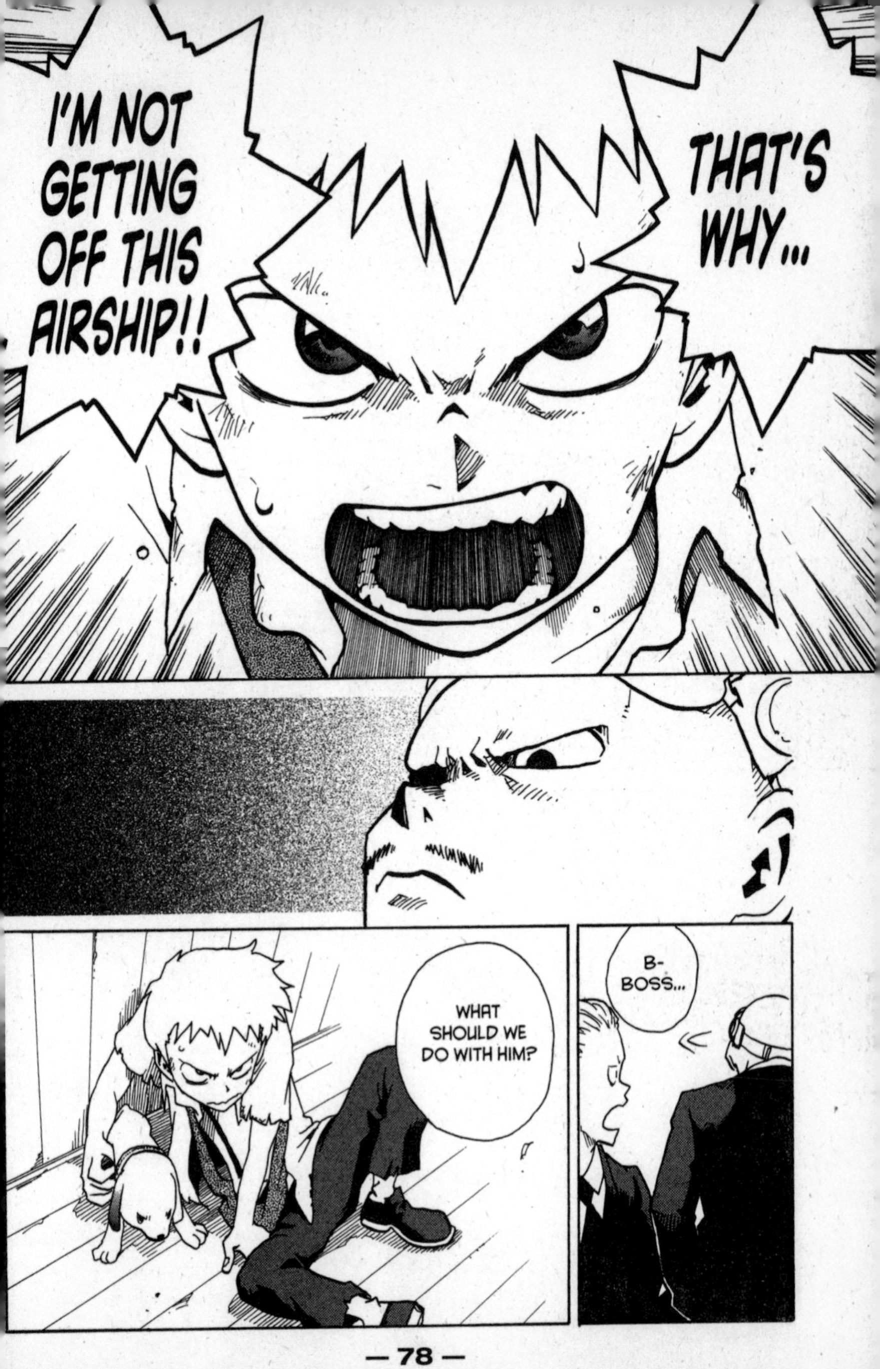
THAT'S WHY...
I'M NOT GETTING OFF THIS AIRSHIP!!
B-BOSS...
WHAT SHOULD WE DO WITH HIM?

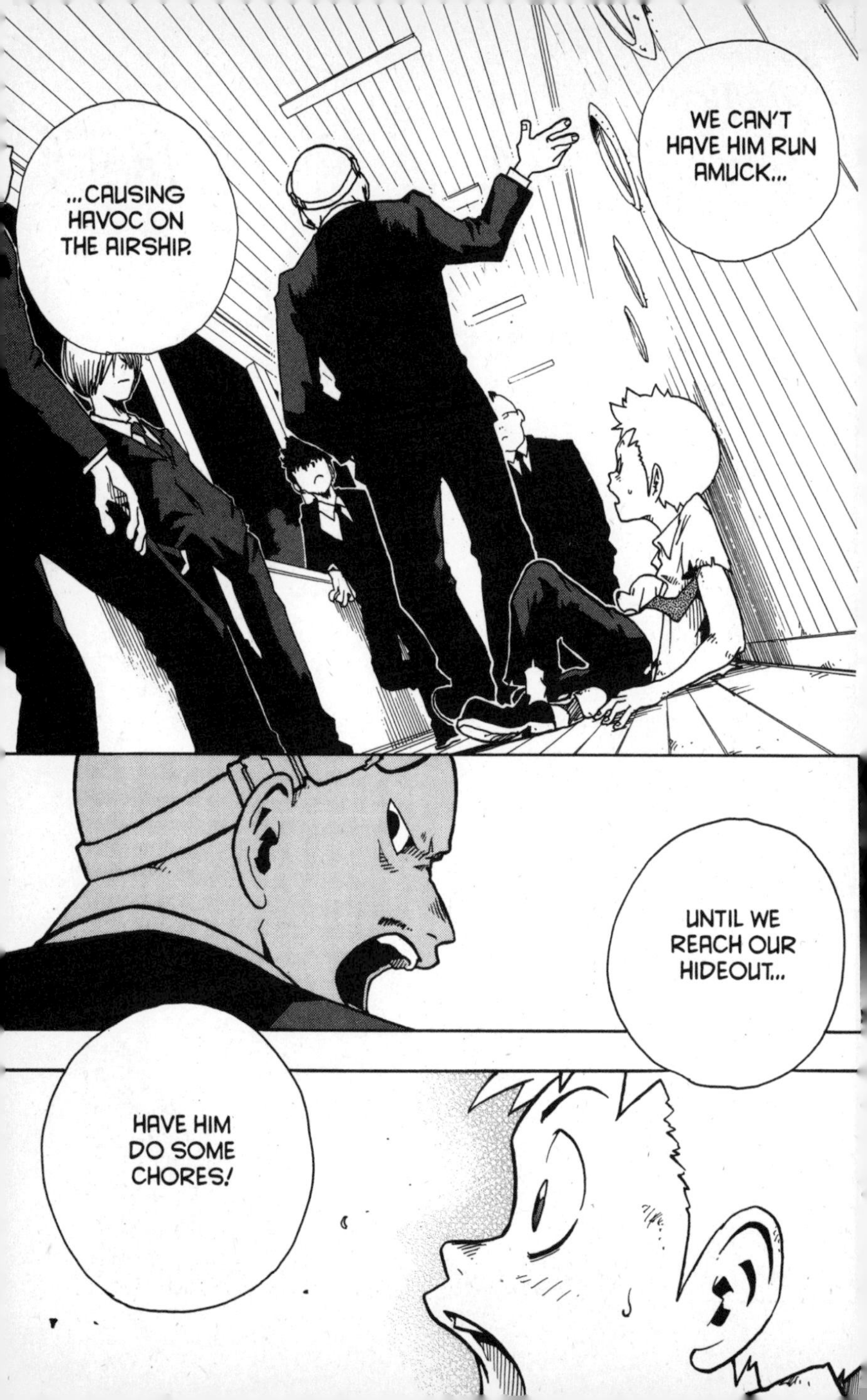
WE CAN'T HAVE HIM RUN AMUCK...
...CAUSING HAVOC ON THE AIRSHIP.
UNTIL WE REACH OUR HIDEOUT...
HAVE HIM DO SOME CHORES!

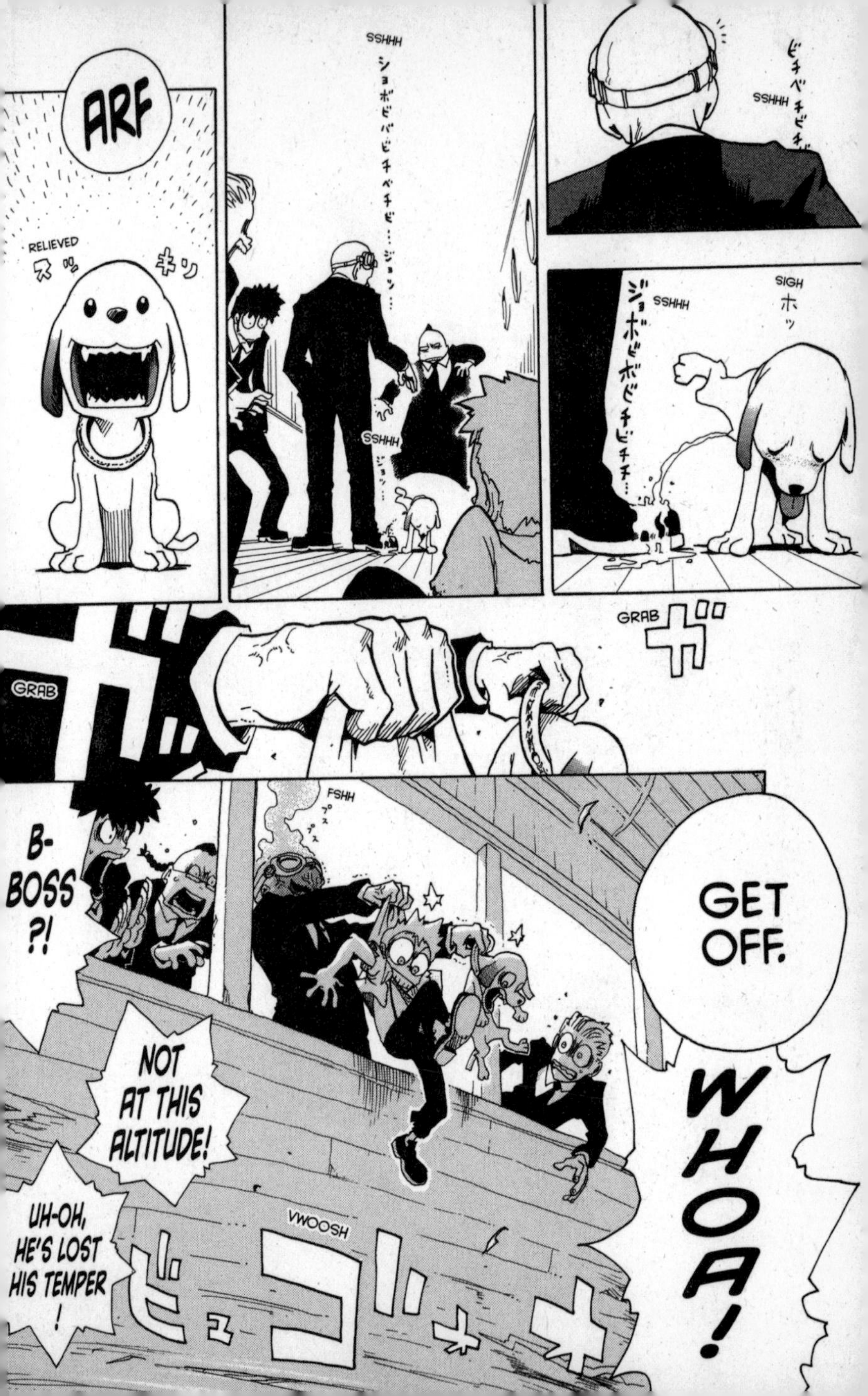
SSHHH
SIGH
SSHHH
SSHHH
SSHHH
ARF
RELIEVED
GRAB
GRAB
GET OFF.
WHOA!
B-BOSS?!
FSHH
NOT AT THIS ALTITUDE!
UH-OH, HE'S LOST HIS TEMPER!
VWOOSH

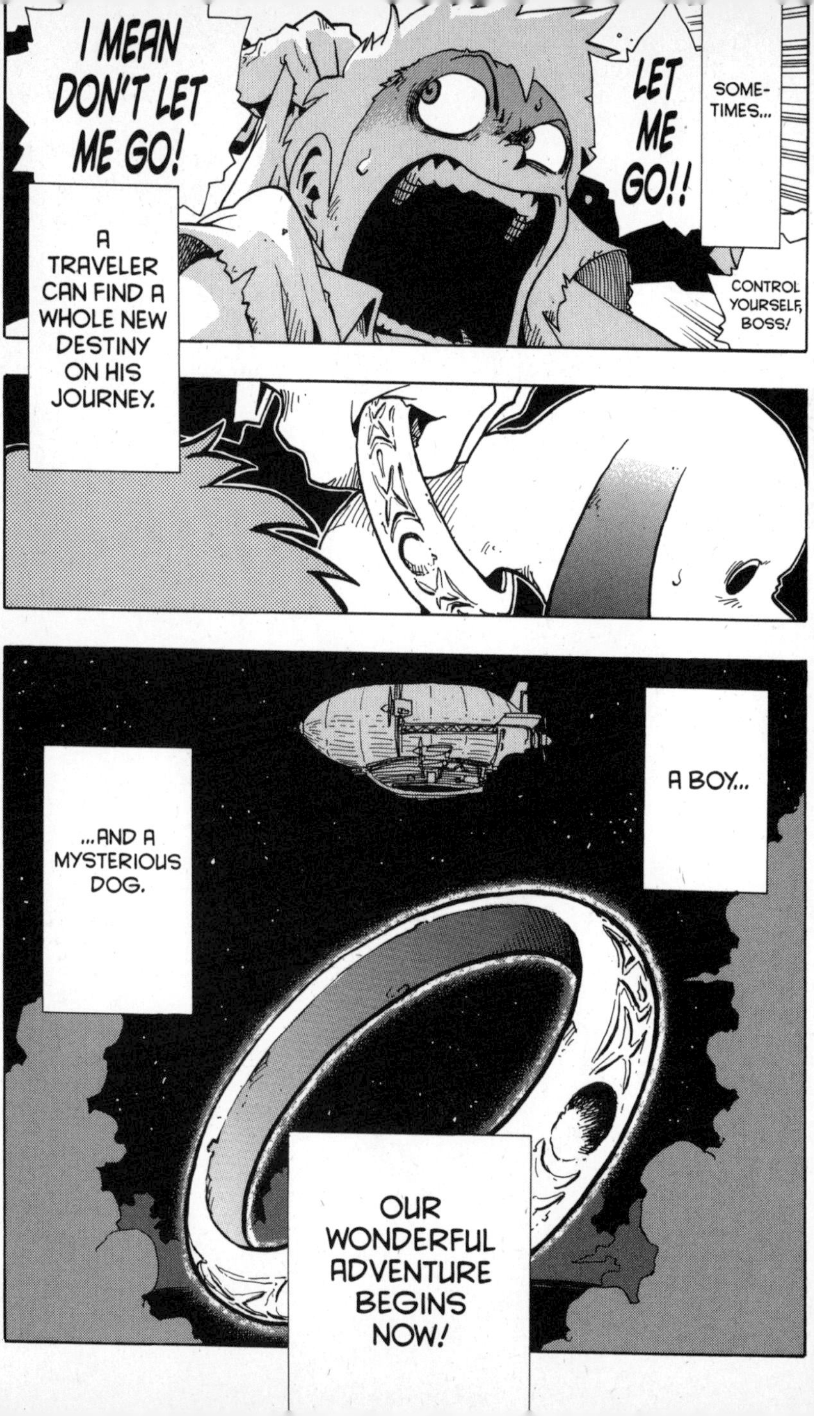
SOME-TIMES...
LET ME GO!!
CONTROL YOURSELF, BOSS!
I MEAN DON'T LET ME GO!
A TRAVELER CAN FIND A WHOLE NEW DESTINY ON HIS JOURNEY.
A BOY...
...AND A MYSTERIOUS DOG.
OUR WONDERFUL ADVENTURE BEGINS NOW!

TOTO! The Rough Character Sketches!

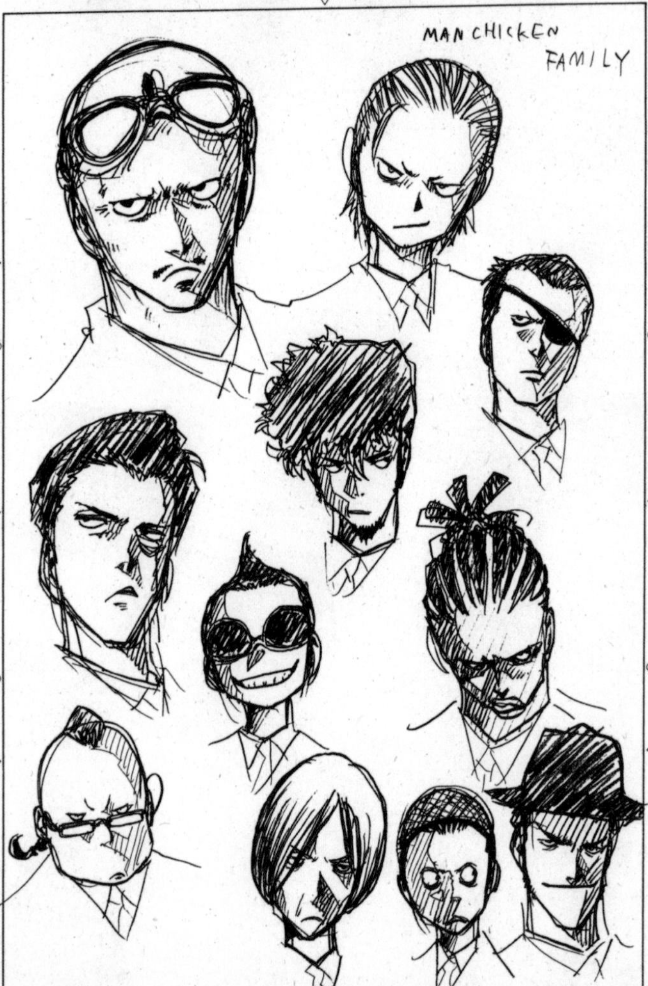
MAN CHICKEN FAMILY

THESE ARE THE FACES OF THE MAN CHICKEN FAMILY. THEY KEPT THE SAME LOOK FROM MY PREVIOUS MANGA. THEIR NAMES ARE ON PAGE 191.

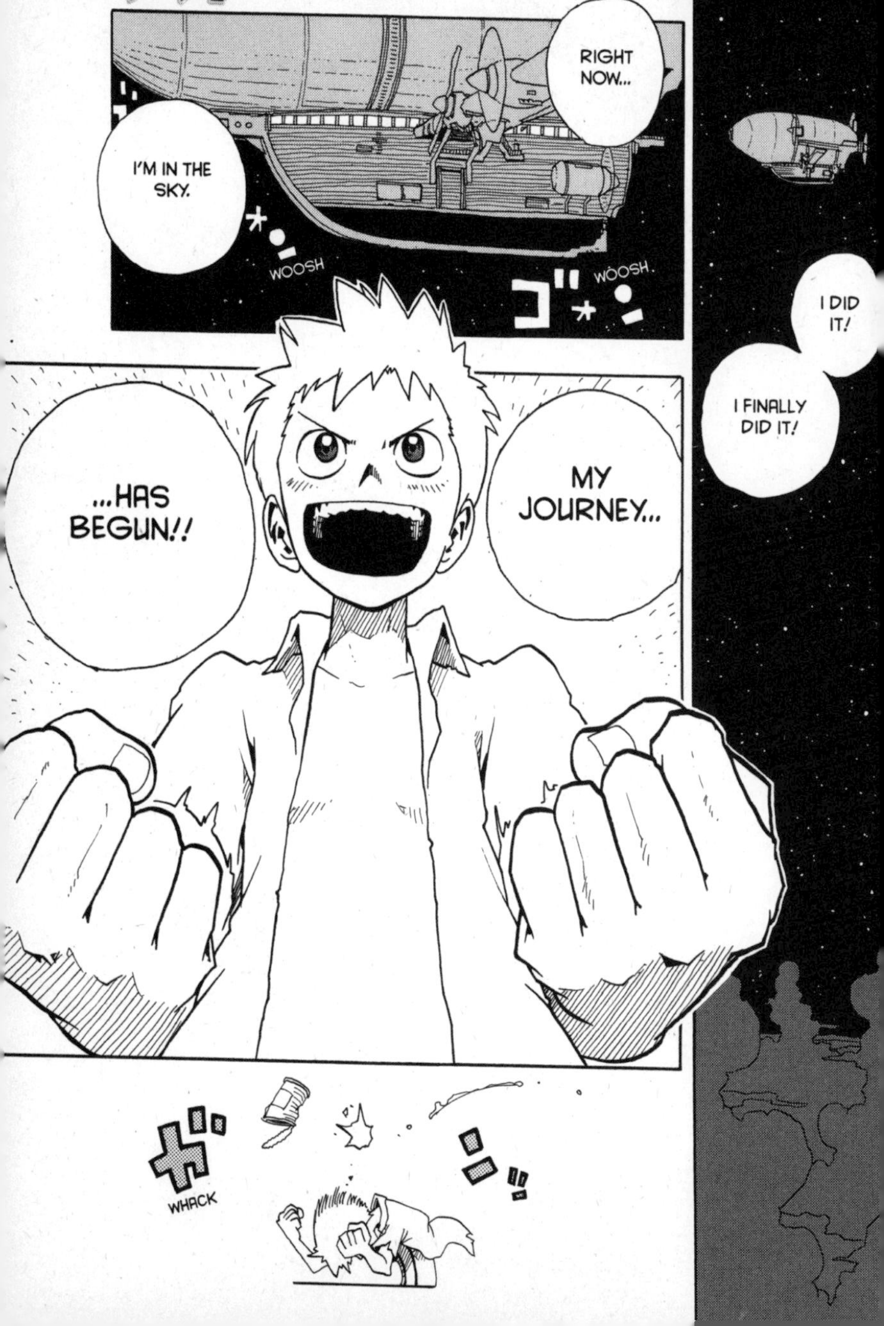
I DID IT!
I FINALLY DID IT!
RIGHT NOW...
I'M IN THE SKY.
WOOSH
WOOSH
MY JOURNEY...
...HAS BEGUN!!
WHACK

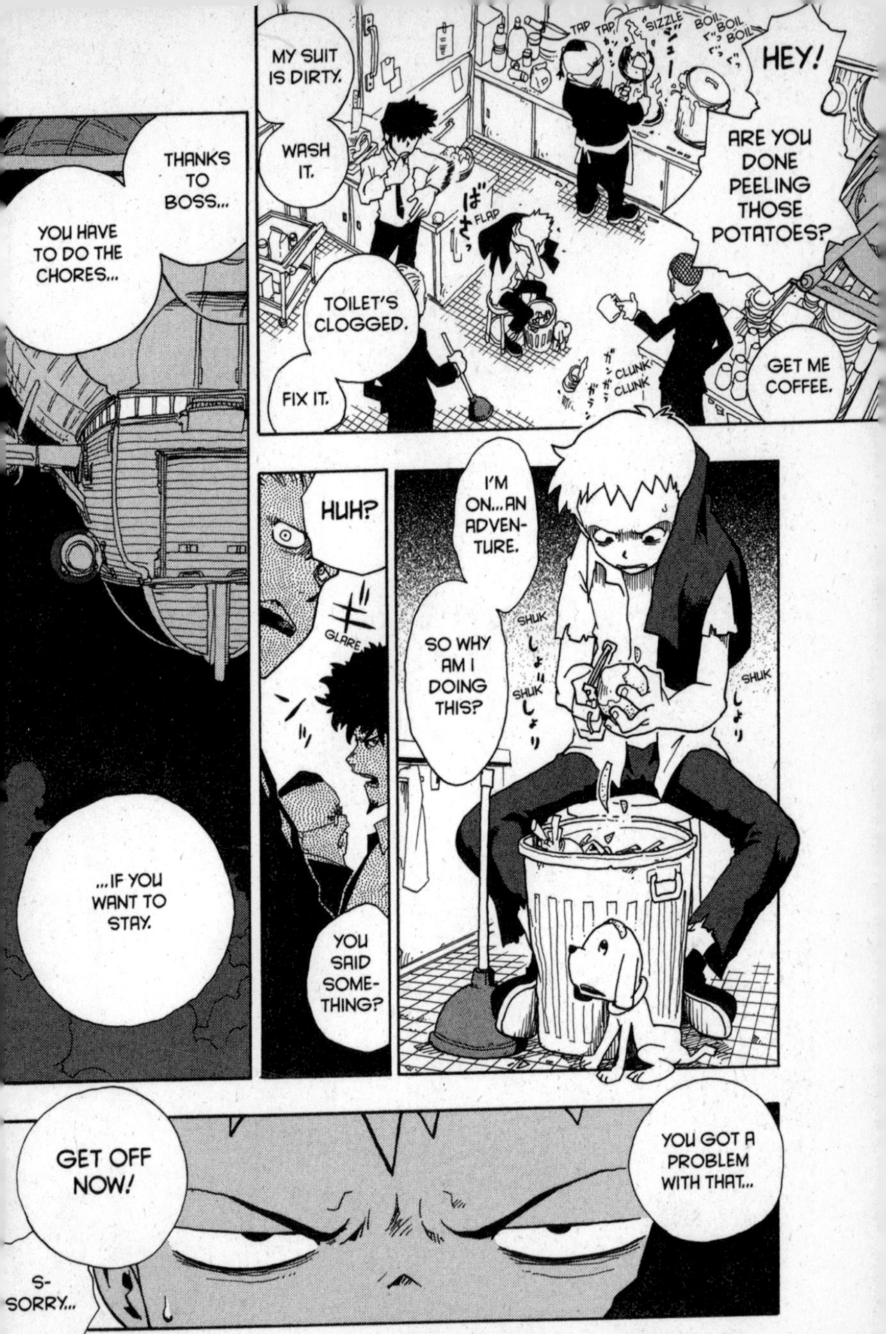
HEY!
ARE YOU DONE PEELING THOSE POTATOES?
TAP TAP
SIZZLE
BOIL BOIL BOIL
GET ME COFFEE.
MY SUIT IS DIRTY.
WASH IT.
FLAP
CLUNK CLUNK
TOILET'S CLOGGED.
FIX IT.
I'M ON...AN ADVENTURE.
SO WHY AM I DOING THIS?
SHUK
SHUK
SHUK
HUH?
GLARE
YOU SAID SOMETHING?
THANKS TO BOSS...
YOU HAVE TO DO THE CHORES...
...IF YOU WANT TO STAY.
YOU GOT A PROBLEM WITH THAT...
GET OFF NOW!
S-SORRY...

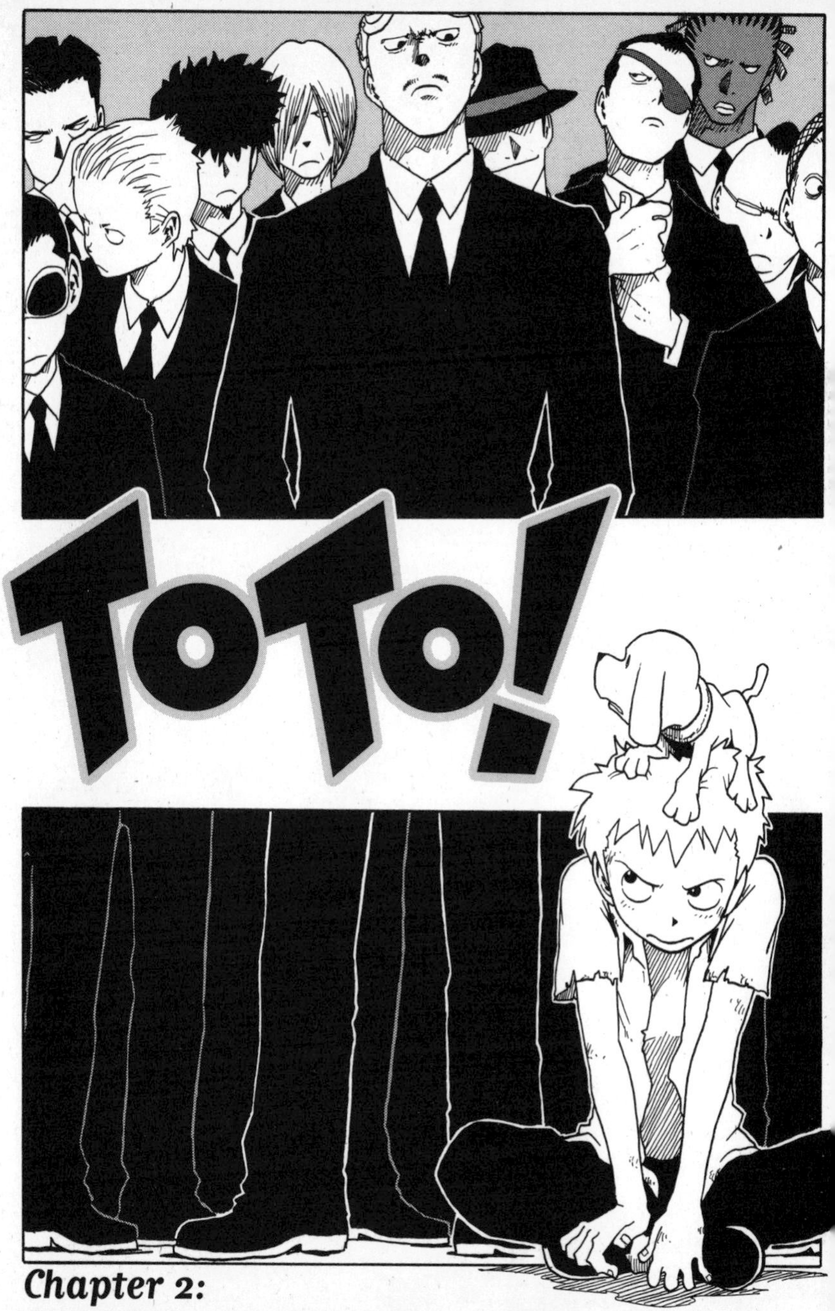
TOTO!

Chapter 2:
KAKASHI AND THE MAN CHICKEN FAMILY

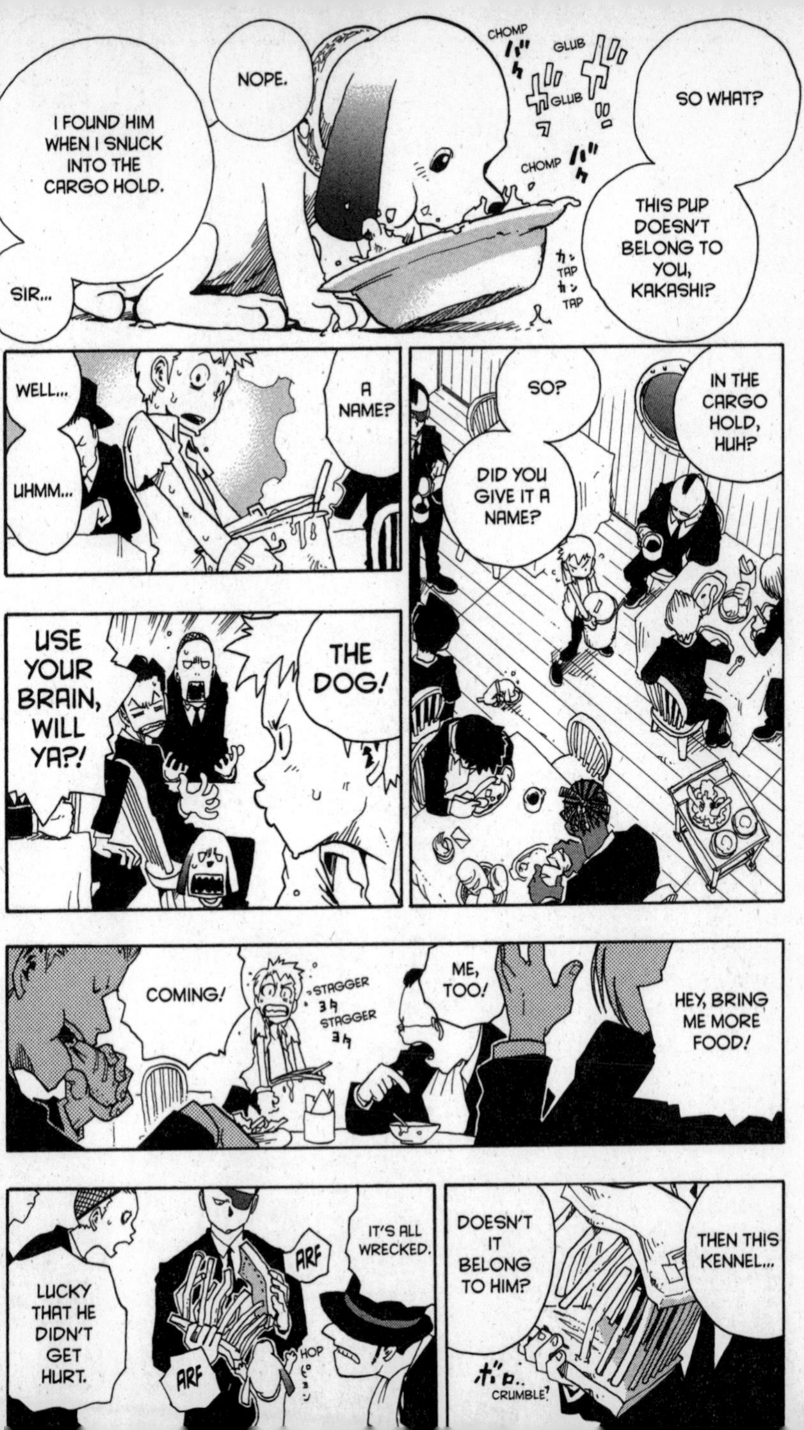
SO WHAT?
THIS PUP DOESN'T BELONG TO YOU, KAKASHI?
CHOMP
GLUB
GLUB
CHOMP
TAP
TAP
NOPE.
I FOUND HIM WHEN I SNUCK INTO THE CARGO HOLD.
SIR...
IN THE CARGO HOLD, HUH?
SO?
DID YOU GIVE IT A NAME?
A NAME?
WELL...
UHMM...
THE DOG!
USE YOUR BRAIN, WILL YA?!
HEY, BRING ME MORE FOOD!
ME, TOO!
STAGGER
STAGGER
COMING!
THEN THIS KENNEL...
DOESN'T IT BELONG TO HIM?
CRUMBLE
IT'S ALL WRECKED.
ARF
HOP
ARF
LUCKY THAT HE DIDN'T GET HURT.

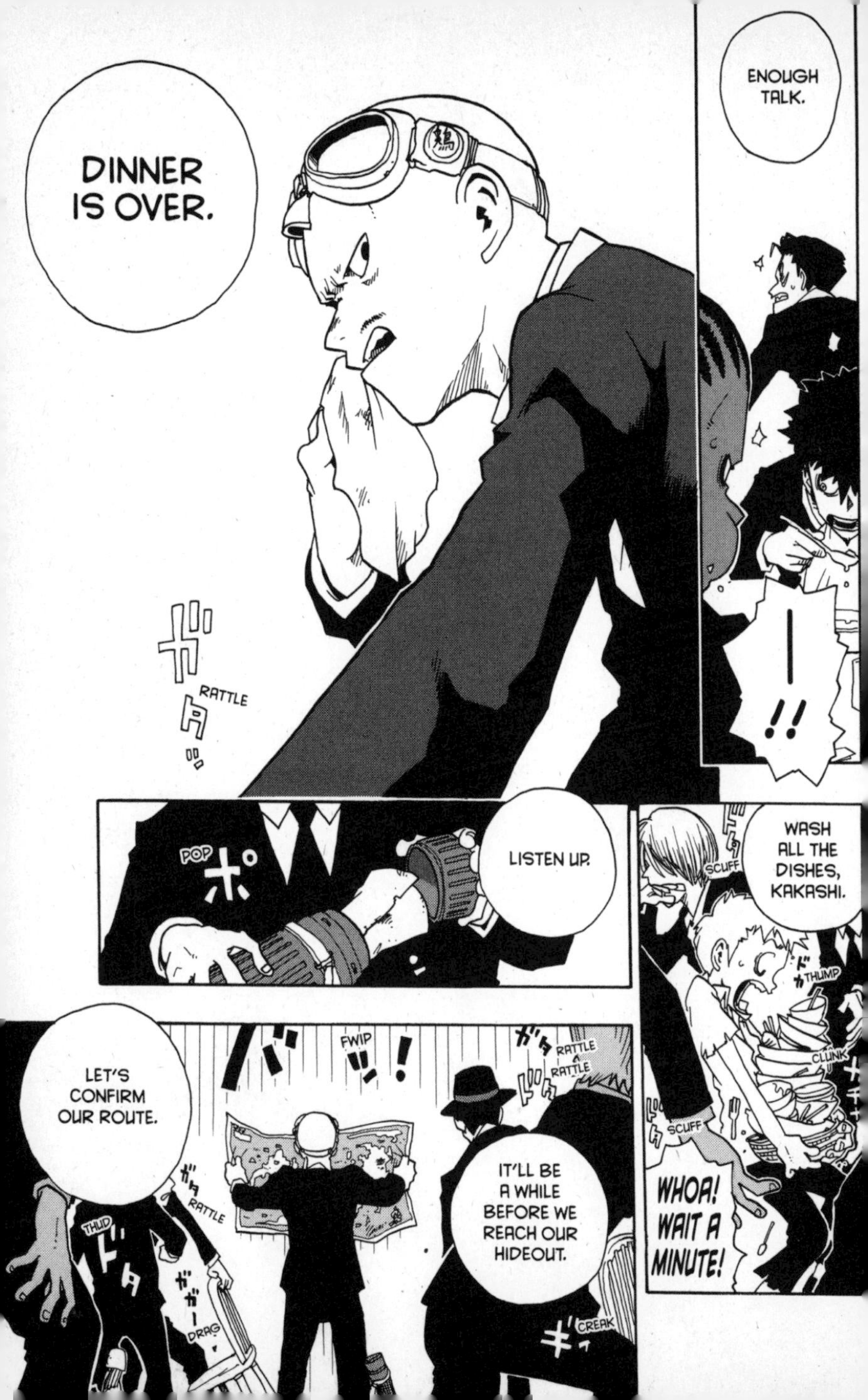
ENOUGH TALK.
!!
DINNER IS OVER.
RATTLE
WASH ALL THE DISHES, KAKASHI.
SCUFF
THUMP
CLUNK
SCUFF
WHOA! WAIT A MINUTE!
LISTEN UP.
POP
IT'LL BE A WHILE BEFORE WE REACH OUR HIDEOUT.
CREAK
RATTLE
RATTLE
FWIP
LET'S CONFIRM OUR ROUTE.
RATTLE
THUD
DRAG

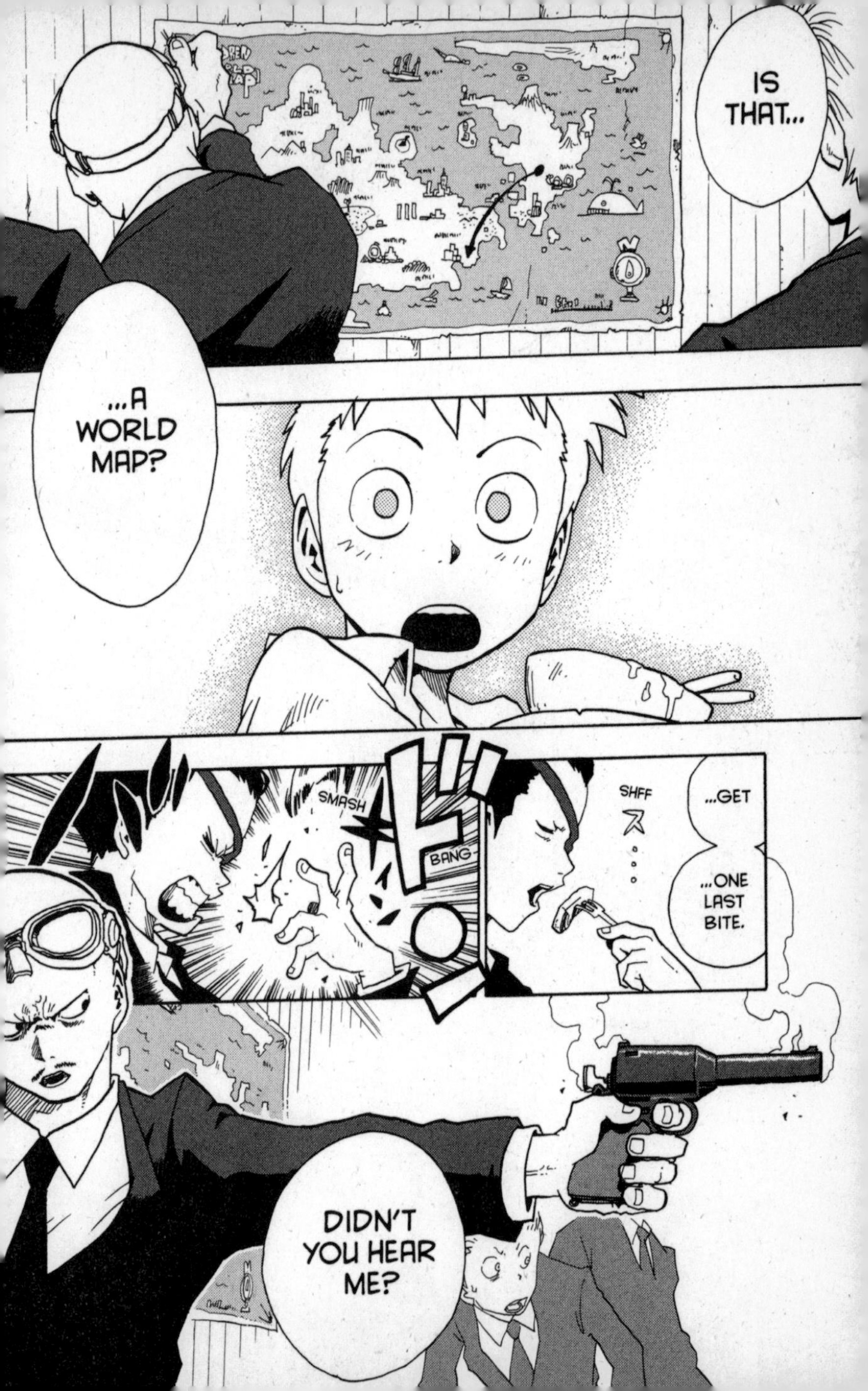
IS THAT...
...A WORLD MAP?
SHFF
ス...
...GET
...ONE LAST BITE.
SMASH
BANG
DIDN'T YOU HEAR ME?

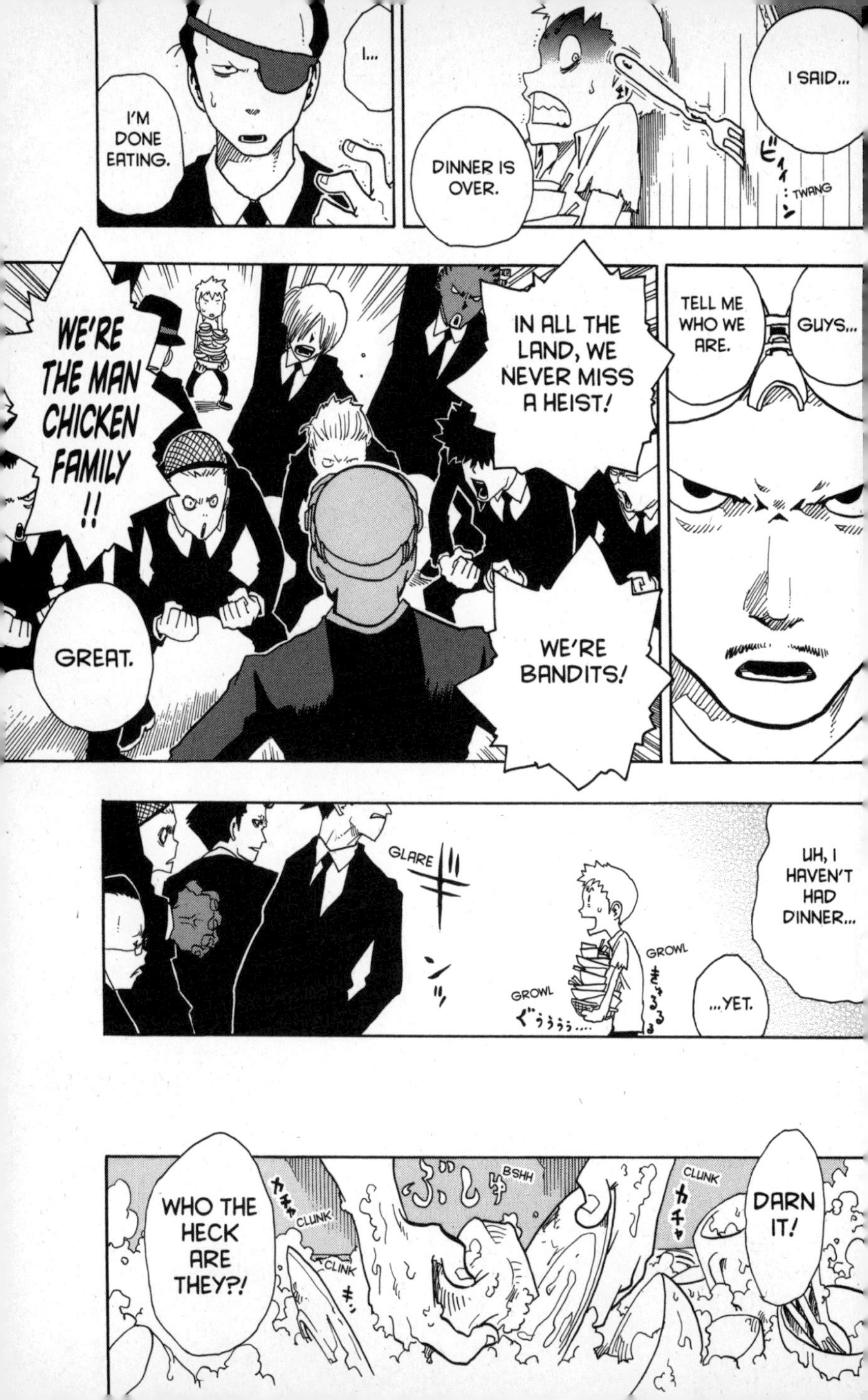
I SAID...
ビィィン
TWANG
DINNER IS OVER.
I...
I'M DONE EATING.
GUYS...
TELL ME WHO WE ARE.
IN ALL THE LAND, WE NEVER MISS A HEIST!
WE'RE BANDITS!
WE'RE THE MAN CHICKEN FAMILY!!
GREAT.
UH, I HAVEN'T HAD DINNER...
...YET.
きゅるる
GROWL
ぐぅぅぅぅ....
GROWL
GLARE
DARN IT!
カチャ
CLINK
ふしゅ
BSHH
カチャ
CLINK
CLINK
WHO THE HECK ARE THEY?!

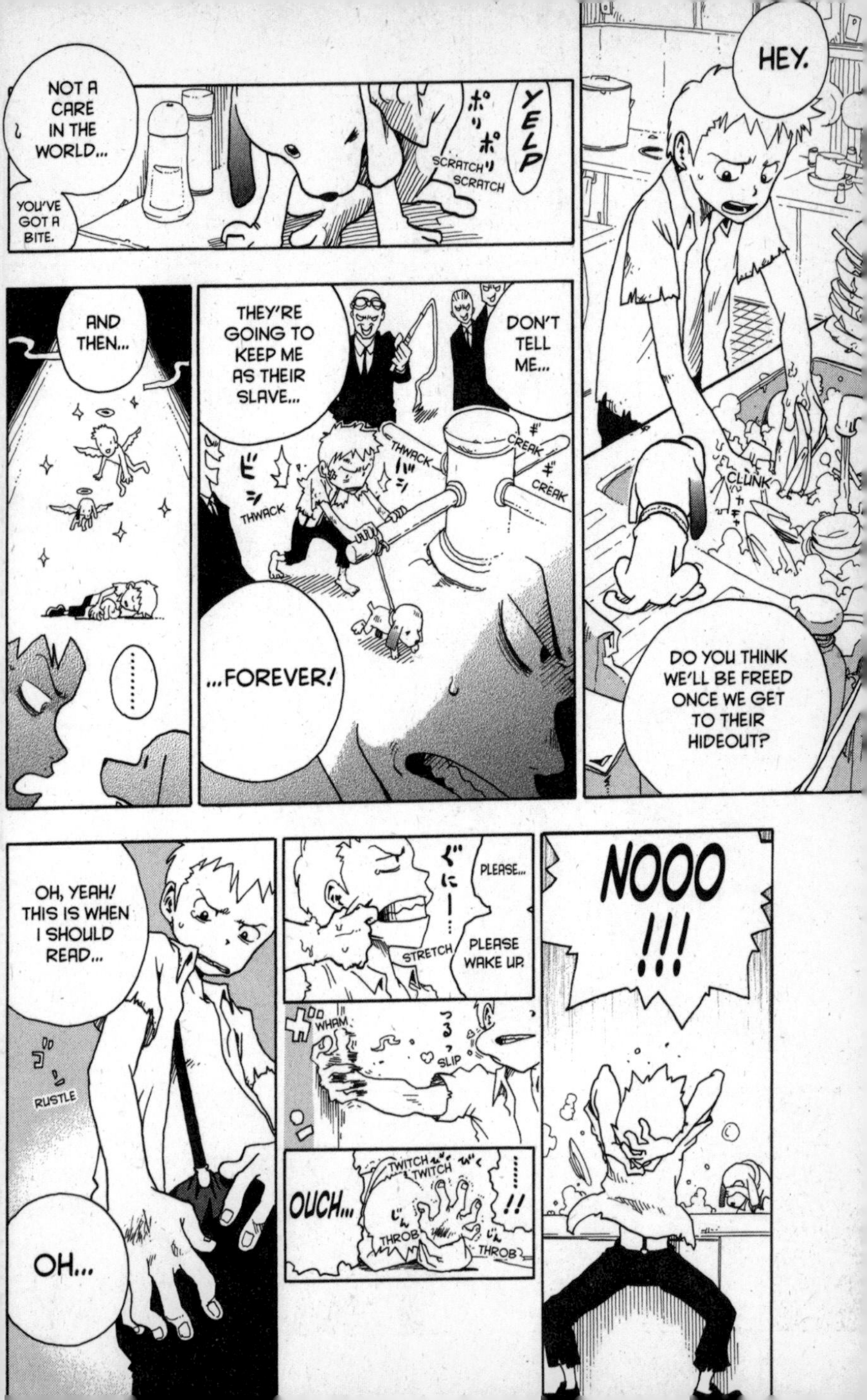
HEY.
CLUNK
DO YOU THINK WE'LL BE FREED ONCE WE GET TO THEIR HIDEOUT?
YELP
ポリポリ
SCRATCH SCRATCH
NOT A CARE IN THE WORLD...
YOU'VE GOT A BITE.
DON'T TELL ME...
THEY'RE GOING TO KEEP ME AS THEIR SLAVE...
CREAK
CREAK
THWACK
THWACK
...FOREVER!
AND THEN...
......
NOOO!!!
ぐにー...
PLEASE...
PLEASE WAKE UP.
STRETCH
つるっ
SLIP
WHAM
TWITCH TWITCH
......!!
OUCH...
THROB
THROB
OH, YEAH! THIS IS WHEN I SHOULD READ...
RUSTLE
OH...

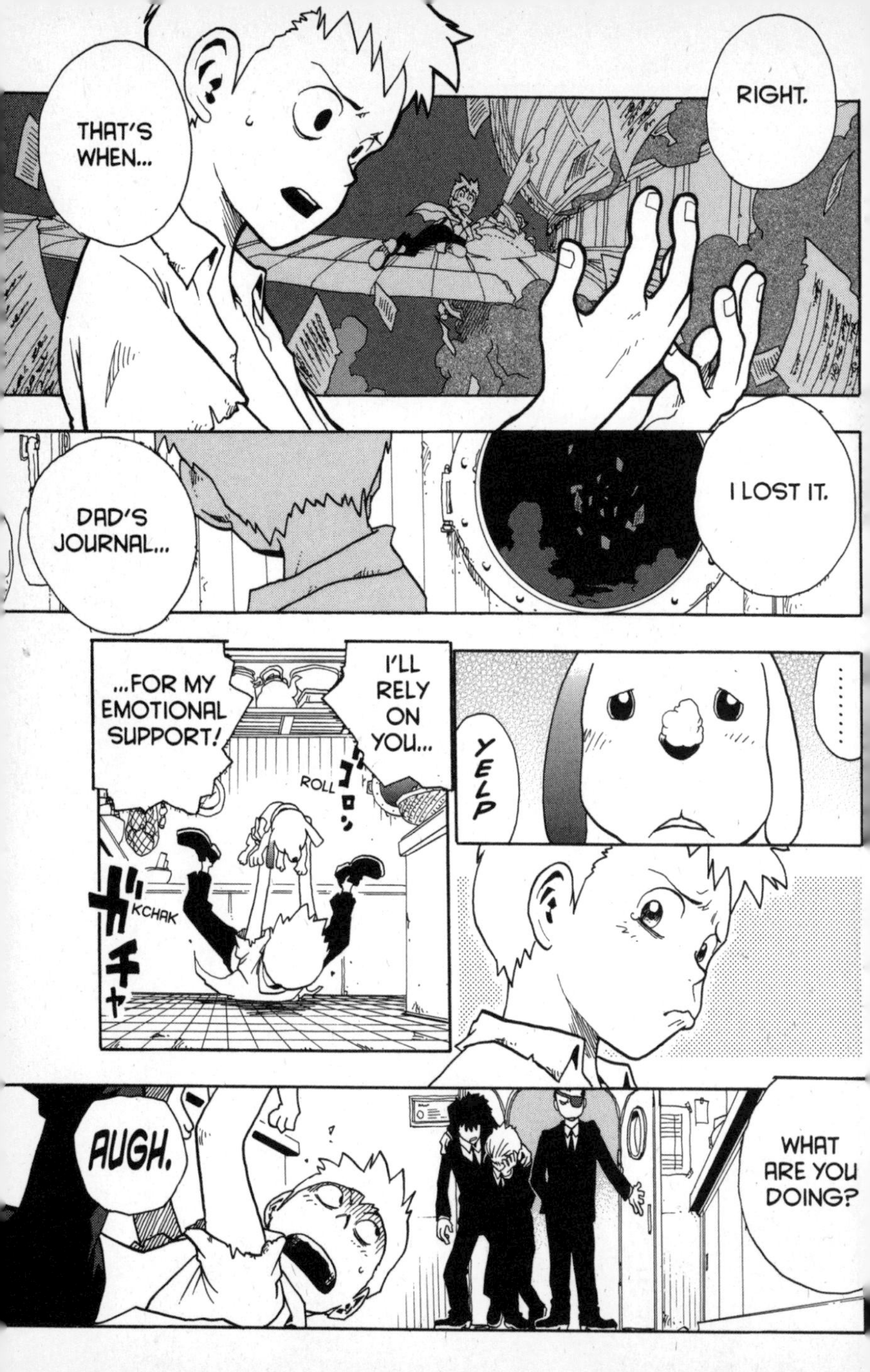
RIGHT.
THAT'S WHEN...
I LOST IT.
DAD'S JOURNAL...
......
YELP
I'LL RELY ON YOU...
...FOR MY EMOTIONAL SUPPORT!
ゴロン
ROLL
ガチャ
KCHAK
WHAT ARE YOU DOING?
AUGH.

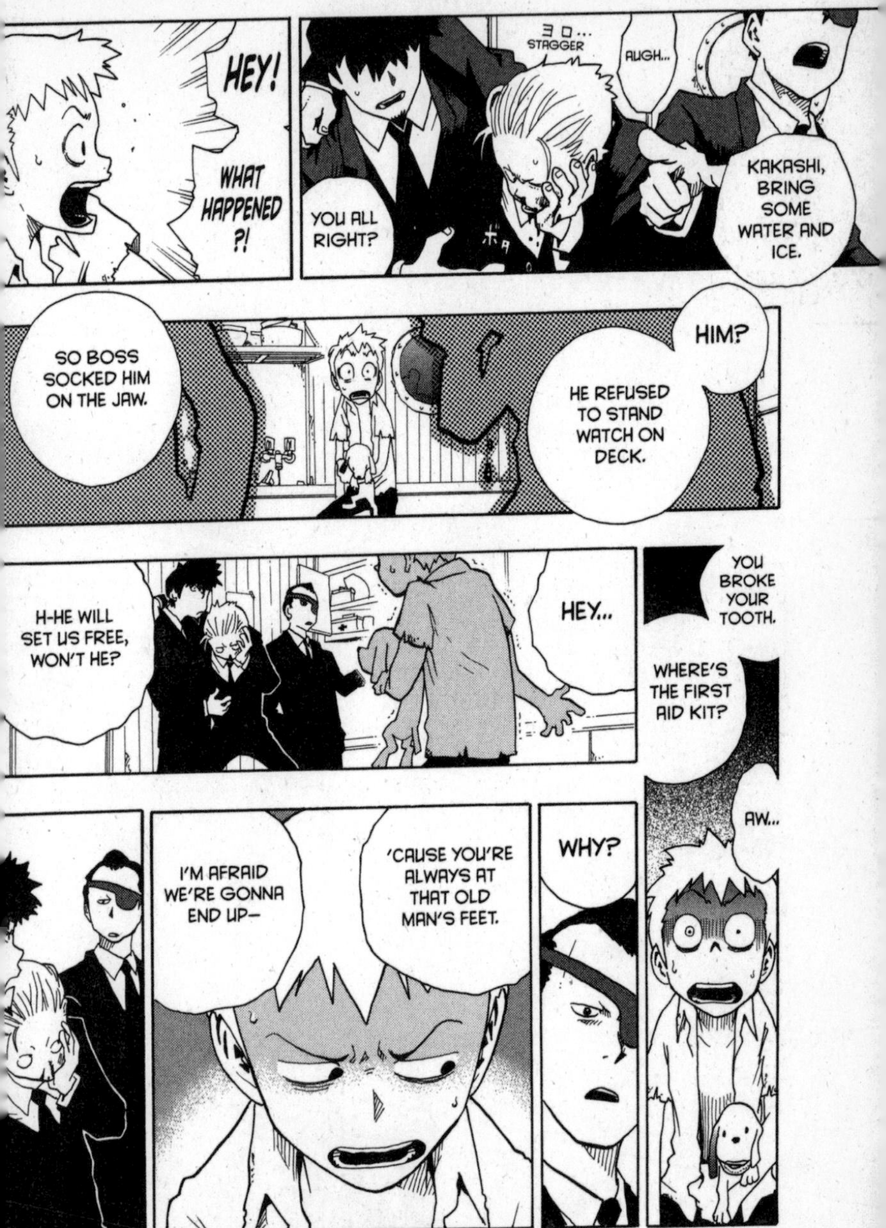
AUGH...
ヨロ…
STAGGER
KAKASHI, BRING SOME WATER AND ICE.
YOU ALL RIGHT?
ボタ
HEY!
WHAT HAPPENED?!
HIM?
HE REFUSED TO STAND WATCH ON DECK.
SO BOSS SOCKED HIM ON THE JAW.
YOU BROKE YOUR TOOTH.
WHERE'S THE FIRST AID KIT?
AW...
HEY...
H-HE WILL SET US FREE, WON'T HE?
WHY?
'CAUSE YOU'RE ALWAYS AT THAT OLD MAN'S FEET.
I'M AFRAID WE'RE GONNA END UP—

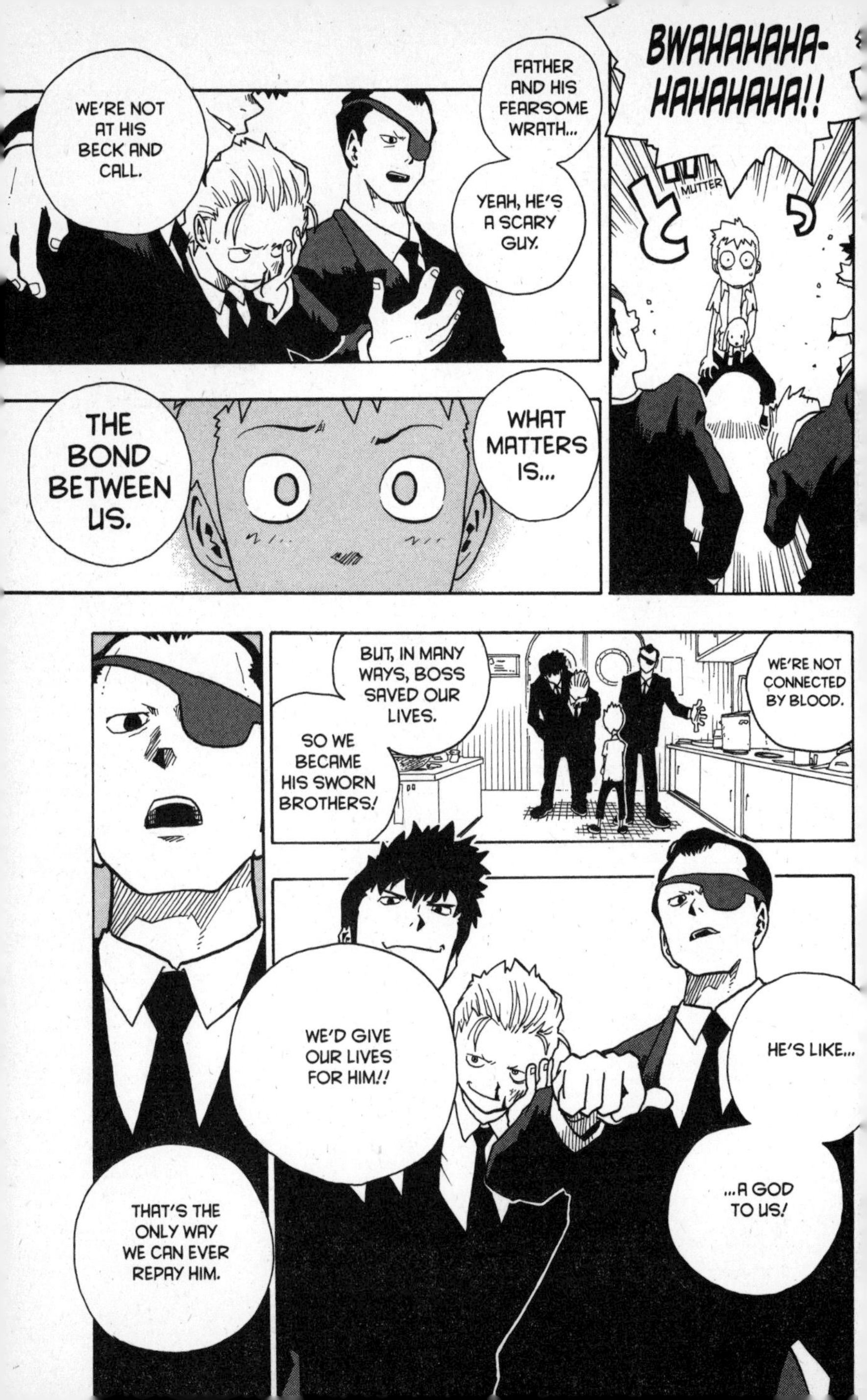
BWAHAHAHA-HAHAHAHA!!
MUTTER
FATHER AND HIS FEARSOME WRATH...
YEAH, HE'S A SCARY GUY.
WE'RE NOT AT HIS BECK AND CALL.
WHAT MATTERS IS...
THE BOND BETWEEN US.
WE'RE NOT CONNECTED BY BLOOD.
BUT, IN MANY WAYS, BOSS SAVED OUR LIVES.
SO WE BECAME HIS SWORN BROTHERS!
HE'S LIKE...
...A GOD TO US!
WE'D GIVE OUR LIVES FOR HIM!!
THAT'S THE ONLY WAY WE CAN EVER REPAY HIM.

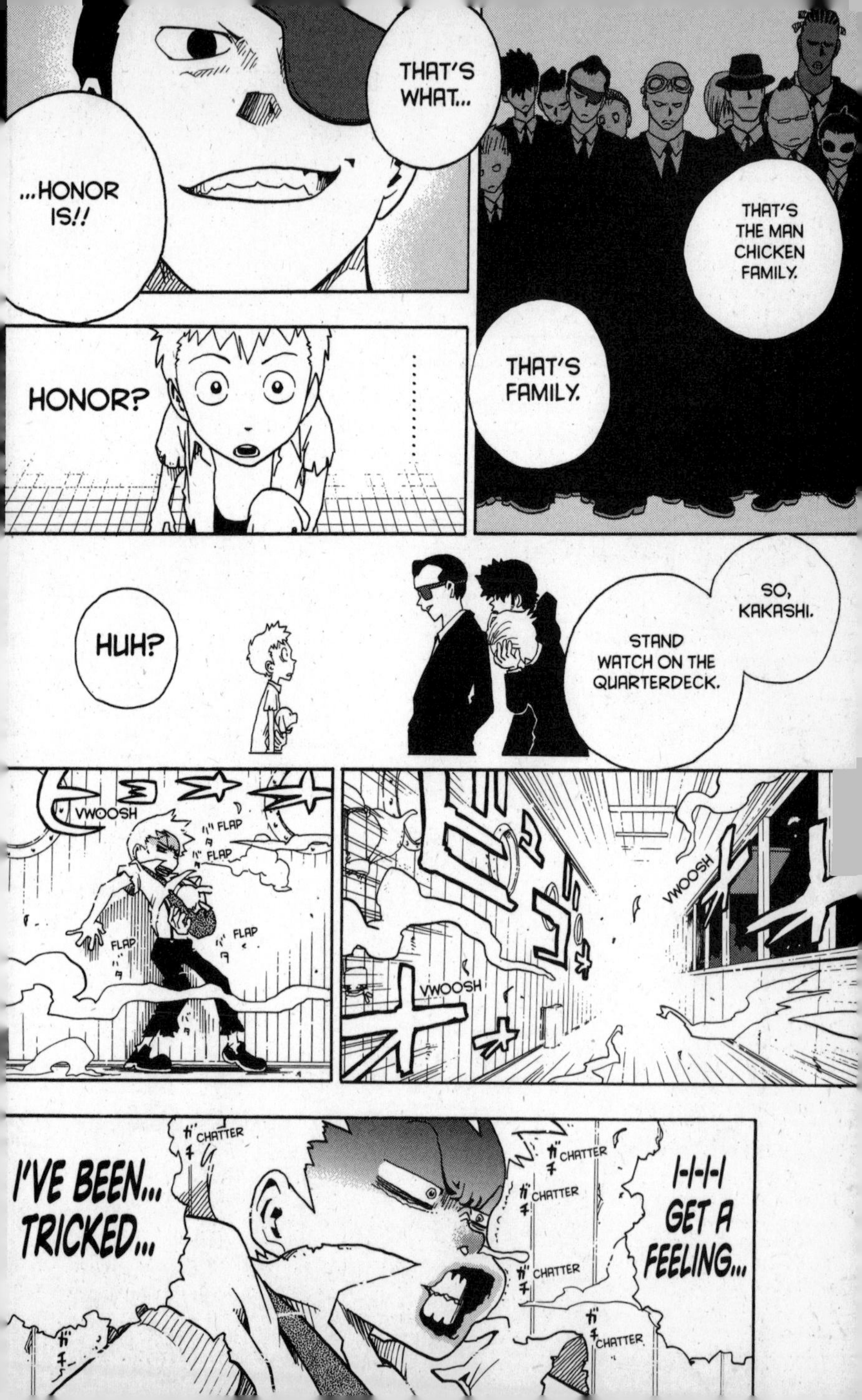
THAT'S THE MAN CHICKEN FAMILY.
THAT'S FAMILY.
THAT'S WHAT...
...HONOR IS!!
HONOR?
SO, KAKASHI.
STAND WATCH ON THE QUARTERDECK.
HUH?
VWOOSH
VWOOSH
VWOOSH
FLAP
FLAP
FLAP
FLAP
I-I-I-I GET A FEELING...
CHATTER
CHATTER
CHATTER
CHATTER
CHATTER
I'VE BEEN... TRICKED...

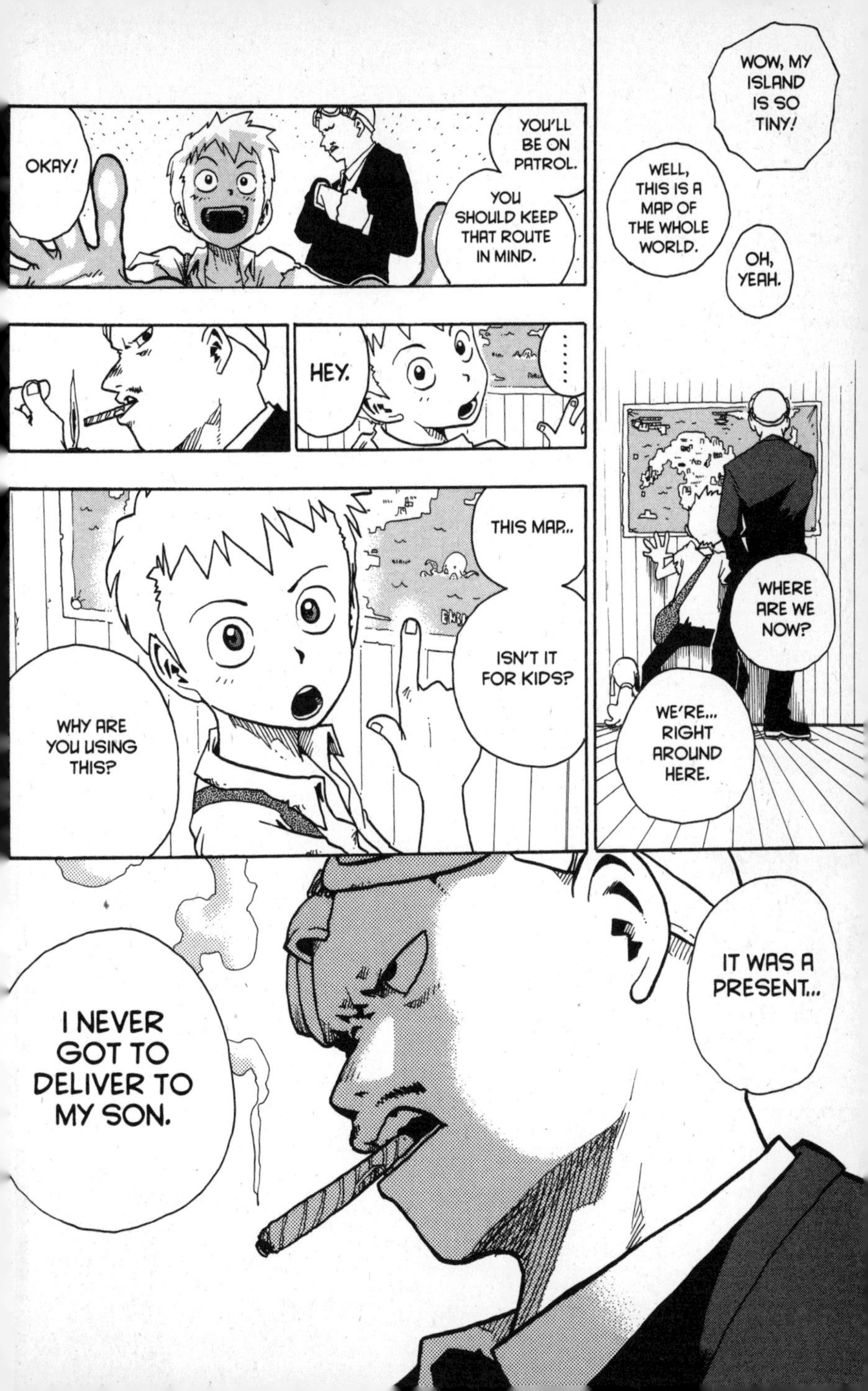
WOW, MY ISLAND IS SO TINY!
WELL, THIS IS A MAP OF THE WHOLE WORLD.
OH, YEAH.
WHERE ARE WE NOW?
WE'RE... RIGHT AROUND HERE.
YOU'LL BE ON PATROL.
YOU SHOULD KEEP THAT ROUTE IN MIND.
OKAY!
......
HEY.
THIS MAP...
ISN'T IT FOR KIDS?
WHY ARE YOU USING THIS?
IT WAS A PRESENT...
I NEVER GOT TO DELIVER TO MY SON.

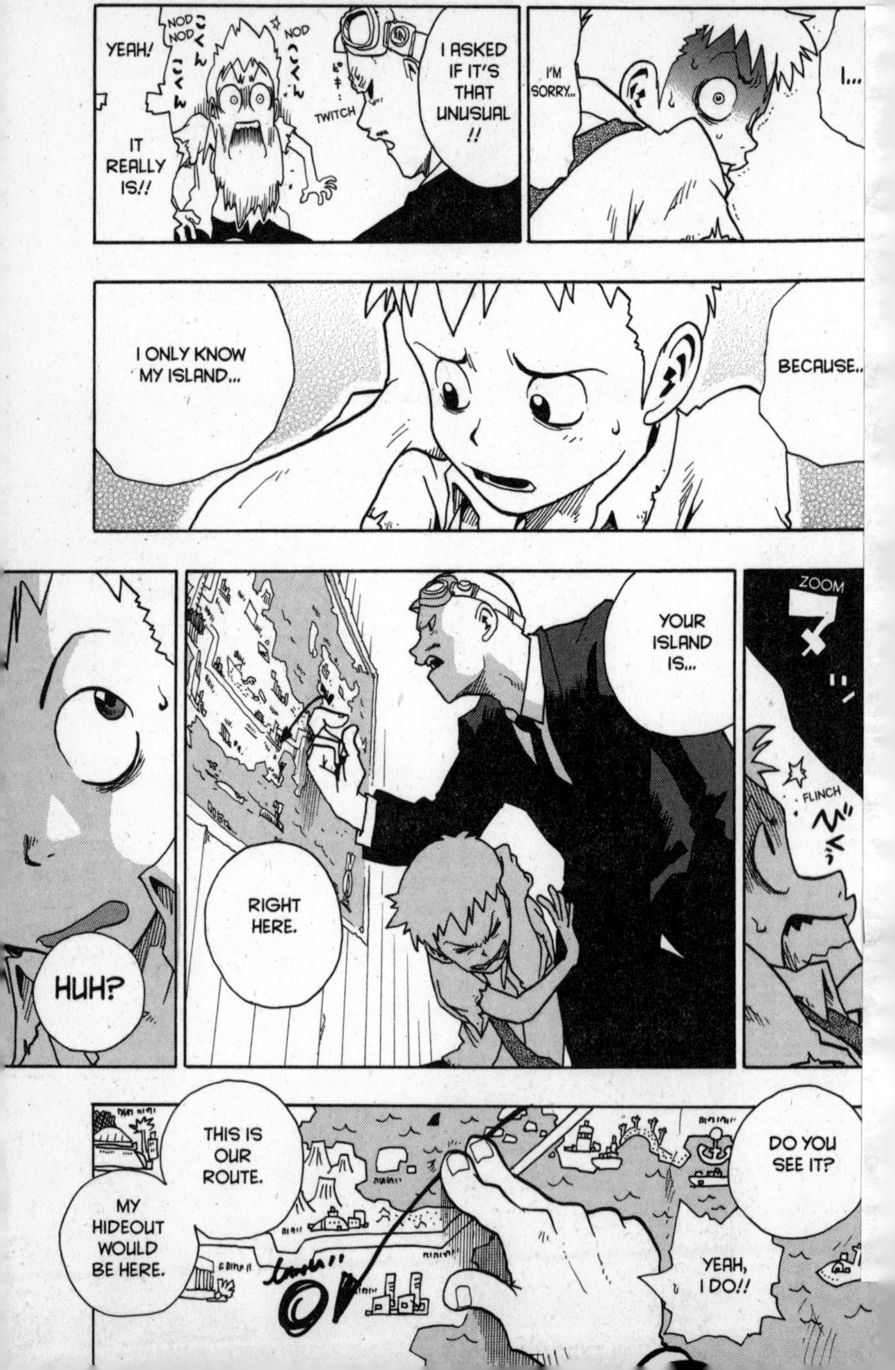
I...
I'M SORRY...
I ASKED IF IT'S THAT UNUSUAL!!
TWITCH
NOD
NOD NOD
YEAH!
IT REALLY IS!!
BECAUSE...
I ONLY KNOW MY ISLAND...
ZOOM
FLINCH
YOUR ISLAND IS...
RIGHT HERE.
HUH?
DO YOU SEE IT?
YEAH, I DO!!
THIS IS OUR ROUTE.
MY HIDEOUT WOULD BE HERE.

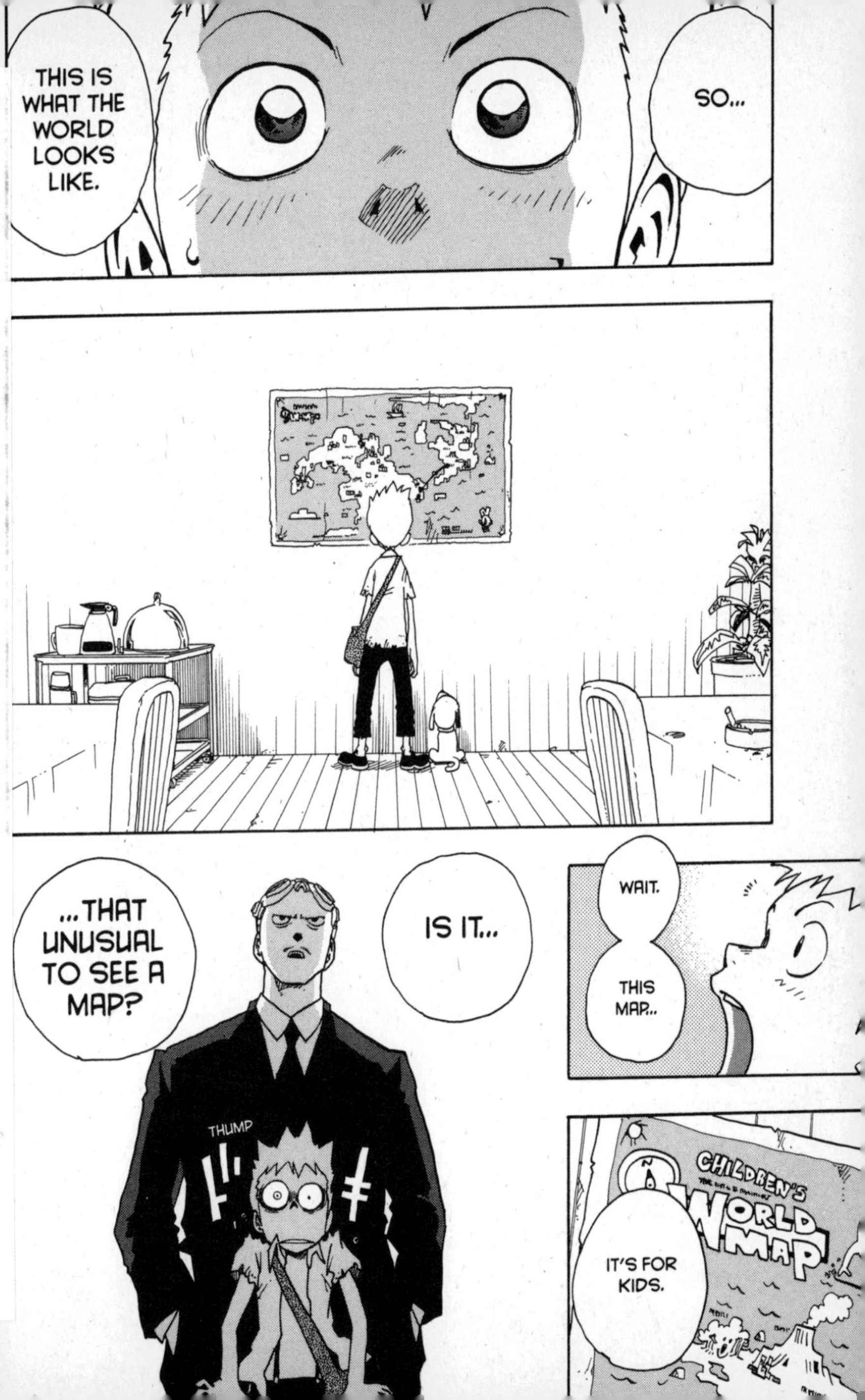
SO...
THIS IS WHAT THE WORLD LOOKS LIKE.
WAIT. THIS MAP...
CHILDREN'S WORLD MAP
IT'S FOR KIDS.
IS IT...
...THAT UNUSUAL TO SEE A MAP?
THUMP

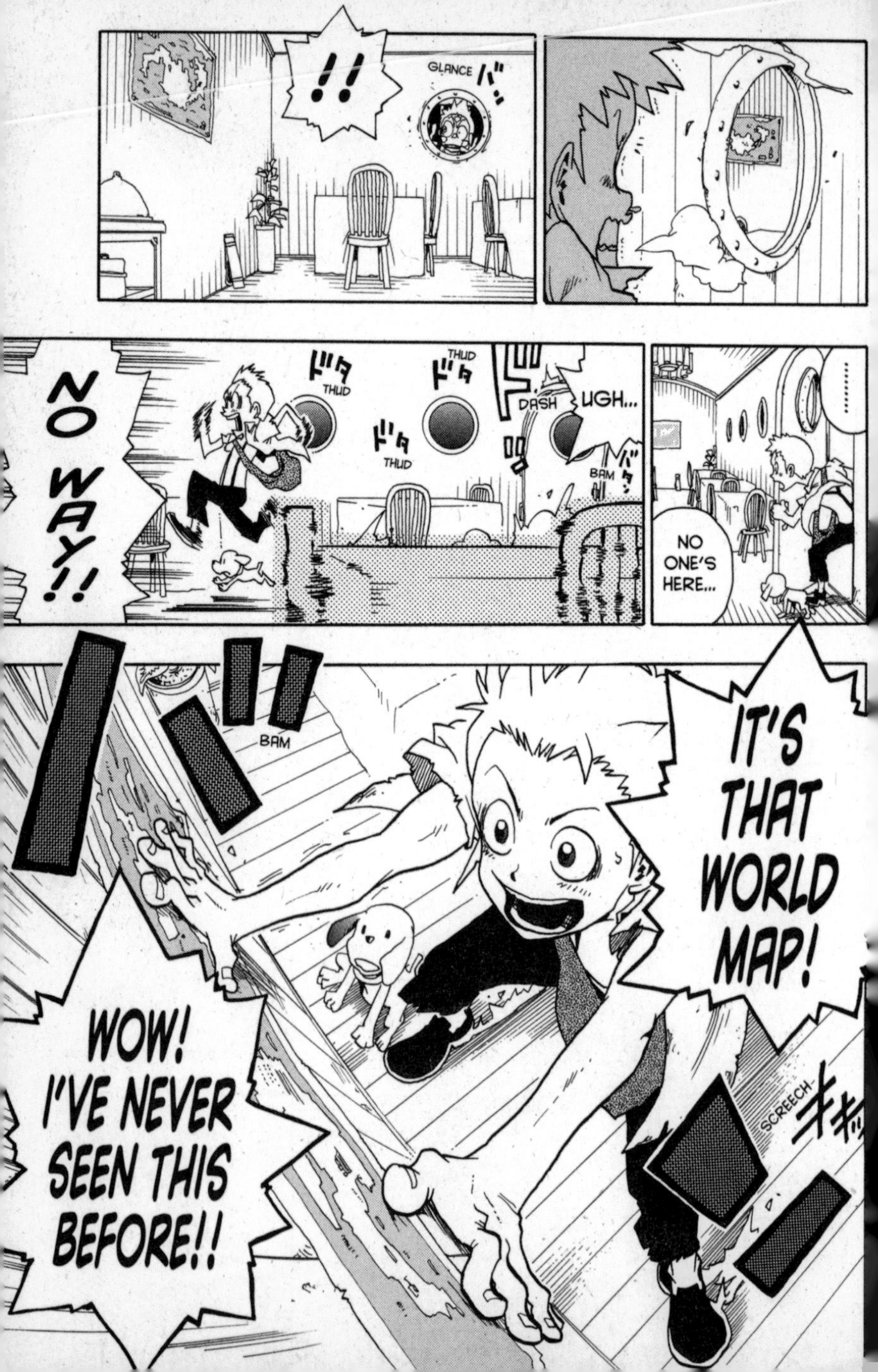
!!
GLANCE バッ
......
NO ONE'S HERE...
UGH...
DASH
BAM
THUD ドタ
THUD ドタ
THUD ドタ
NO WAY!!
IT'S THAT WORLD MAP!
BAM
SCREECH
WOW! I'VE NEVER SEEN THIS BEFORE!!

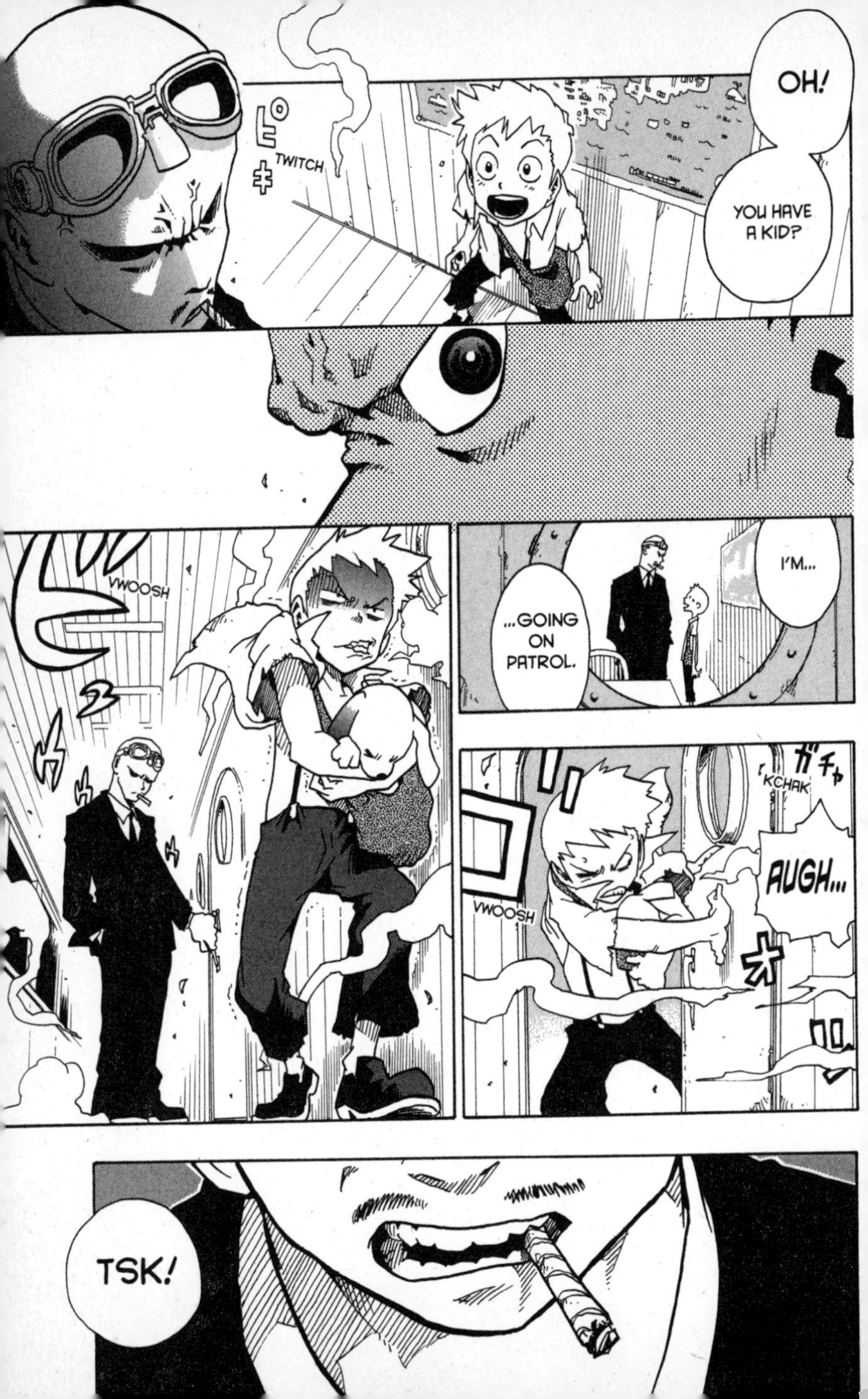
OH!
YOU HAVE A KID?
TWITCH
I'M...
...GOING ON PATROL.
VWOOSH
KCHAK
AUGH...
VWOOSH
TSK!

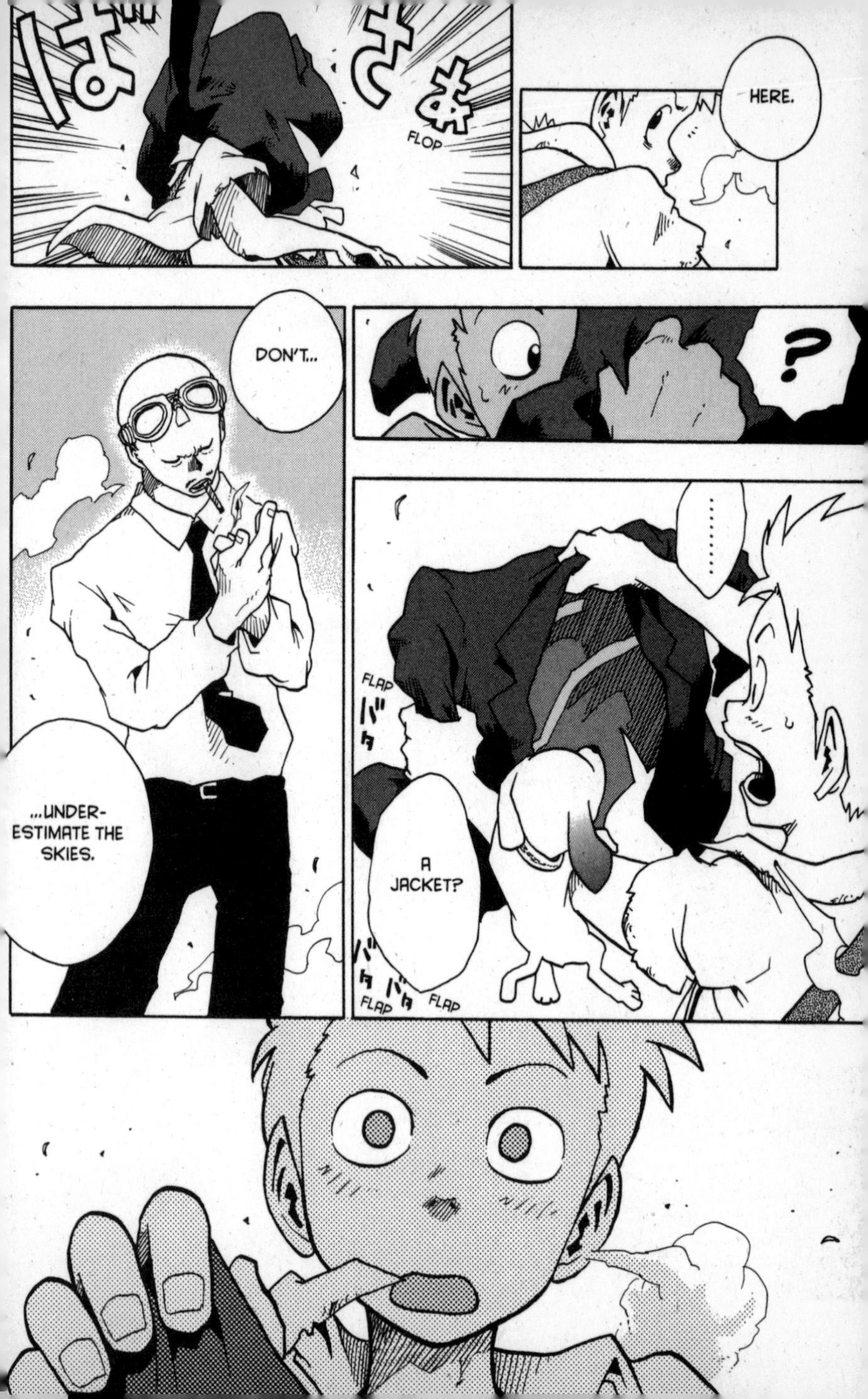
HERE.
ばさ
FLOP
?
......
A JACKET?
バタ
FLAP
バタ
バタ
FLAP
FLAP
DON'T...
...UNDER-ESTIMATE THE SKIES.

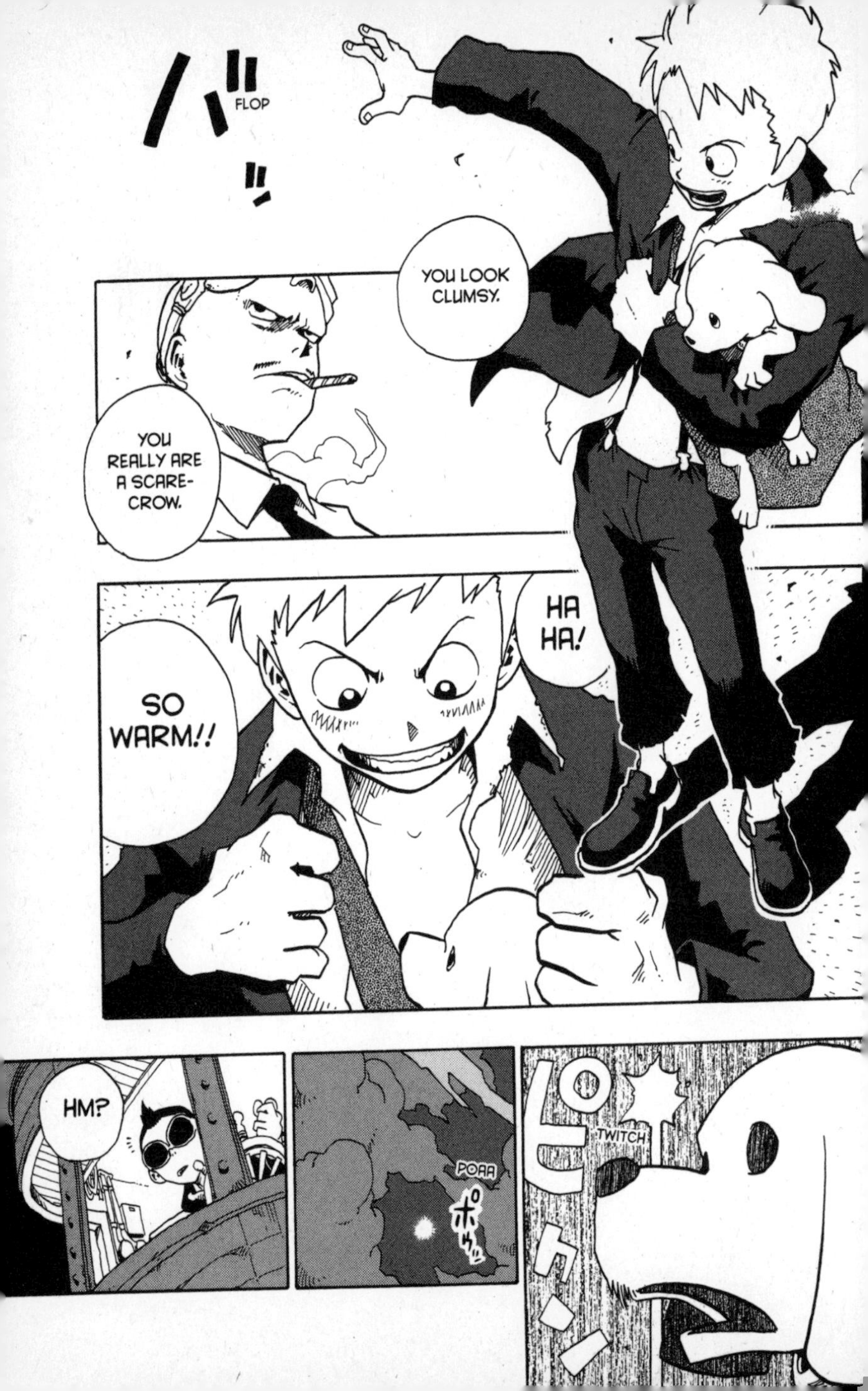
FLOP
YOU LOOK CLUMSY.
YOU REALLY ARE A SCARE-CROW.
HA HA!
SO WARM!!
TWITCH
POAA
HM?

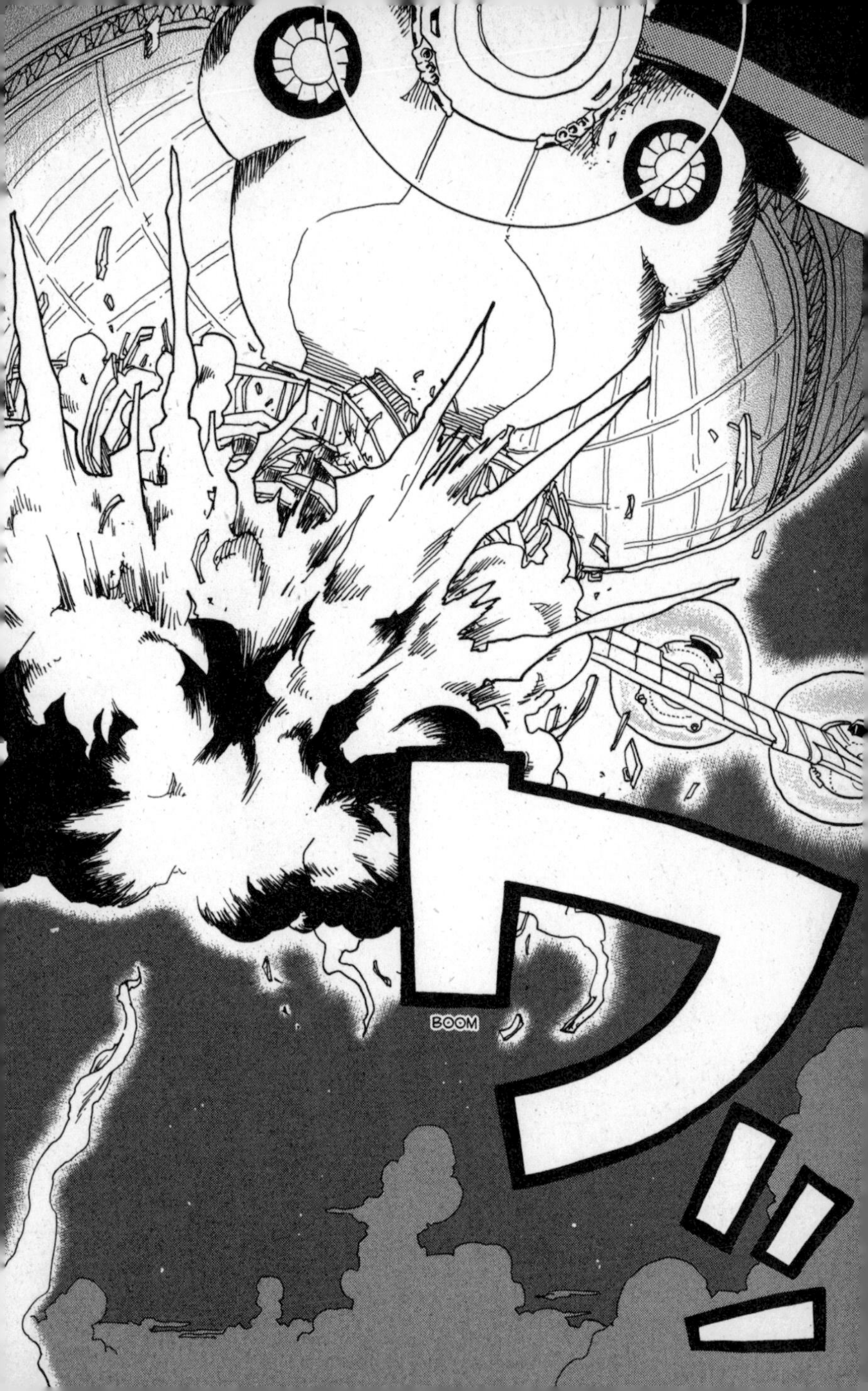
BOOM

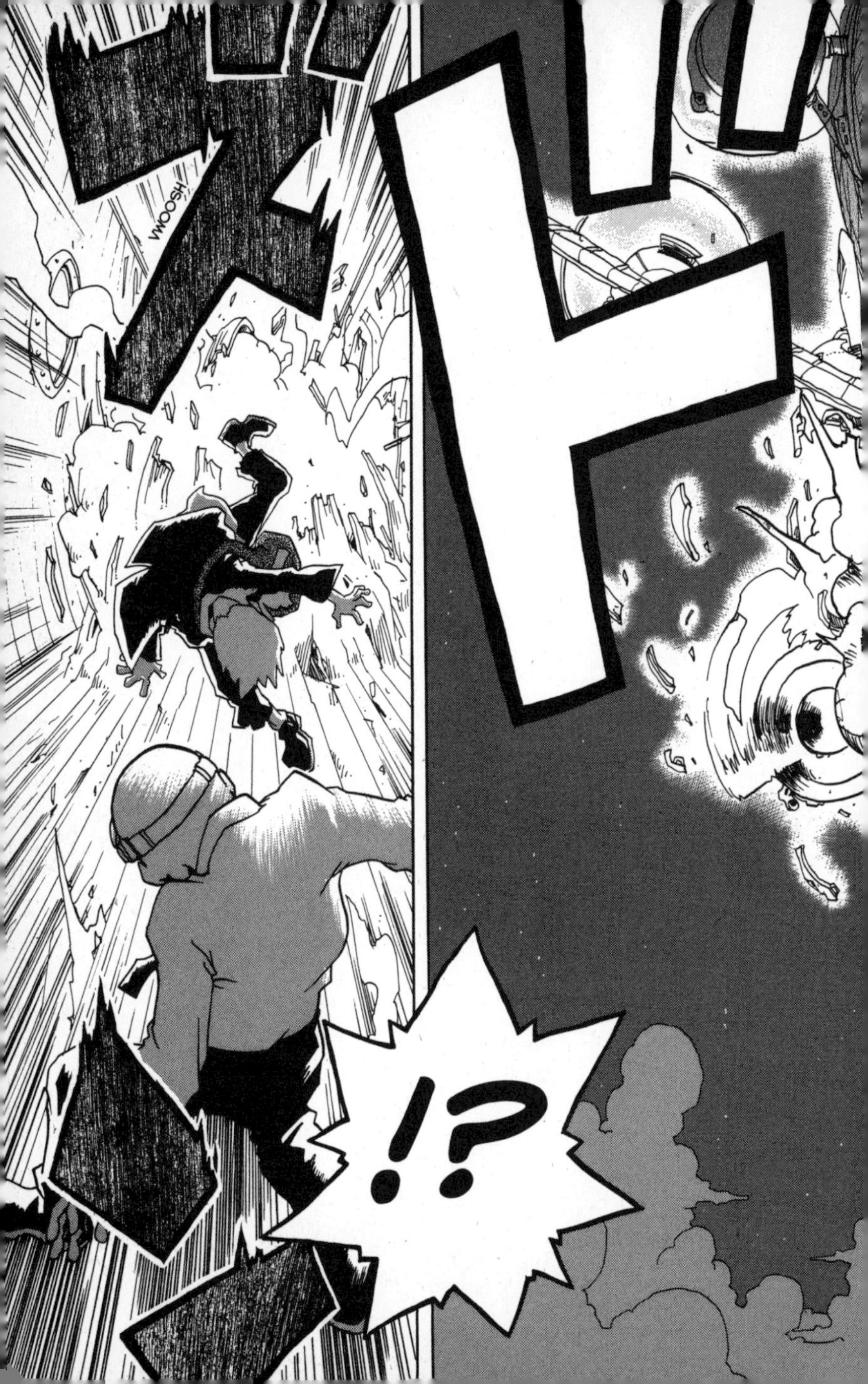
VWOOSH
!?

OUCH!

AW!

KAKASHI!

THUD

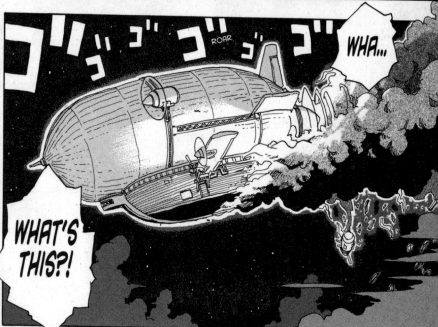

ROAR

WHA...

WHAT'S THIS?!

A MISSILE ATTACK?!

— 104 —

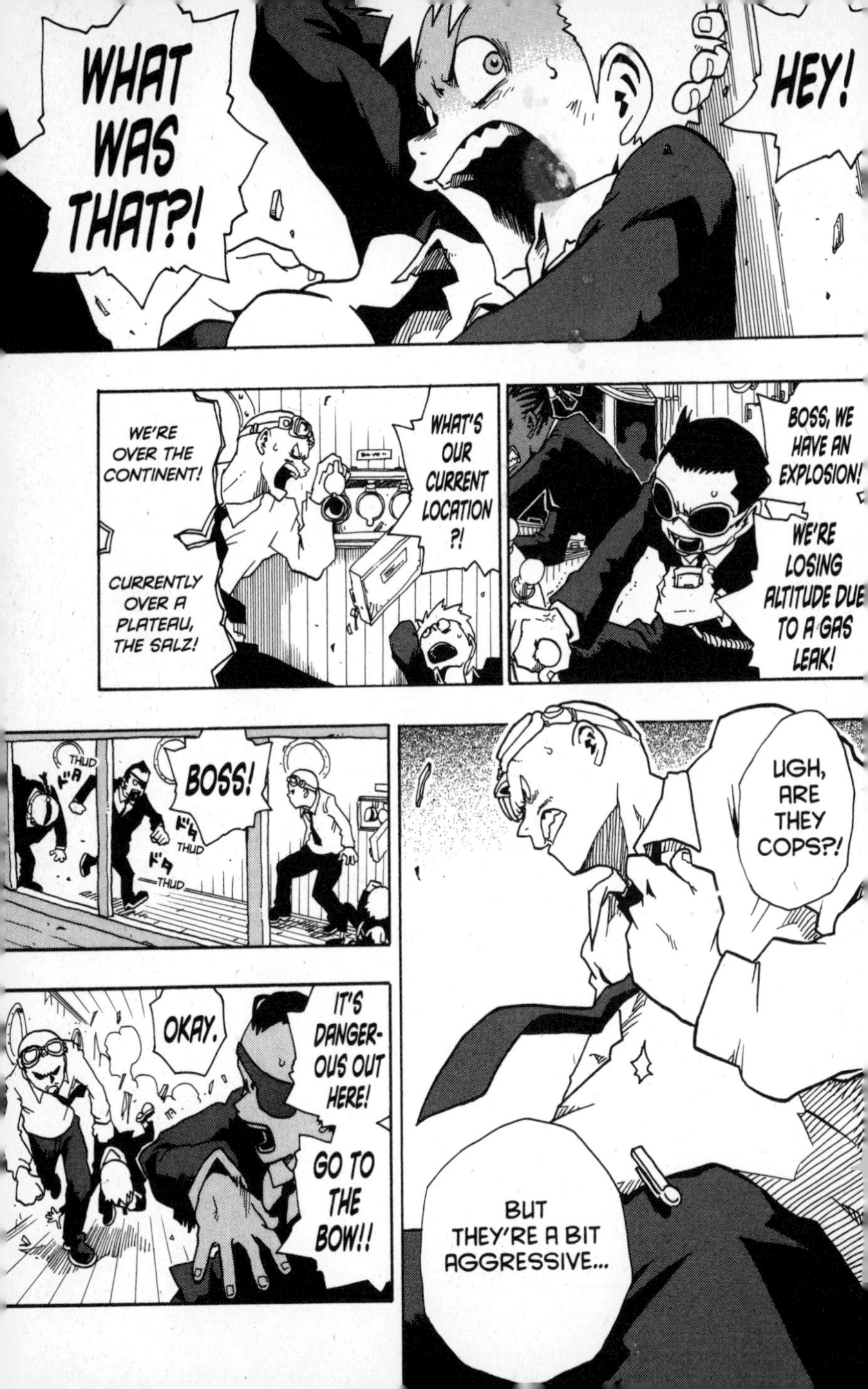
HEY!
WHAT WAS THAT?!
BOSS, WE HAVE AN EXPLOSION!
WE'RE LOSING ALTITUDE DUE TO A GAS LEAK!
WHAT'S OUR CURRENT LOCATION?!
WE'RE OVER THE CONTINENT!
CURRENTLY OVER A PLATEAU, THE SALZ!
UGH, ARE THEY COPS?!
BUT THEY'RE A BIT AGGRESSIVE...
BOSS!
THUD
THUD
THUD
IT'S DANGER-OUS OUT HERE!
GO TO THE BOW!!
OKAY.

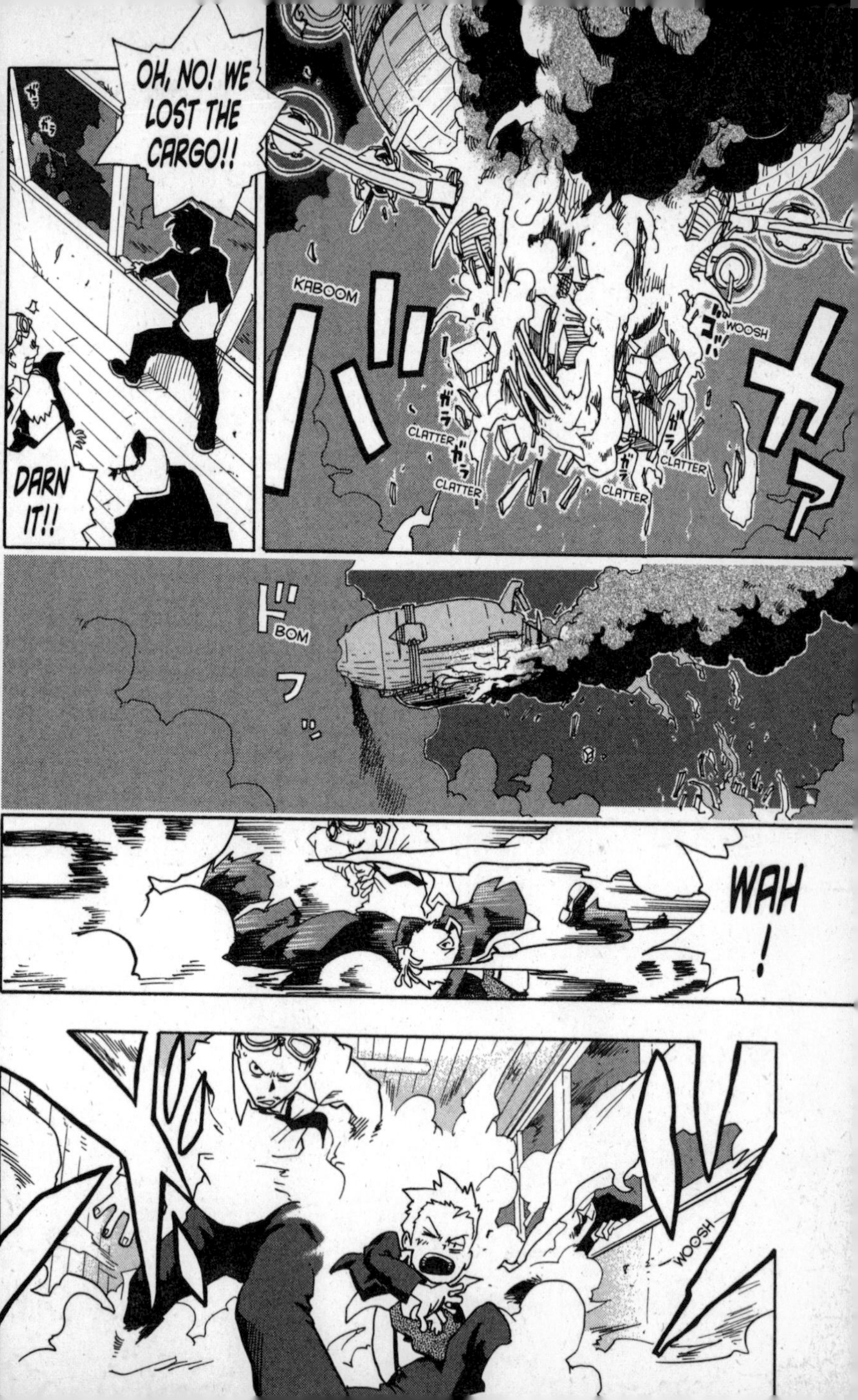
KABOOM
WOOSH
CLATTER
CLATTER
CLATTER
CLATTER
OH, NO! WE LOST THE CARGO!!
DARN IT!!
BOM
WAH!
WOOSH

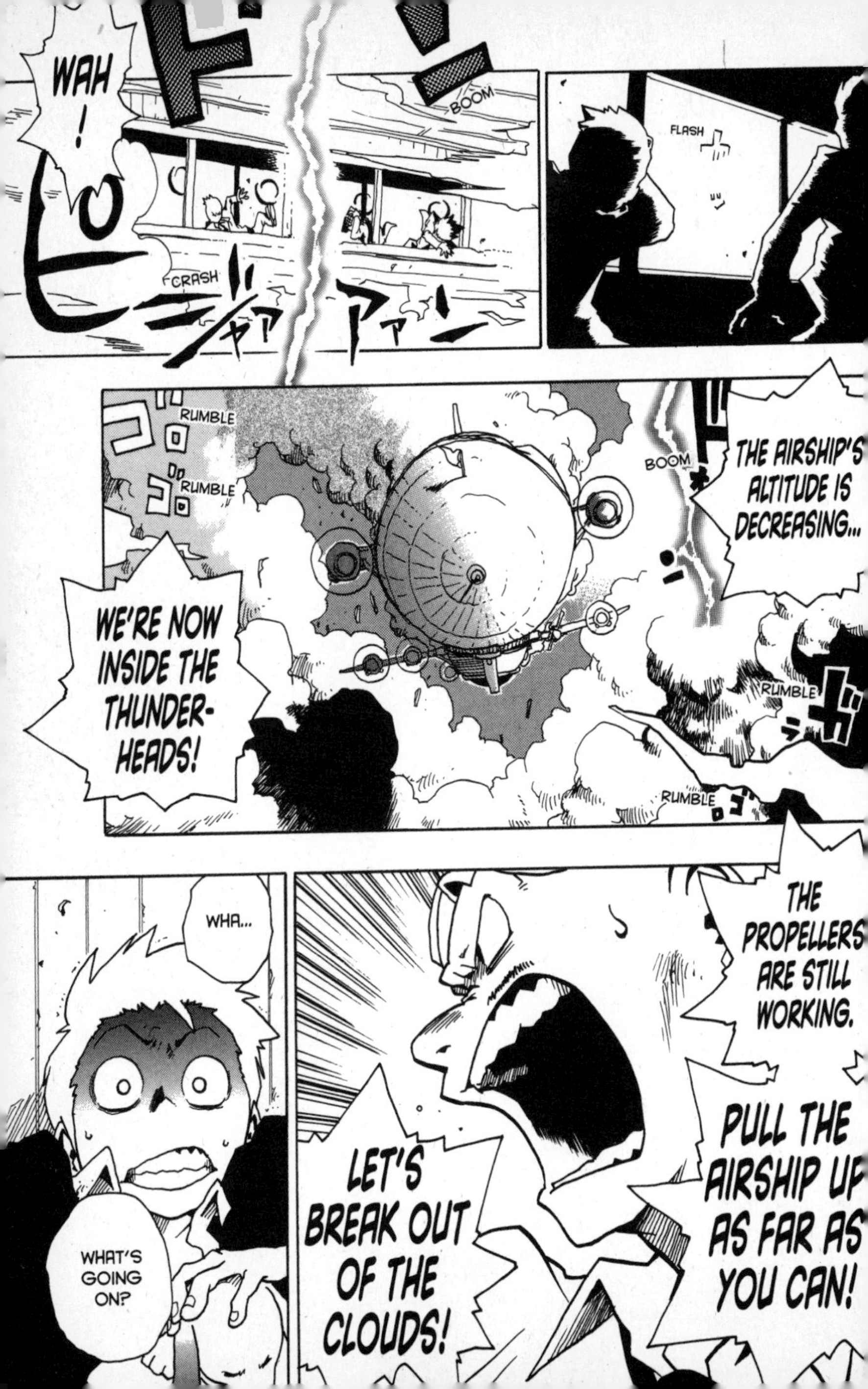
FLASH
BOOM
WAH!
CRASH
THE AIRSHIP'S ALTITUDE IS DECREASING...
BOOM
RUMBLE
RUMBLE
RUMBLE
RUMBLE
WE'RE NOW INSIDE THE THUNDER-HEADS!
THE PROPELLERS ARE STILL WORKING.
PULL THE AIRSHIP UP AS FAR AS YOU CAN!
LET'S BREAK OUT OF THE CLOUDS!
WHA...
WHAT'S GOING ON?

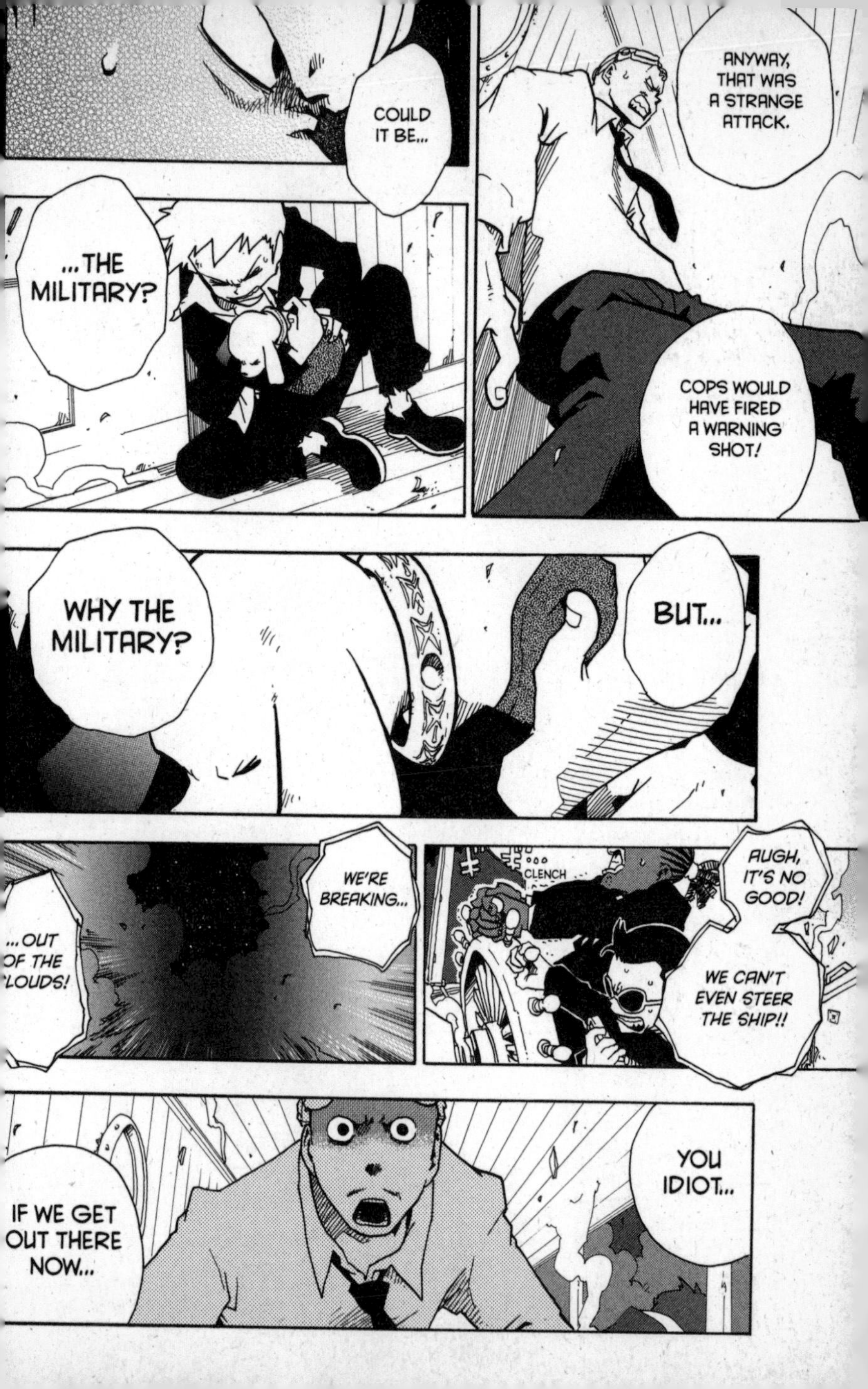
ANYWAY, THAT WAS A STRANGE ATTACK.
COPS WOULD HAVE FIRED A WARNING SHOT!
COULD IT BE...
...THE MILITARY?
BUT...
WHY THE MILITARY?
CLENCH
AUGH, IT'S NO GOOD!
WE CAN'T EVEN STEER THE SHIP!!
WE'RE BREAKING...
...OUT OF THE LOUDS!
YOU IDIOT...
IF WE GET OUT THERE NOW...

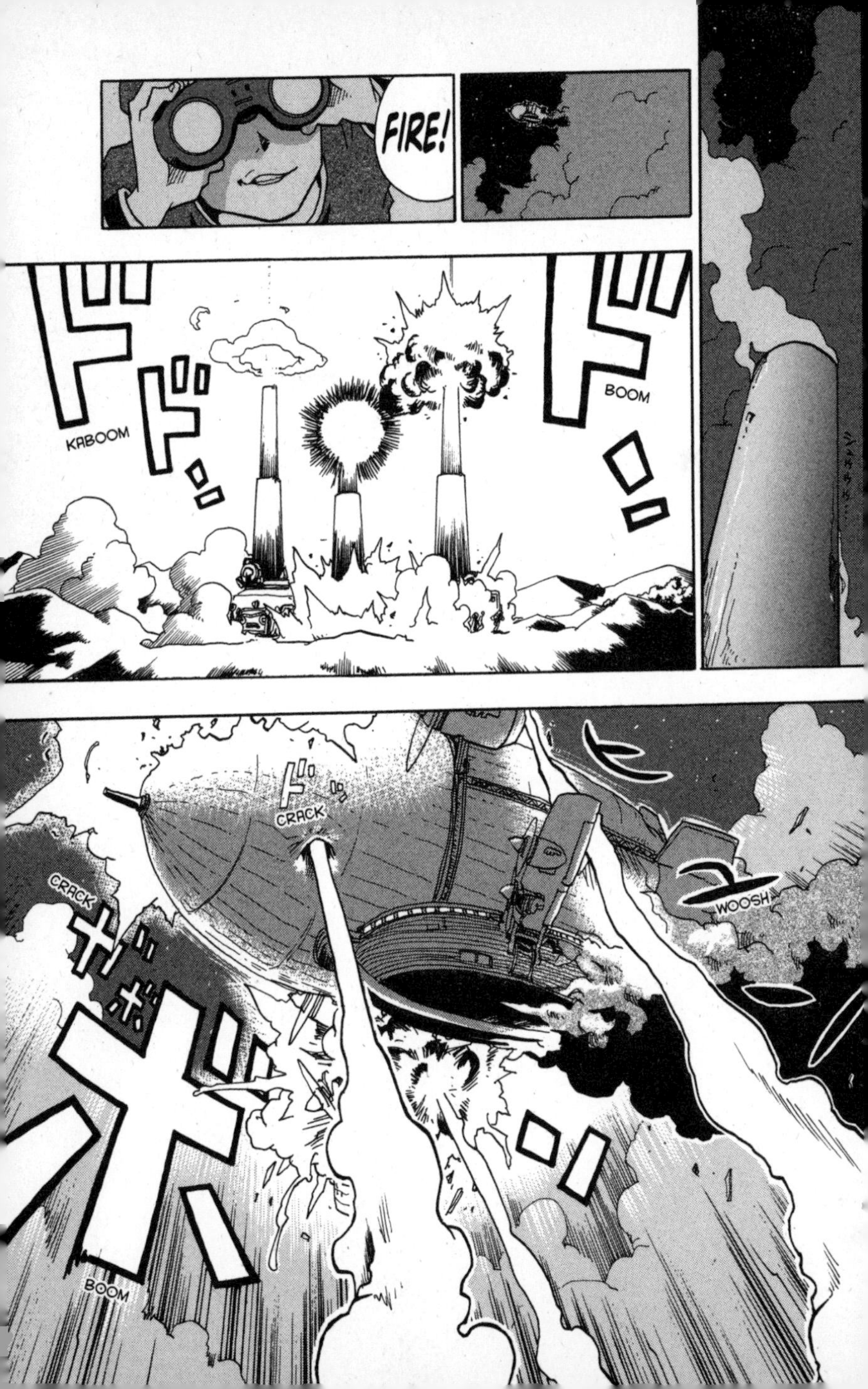
FIRE!
BOOM
KABOOM
WOOSH
CRACK
CRACK
BOOM

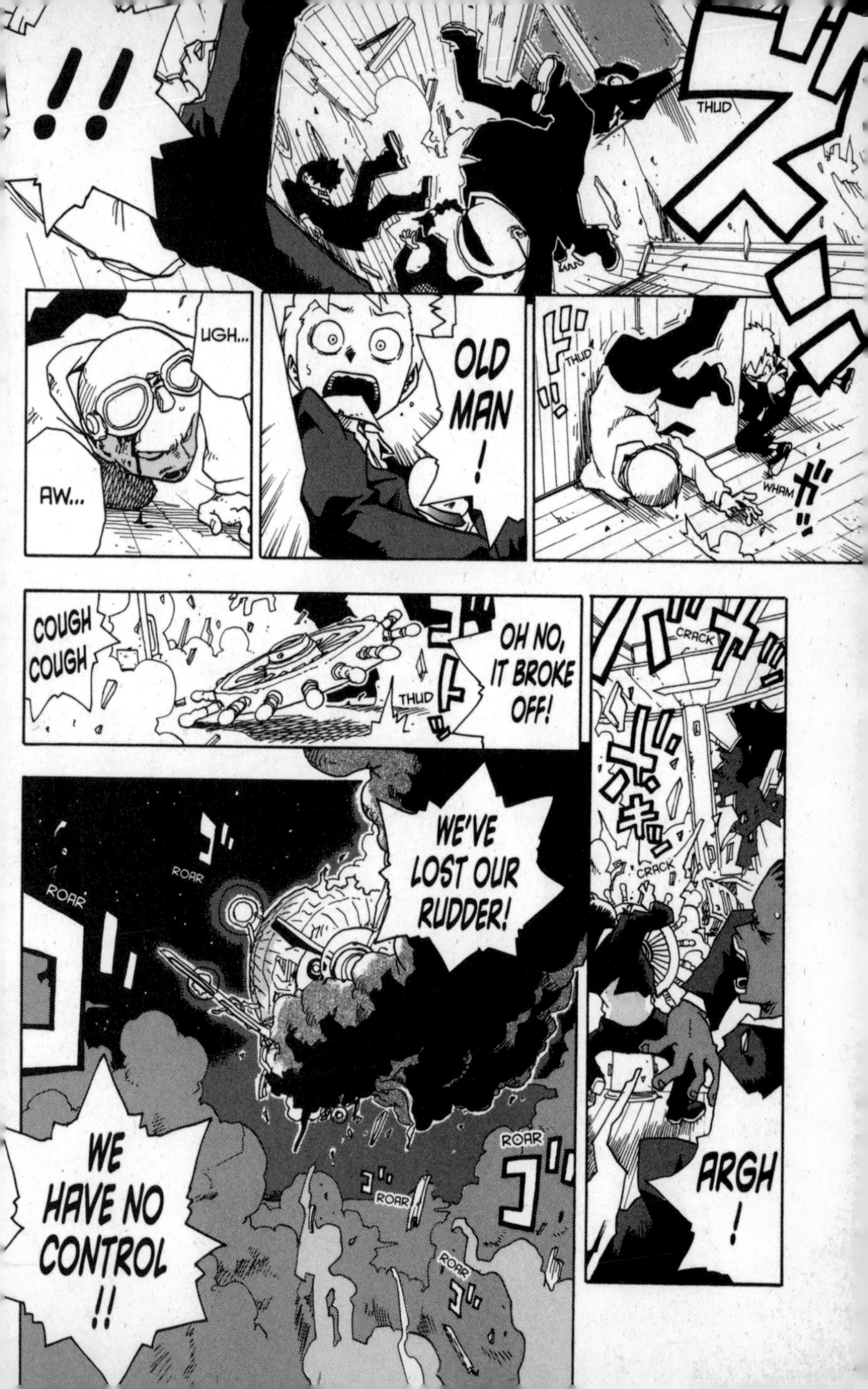
THUD
!!
THUD
WHAM
OLD MAN!
UGH...
AW...
CRACK
CRACK
ARGH!
OH NO, IT BROKE OFF!
THUD
COUGH COUGH
WE'VE LOST OUR RUDDER!
ROAR
ROAR
ROAR
ROAR
ROAR
WE HAVE NO CONTROL!!

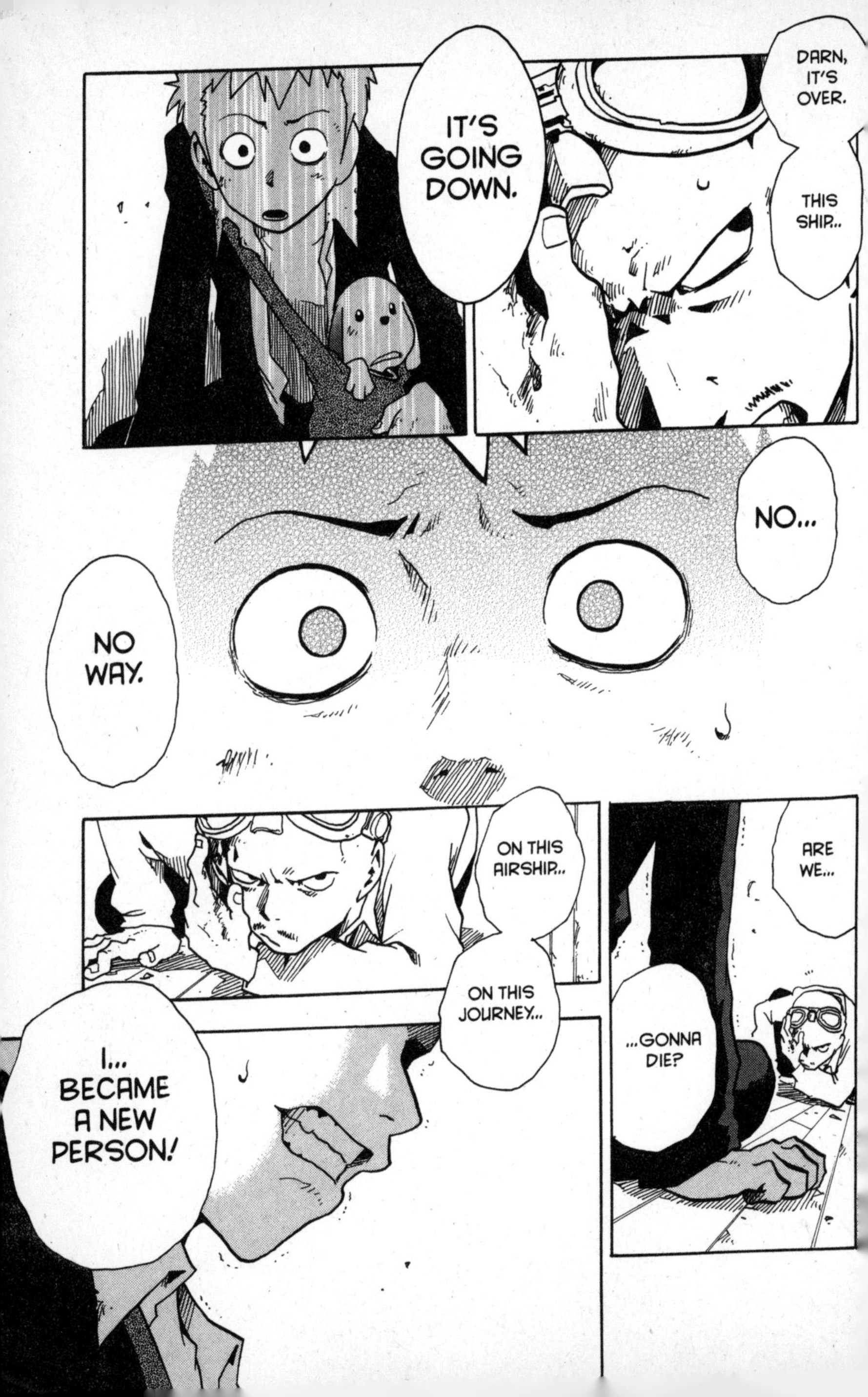
DARN, IT'S OVER.
THIS SHIP...
IT'S GOING DOWN.
NO...
NO WAY.
ARE WE...
...GONNA DIE?
ON THIS AIRSHIP...
ON THIS JOURNEY...
I... BECAME A NEW PERSON!

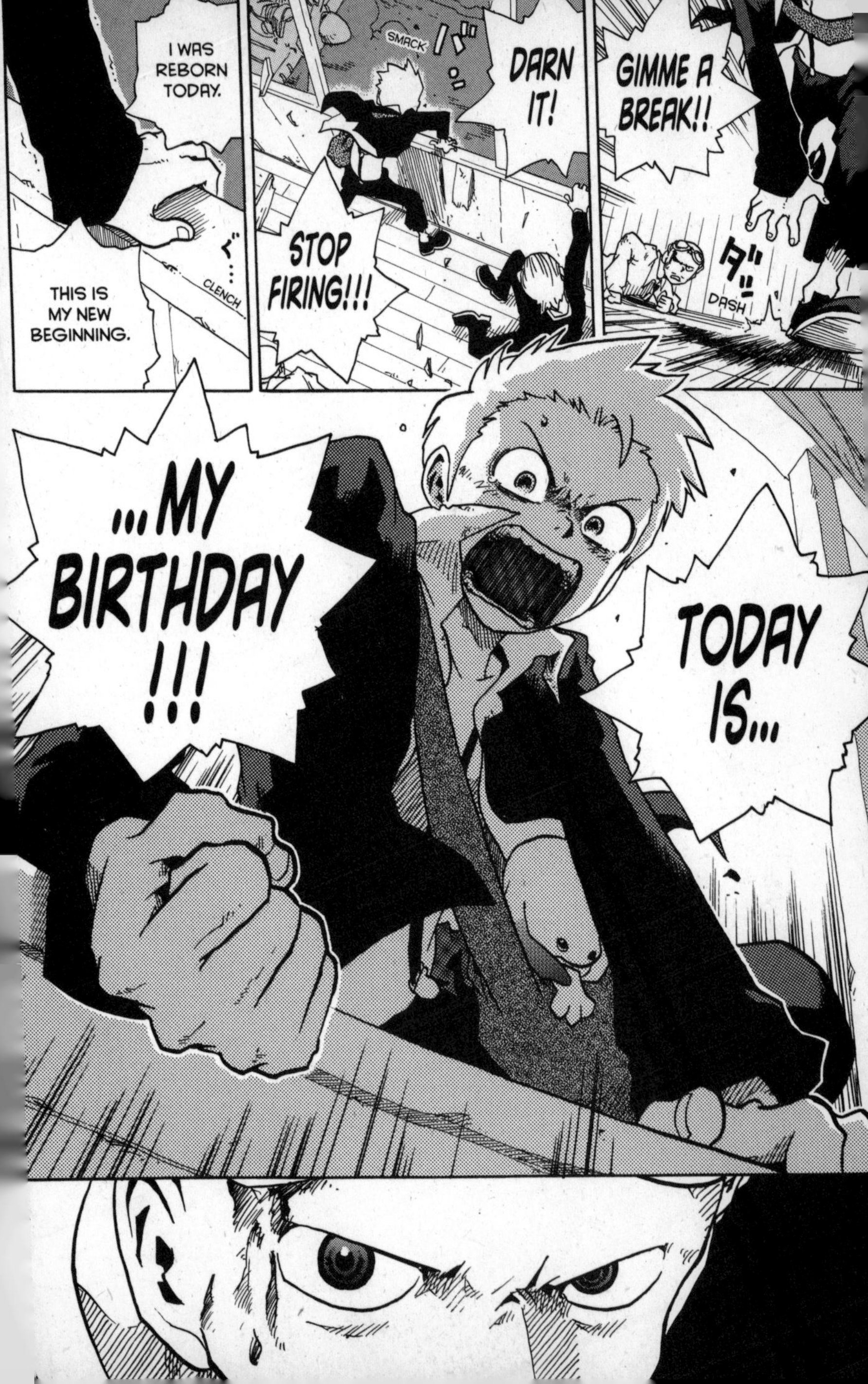
GIMME A BREAK!!
ダッ
DASH
SMACK
DARN IT!
STOP FIRING!!!
I WAS REBORN TODAY.
CLENCH
THIS IS MY NEW BEGINNING.
TODAY IS...
...MY BIRTHDAY!!!

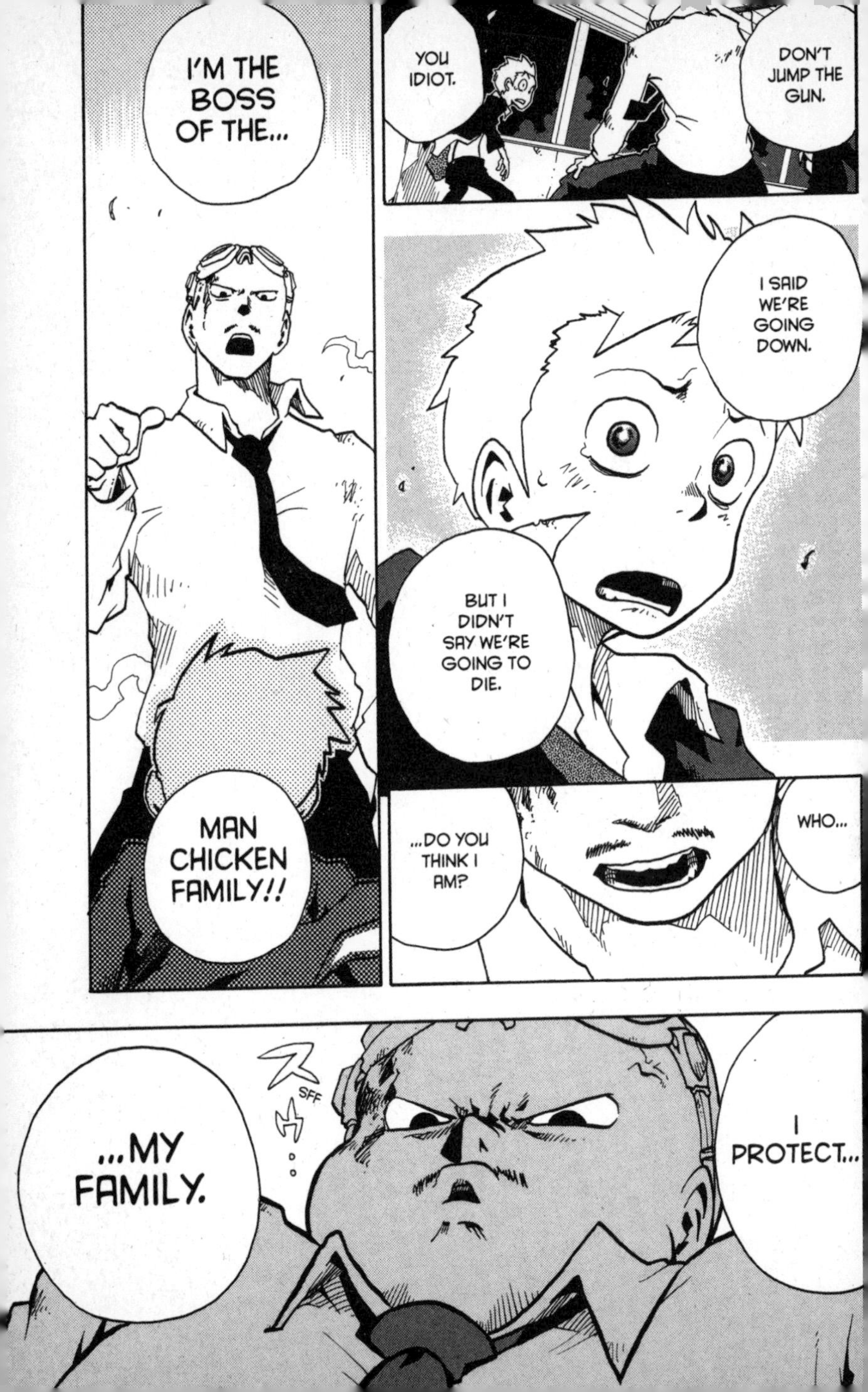
DON'T JUMP THE GUN.
YOU IDIOT.
I SAID WE'RE GOING DOWN.
BUT I DIDN'T SAY WE'RE GOING TO DIE.
WHO...
...DO YOU THINK I AM?
I'M THE BOSS OF THE...
MAN CHICKEN FAMILY!!
I PROTECT...
SFF
...MY FAMILY.

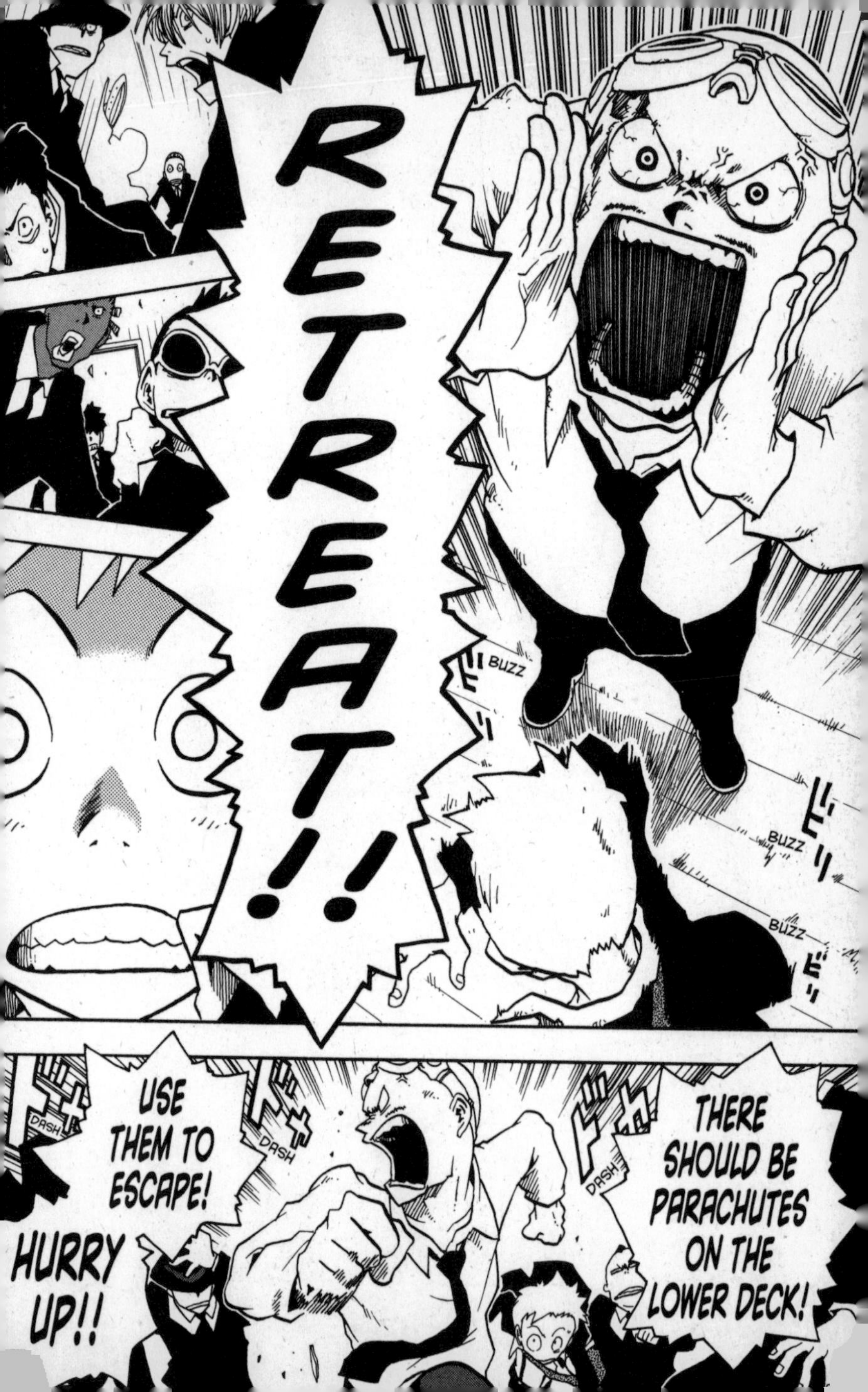
RETREAT!!
BUZZ
BUZZ
BUZZ
DASH
THERE SHOULD BE PARACHUTES ON THE LOWER DECK!
DASH
USE THEM TO ESCAPE!
DASH
HURRY UP!!

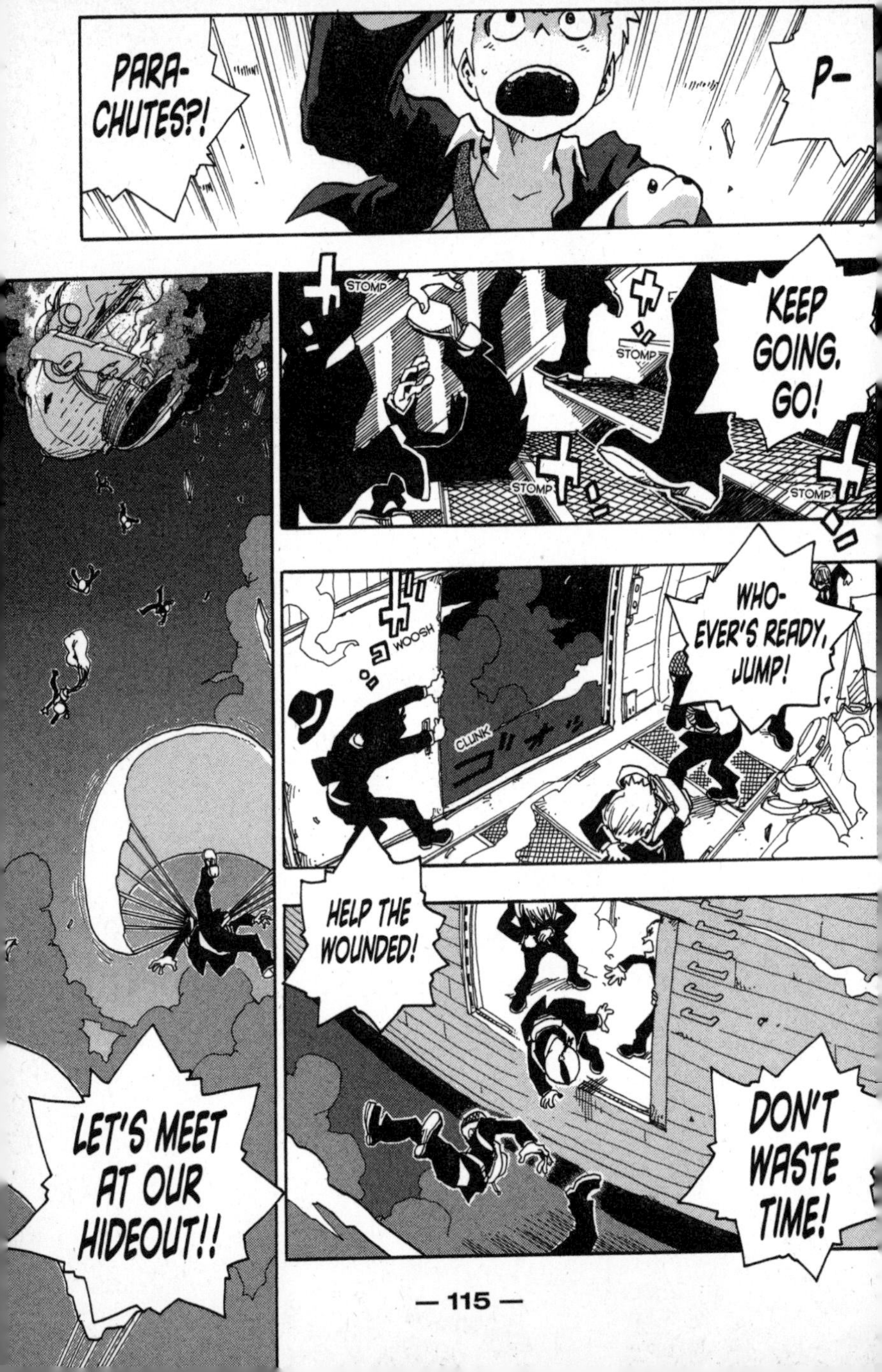
P-
PARA-CHUTES?!
KEEP GOING. GO!
STOMP
STOMP
STOMP
STOMP
STOMP
WHO-EVER'S READY, JUMP!
WOOSH
CLUNK
DON'T WASTE TIME!
HELP THE WOUNDED!
LET'S MEET AT OUR HIDEOUT!!

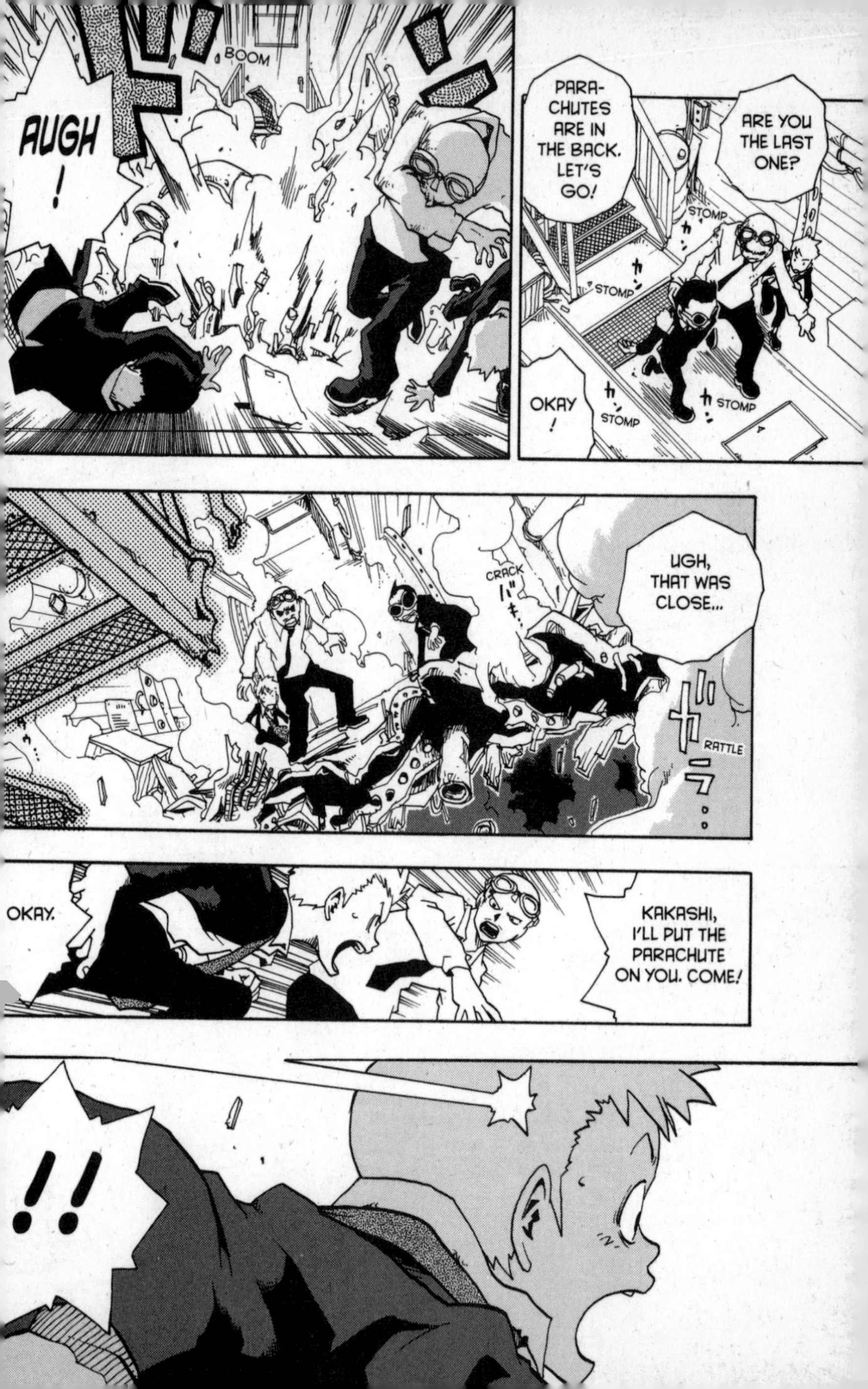
ARE YOU THE LAST ONE?
PARA-CHUTES ARE IN THE BACK. LET'S GO!
STOMP
STOMP
STOMP
STOMP
OKAY!
BOOM
AUGH!
CRACK
UGH, THAT WAS CLOSE...
RATTLE
KAKASHI, I'LL PUT THE PARACHUTE ON YOU. COME!
OKAY.
!!

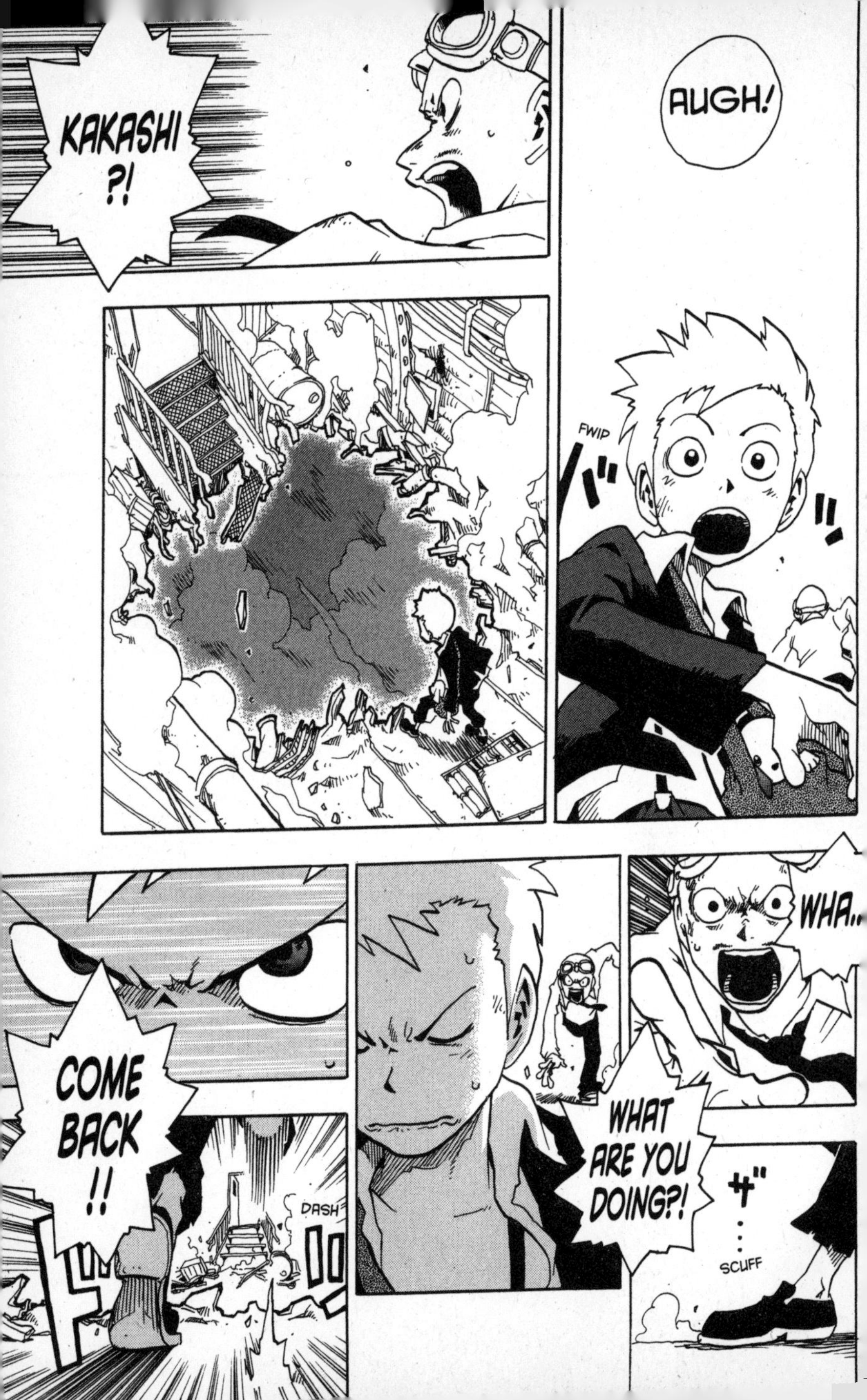
AUGH!
FWIP
KAKASHI?!
WHA...
WHAT ARE YOU DOING?!
SCUFF
COME BACK!!
DASH

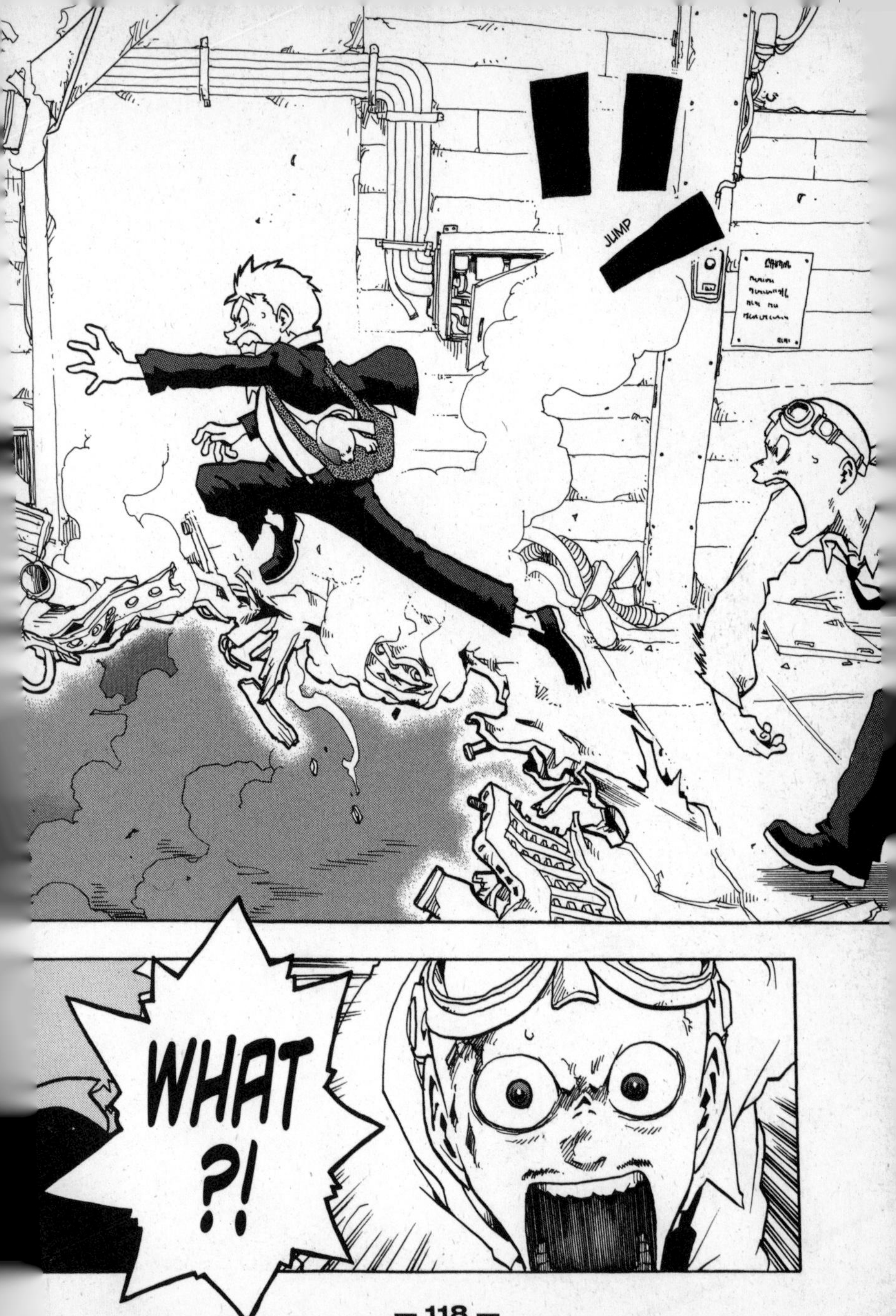
JUMP
WHAT ?!

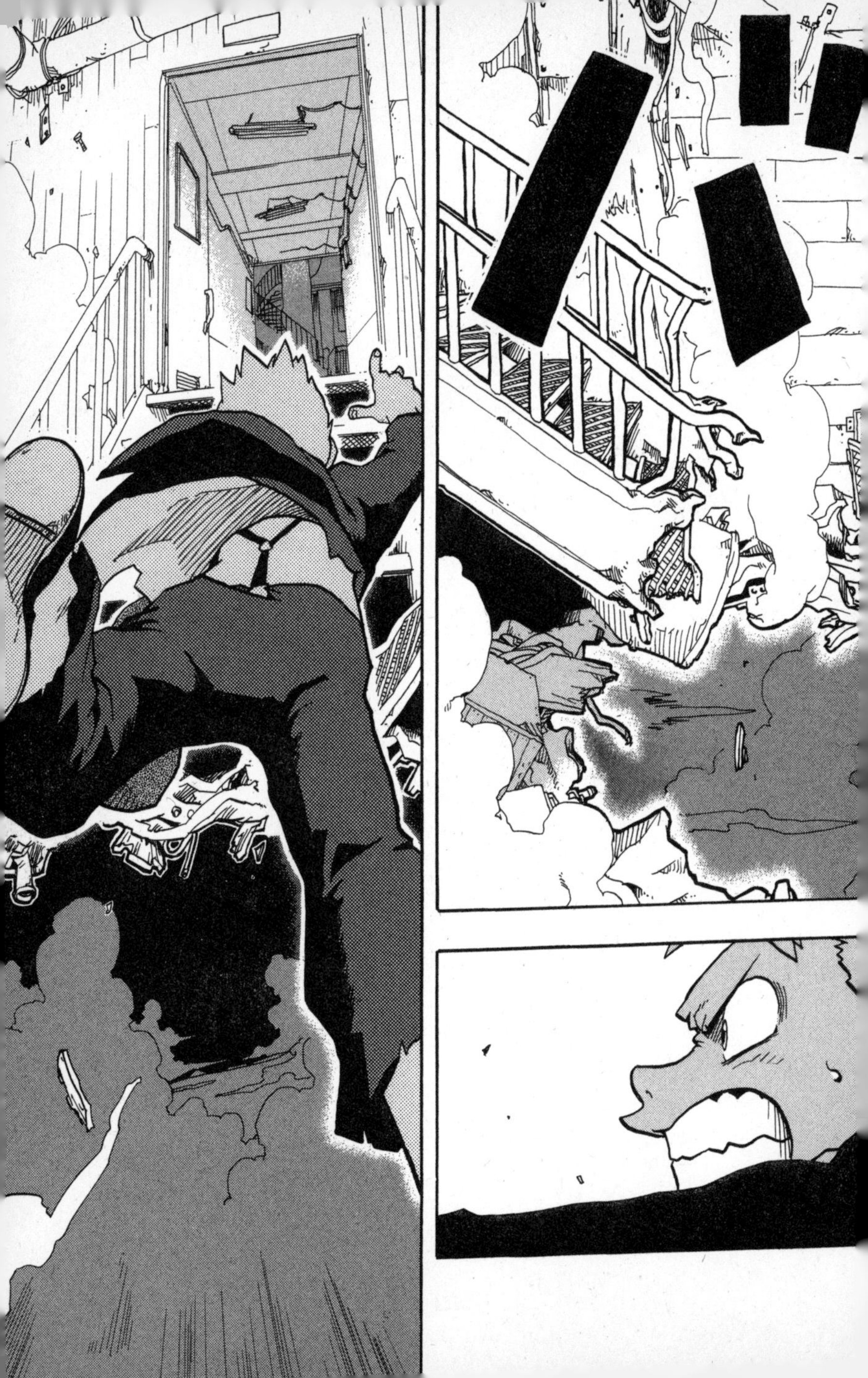
バ

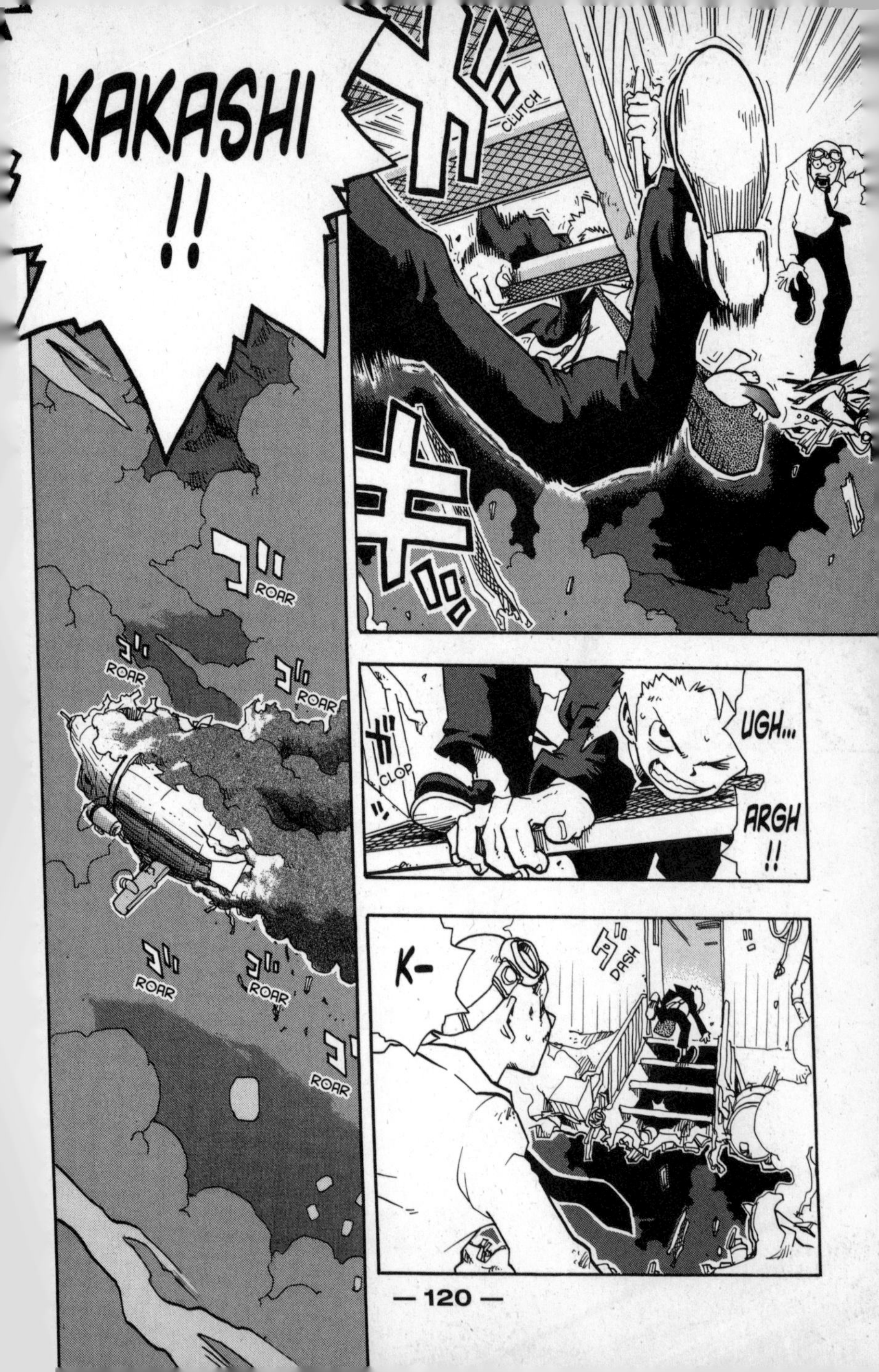
CLUTCH
CLOP
UGH... ARGH!!
DASH
K-
KAKASHI!!
ROAR
ROAR
ROAR
ROAR
ROAR
ROAR

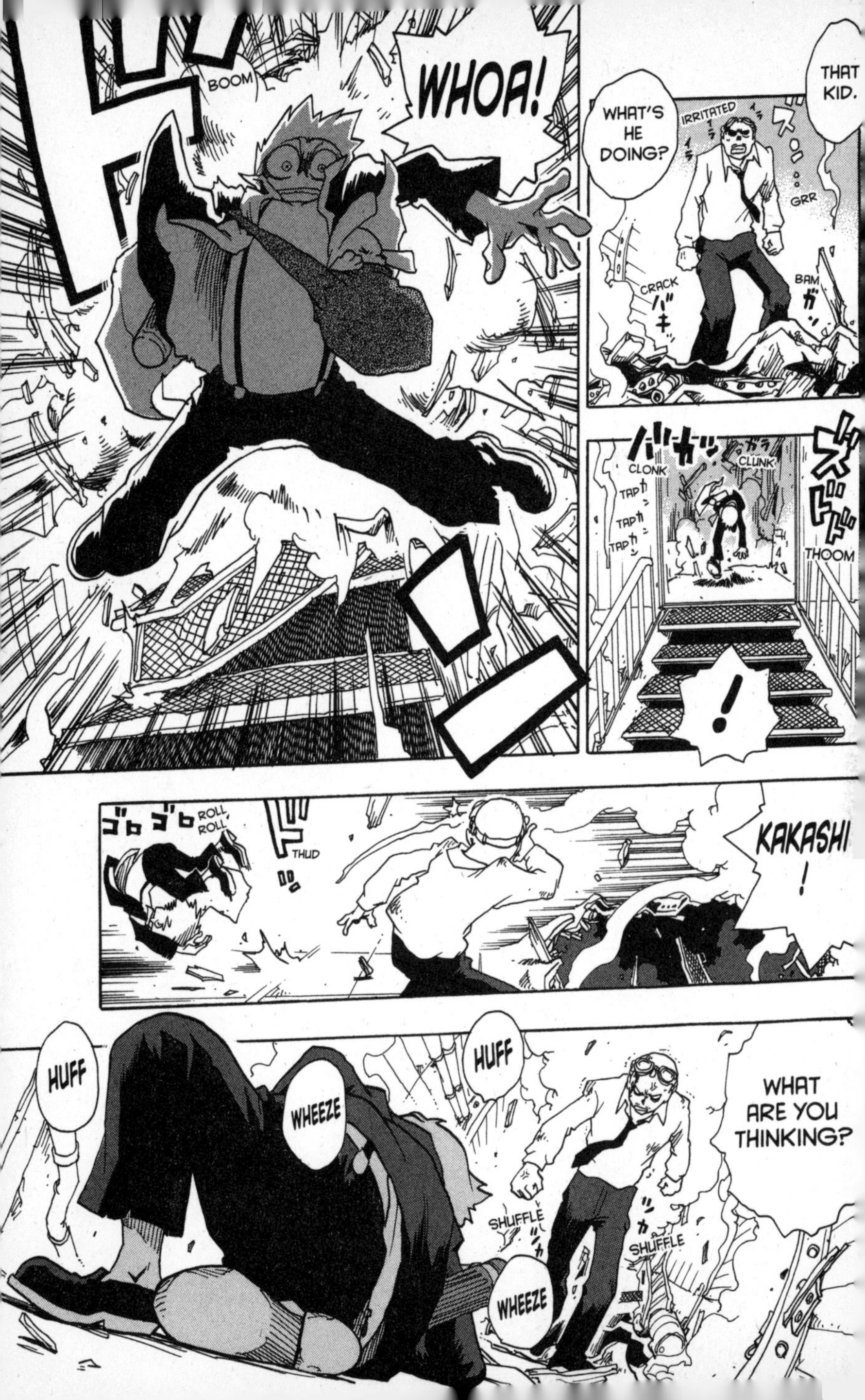
THAT KID.
WHAT'S HE DOING?
IRRITATED
GRR
CRACK
BAM
THOOM
CLUNK
CLONK
TAP
TAP
TAP
!
WHOA!
BOOM
KAKASHI!
THUD
ROLL, ROLL
WHAT ARE YOU THINKING?
SHUFFLE
SHUFFLE
WHEEZE
HUFF
WHEEZE
HUFF

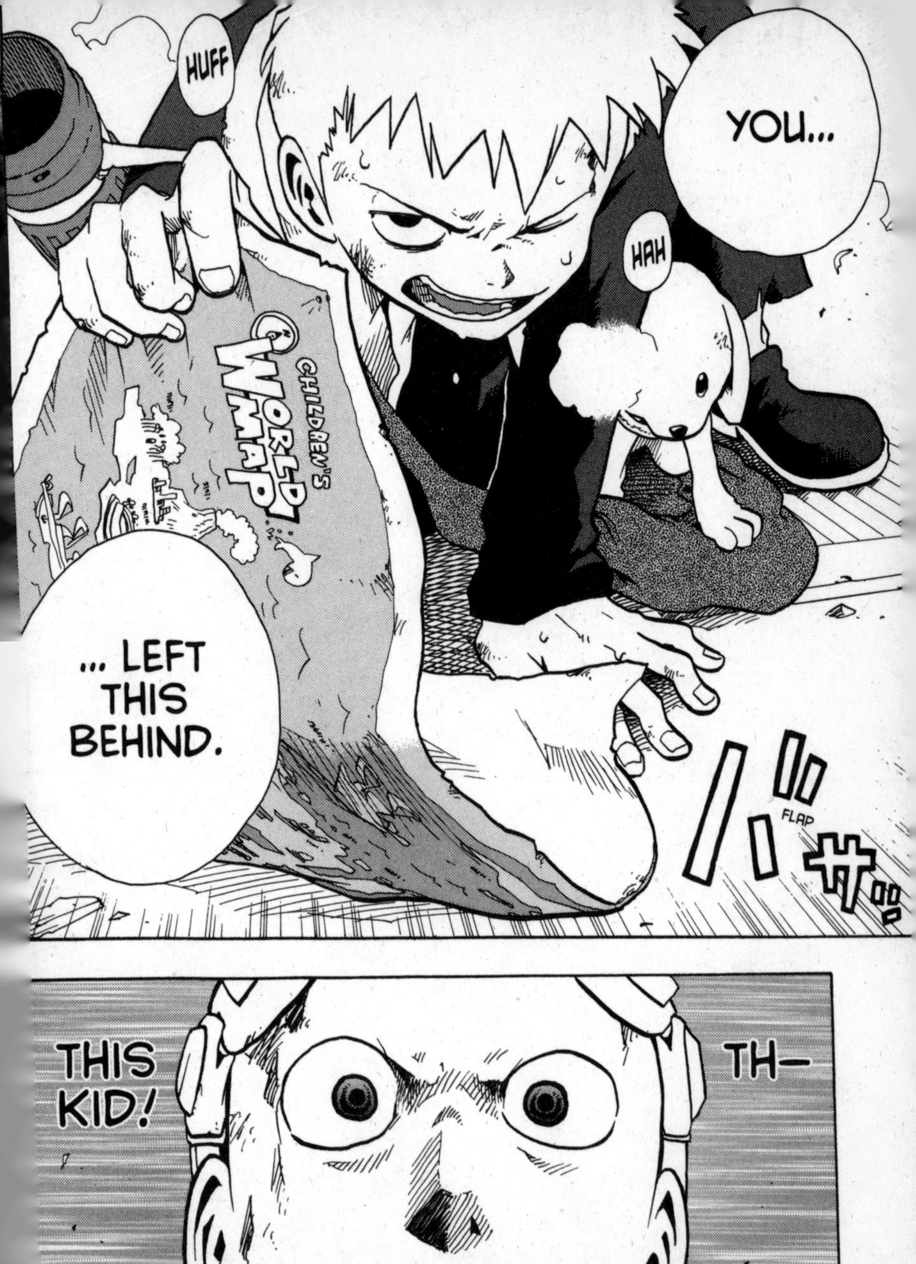
YOU...
HAH
HUFF
CHILDREN'S WORLD MAP
... LEFT THIS BEHIND.
FLAP
TH—
THIS KID!

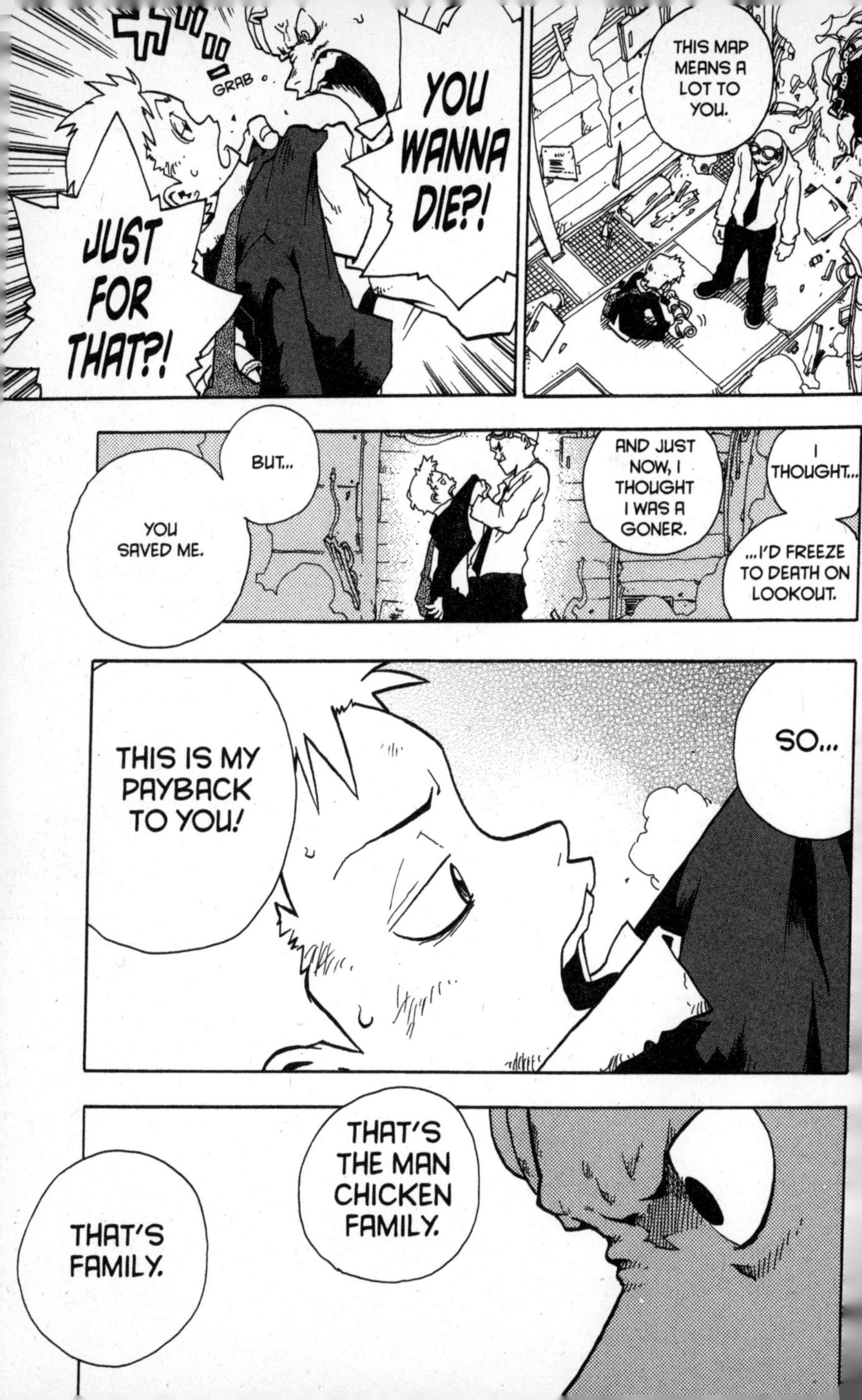
THIS MAP MEANS A LOT TO YOU.
YOU WANNA DIE?!
GRAB
JUST FOR THAT?!
I THOUGHT...
...I'D FREEZE TO DEATH ON LOOKOUT.
AND JUST NOW, I THOUGHT I WAS A GONER.
BUT...
YOU SAVED ME.
SO...
THIS IS MY PAYBACK TO YOU!
THAT'S THE MAN CHICKEN FAMILY.
THAT'S FAMILY.

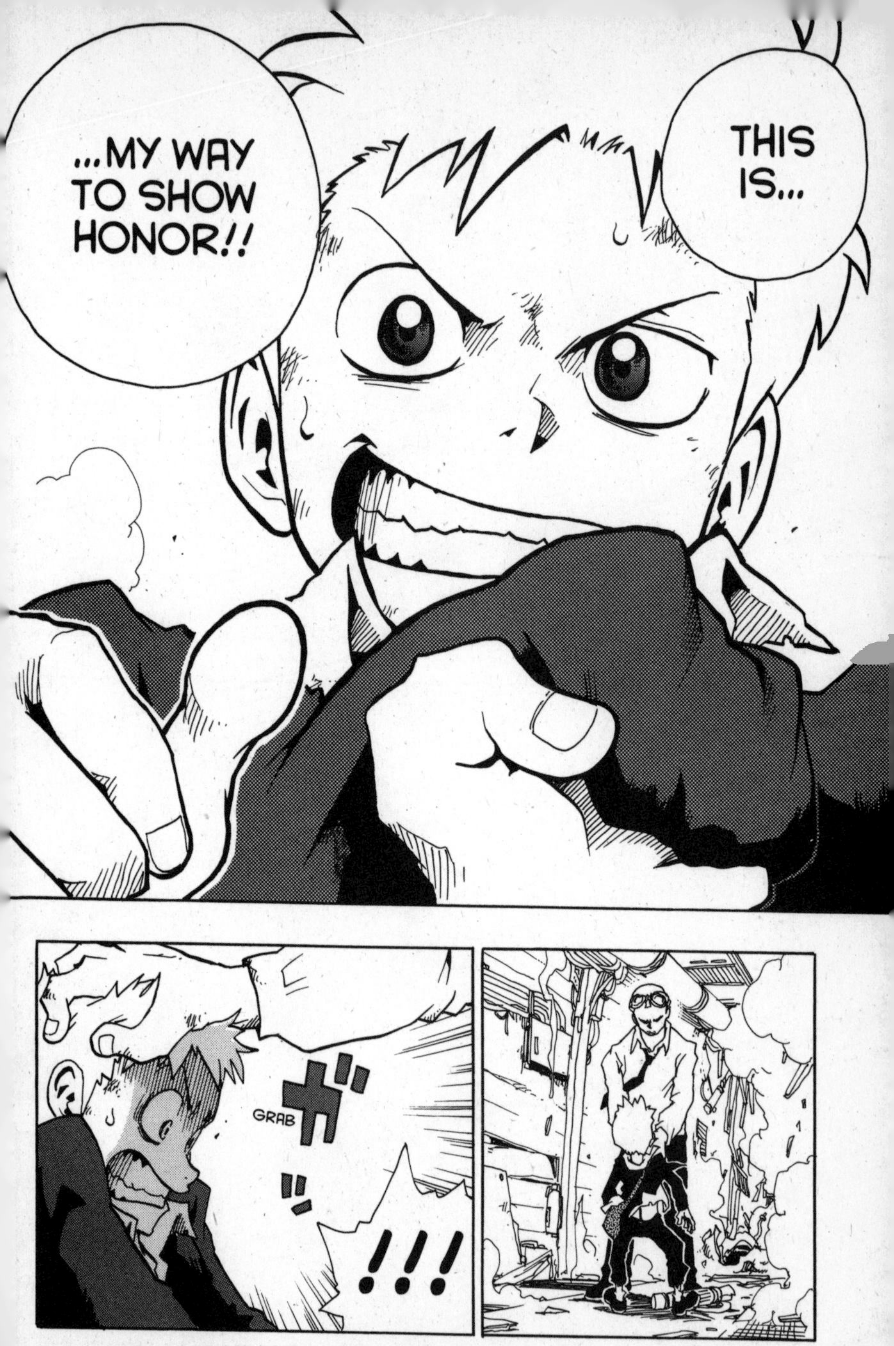
THIS IS...
...MY WAY TO SHOW HONOR!!
ガッ
GRAB
!!!

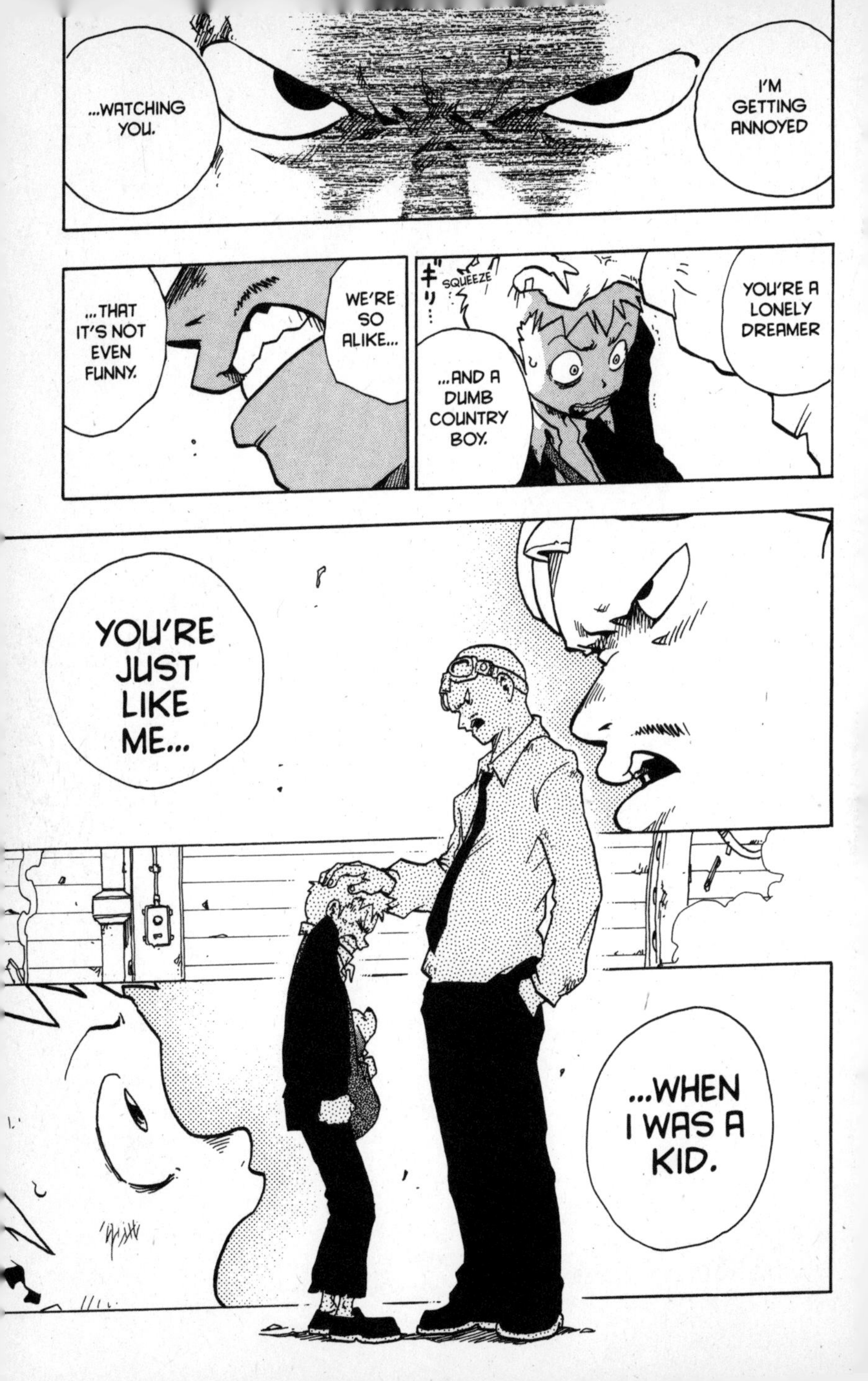
I'M GETTING ANNOYED
...WATCHING YOU.
YOU'RE A LONELY DREAMER
ギリ…
SQUEEZE
...AND A DUMB COUNTRY BOY.
WE'RE SO ALIKE...
...THAT IT'S NOT EVEN FUNNY.
YOU'RE JUST LIKE ME...
...WHEN I WAS A KID.

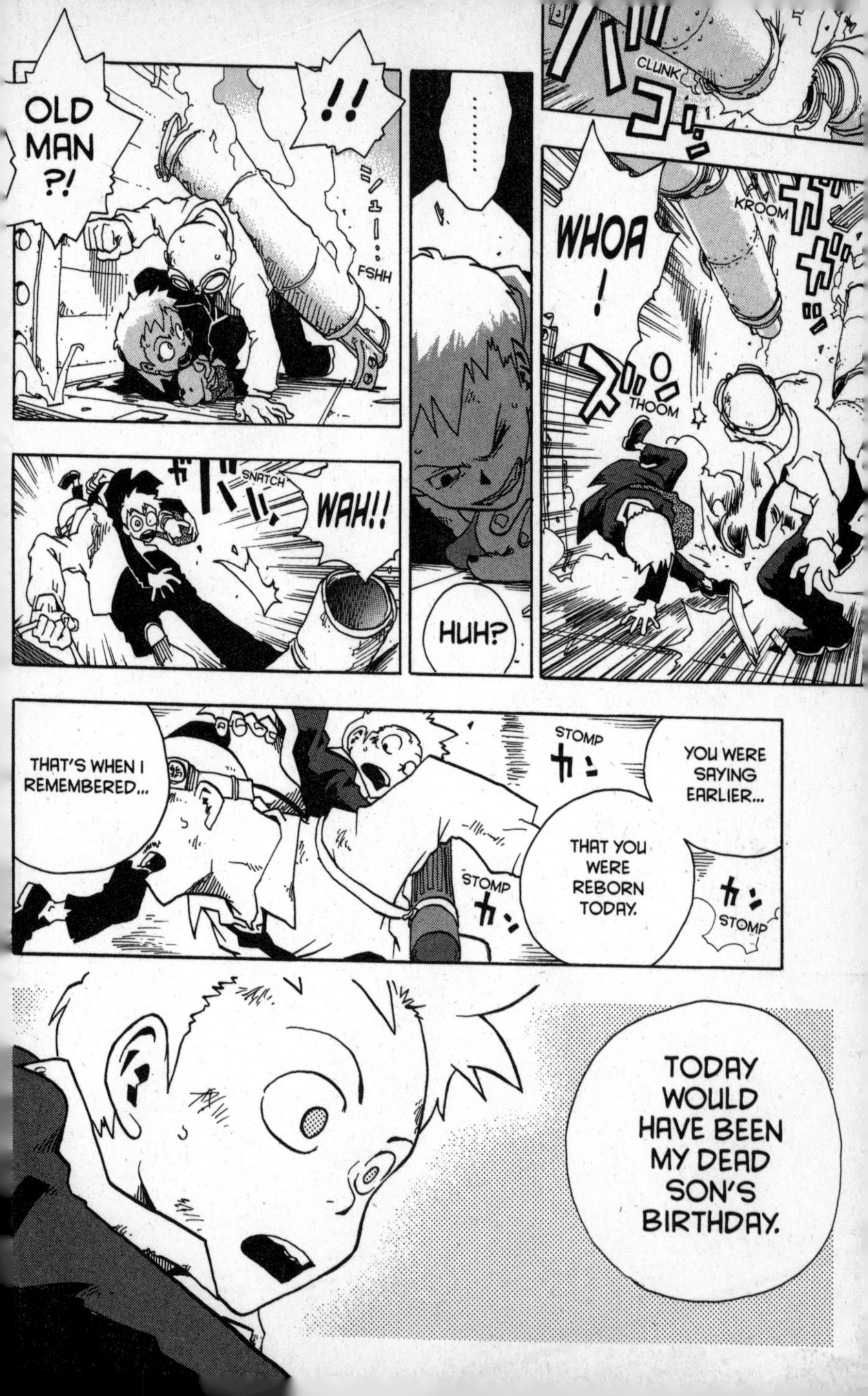
CLUNK
WHOA!
KROOM
THOOM
......
HUH?
!!
OLD MAN?!
FSHH
SNATCH
WAH!!
STOMP
YOU WERE SAYING EARLIER...
THAT YOU WERE REBORN TODAY.
STOMP
STOMP
THAT'S WHEN I REMEMBERED...
TODAY WOULD HAVE BEEN MY DEAD SON'S BIRTHDAY.

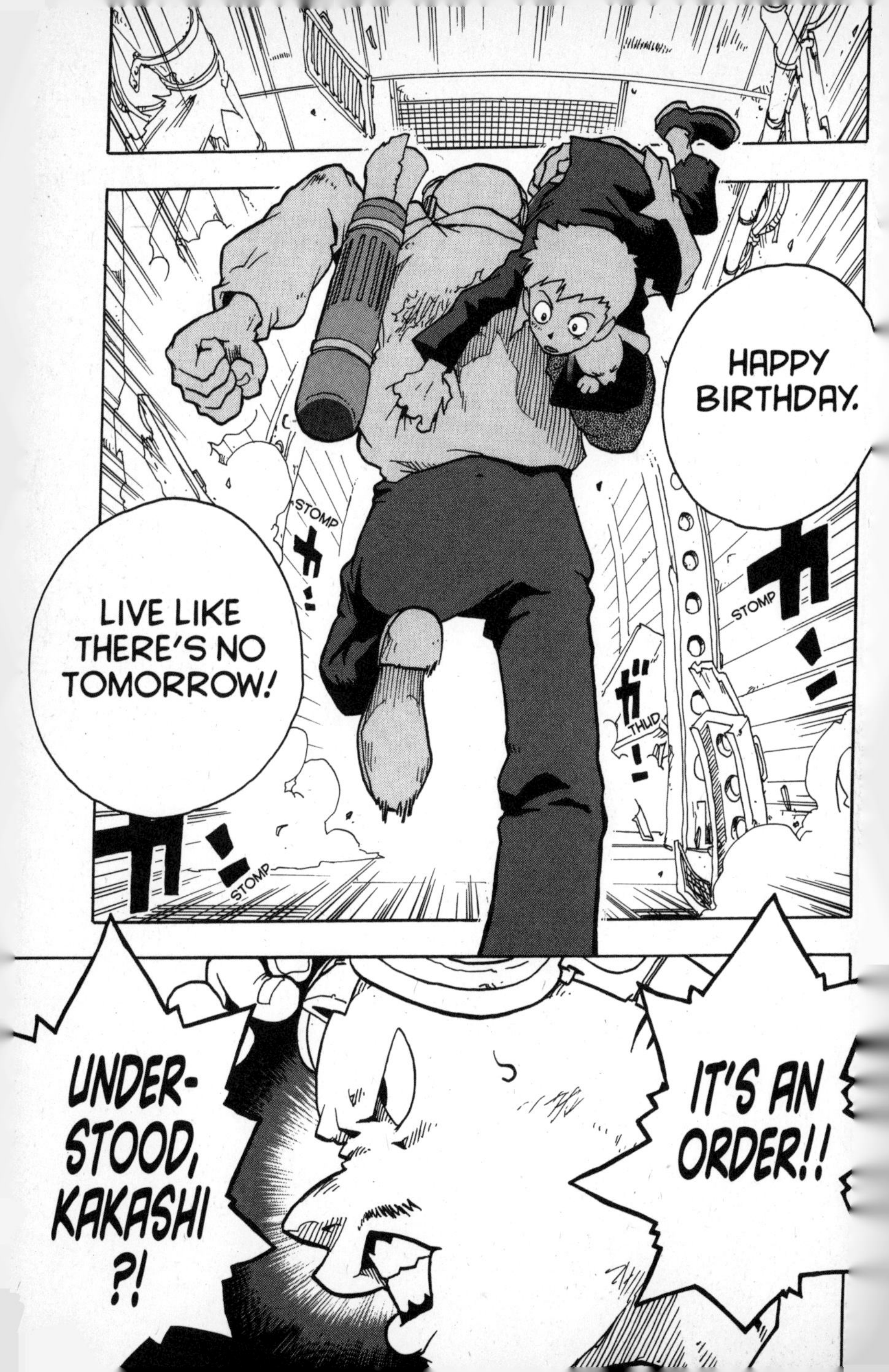
HAPPY BIRTHDAY.
STOMP
STOMP
LIVE LIKE THERE'S NO TOMORROW!
THUD
STOMP
IT'S AN ORDER!!
UNDER-STOOD, KAKASHI ?!

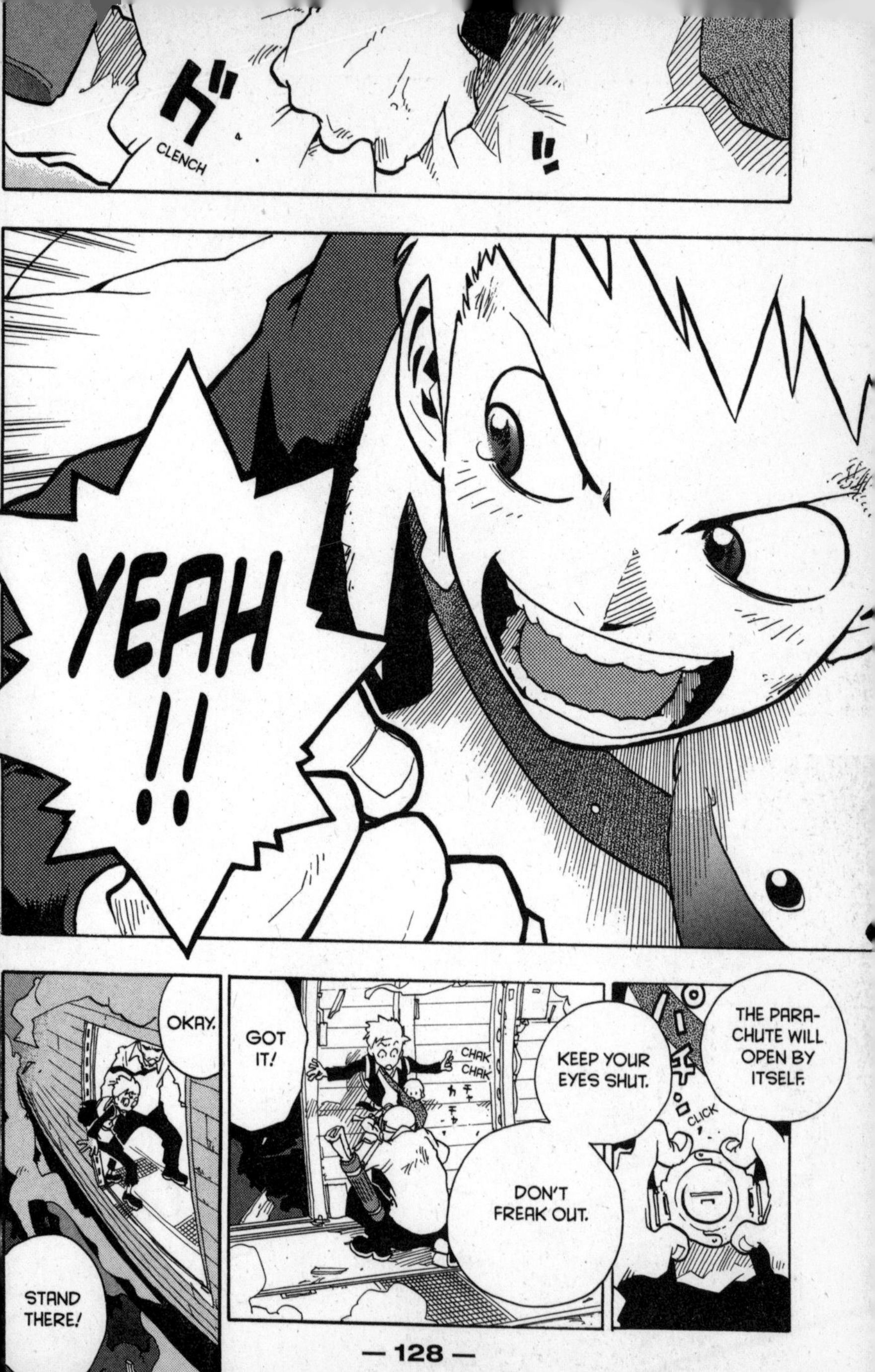
CLENCH
YEAH!!
THE PARA-CHUTE WILL OPEN BY ITSELF.
CLICK
KEEP YOUR EYES SHUT.
DON'T FREAK OUT.
CHAK CHAK
GOT IT!
OKAY.
STAND THERE!

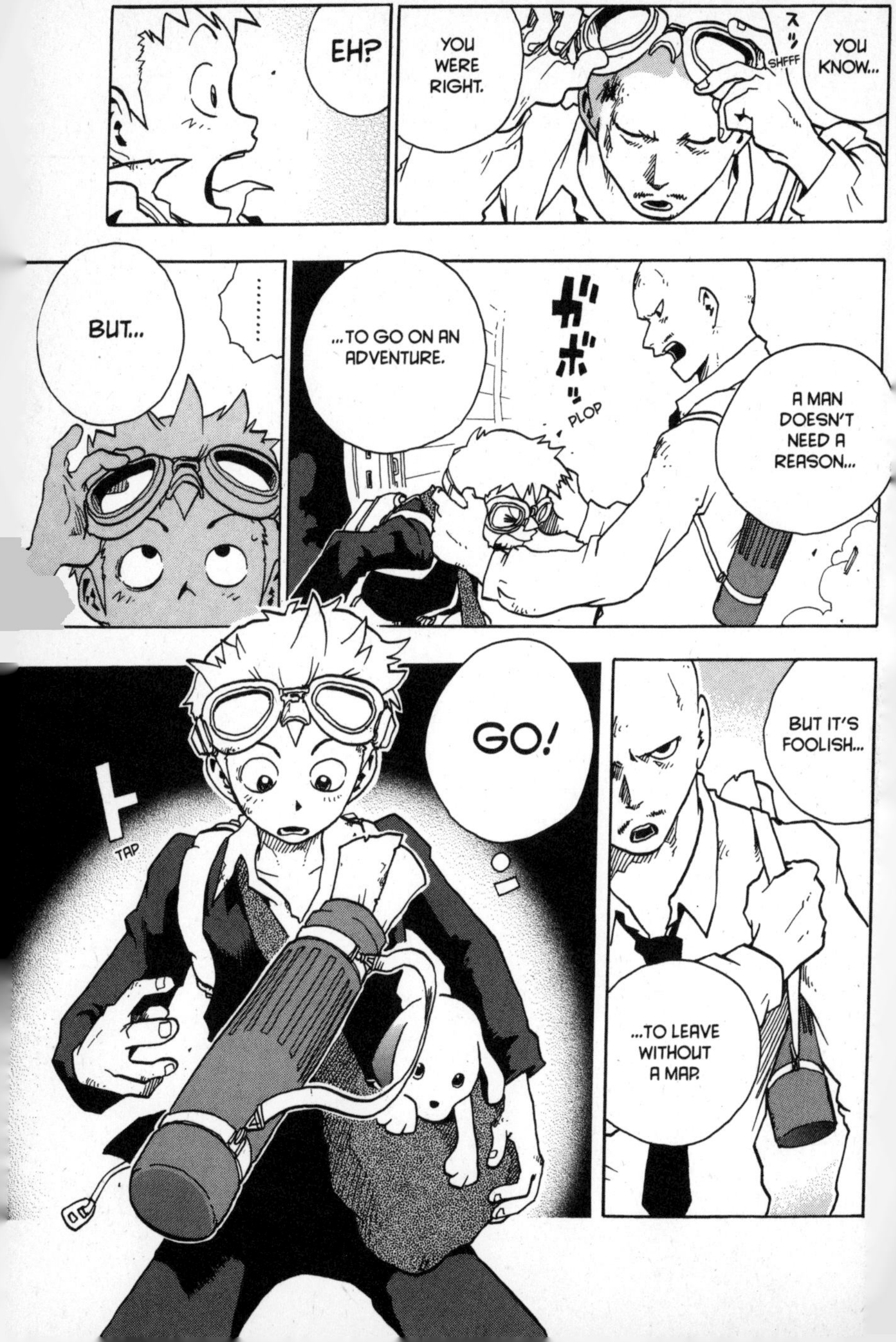
スッ
SHFFF
YOU KNOW...
YOU WERE RIGHT.
EH?
A MAN DOESN'T NEED A REASON...
ガボッ
PLOP
...TO GO ON AN ADVENTURE.
......
BUT...
BUT IT'S FOOLISH...
...TO LEAVE WITHOUT A MAP.
GO!
ト
TAP

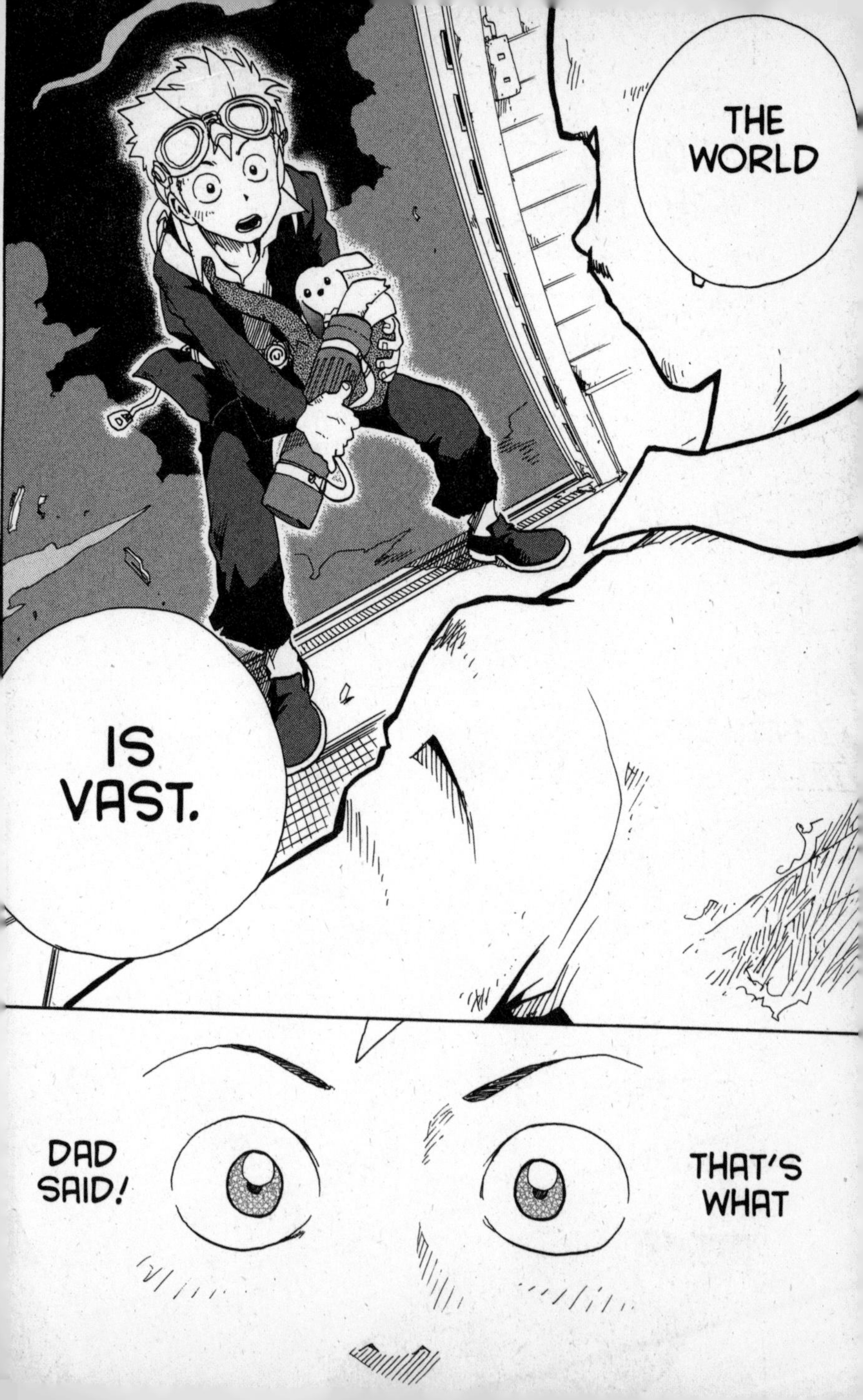
THE WORLD
IS VAST.
THAT'S WHAT
DAD SAID!

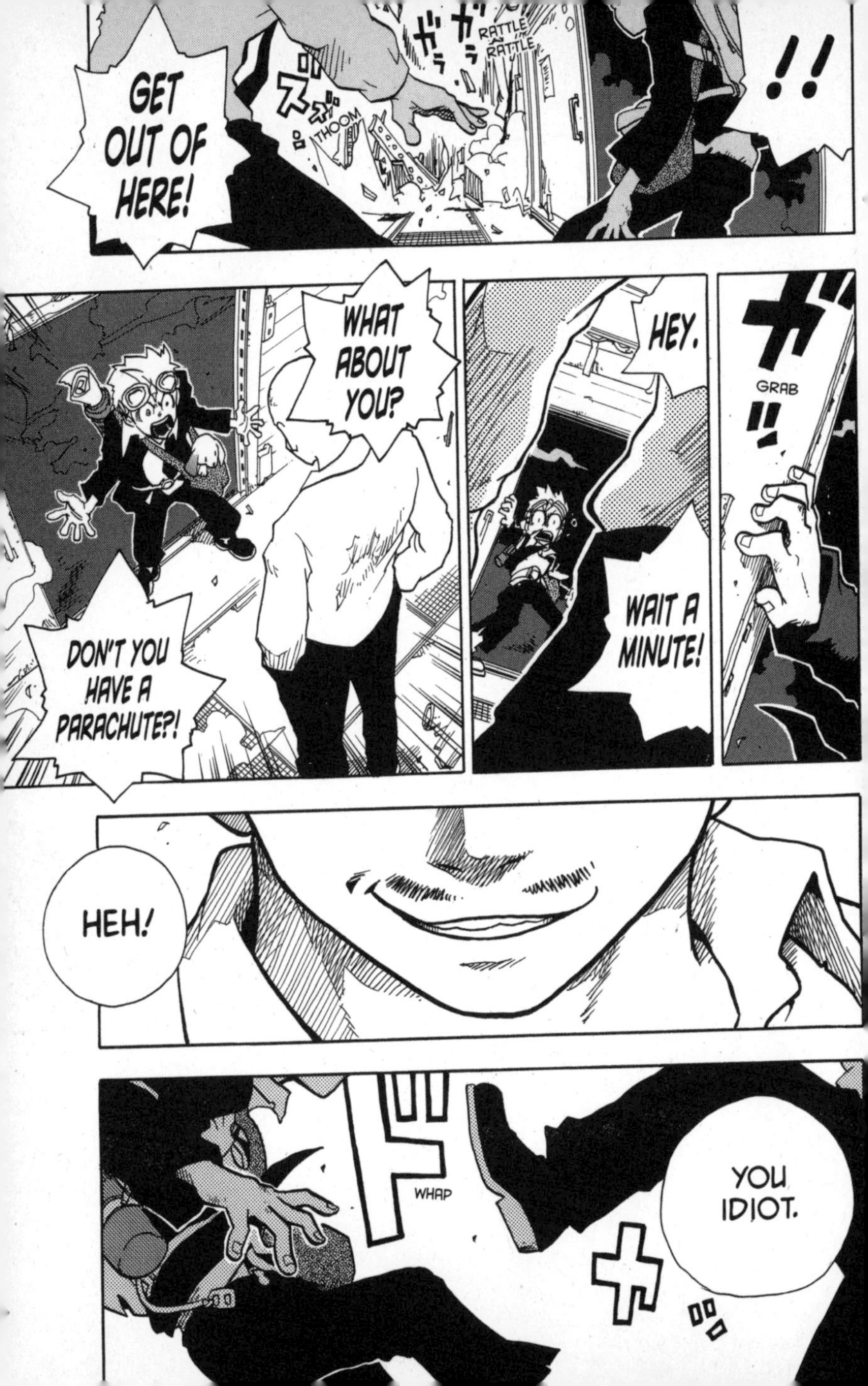
!!
RATTLE RATTLE
THOOM
GET OUT OF HERE!
GRAB
HEY.
WAIT A MINUTE!
WHAT ABOUT YOU?
DON'T YOU HAVE A PARACHUTE?!
HEH!
YOU IDIOT.
WHAP

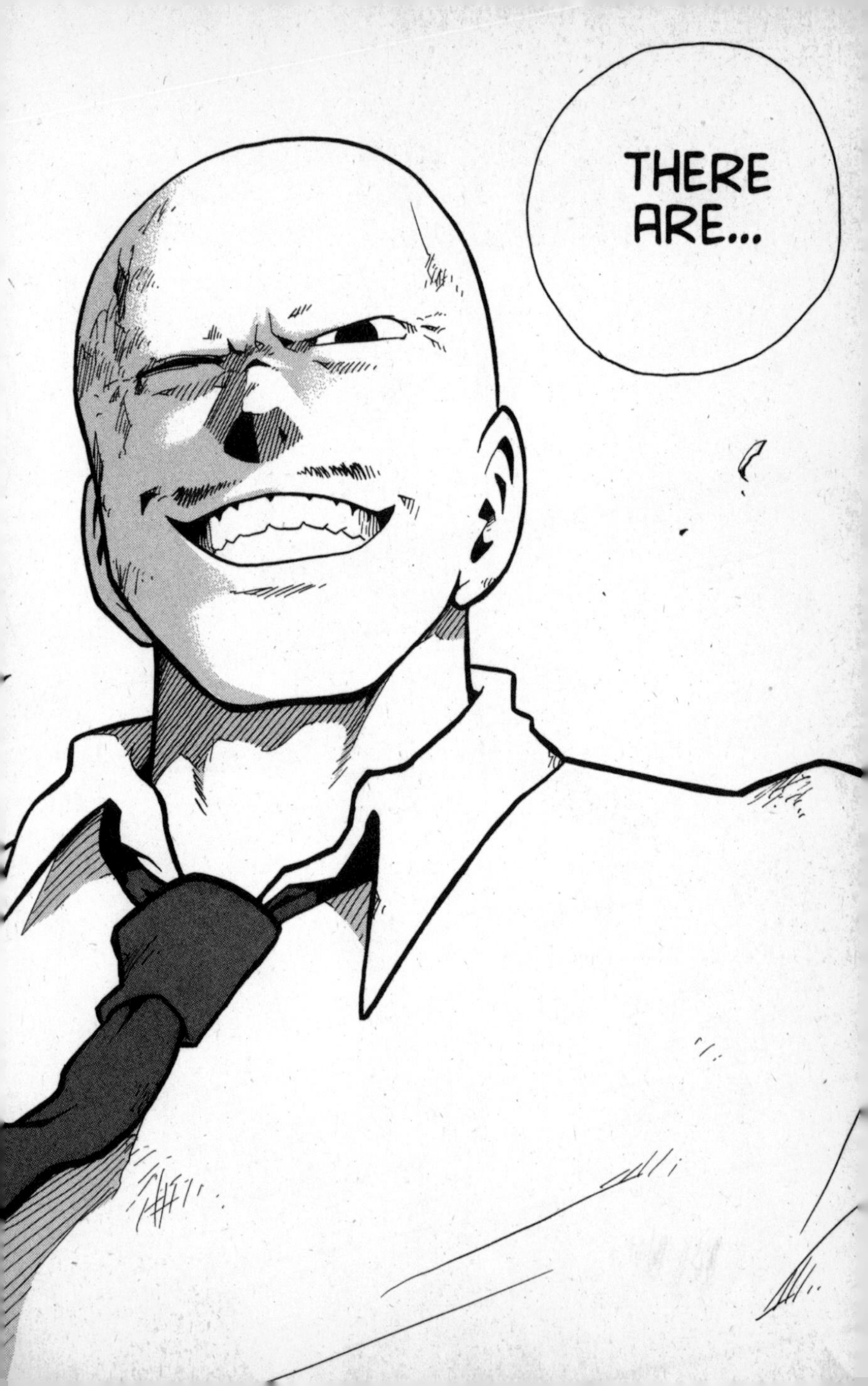
THERE ARE...

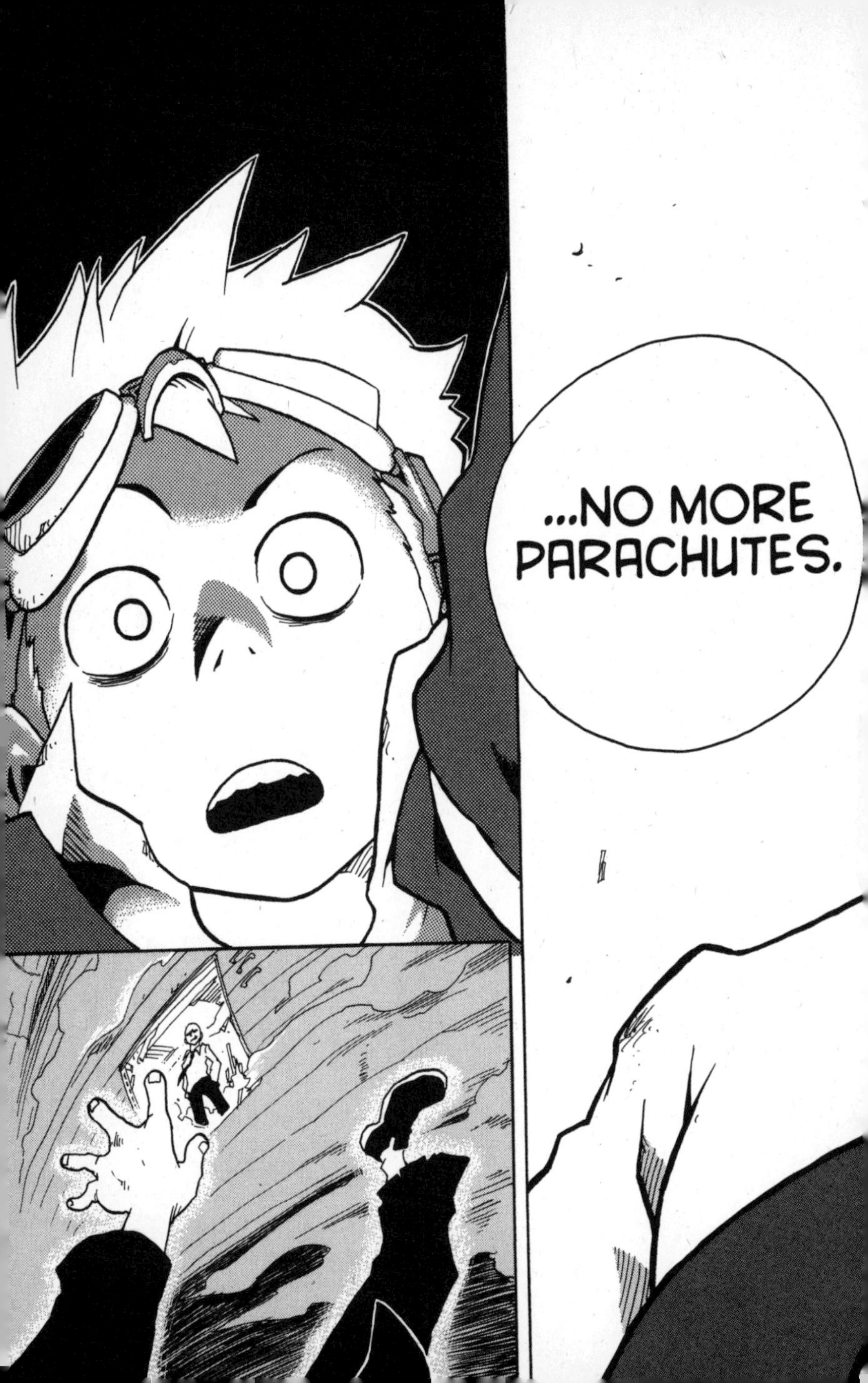
...NO MORE PARACHUTES.

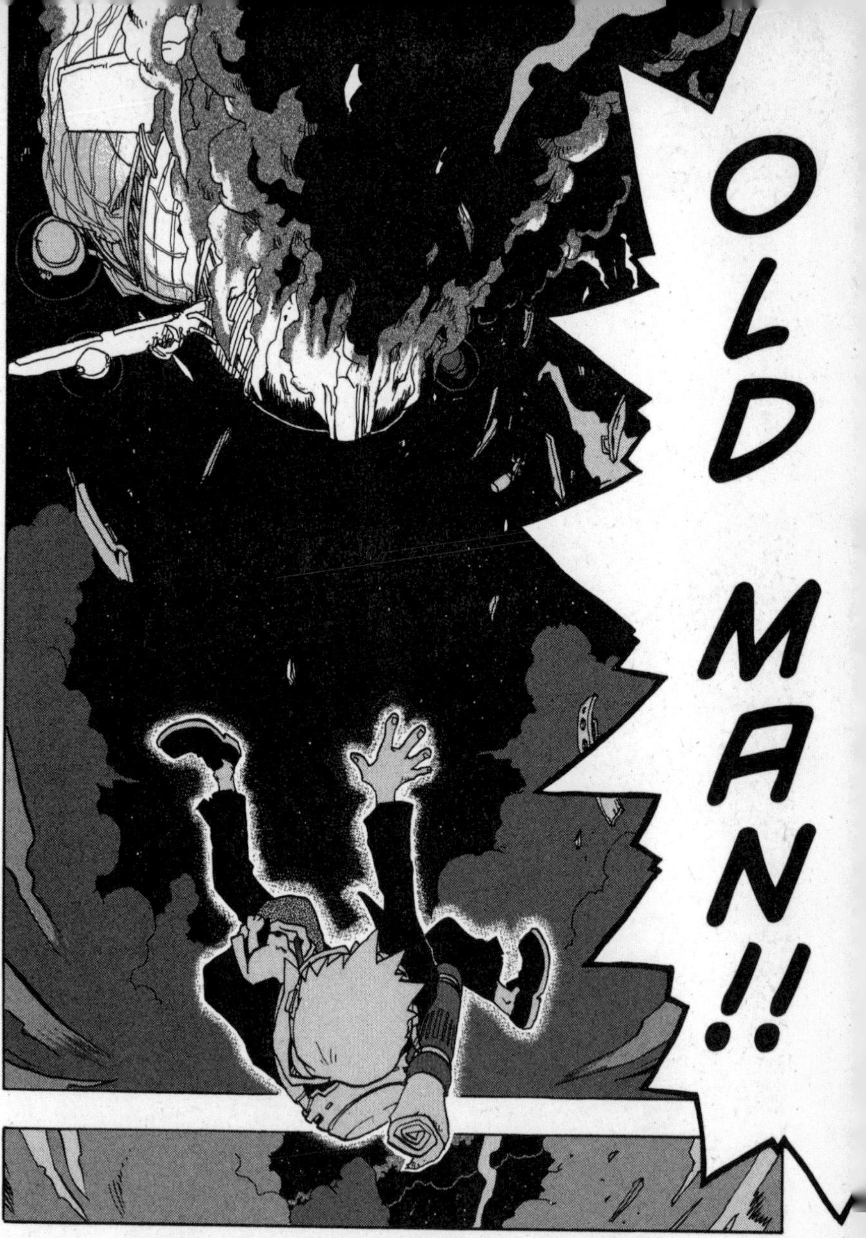
OLD MAN!!

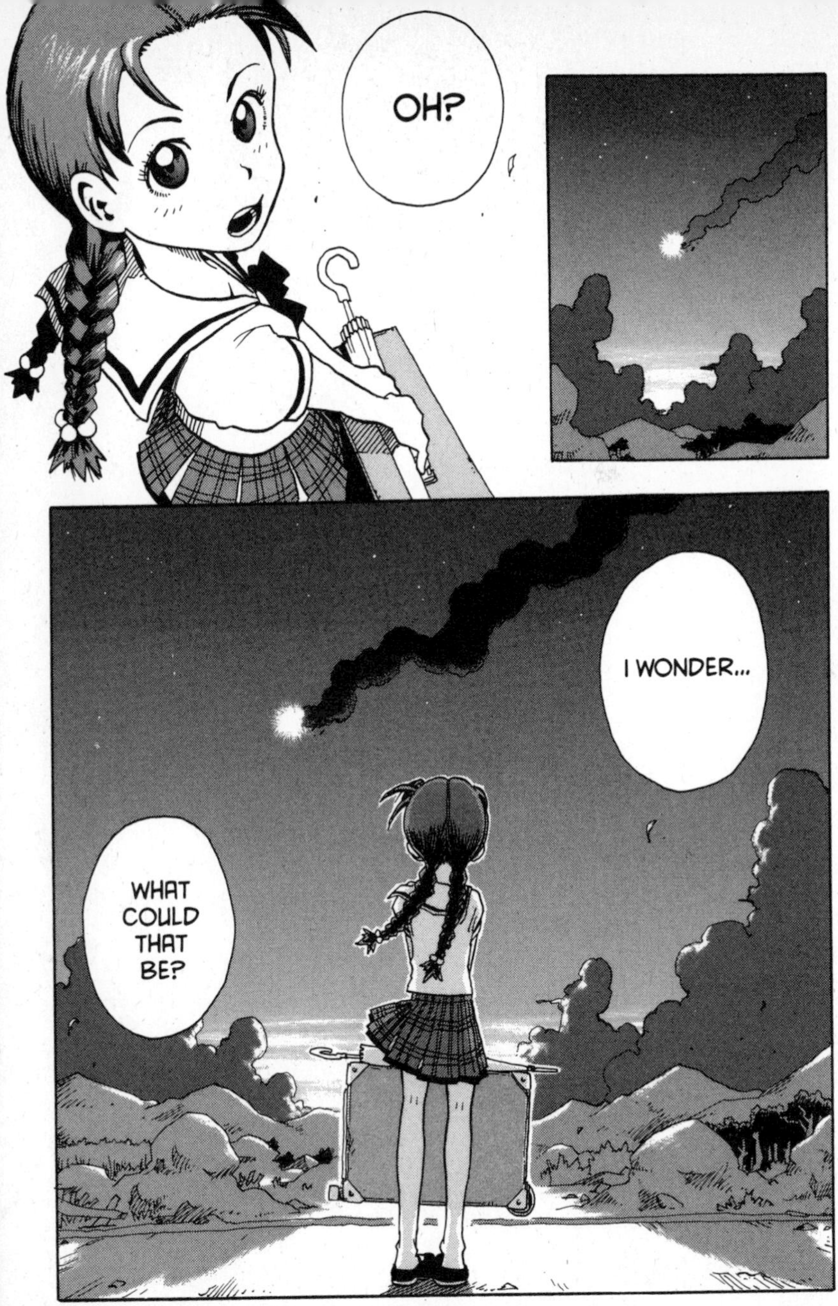
OH?
I WONDER...
WHAT COULD THAT BE?

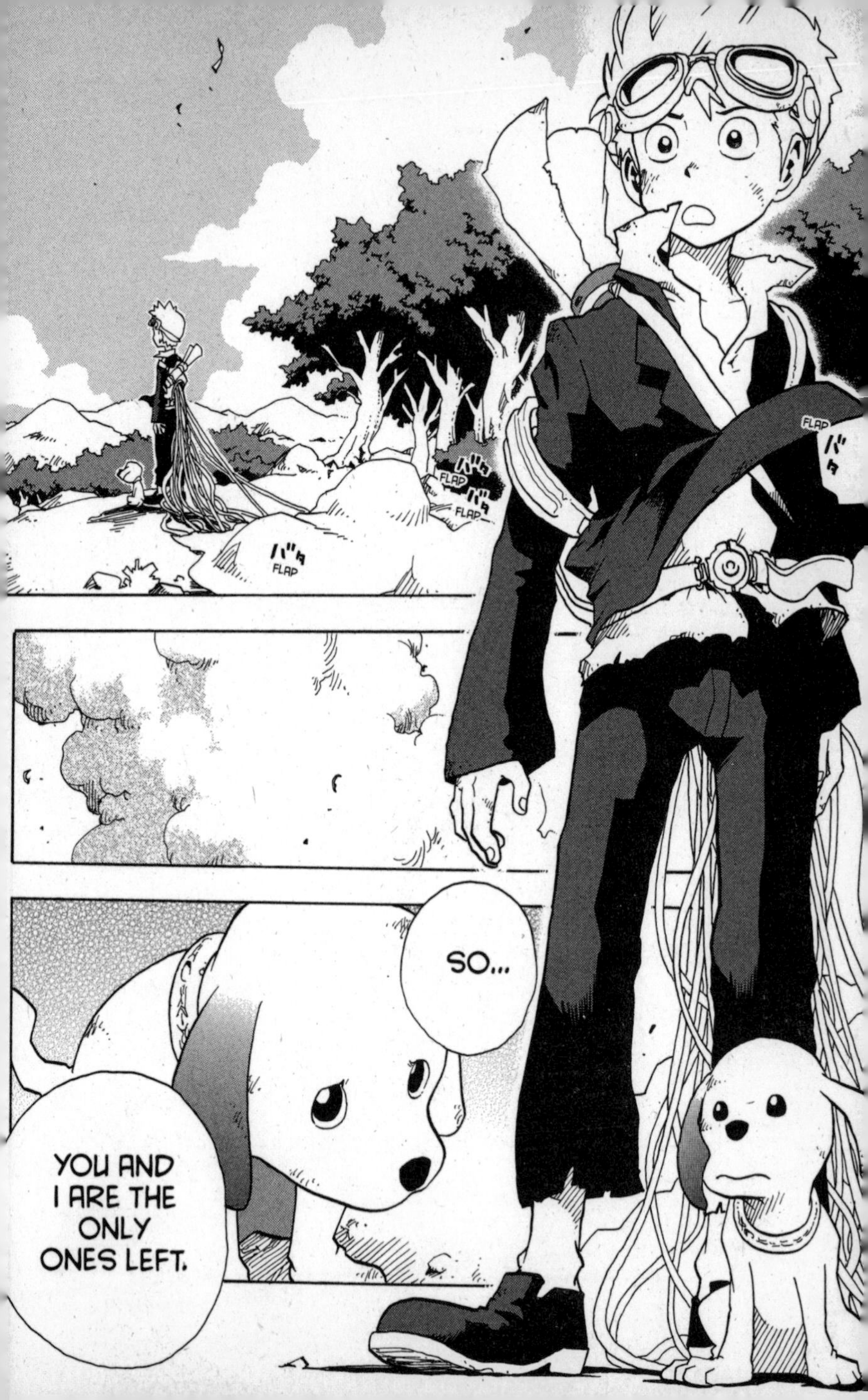

FLAP
バタ
バタ
FLAP
バタ
FLAP
バタ
FLAP
SO...
YOU AND I ARE THE ONLY ONES LEFT.

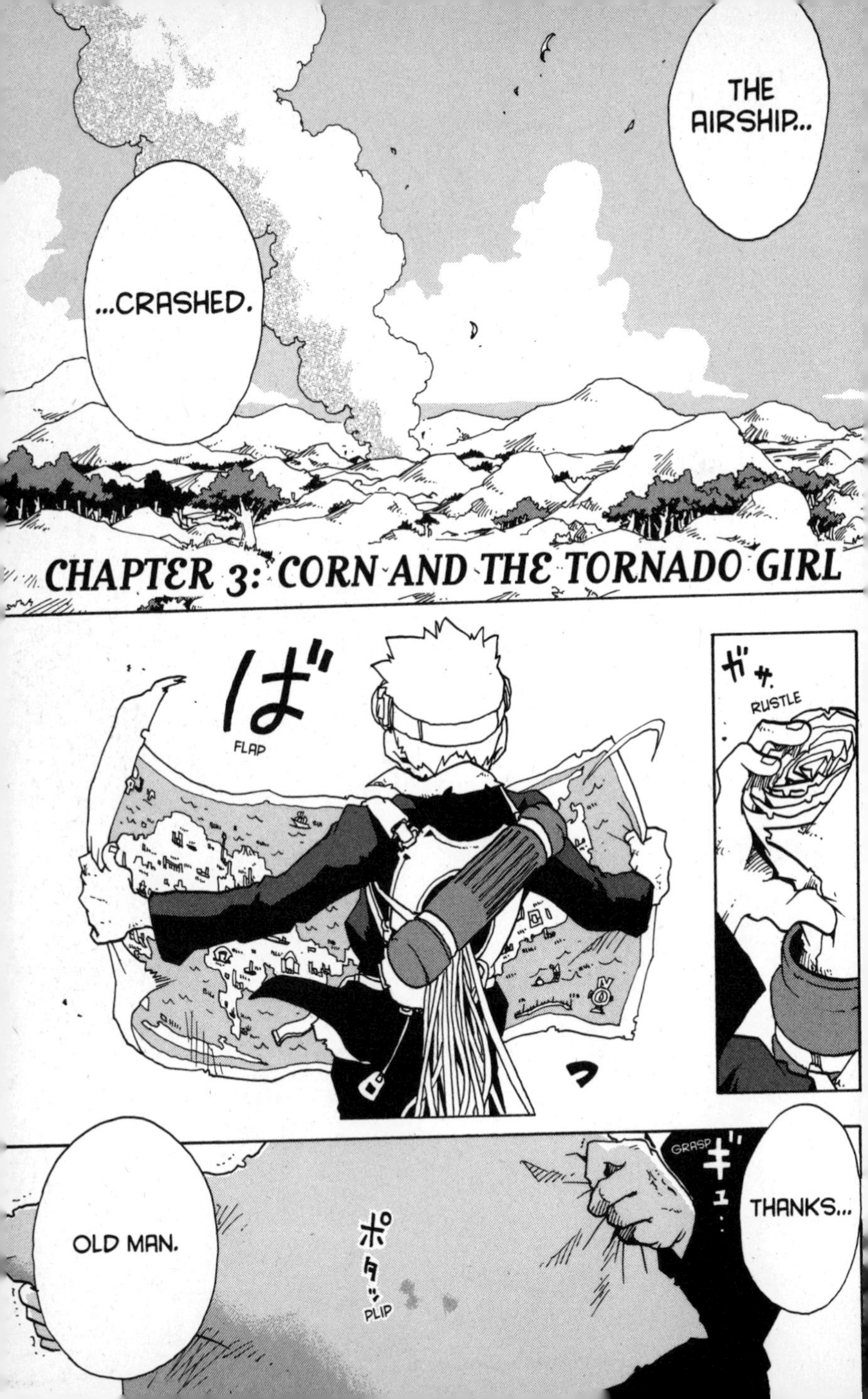
THE AIRSHIP...
...CRASHED.
CHAPTER 3: CORN AND THE TORNADO GIRL
ガサ
RUSTLE
ば
FLAP
ギュ
GRASP
THANKS...
ポタッ
PLIP
OLD MAN.

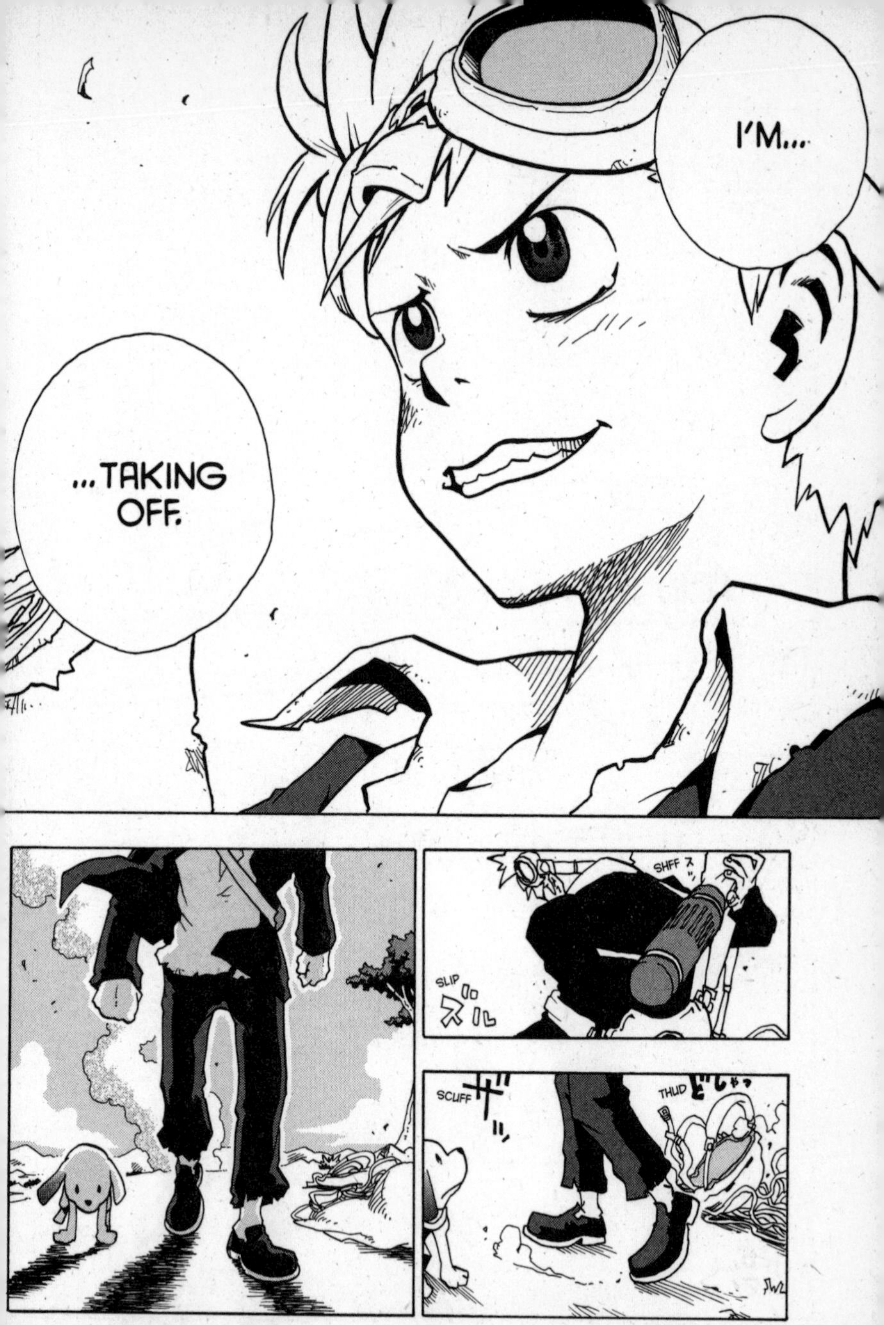
I'M...
...TAKING OFF.
SHFF
SLIP
SCUFF
THUD

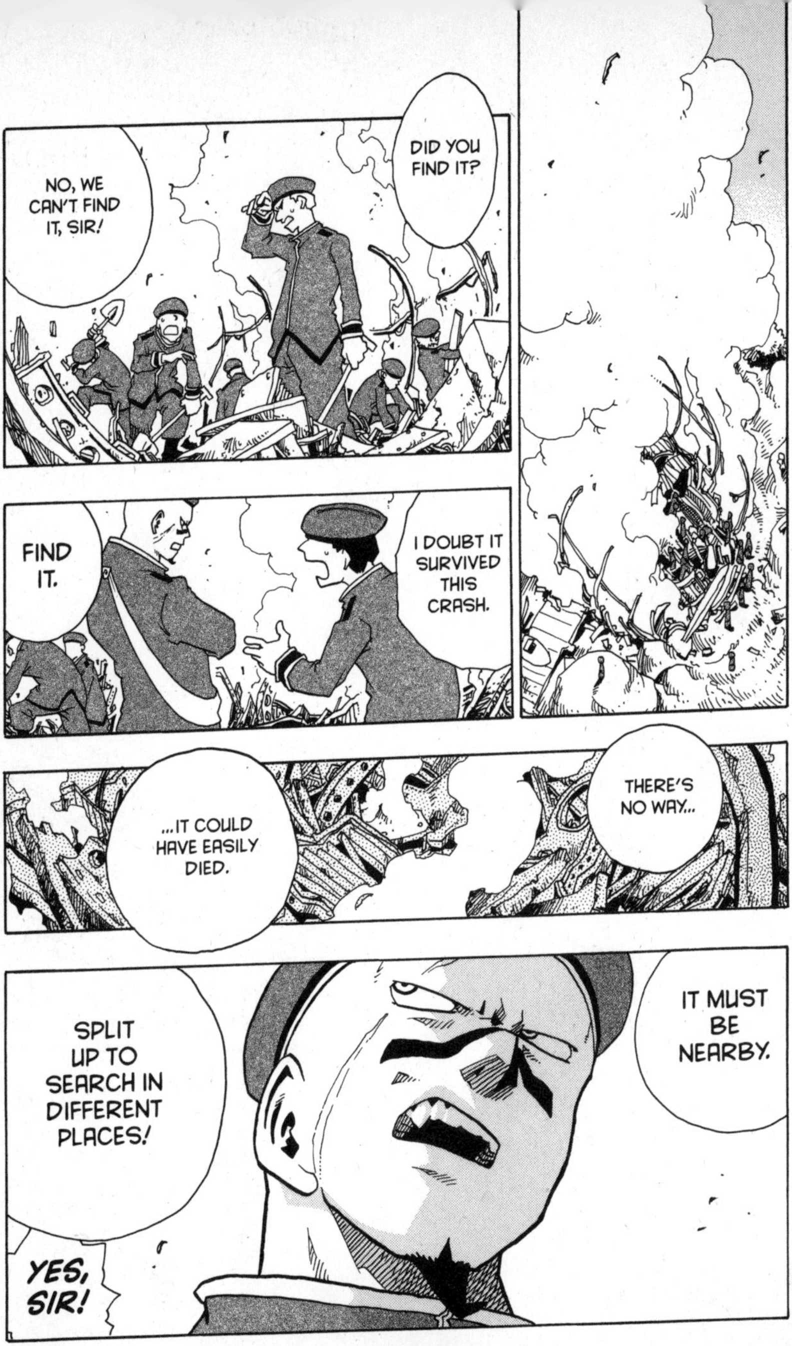
DID YOU FIND IT?
NO, WE CAN'T FIND IT, SIR!
I DOUBT IT SURVIVED THIS CRASH.
FIND IT.
THERE'S NO WAY...
...IT COULD HAVE EASILY DIED.
IT MUST BE NEARBY.
SPLIT UP TO SEARCH IN DIFFERENT PLACES!
YES, SIR!

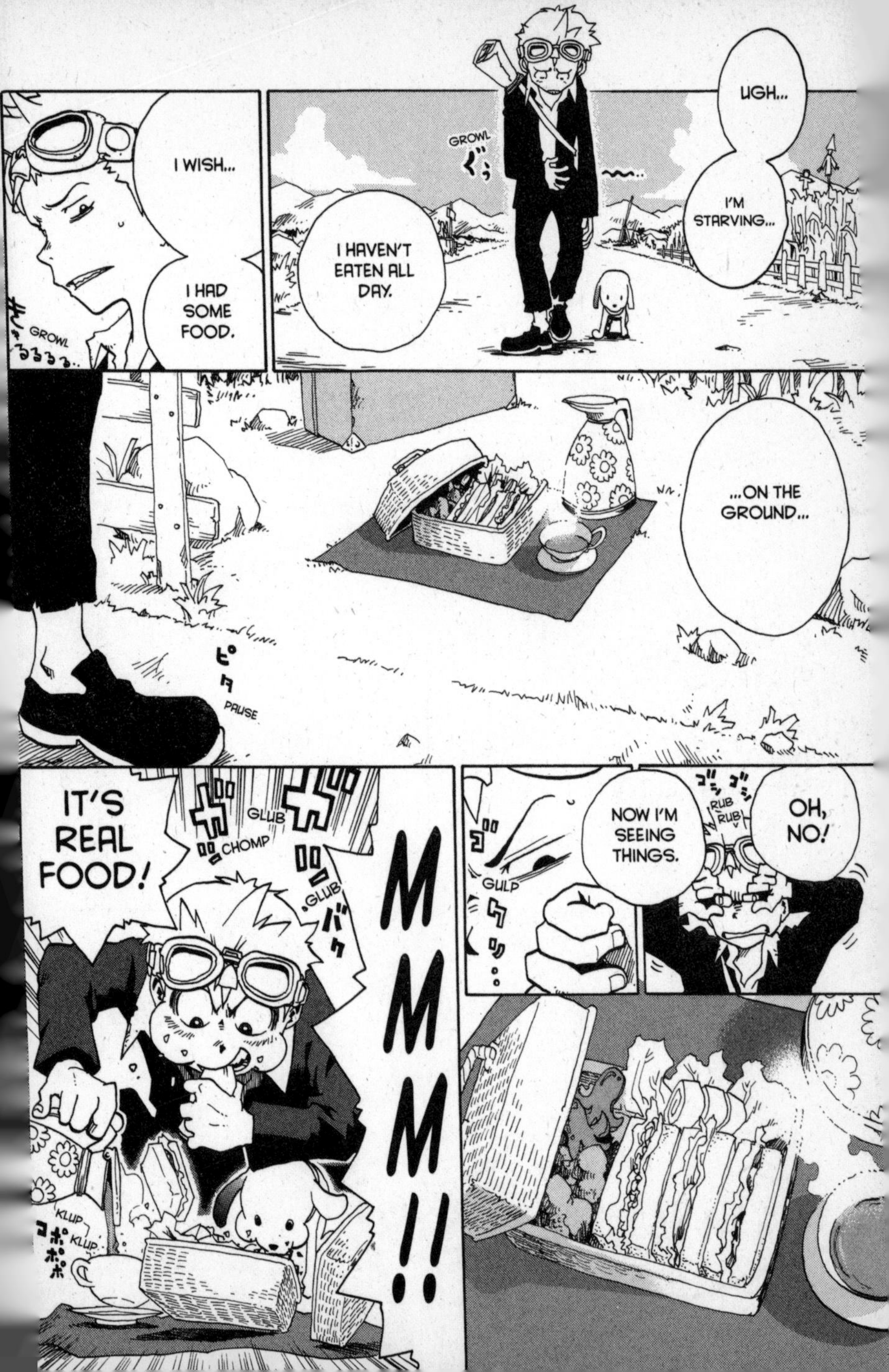

UGH...
I'M STARVING...
~~...
GROWL ぐぅ
I HAVEN'T EATEN ALL DAY.
I WISH...
I HAD SOME FOOD.
GROWL きゅるるるる..
...ON THE GROUND...
ピタ PAUSE
OH, NO!
ゴシ ゴシ RUB RUB
NOW I'M SEEING THINGS.
GULP ゴクッ
IT'S REAL FOOD!
GLUB
CHOMP
GLUB バク
MMMM!!
KLUP KLUP コポポポ

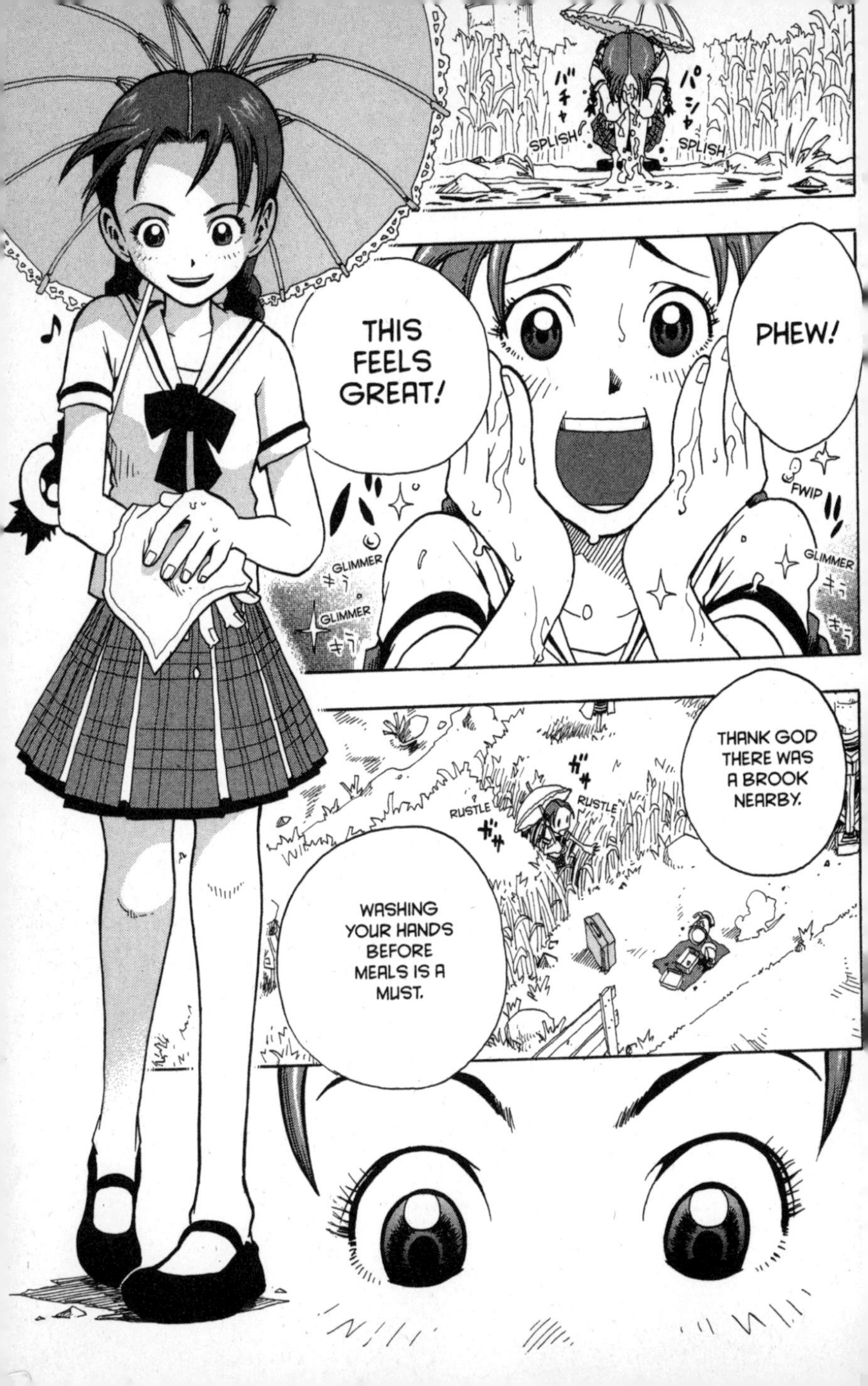
パシャ
SPLISH
バチャ
SPLISH
PHEW!
FWIP
GLIMMER
キラ
THIS FEELS GREAT!
GLIMMER
キラ
GLIMMER
キラ
THANK GOD THERE WAS A BROOK NEARBY.
RUSTLE
ガサ
RUSTLE
ガサ
WASHING YOUR HANDS BEFORE MEALS IS A MUST.

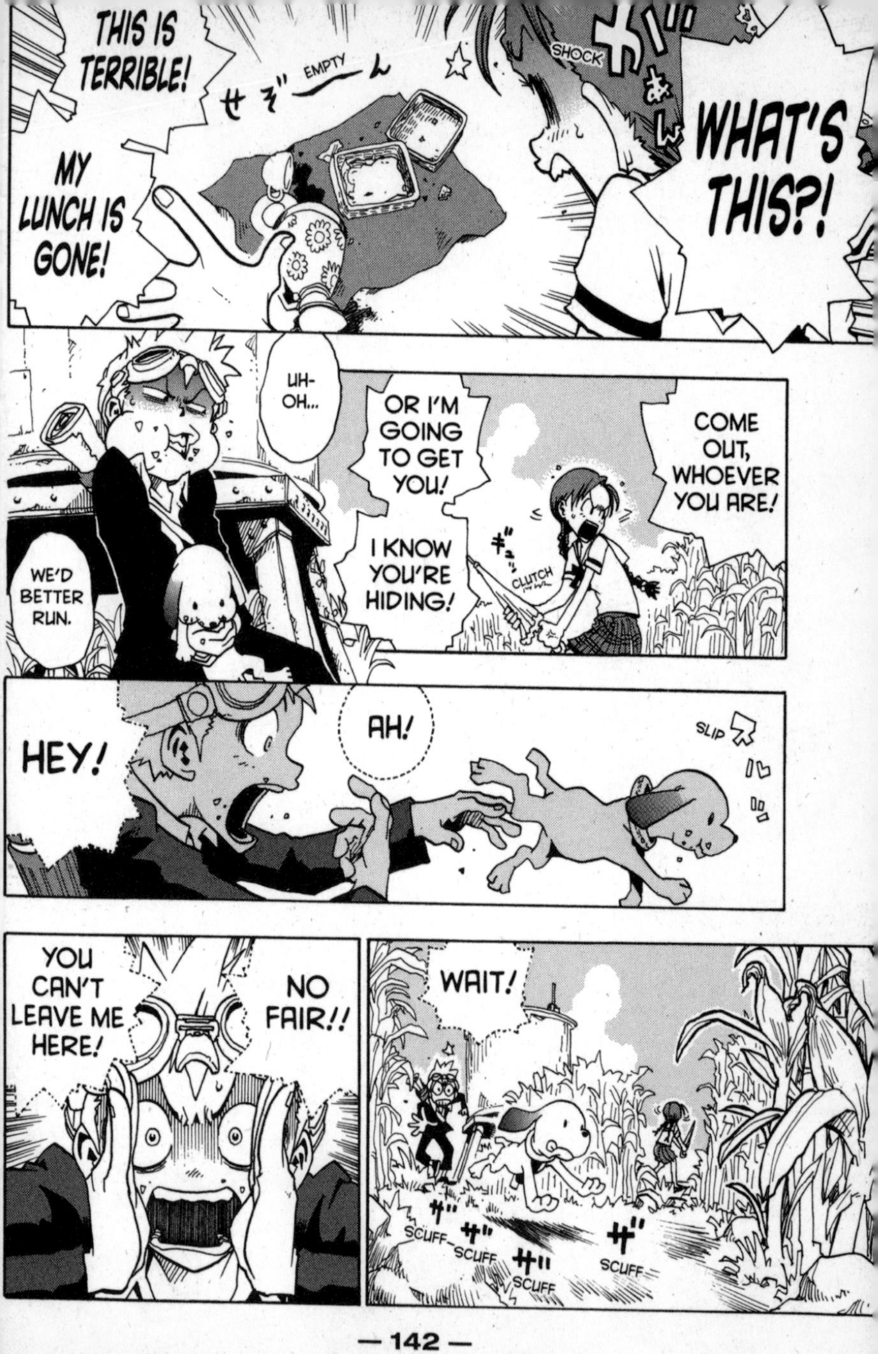
SHOCK
WHAT'S THIS?!
EMPTY
THIS IS TERRIBLE!
MY LUNCH IS GONE!
COME OUT, WHOEVER YOU ARE!
OR I'M GOING TO GET YOU!
I KNOW YOU'RE HIDING!
CLUTCH
UH-OH...
WE'D BETTER RUN.
SLIP
AH!
HEY!
WAIT!
SCUFF
SCUFF
SCUFF
SCUFF
NO FAIR!!
YOU CAN'T LEAVE ME HERE!

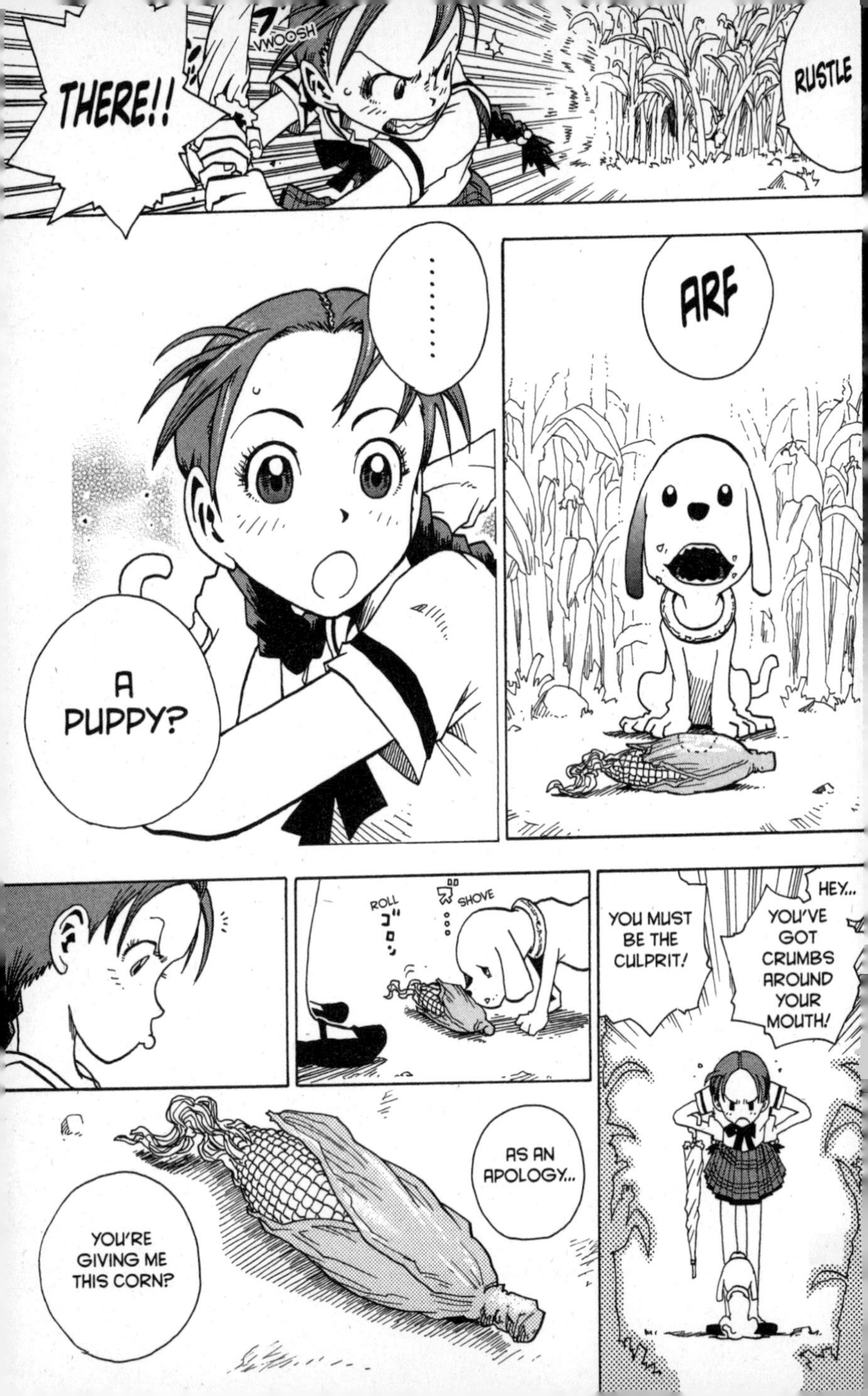
RUSTLE
VWOOSH
THERE!!
ARF
......
A PUPPY?
HEY... YOU'VE GOT CRUMBS AROUND YOUR MOUTH!
YOU MUST BE THE CULPRIT!
SHOVE
ROLL
AS AN APOLOGY...
YOU'RE GIVING ME THIS CORN?

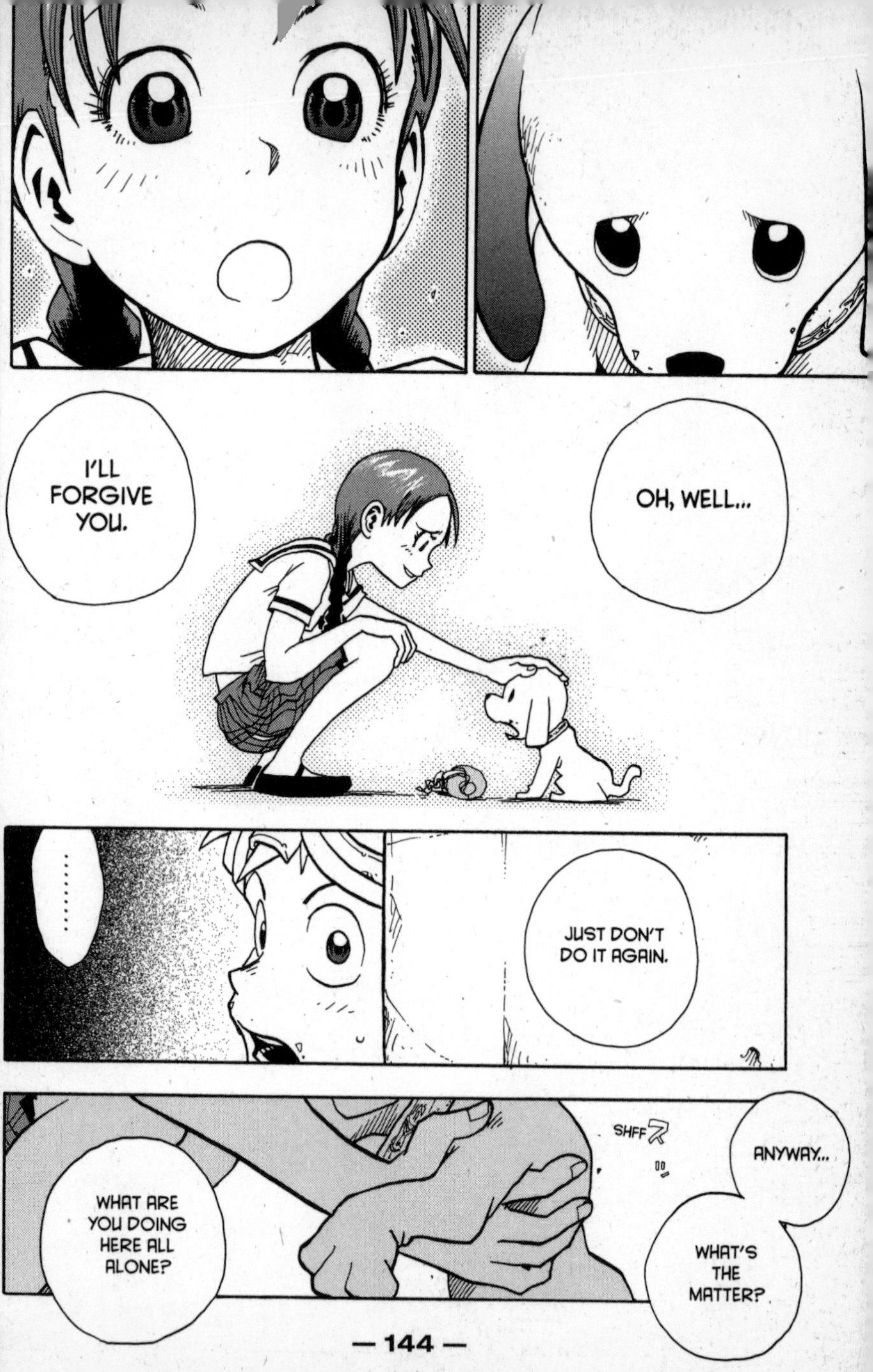
OH, WELL...
I'LL FORGIVE YOU.
JUST DON'T DO IT AGAIN.
......
ANYWAY...
WHAT'S THE MATTER?
SHFF
WHAT ARE YOU DOING HERE ALL ALONE?

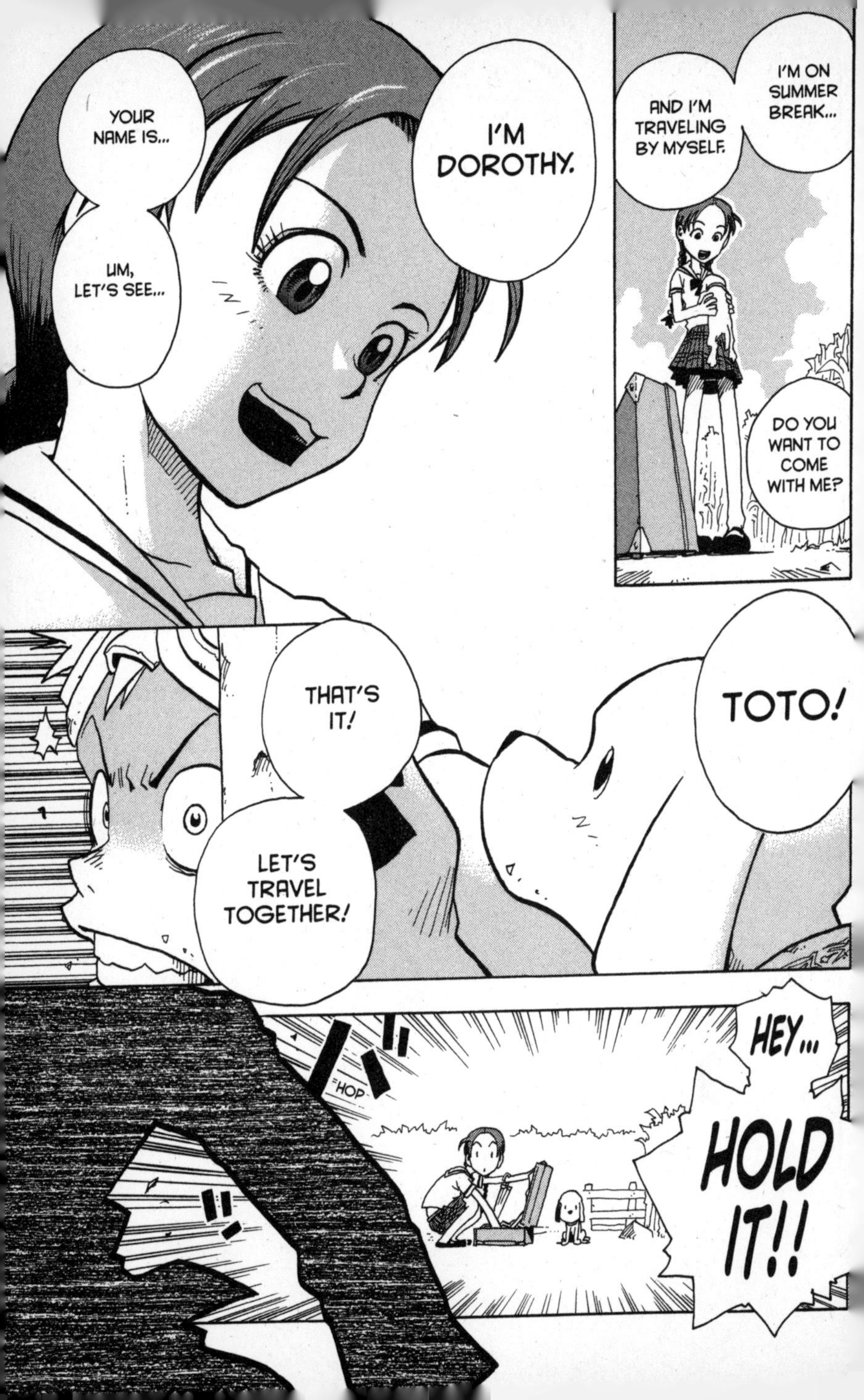
I'M ON SUMMER BREAK...
AND I'M TRAVELING BY MYSELF.
DO YOU WANT TO COME WITH ME?
I'M DOROTHY.
YOUR NAME IS...
UM, LET'S SEE...
TOTO!
THAT'S IT!
LET'S TRAVEL TOGETHER!
HEY... HOLD IT!!
HOP

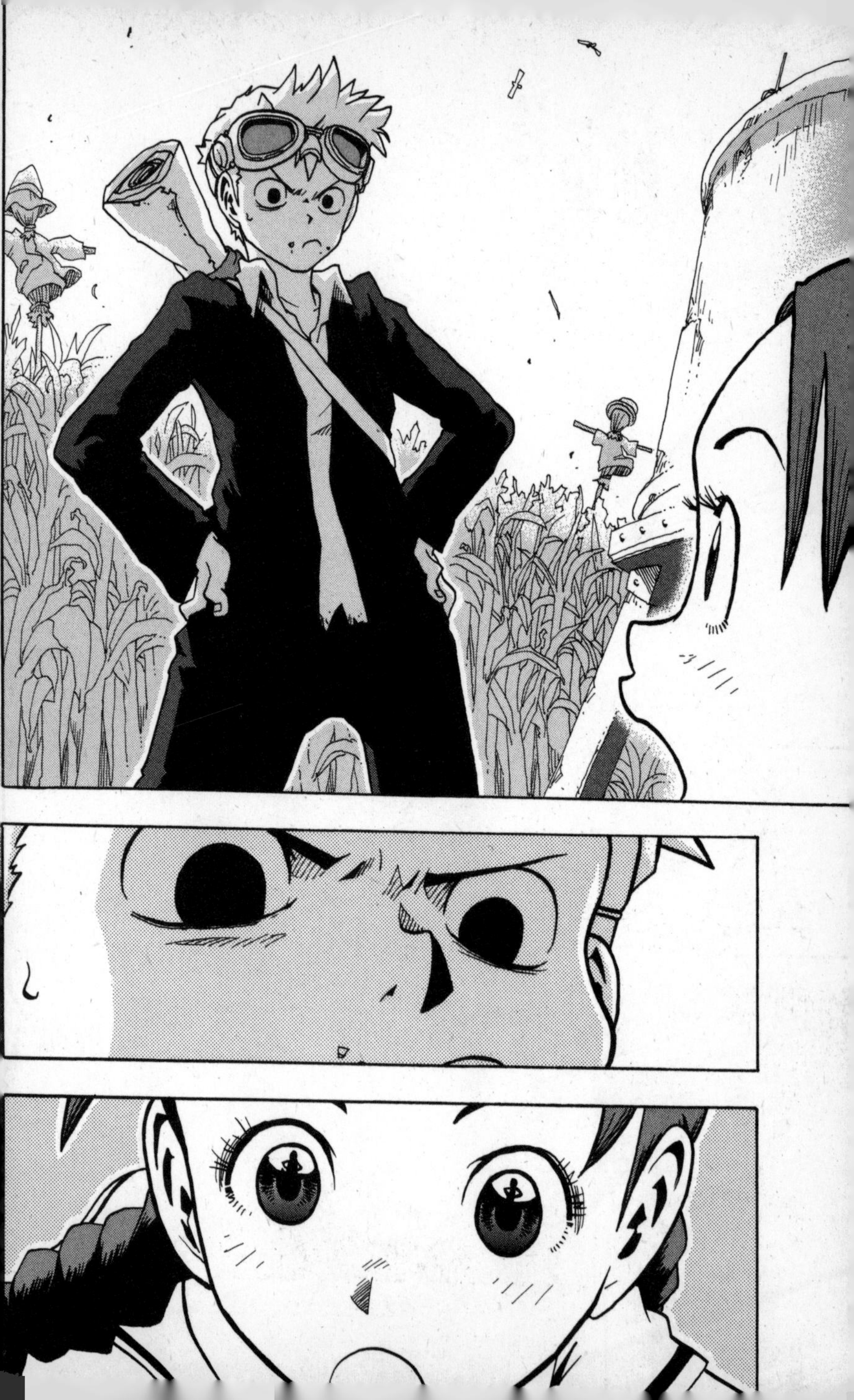

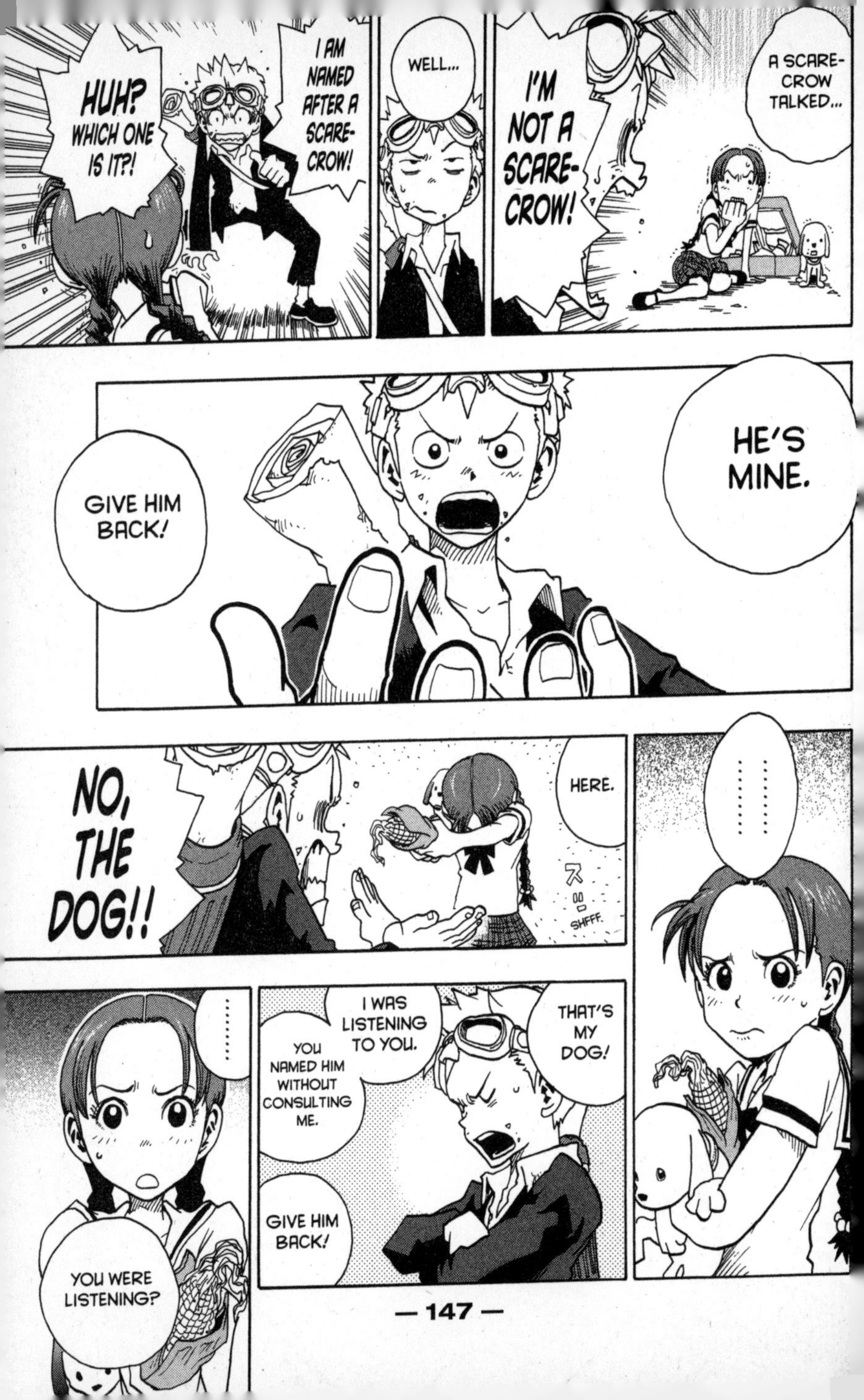
A SCARE-CROW TALKED...
I'M NOT A SCARE-CROW!
WELL...
I AM NAMED AFTER A SCARE-CROW!
HUH? WHICH ONE IS IT?!
HE'S MINE.
GIVE HIM BACK!
......
HERE.
スー SHFFF.
NO, THE DOG!!
THAT'S MY DOG!
I WAS LISTENING TO YOU.
YOU NAMED HIM WITHOUT CONSULTING ME.
GIVE HIM BACK!
......
YOU WERE LISTENING?

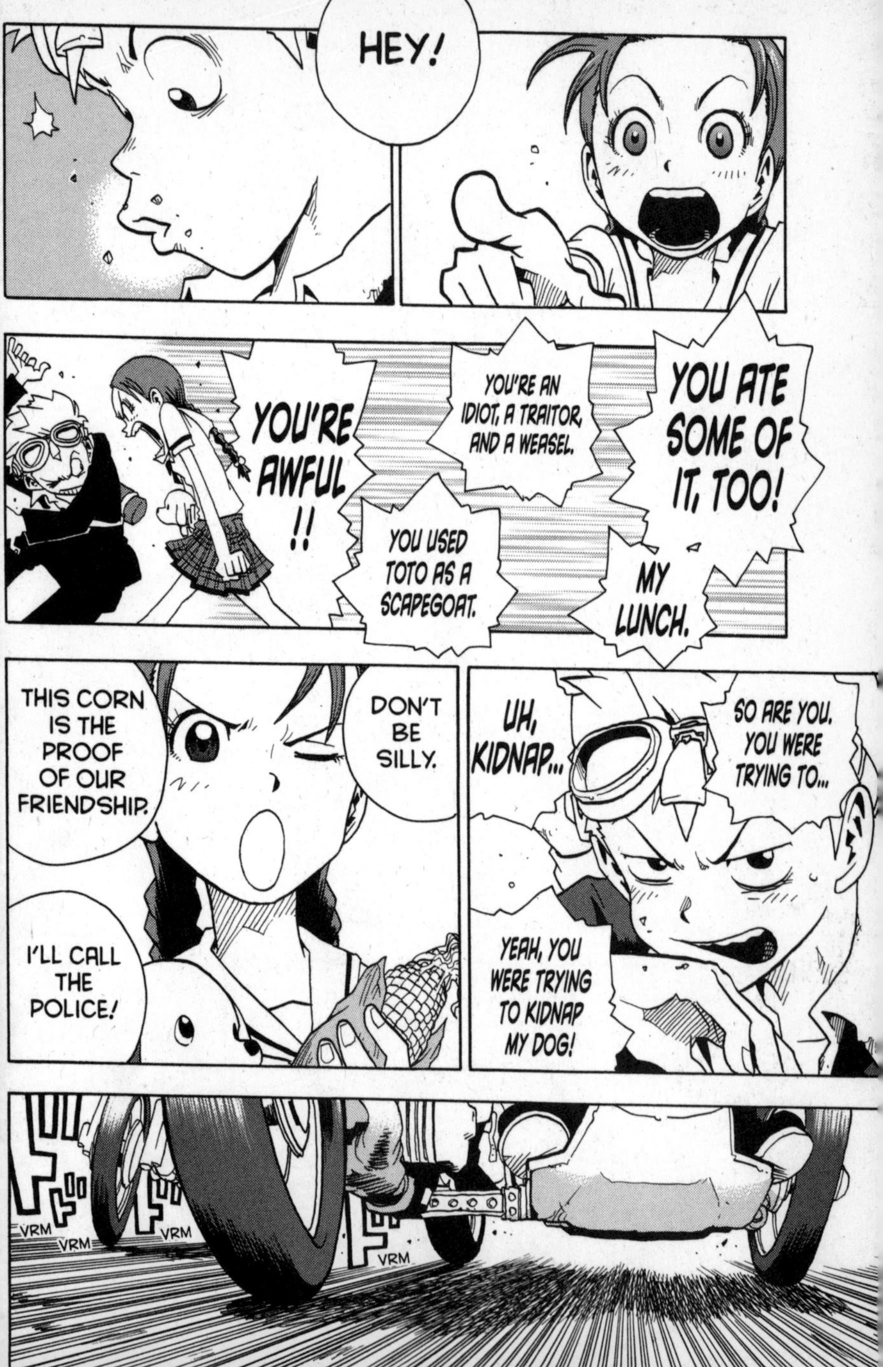
HEY!
YOU ATE SOME OF IT, TOO!
MY LUNCH.
YOU'RE AN IDIOT, A TRAITOR, AND A WEASEL.
YOU USED TOTO AS A SCAPEGOAT.
YOU'RE AWFUL !!
SO ARE YOU. YOU WERE TRYING TO...
UH, KIDNAP...
YEAH, YOU WERE TRYING TO KIDNAP MY DOG!
DON'T BE SILLY.
THIS CORN IS THE PROOF OF OUR FRIENDSHIP.
I'LL CALL THE POLICE!
VRM
VRM
VRM
VRM

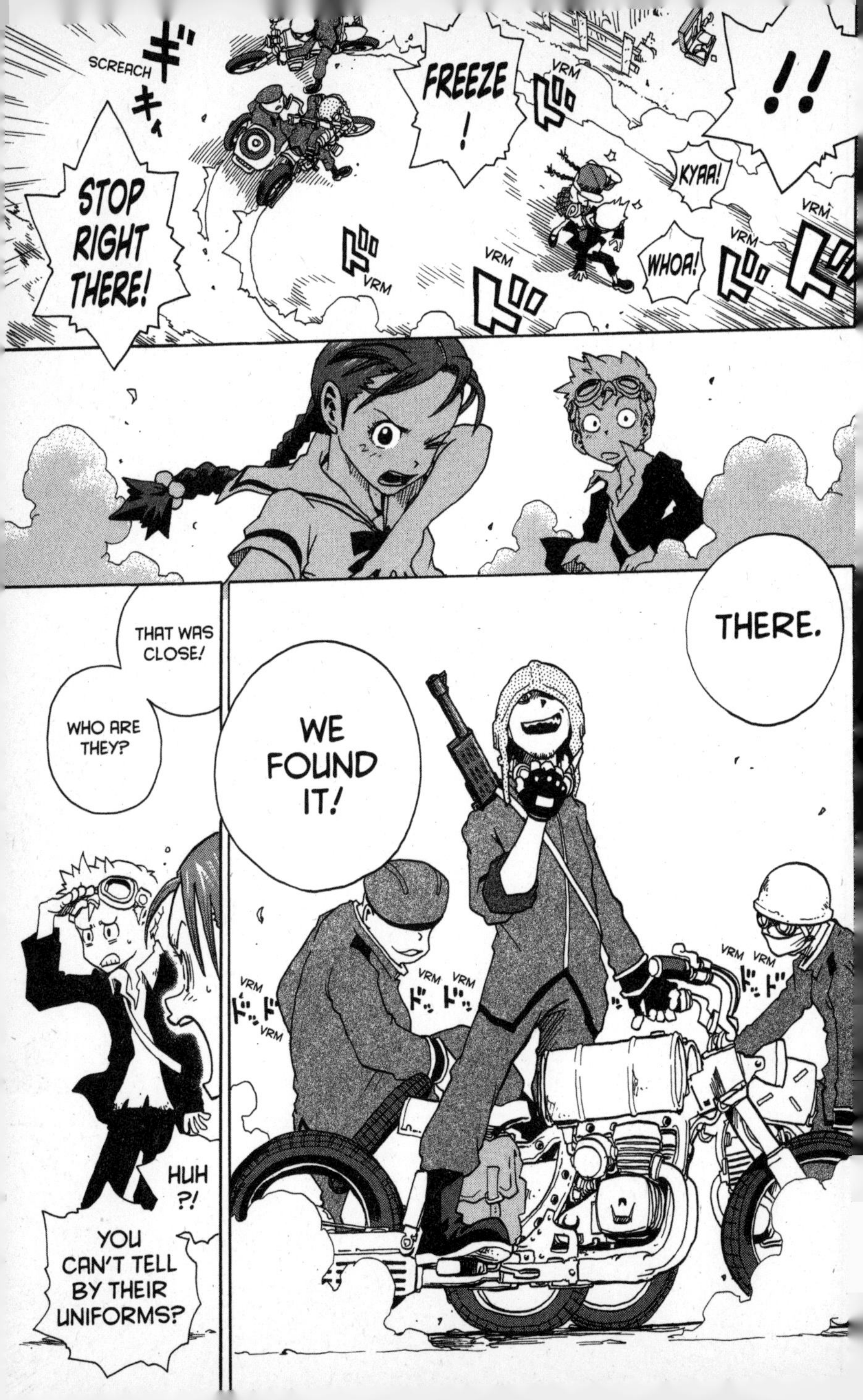
!!
VRM
KYAA!
VRM
WHOA!
FREEZE!
VRM
VRM
VRM
SCREACH
ギキィ
STOP RIGHT THERE!
THERE.
WE FOUND IT!
VRM VRM
VRM VRM
VRM VRM
THAT WAS CLOSE!
WHO ARE THEY?
HUH?!
YOU CAN'T TELL BY THEIR UNIFORMS?

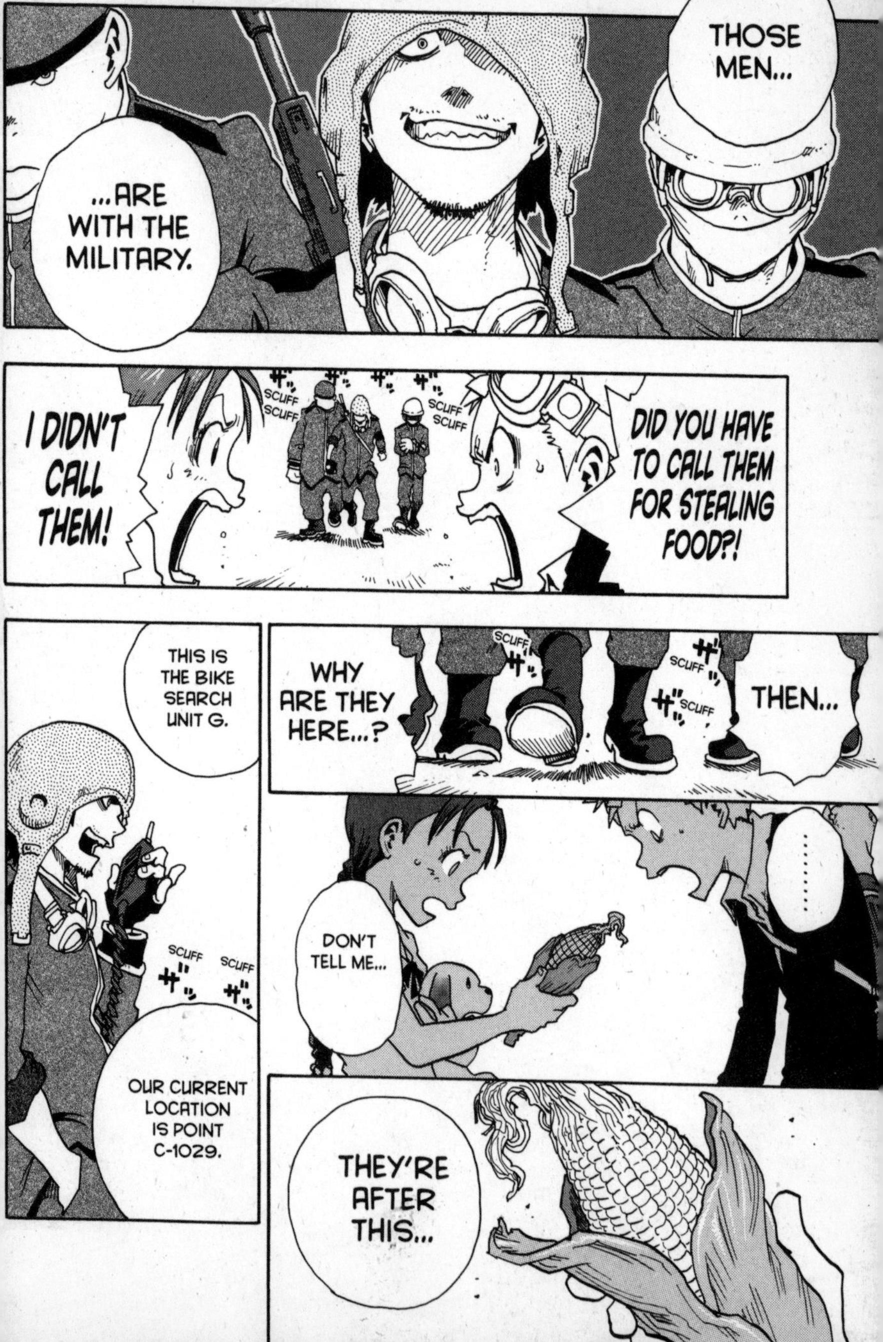
THOSE MEN...
...ARE WITH THE MILITARY.
DID YOU HAVE TO CALL THEM FOR STEALING FOOD?!
SCUFF SCUFF
SCUFF SCUFF
I DIDN'T CALL THEM!
THEN...
SCUFF
SCUFF
SCUFF
WHY ARE THEY HERE...?
......
DON'T TELL ME...
THEY'RE AFTER THIS...
THIS IS THE BIKE SEARCH UNIT G.
SCUFF SCUFF
OUR CURRENT LOCATION IS POINT C-1029.

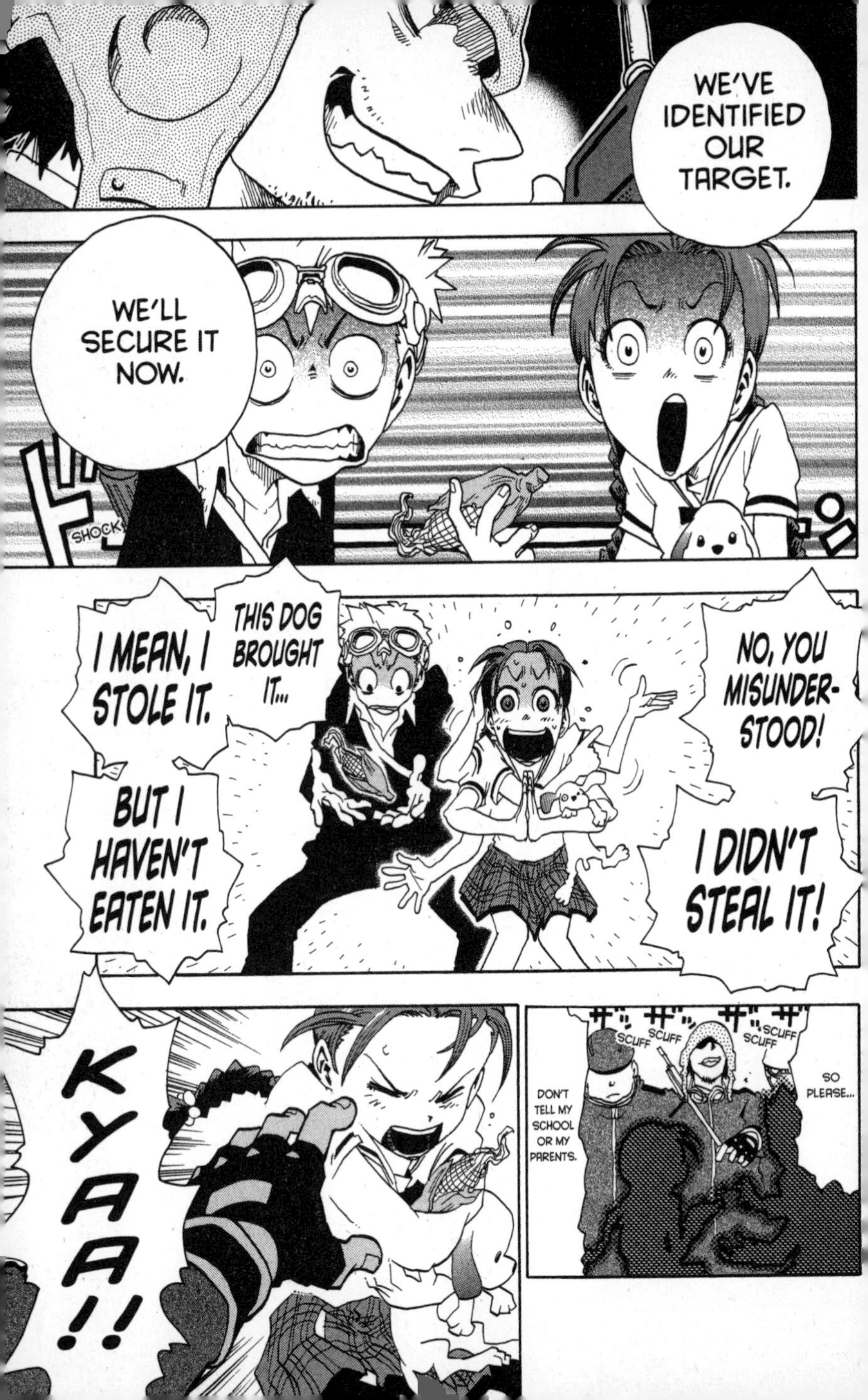
WE'VE IDENTIFIED OUR TARGET.
WE'LL SECURE IT NOW.
SHOCK
NO, YOU MISUNDER-STOOD!
I DIDN'T STEAL IT!
THIS DOG BROUGHT IT...
I MEAN, I STOLE IT.
BUT I HAVEN'T EATEN IT.
SCUFF SCUFF
SCUFF SCUFF
SCUFF
SO PLEASE...
DON'T TELL MY SCHOOL OR MY PARENTS.
KYAAA!!

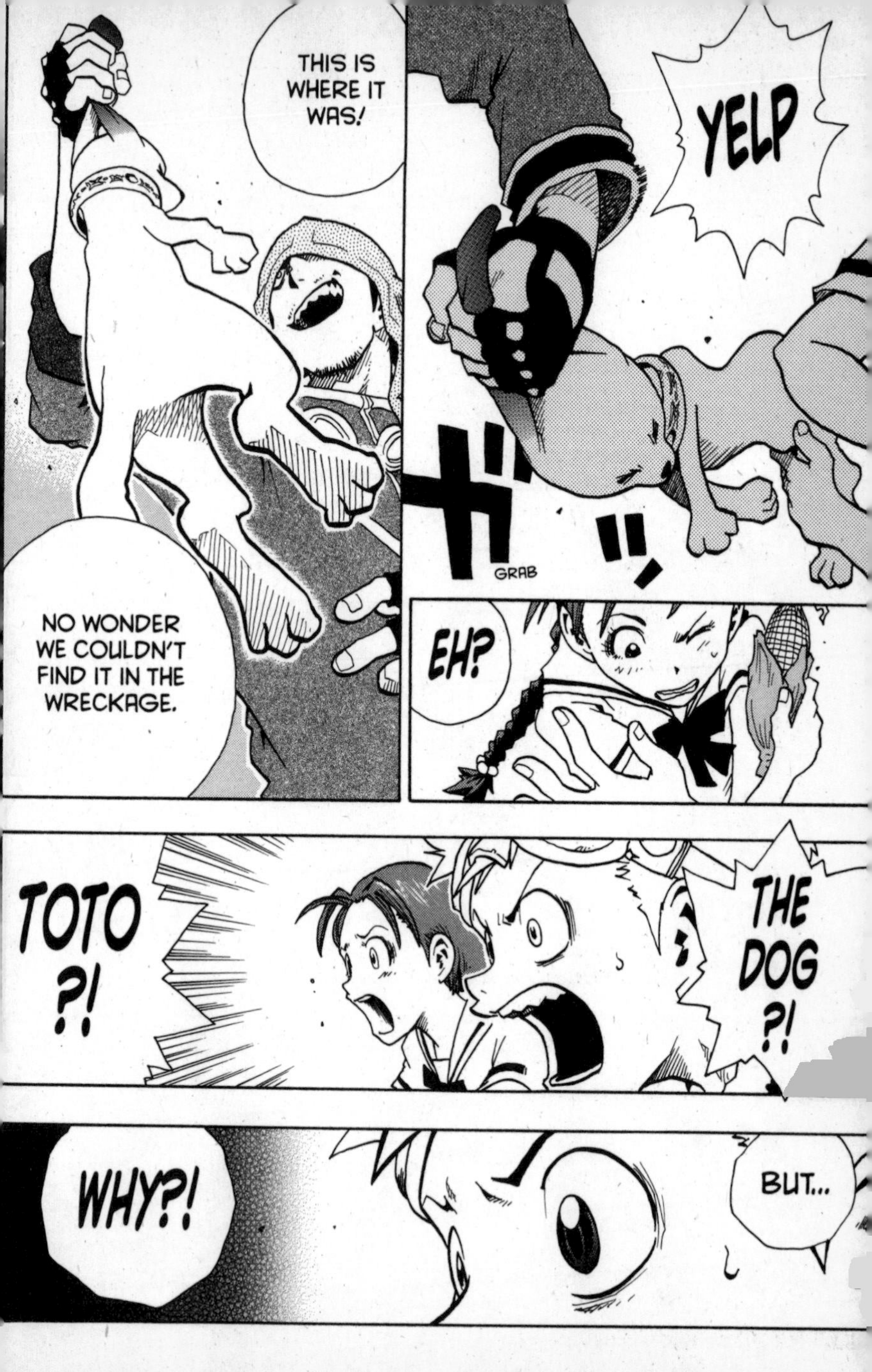
YELP
ガッ
GRAB
EH?
THIS IS WHERE IT WAS!
NO WONDER WE COULDN'T FIND IT IN THE WRECKAGE.
THE DOG ?!
TOTO ?!
BUT...
WHY?!

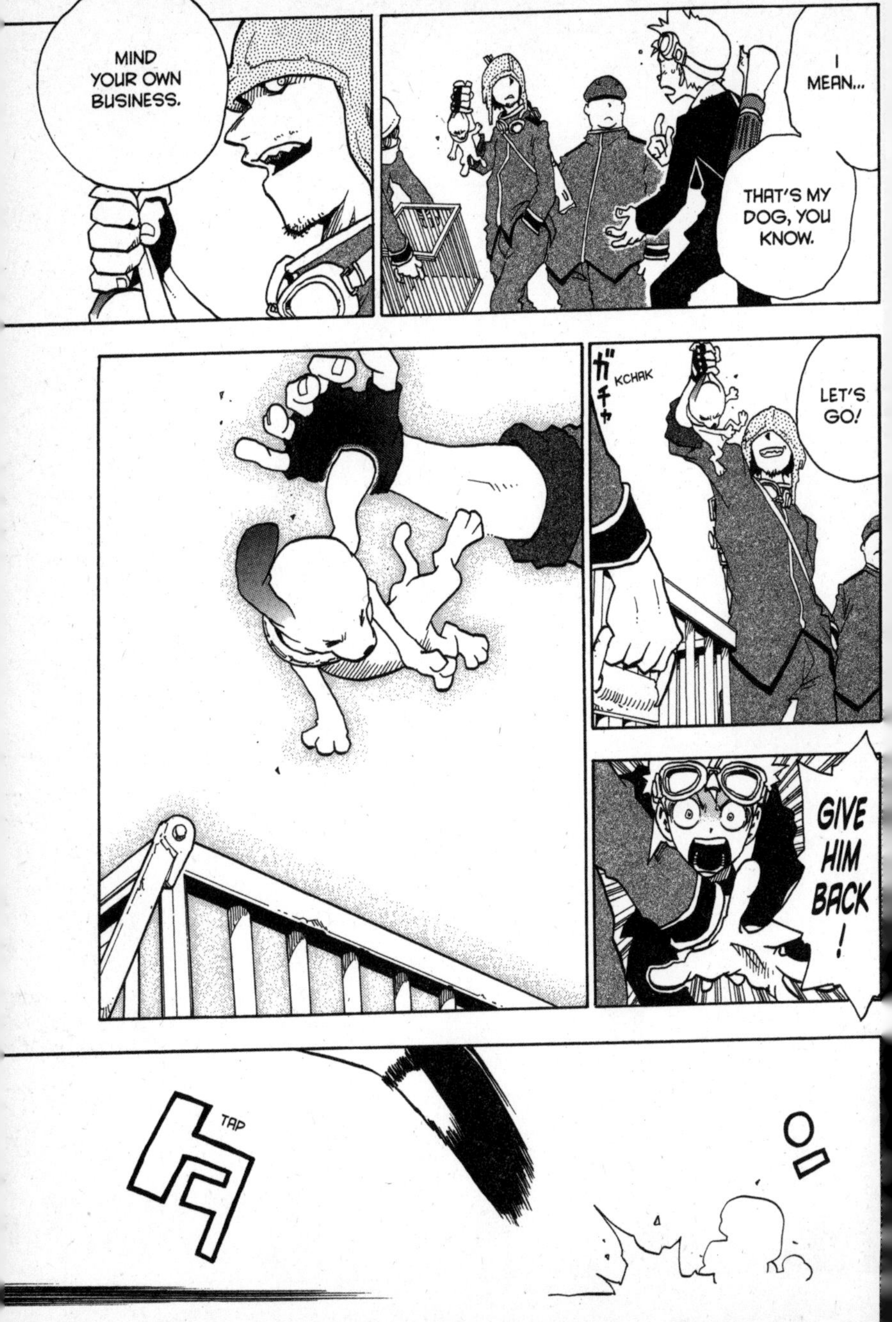
I MEAN...
THAT'S MY DOG, YOU KNOW.
MIND YOUR OWN BUSINESS.
ガチャ
KCHAK
LET'S GO!
GIVE HIM BACK!
ト
TAP

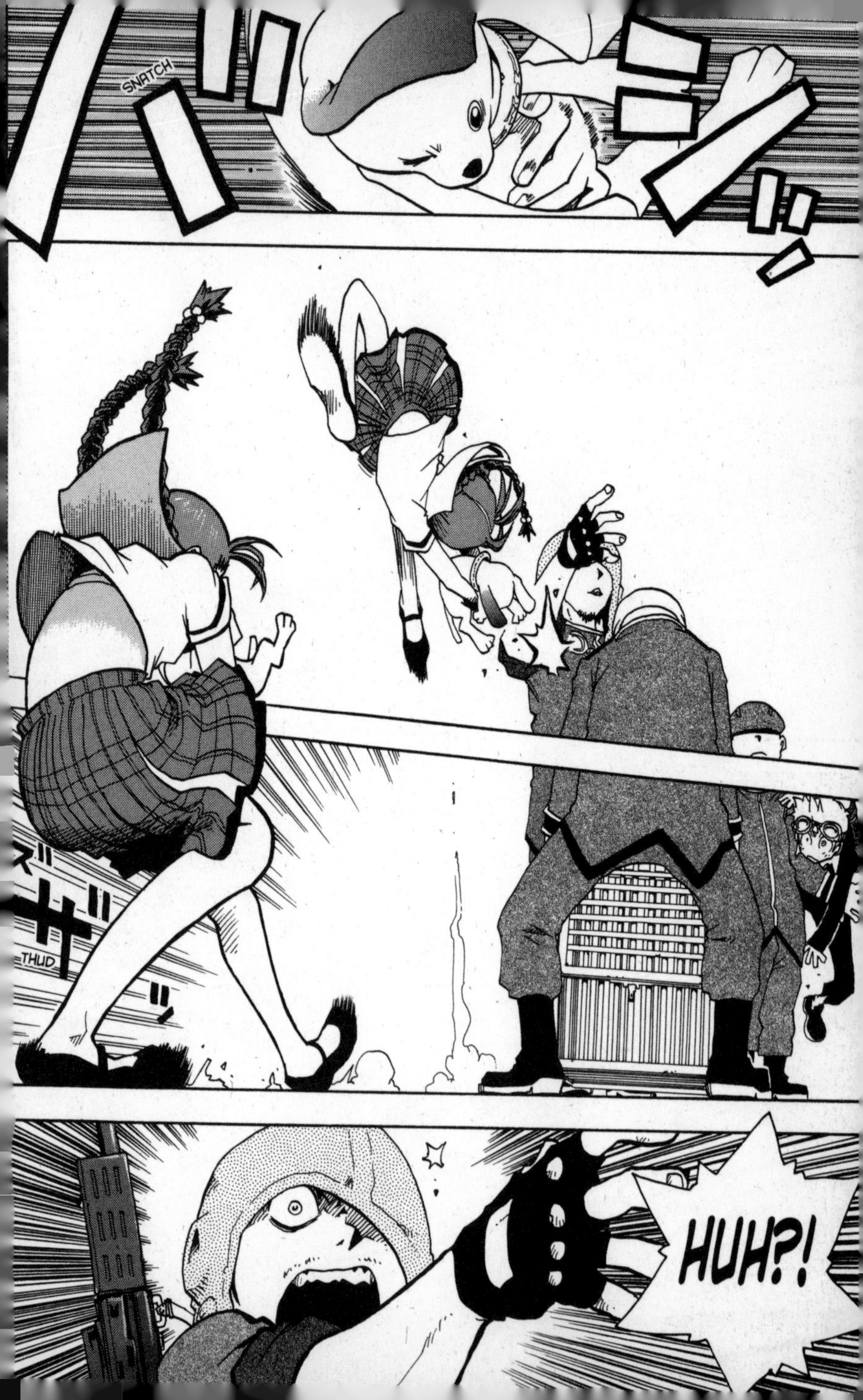
SNATCH
THUD
HUH?!

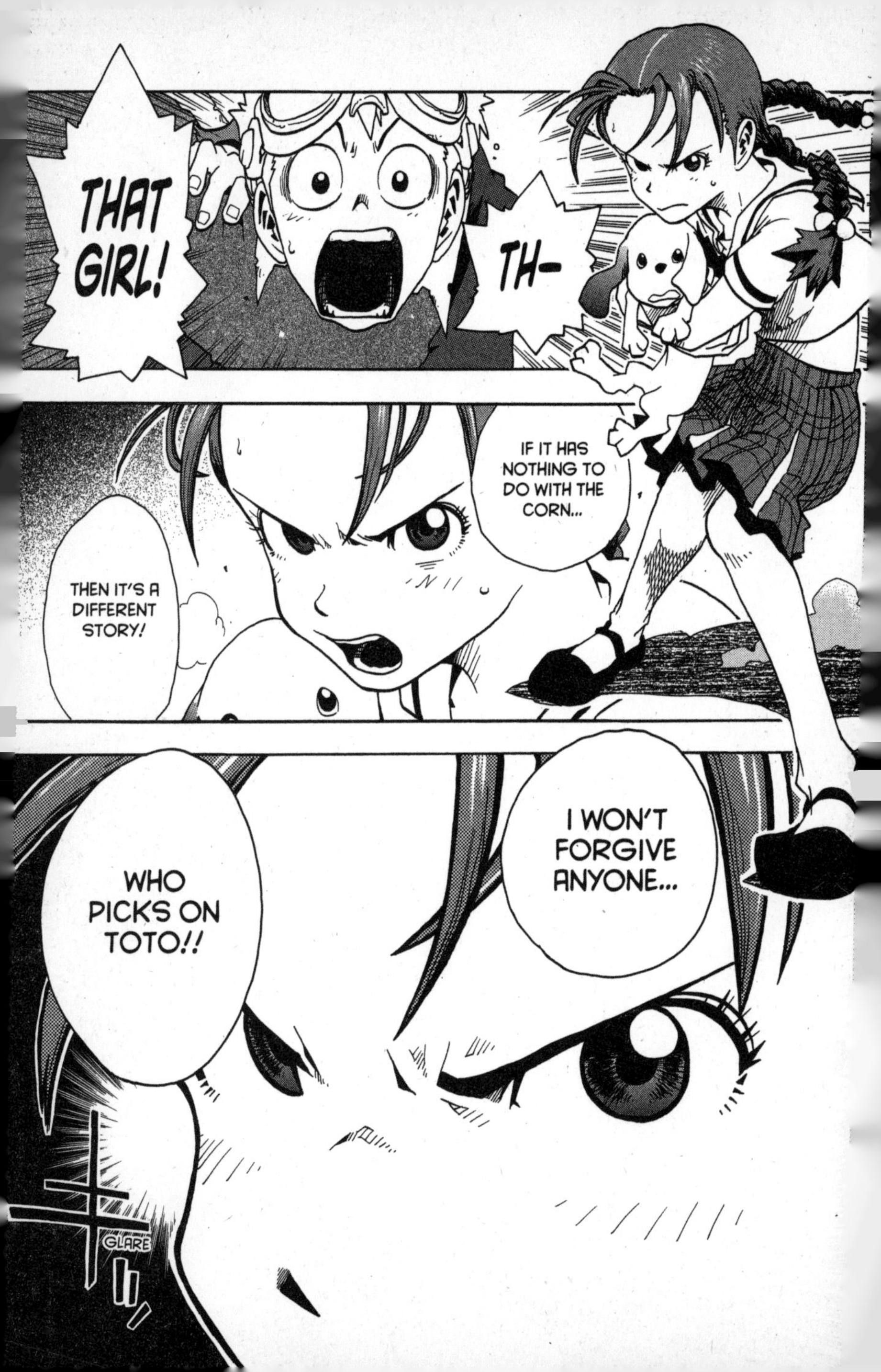
TH-
THAT GIRL!
IF IT HAS NOTHING TO DO WITH THE CORN...
THEN IT'S A DIFFERENT STORY!
I WON'T FORGIVE ANYONE...
WHO PICKS ON TOTO!!
GLARE

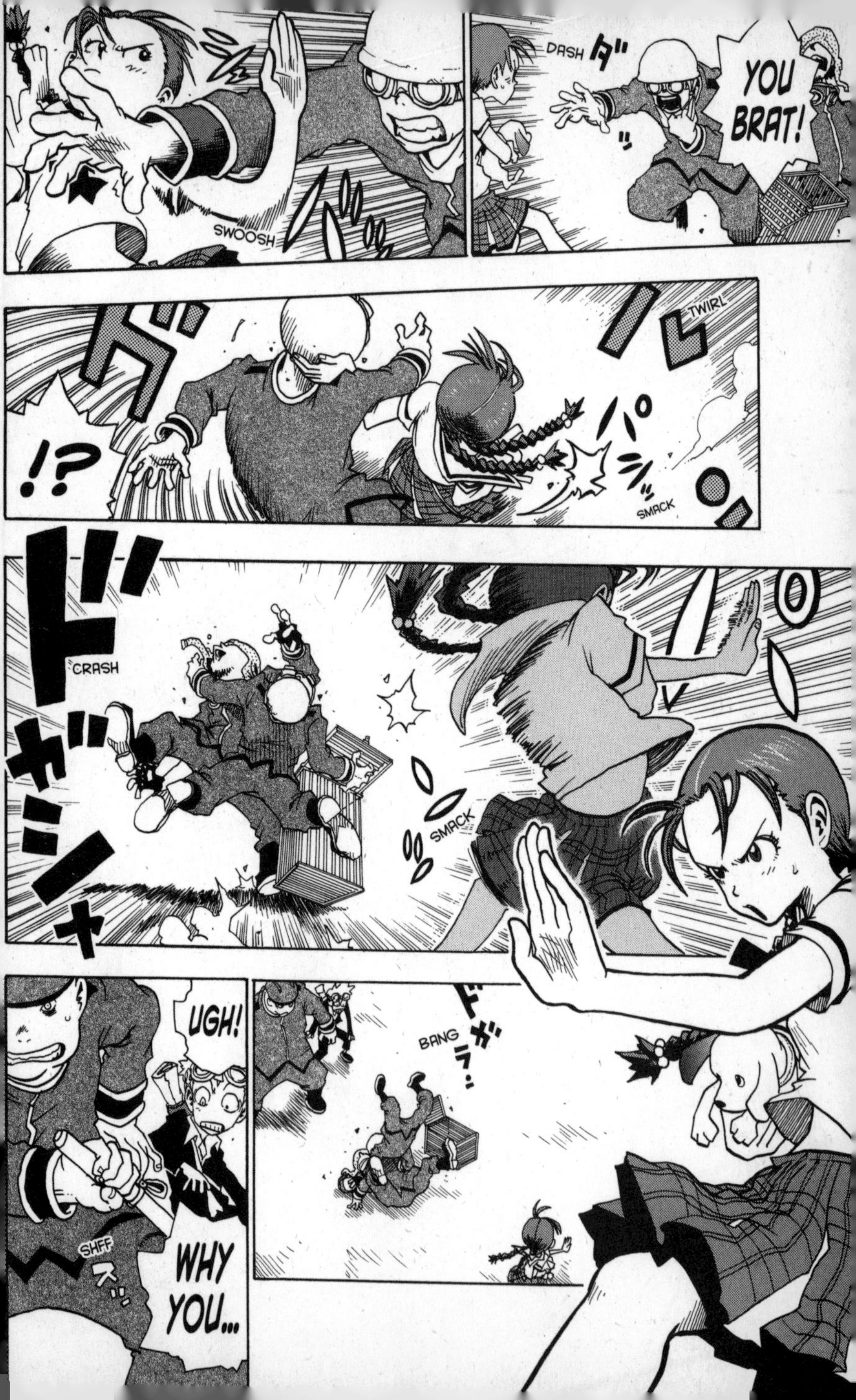
DASH
ダ
YOU BRAT!
ッ
SWOOSH
TWIRL
パシッ
SMACK
!?
CRASH
SMACK
BANG
UGH!
SHFF
WHY YOU...

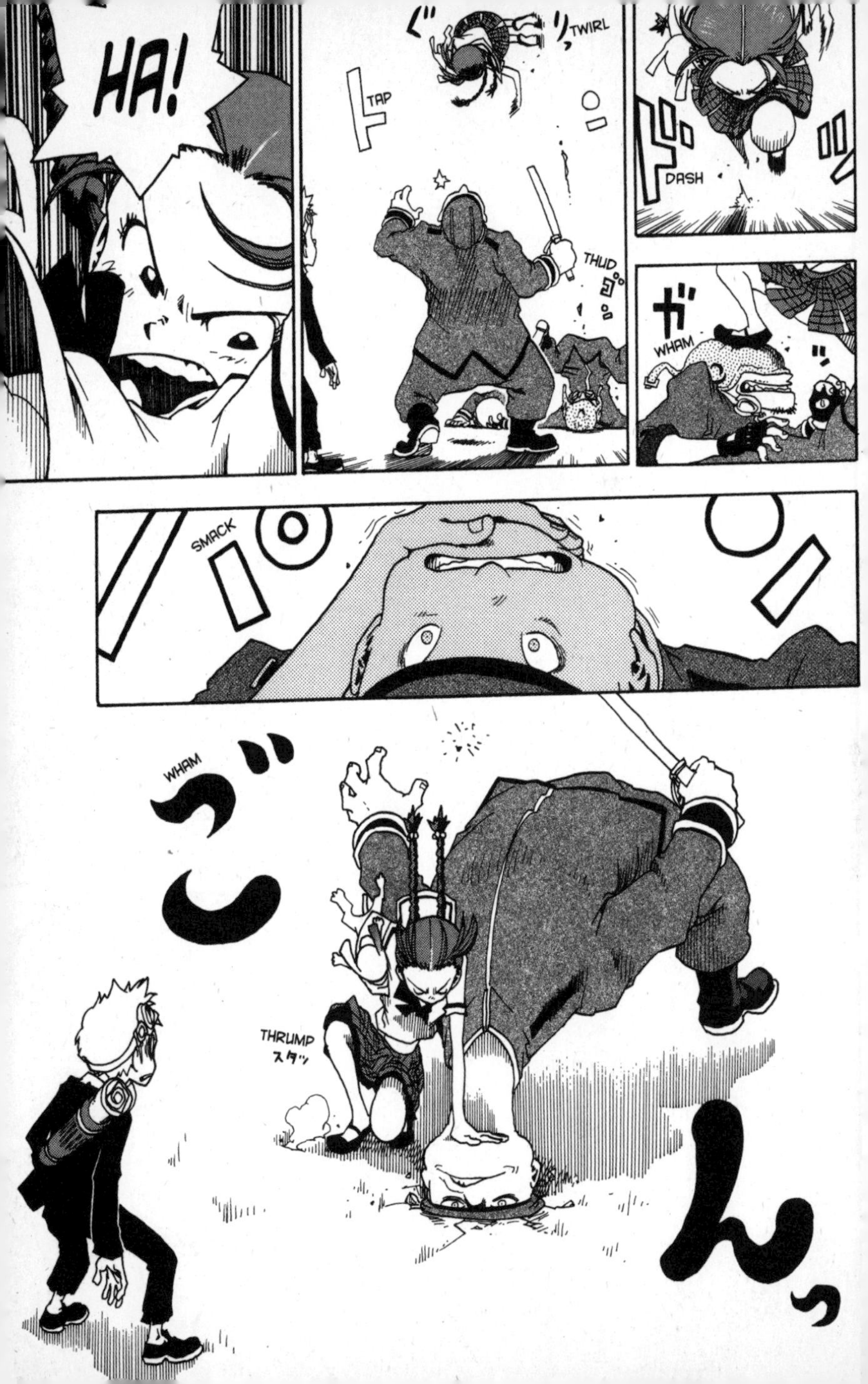
DASH
WHAM
TWIRL
TAP
THUD
HA!
SMACK
WHAM
THRUMP
スタッ

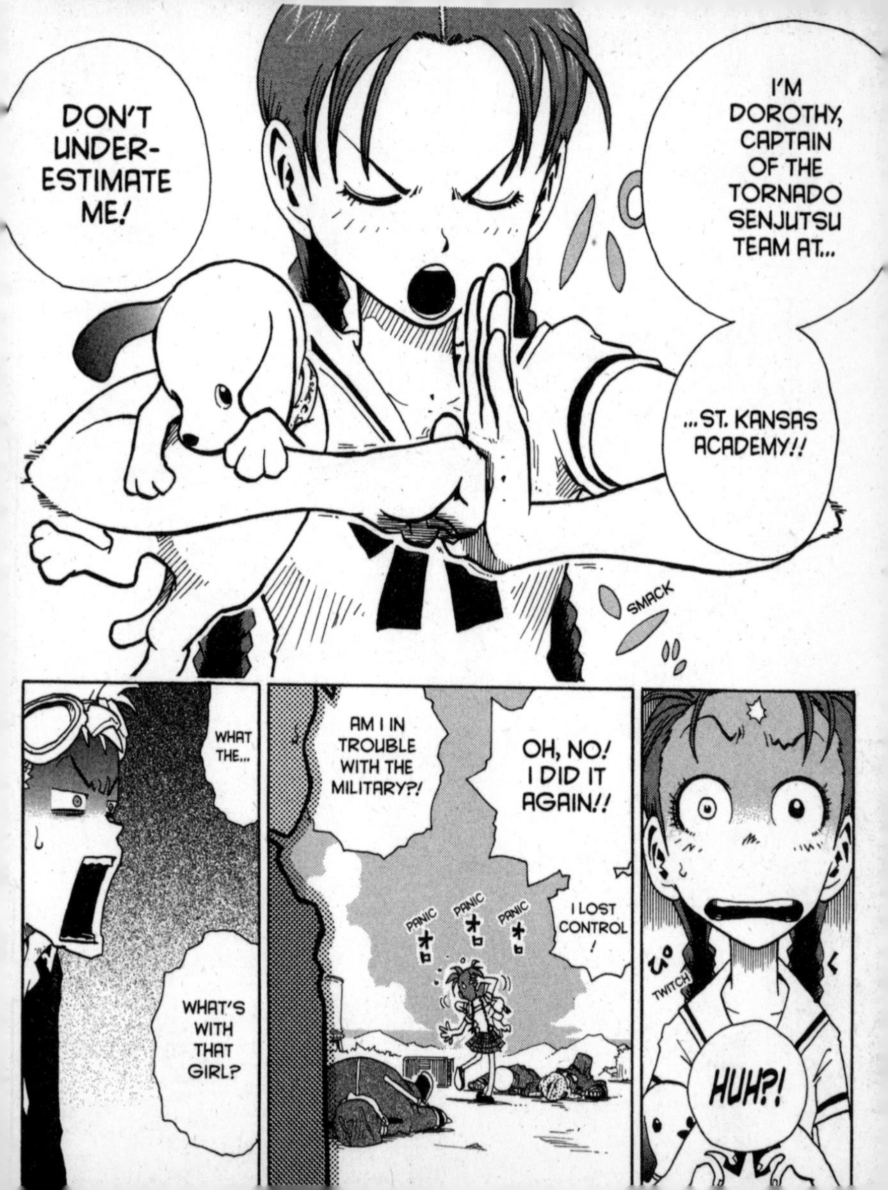
I'M DOROTHY, CAPTAIN OF THE TORNADO SENJUTSU TEAM AT...
...ST. KANSAS ACADEMY!!
DON'T UNDER-ESTIMATE ME!
SMACK
TWITCH
HUH?!
OH, NO! I DID IT AGAIN!!
AM I IN TROUBLE WITH THE MILITARY?!
I LOST CONTROL!
PANIC
PANIC
PANIC
WHAT THE...
WHAT'S WITH THAT GIRL?

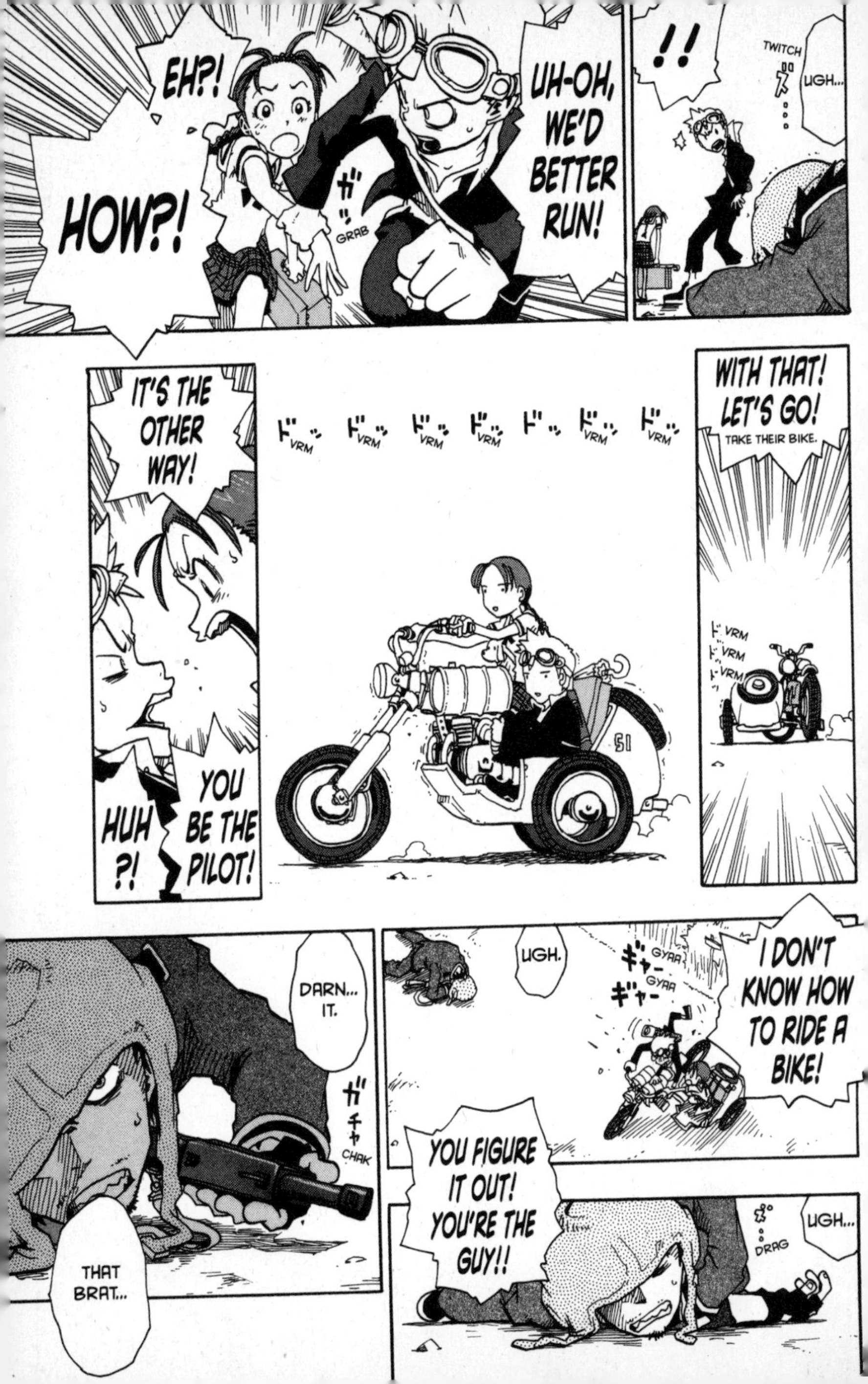
!!
TWITCH
UGH...
UH-OH, WE'D BETTER RUN!
EH?!
GRAB
HOW?!
WITH THAT! LET'S GO!
TAKE THEIR BIKE.
VRM
VRM
VRM
VRM VRM VRM VRM VRM VRM VRM
IT'S THE OTHER WAY!
YOU BE THE PILOT!
HUH?!
I DON'T KNOW HOW TO RIDE A BIKE!
GYAA
GYAA
UGH.
YOU FIGURE IT OUT! YOU'RE THE GUY!!
UGH...
DRAG
DARN... IT.
CHAK
THAT BRAT...

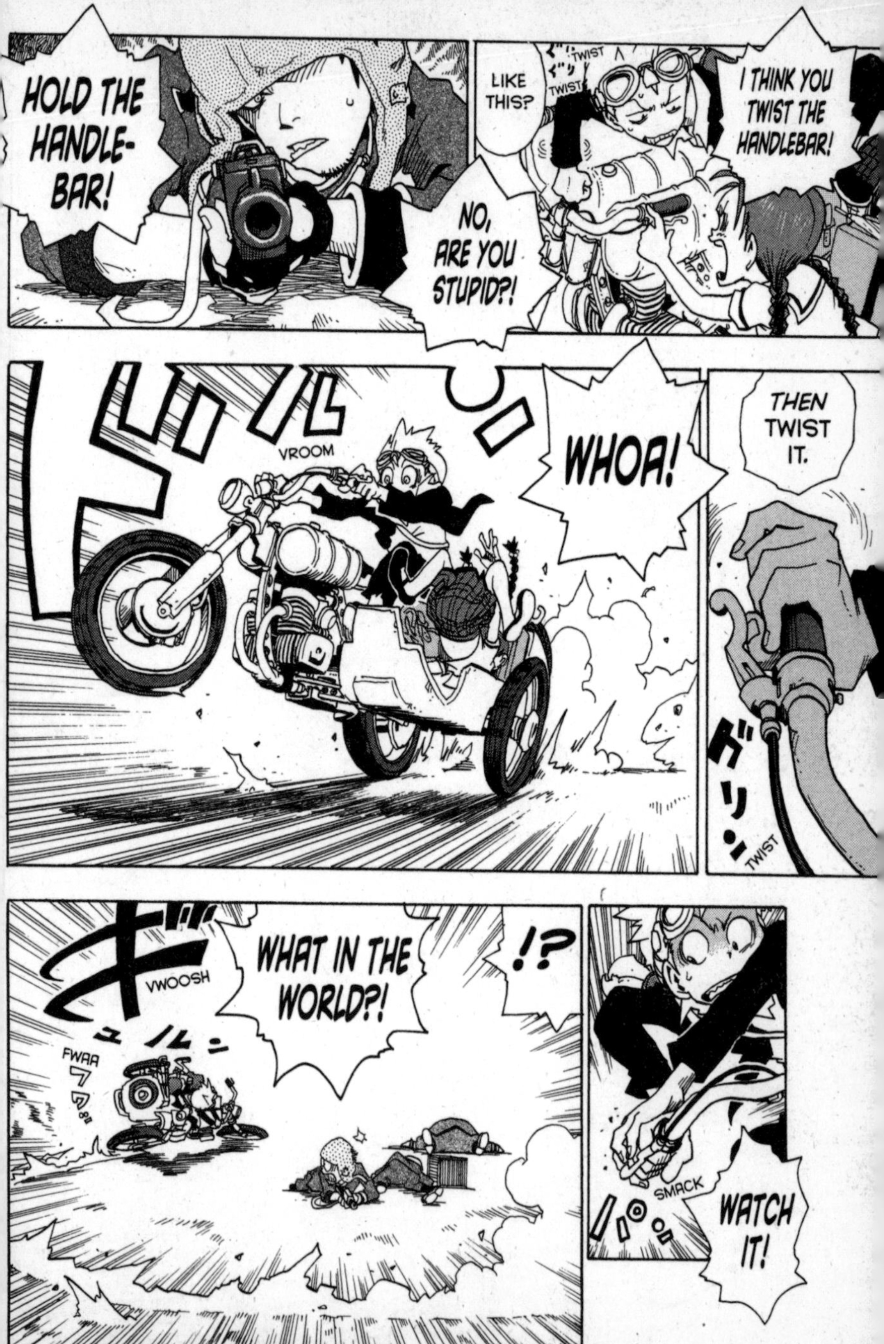
I THINK YOU TWIST THE HANDLEBAR!
TWIST
TWIST
LIKE THIS?
NO, ARE YOU STUPID?!
HOLD THE HANDLE-BAR!
THEN TWIST IT.
TWIST
WHOA!
VROOM
WATCH IT!
SMACK
!?
WHAT IN THE WORLD?!
VWOOSH
FWAA

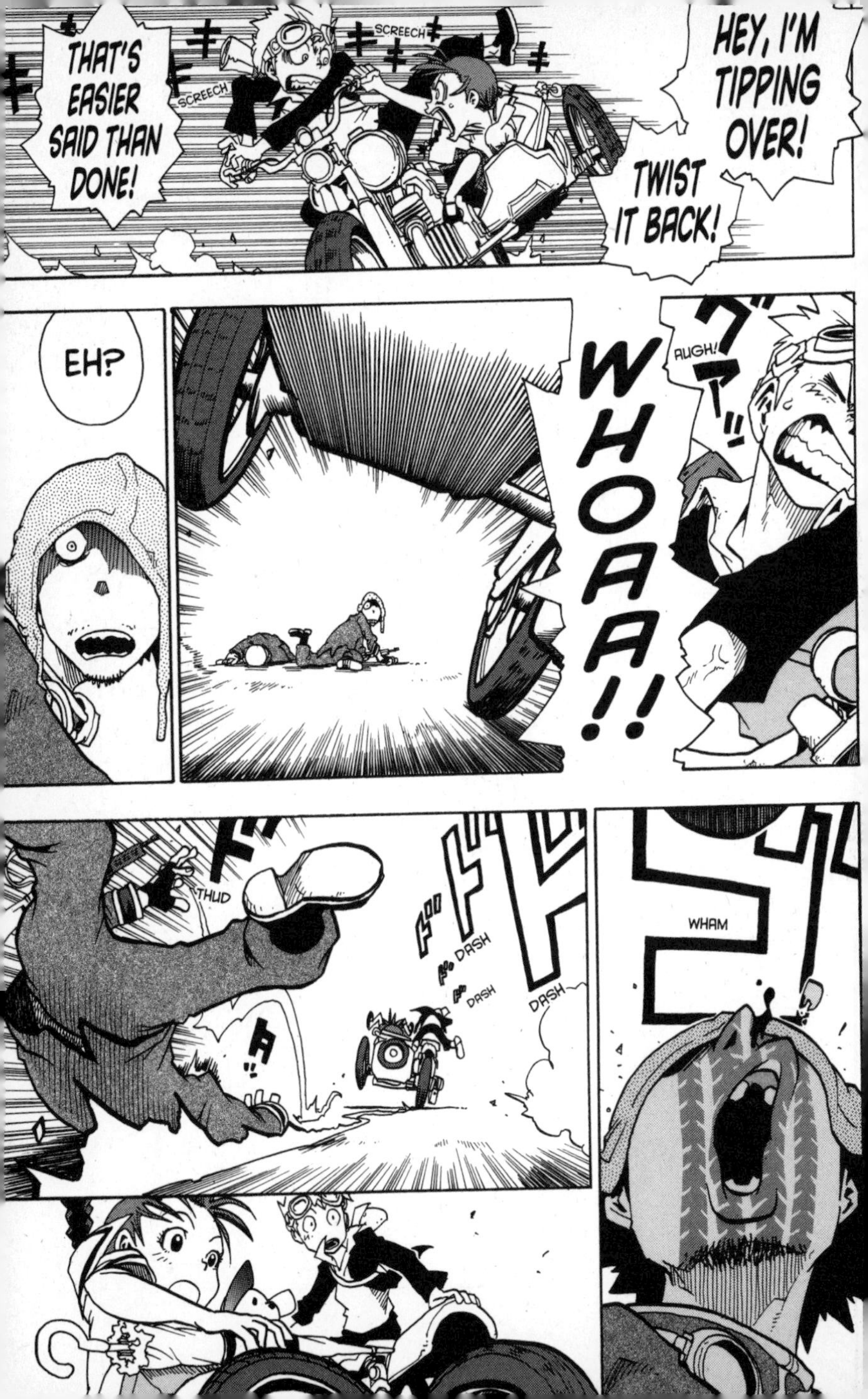
HEY, I'M TIPPING OVER!
TWIST IT BACK!
SCREECH
SCREECH
THAT'S EASIER SAID THAN DONE!
AUGH!
WHOAAA!!
EH?
WHAM
THUD
DASH
DASH
DASH

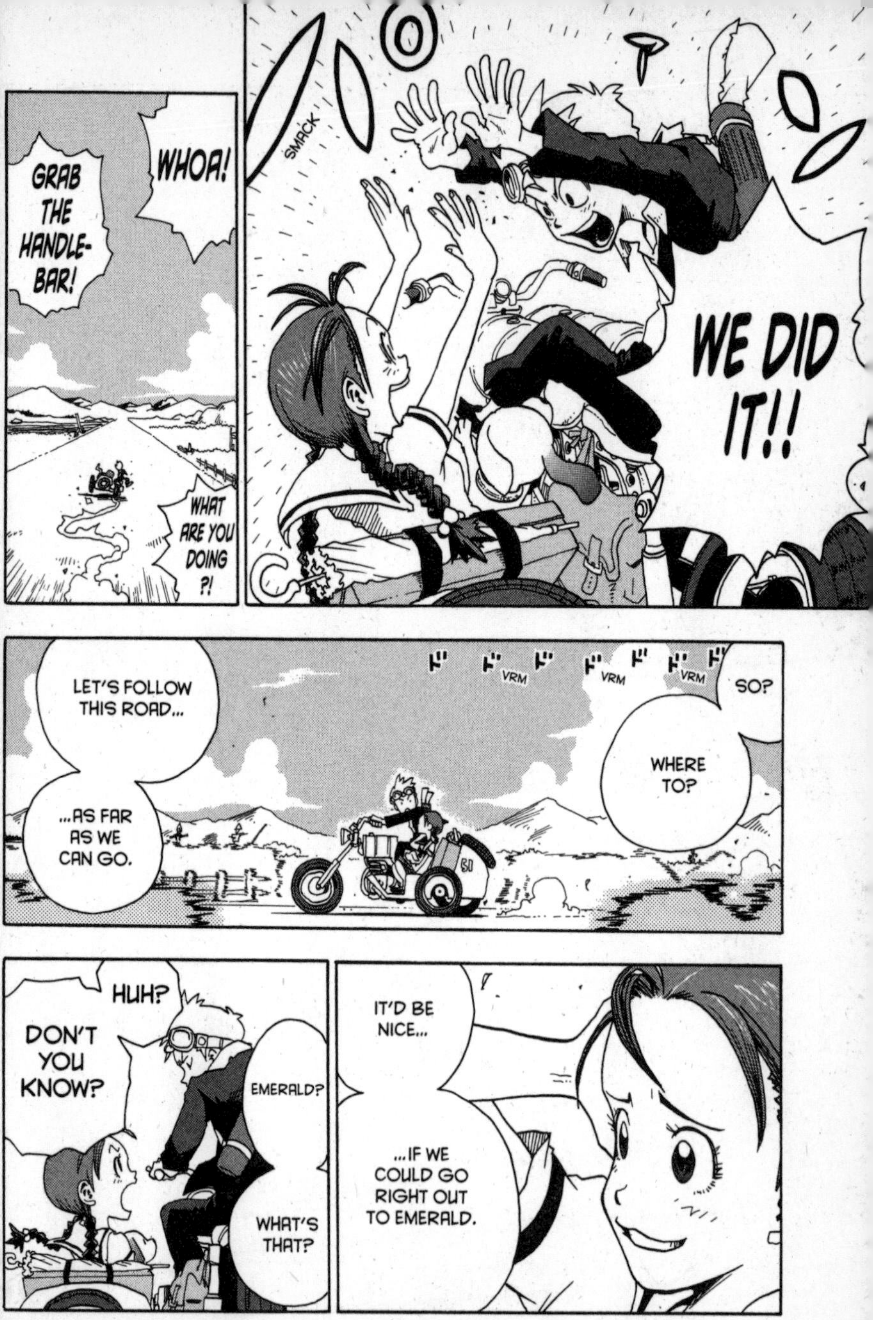
SMACK
WE DID IT!!
WHOA!
GRAB THE HANDLE-BAR!
WHAT ARE YOU DOING ?!
ド VRM ド ド VRM ド ド VRM ド
SO?
WHERE TO?
LET'S FOLLOW THIS ROAD...
...AS FAR AS WE CAN GO.
IT'D BE NICE...
...IF WE COULD GO RIGHT OUT TO EMERALD.
EMERALD?
WHAT'S THAT?
HUH?
DON'T YOU KNOW?

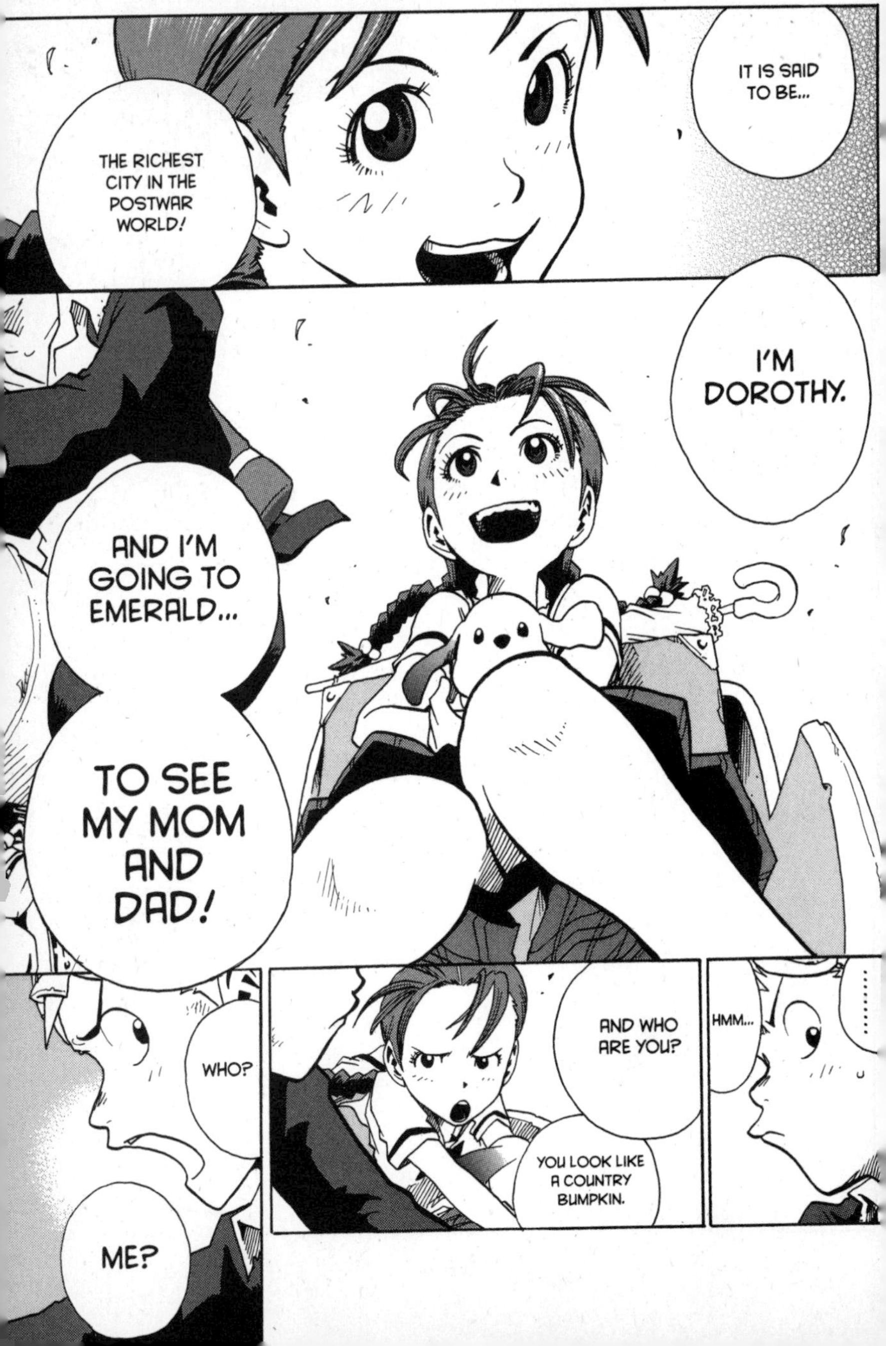
IT IS SAID TO BE...
THE RICHEST CITY IN THE POSTWAR WORLD!
I'M DOROTHY.
AND I'M GOING TO EMERALD...
TO SEE MY MOM AND DAD!
......
HMM...
AND WHO ARE YOU?
YOU LOOK LIKE A COUNTRY BUMPKIN.
WHO?
ME?

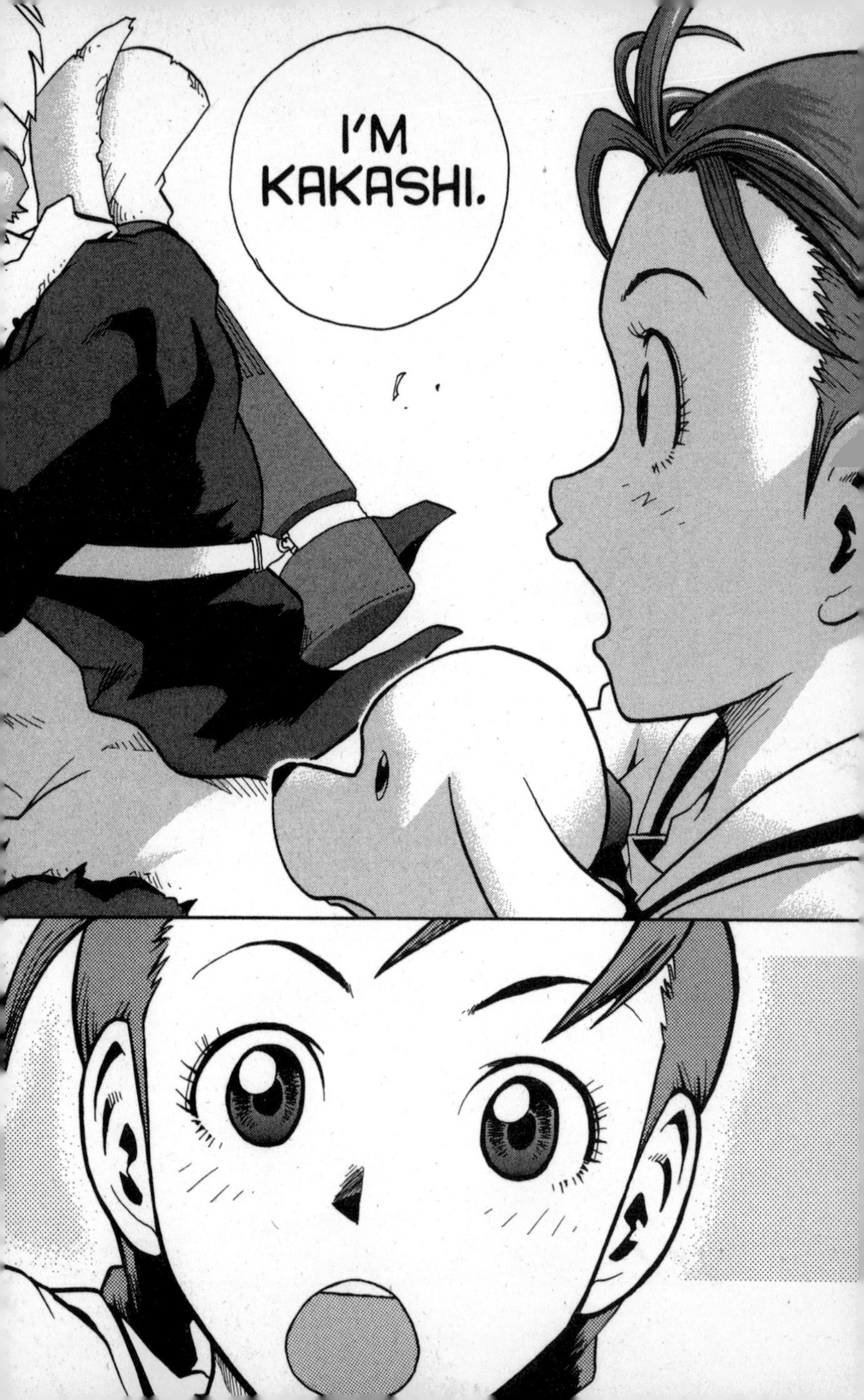
I'M KAKASHI.

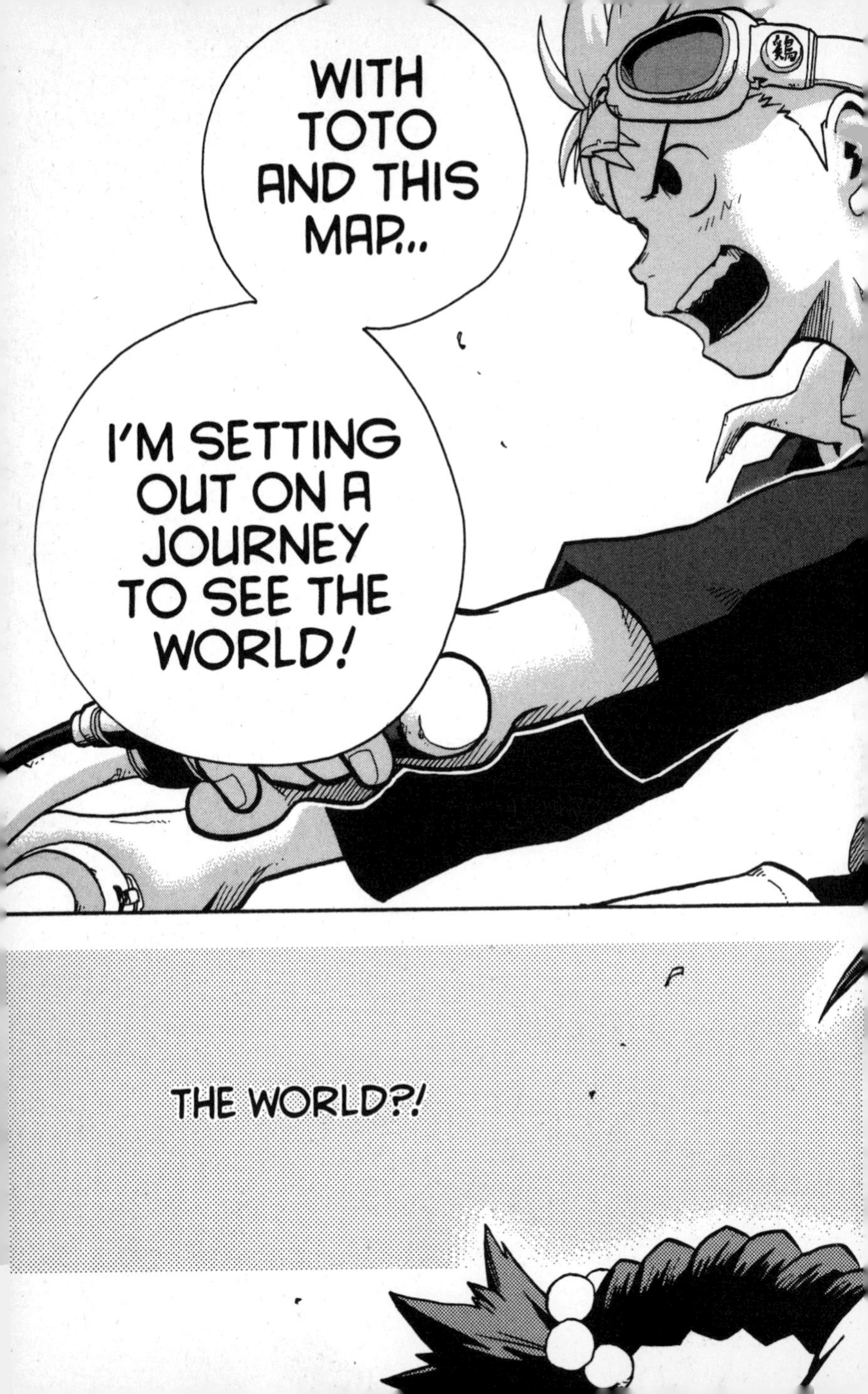
WITH TOTO AND THIS MAP...
I'M SETTING OUT ON A JOURNEY TO SEE THE WORLD!
THE WORLD?!

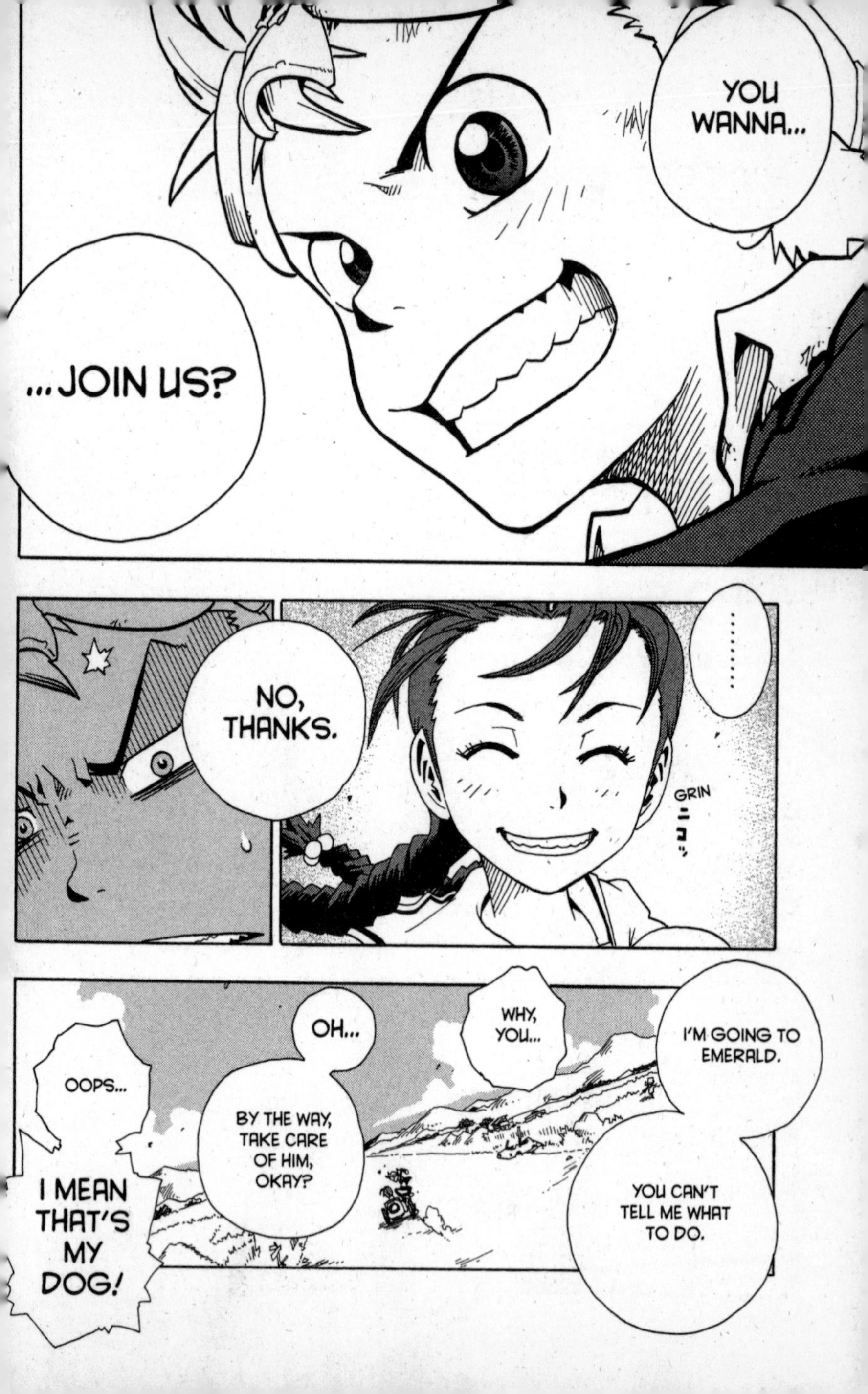
YOU WANNA...
...JOIN US?
......
NO, THANKS.
GRIN
I'M GOING TO EMERALD.
YOU CAN'T TELL ME WHAT TO DO.
WHY, YOU...
OH...
BY THE WAY, TAKE CARE OF HIM, OKAY?
OOPS...
I MEAN THAT'S MY DOG!

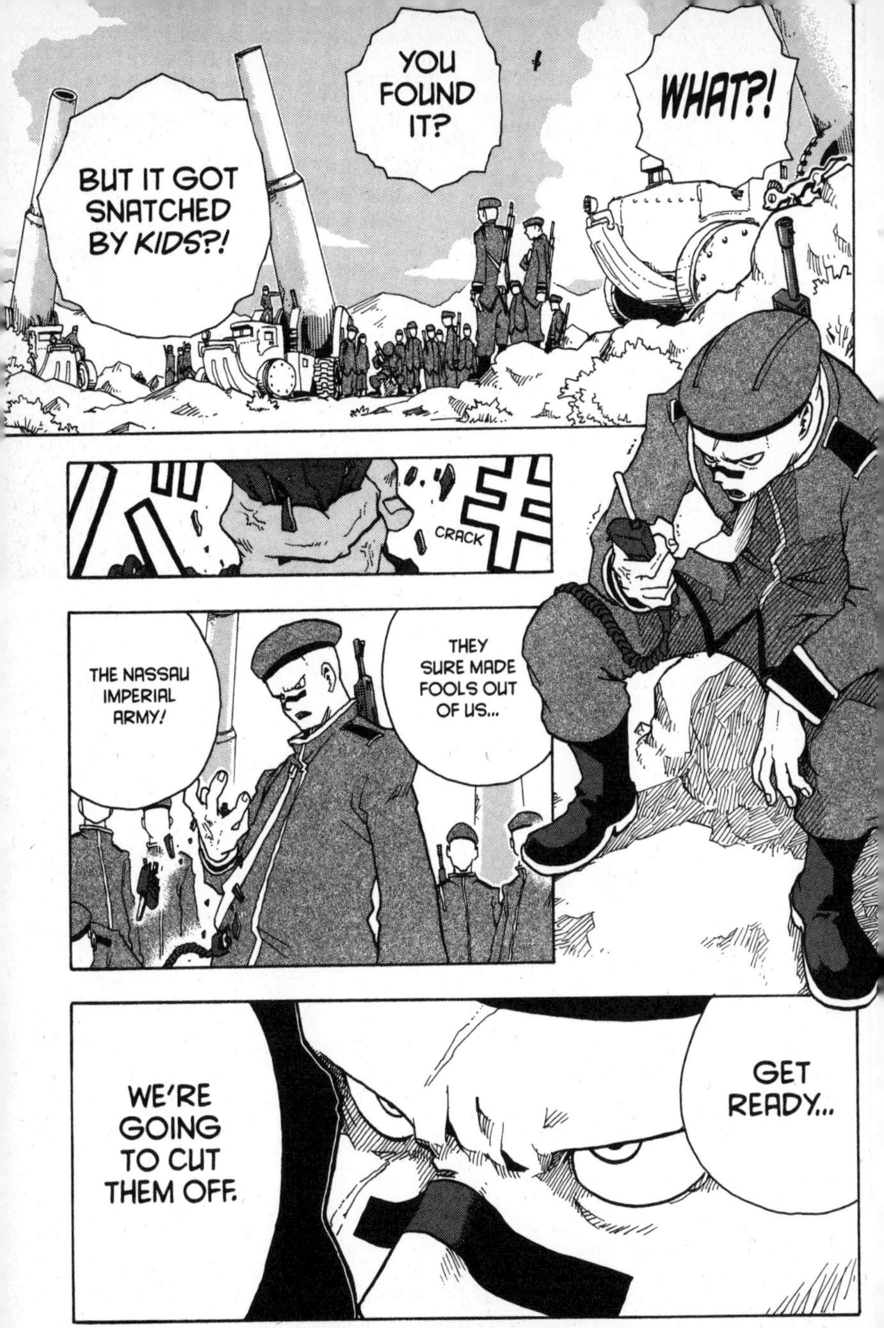
WHAT?!
YOU FOUND IT?
BUT IT GOT SNATCHED BY KIDS?!
CRACK
THEY SURE MADE FOOLS OUT OF US...
THE NASSAU IMPERIAL ARMY!
GET READY...
WE'RE GOING TO CUT THEM OFF.

TOTO! The Rough Character Sketches!

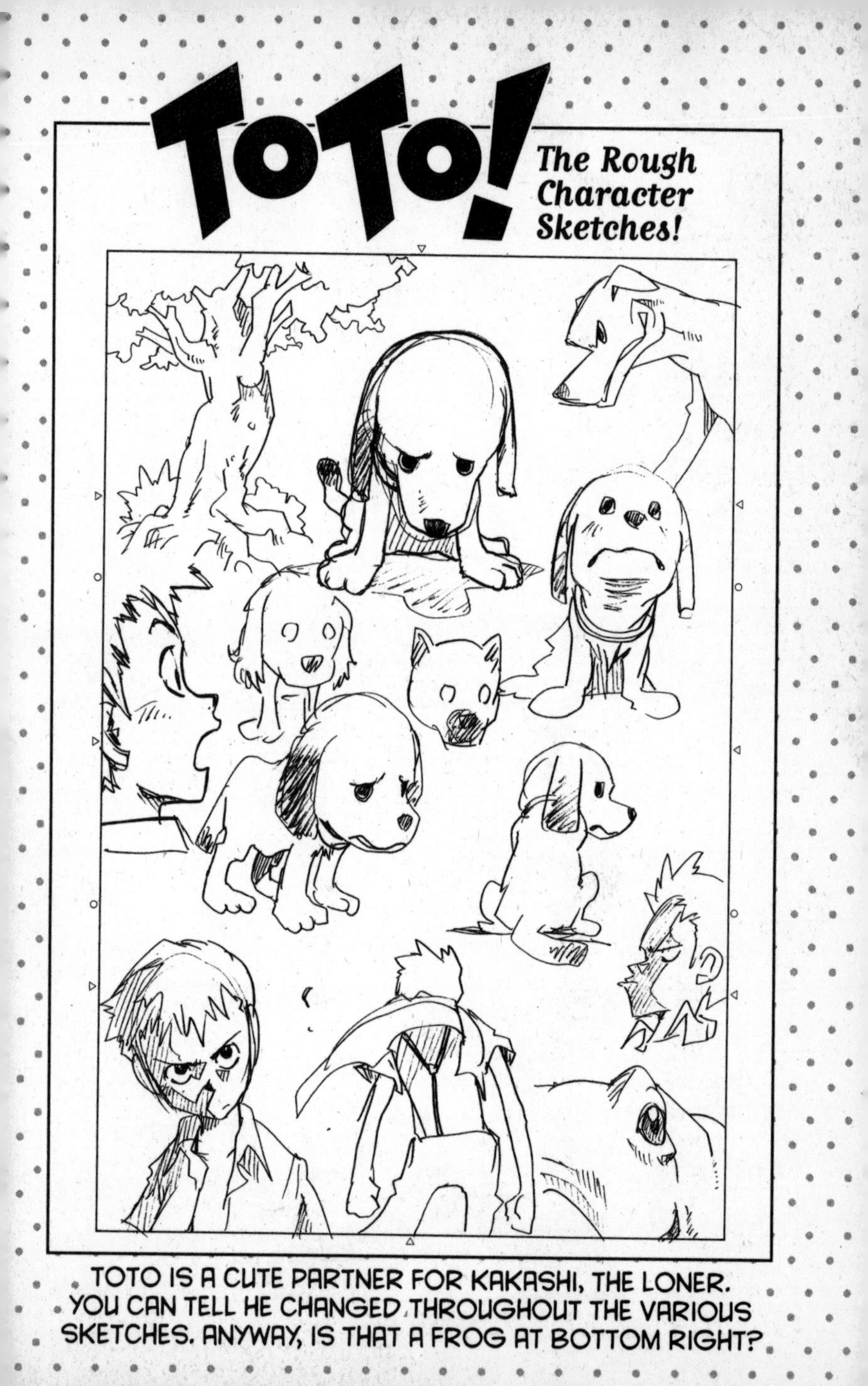

TOTO IS A CUTE PARTNER FOR KAKASHI, THE LONER. YOU CAN TELL HE CHANGED THROUGHOUT THE VARIOUS SKETCHES. ANYWAY, IS THAT A FROG AT BOTTOM RIGHT?

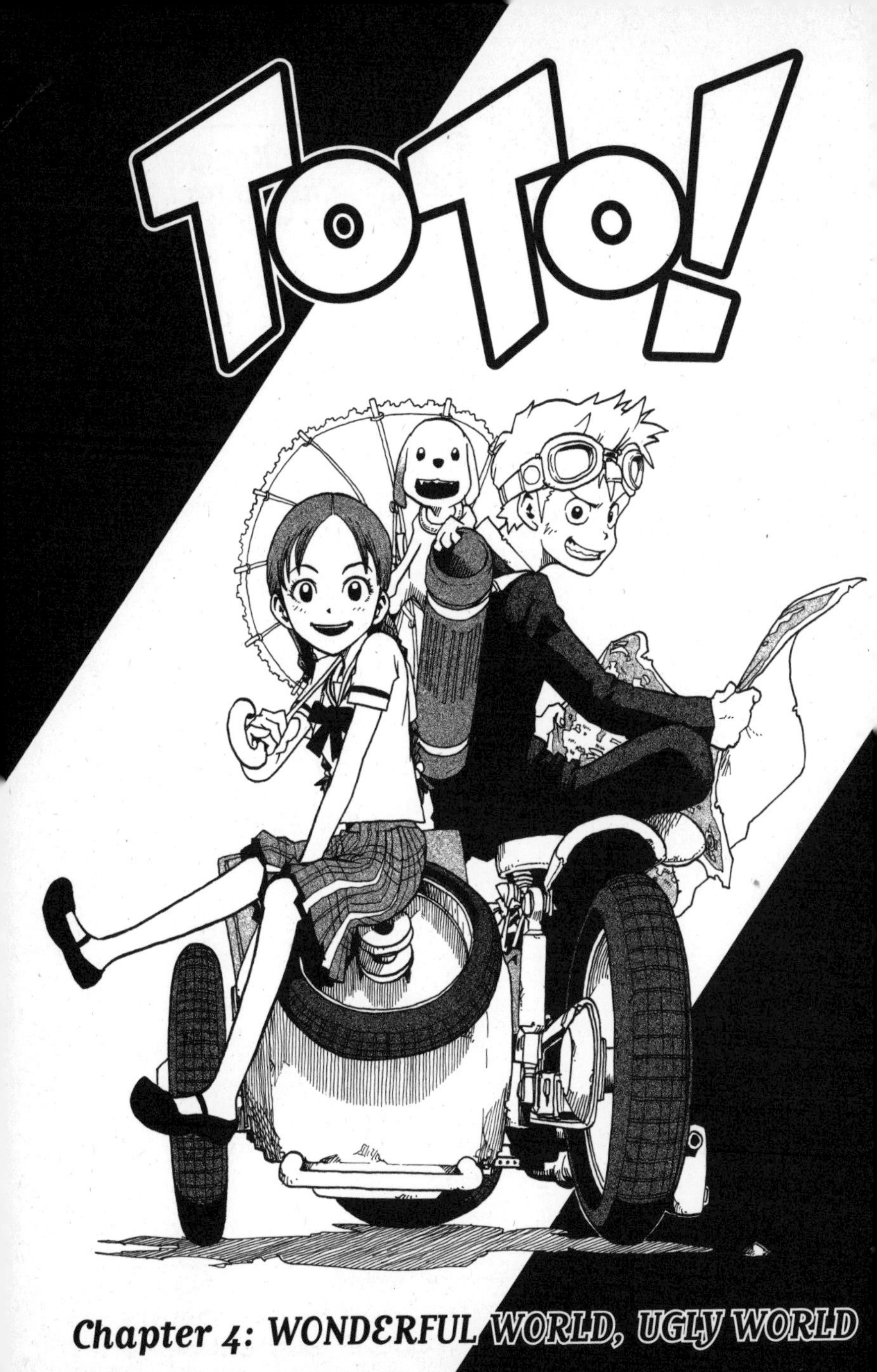
TOTO!

Chapter 4: WONDERFUL WORLD, UGLY WORLD

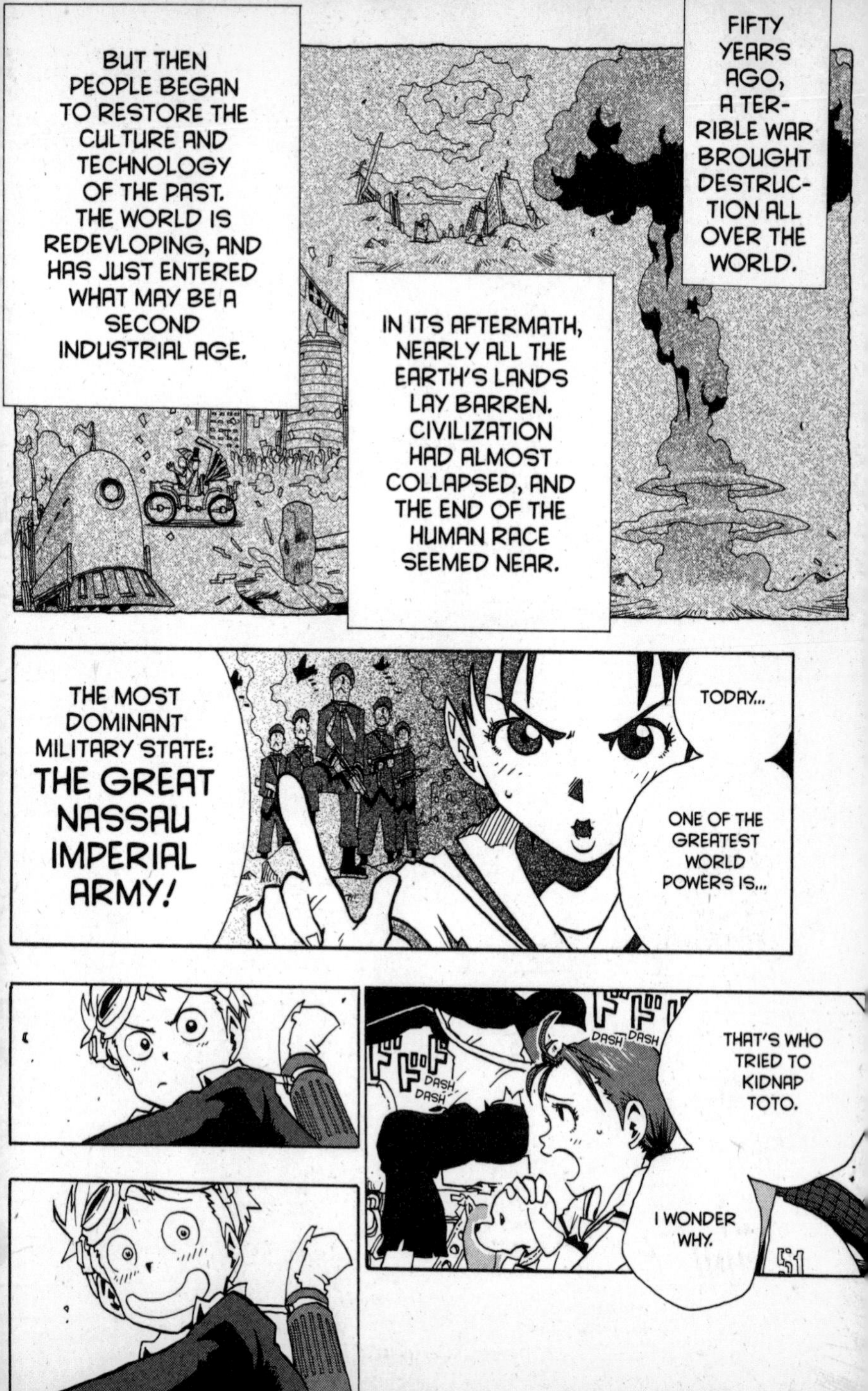
FIFTY YEARS AGO, A TERRIBLE WAR BROUGHT DESTRUCTION ALL OVER THE WORLD.
IN ITS AFTERMATH, NEARLY ALL THE EARTH'S LANDS LAY BARREN. CIVILIZATION HAD ALMOST COLLAPSED, AND THE END OF THE HUMAN RACE SEEMED NEAR.
BUT THEN PEOPLE BEGAN TO RESTORE THE CULTURE AND TECHNOLOGY OF THE PAST. THE WORLD IS REDEVLOPING, AND HAS JUST ENTERED WHAT MAY BE A SECOND INDUSTRIAL AGE.
TODAY...
ONE OF THE GREATEST WORLD POWERS IS...
THE MOST DOMINANT MILITARY STATE: THE GREAT NASSAU IMPERIAL ARMY!
DASH DASH
DASH DASH
THAT'S WHO TRIED TO KIDNAP TOTO.
I WONDER WHY.

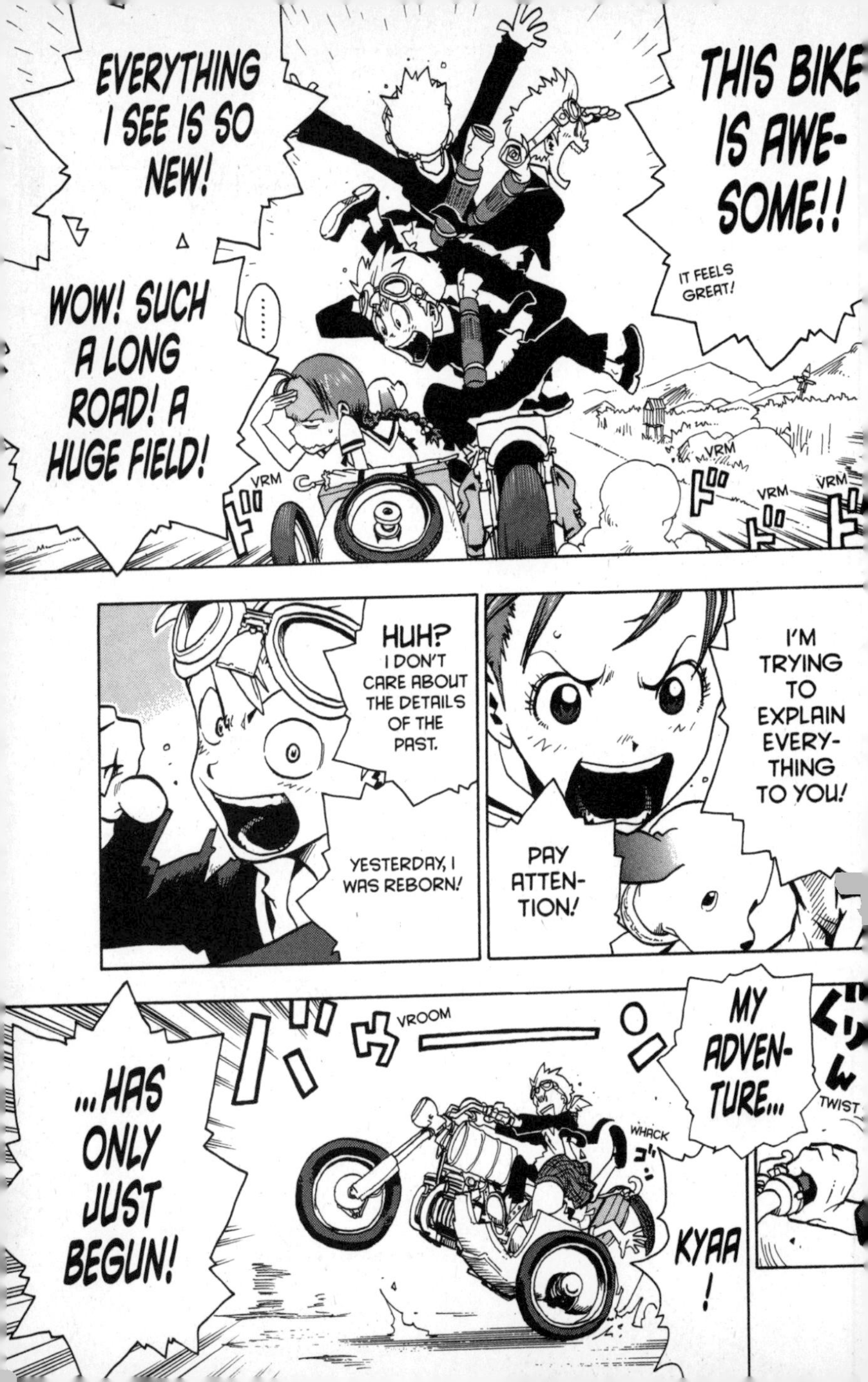
THIS BIKE IS AWE-SOME!!
IT FEELS GREAT!
EVERYTHING I SEE IS SO NEW!
WOW! SUCH A LONG ROAD! A HUGE FIELD!
......
VRM
VRM
VRM
VRM
I'M TRYING TO EXPLAIN EVERY-THING TO YOU!
PAY ATTEN-TION!
HUH? I DON'T CARE ABOUT THE DETAILS OF THE PAST.
YESTERDAY, I WAS REBORN!
TWIST
MY ADVEN-TURE...
VROOM
WHACK
KYAA!
...HAS ONLY JUST BEGUN!

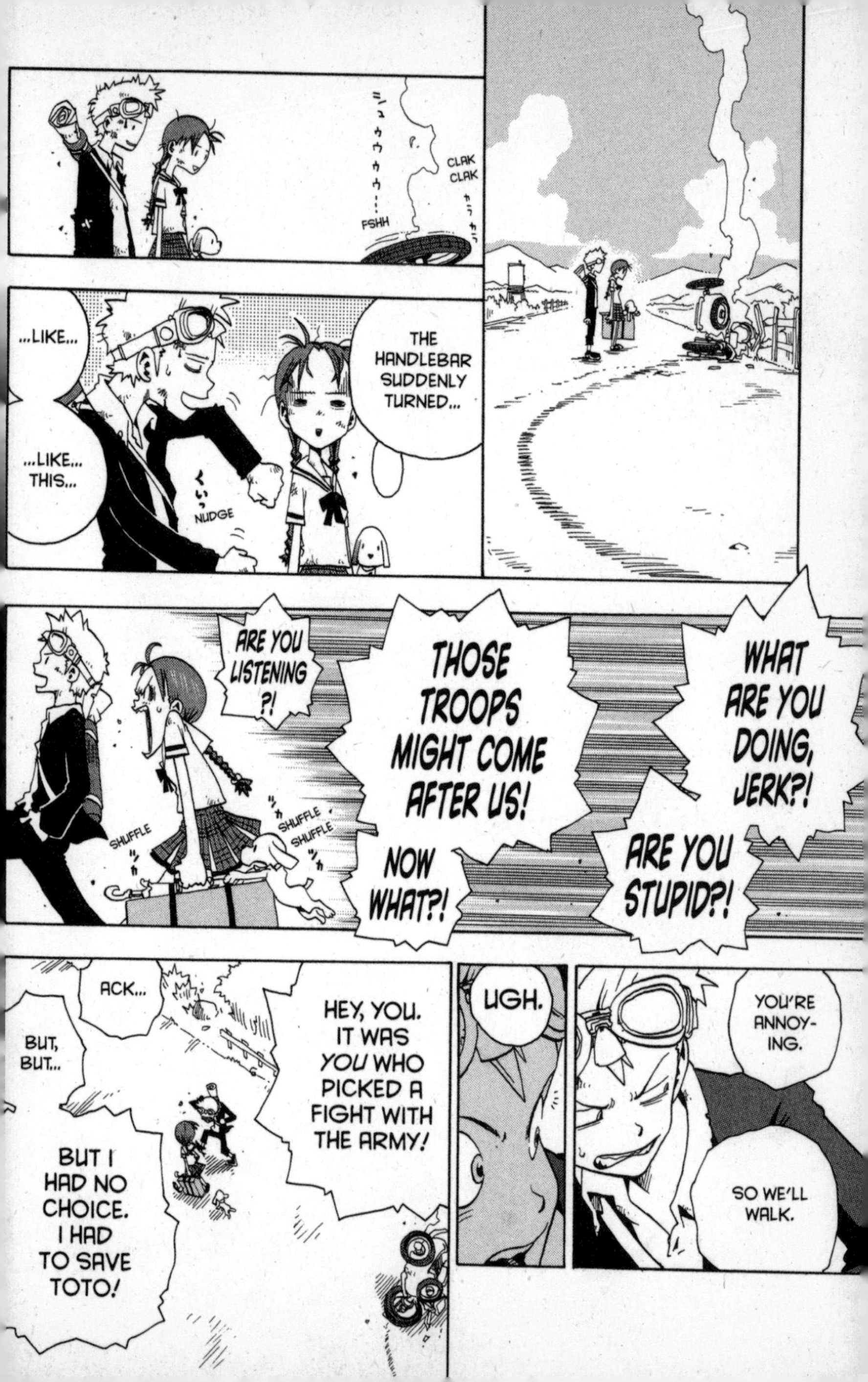
シュウウウウ…
FSHH
CLAK CLAK
カラ カラ
THE HANDLEBAR SUDDENLY TURNED...
...LIKE...
...LIKE... THIS...
くいっ
NUDGE
WHAT ARE YOU DOING, JERK?!
ARE YOU STUPID?!
THOSE TROOPS MIGHT COME AFTER US!
NOW WHAT?!
ARE YOU LISTENING?!
ツカ SHUFFLE SHUFFLE ツカ
SHUFFLE ツカ
YOU'RE ANNOY-ING.
SO WE'LL WALK.
UGH.
HEY, YOU. IT WAS *YOU* WHO PICKED A FIGHT WITH THE ARMY!
ACK...
BUT, BUT...
BUT I HAD NO CHOICE. I HAD TO SAVE TOTO!

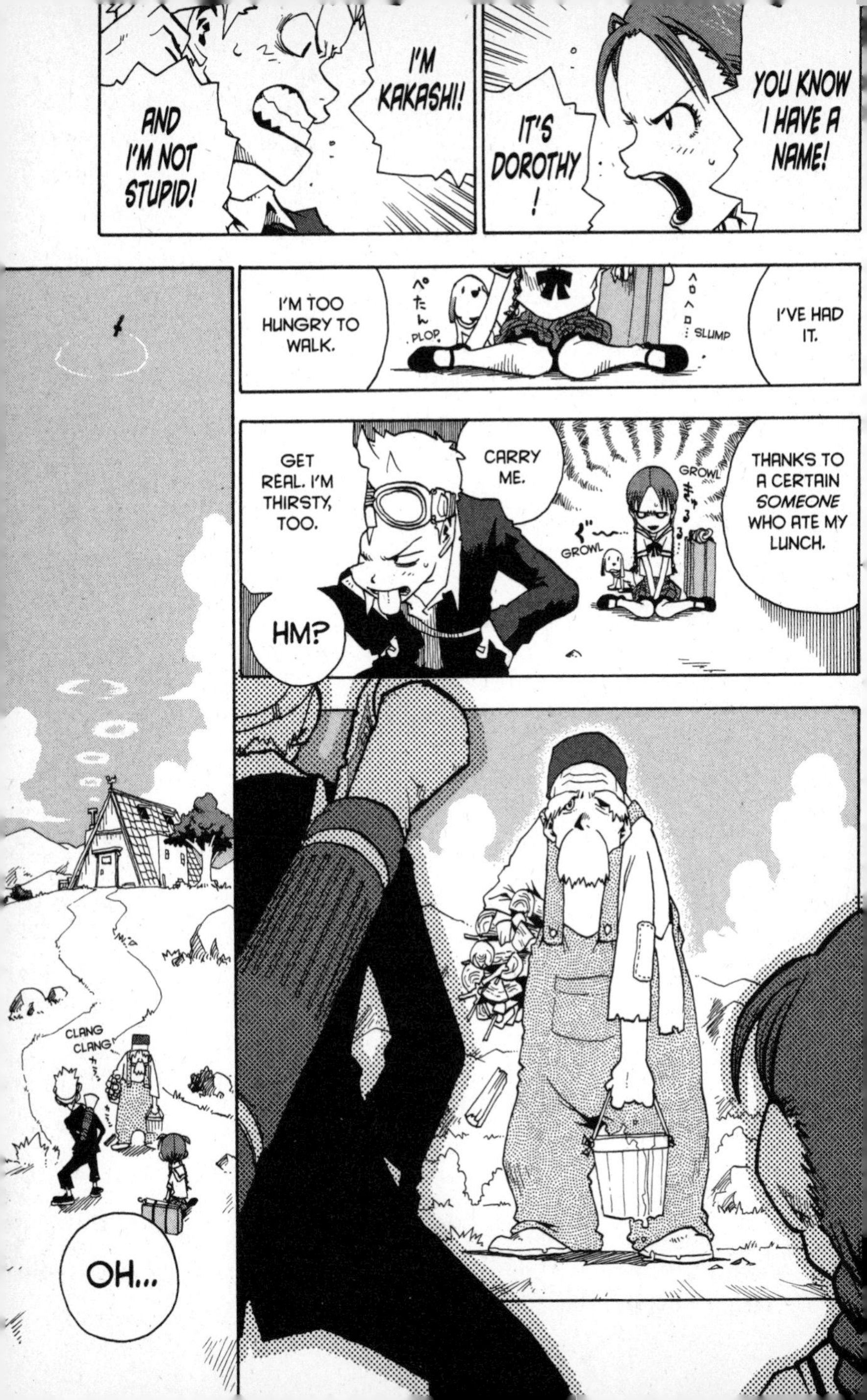
YOU KNOW I HAVE A NAME!
IT'S DOROTHY!
I'M KAKASHI!
AND I'M NOT STUPID!
I'VE HAD IT.
ヘロヘロ… SLUMP
ぺたん PLOP
I'M TOO HUNGRY TO WALK.
THANKS TO A CERTAIN *SOMEONE* WHO ATE MY LUNCH.
GROWL
ぐ〜〜 GROWL
CARRY ME.
GET REAL. I'M THIRSTY, TOO.
HM?
CLANG CLANG
OH...

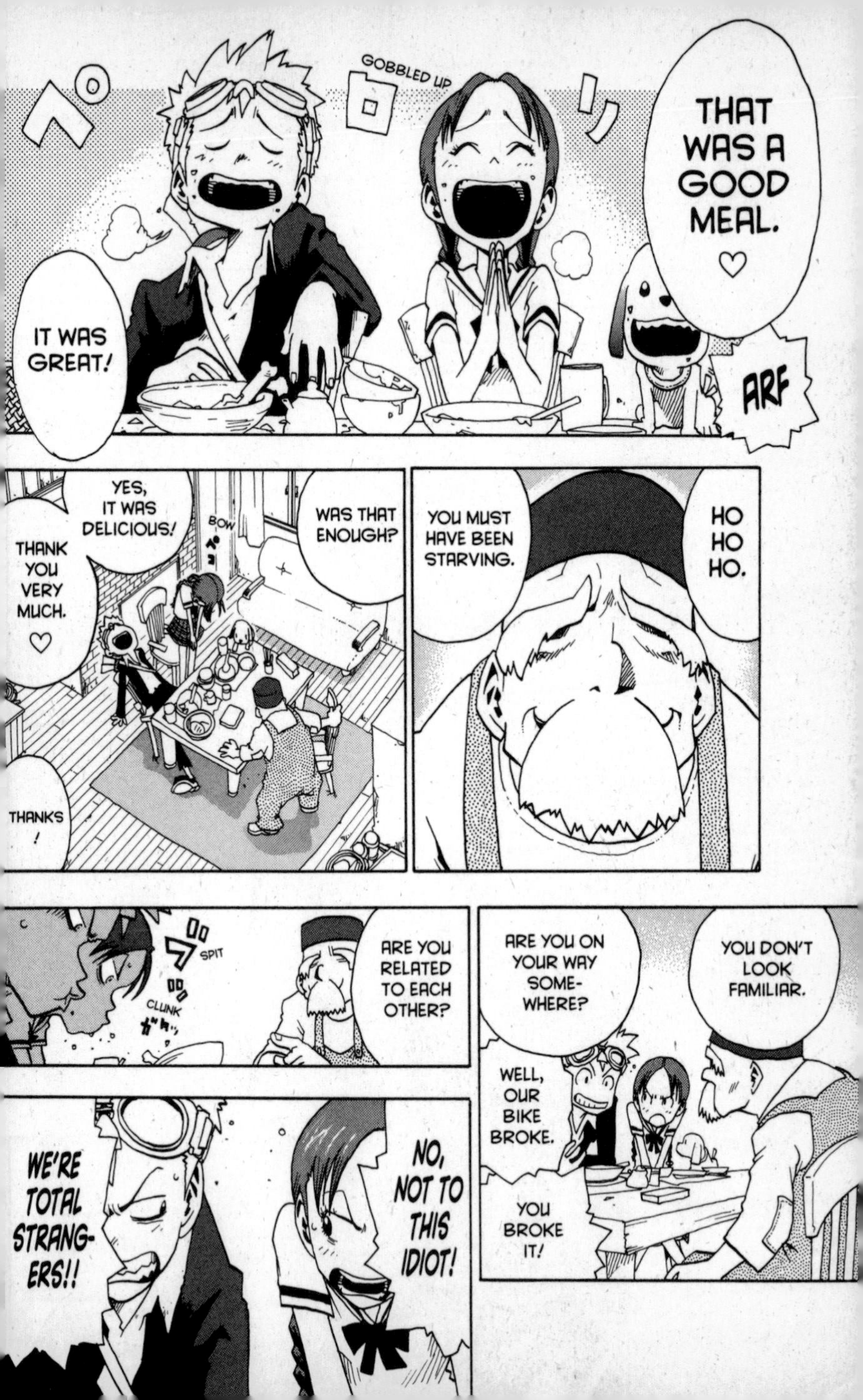
THAT WAS A GOOD MEAL. ♡
ARF
GOBBLED UP
IT WAS GREAT!
HO HO HO.
YOU MUST HAVE BEEN STARVING.
WAS THAT ENOUGH?
YES, IT WAS DELICIOUS!
BOW
THANK YOU VERY MUCH. ♡
THANKS!
YOU DON'T LOOK FAMILIAR.
ARE YOU ON YOUR WAY SOME-WHERE?
WELL, OUR BIKE BROKE.
YOU BROKE IT!
ARE YOU RELATED TO EACH OTHER?
SPIT
CLUNK
NO, NOT TO THIS IDIOT!
WE'RE TOTAL STRANG-ERS!!

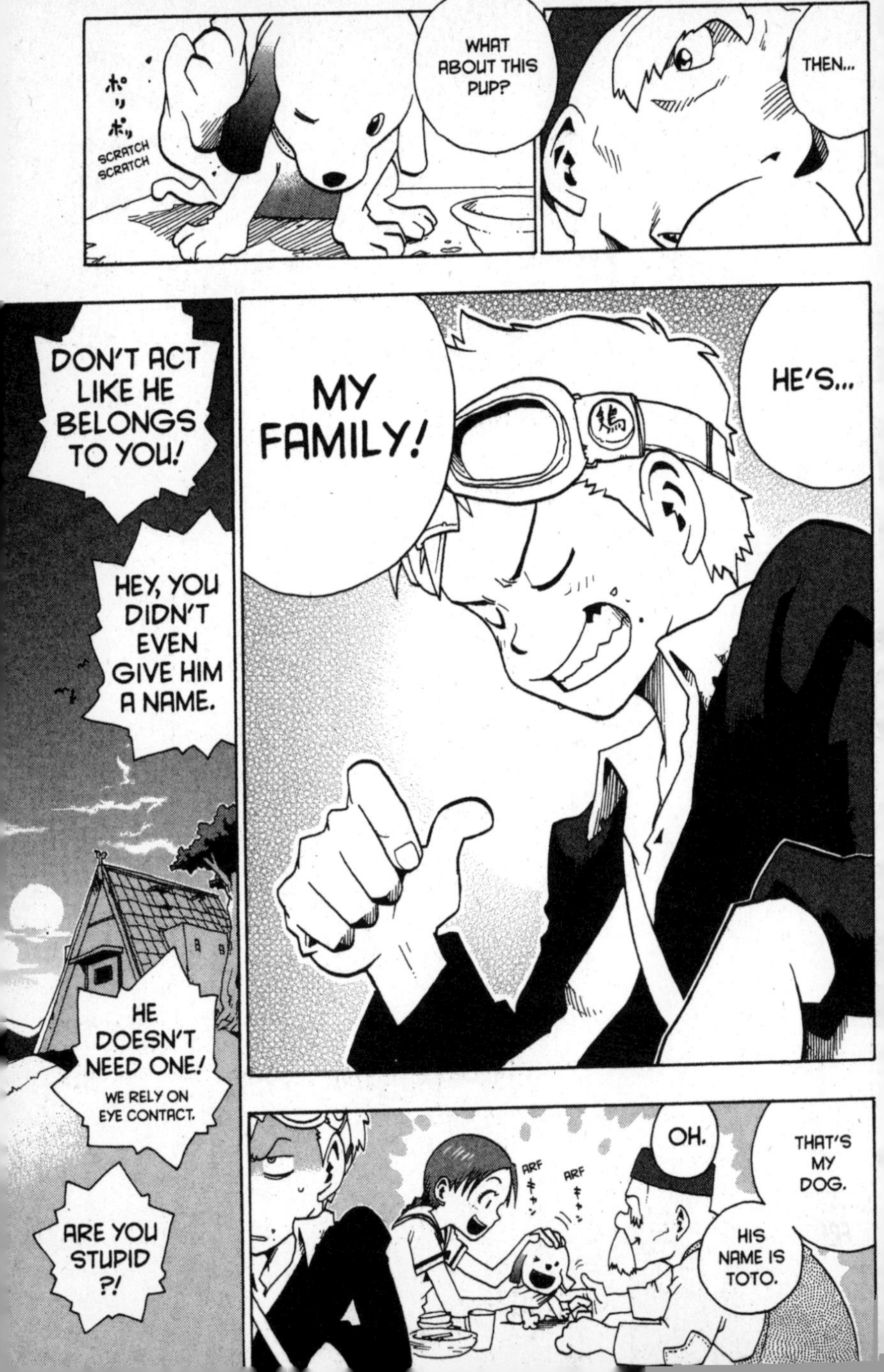
THEN...
WHAT ABOUT THIS PUP?
ポリポリ
SCRATCH SCRATCH
HE'S...
MY FAMILY!
OH.
THAT'S MY DOG.
HIS NAME IS TOTO.
ARF キャン
ARF キャン
DON'T ACT LIKE HE BELONGS TO YOU!
HEY, YOU DIDN'T EVEN GIVE HIM A NAME.
HE DOESN'T NEED ONE!
WE RELY ON EYE CONTACT.
ARE YOU STUPID ?!

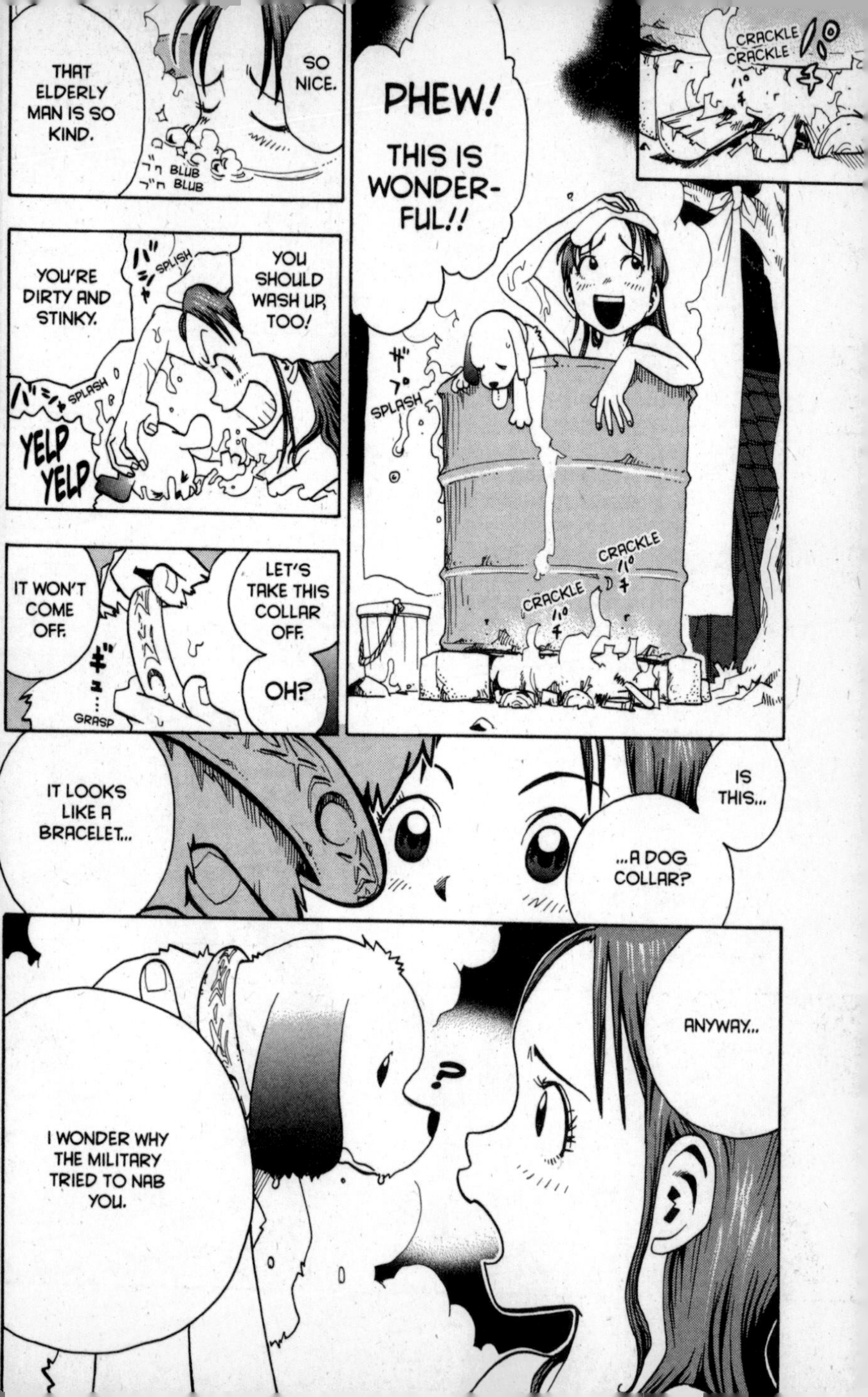
CRACKLE
CRACKLE
PHEW!
THIS IS WONDERFUL!!
SPLASH
CRACKLE
CRACKLE
SO NICE.
THAT ELDERLY MAN IS SO KIND.
BLUB
BLUB
YOU SHOULD WASH UP, TOO!
YOU'RE DIRTY AND STINKY.
SPLASH
SPLASH
YELP
YELP
LET'S TAKE THIS COLLAR OFF.
OH?
IT WON'T COME OFF.
GRASP
IS THIS...
...A DOG COLLAR?
IT LOOKS LIKE A BRACELET...
ANYWAY...
I WONDER WHY THE MILITARY TRIED TO NAB YOU.

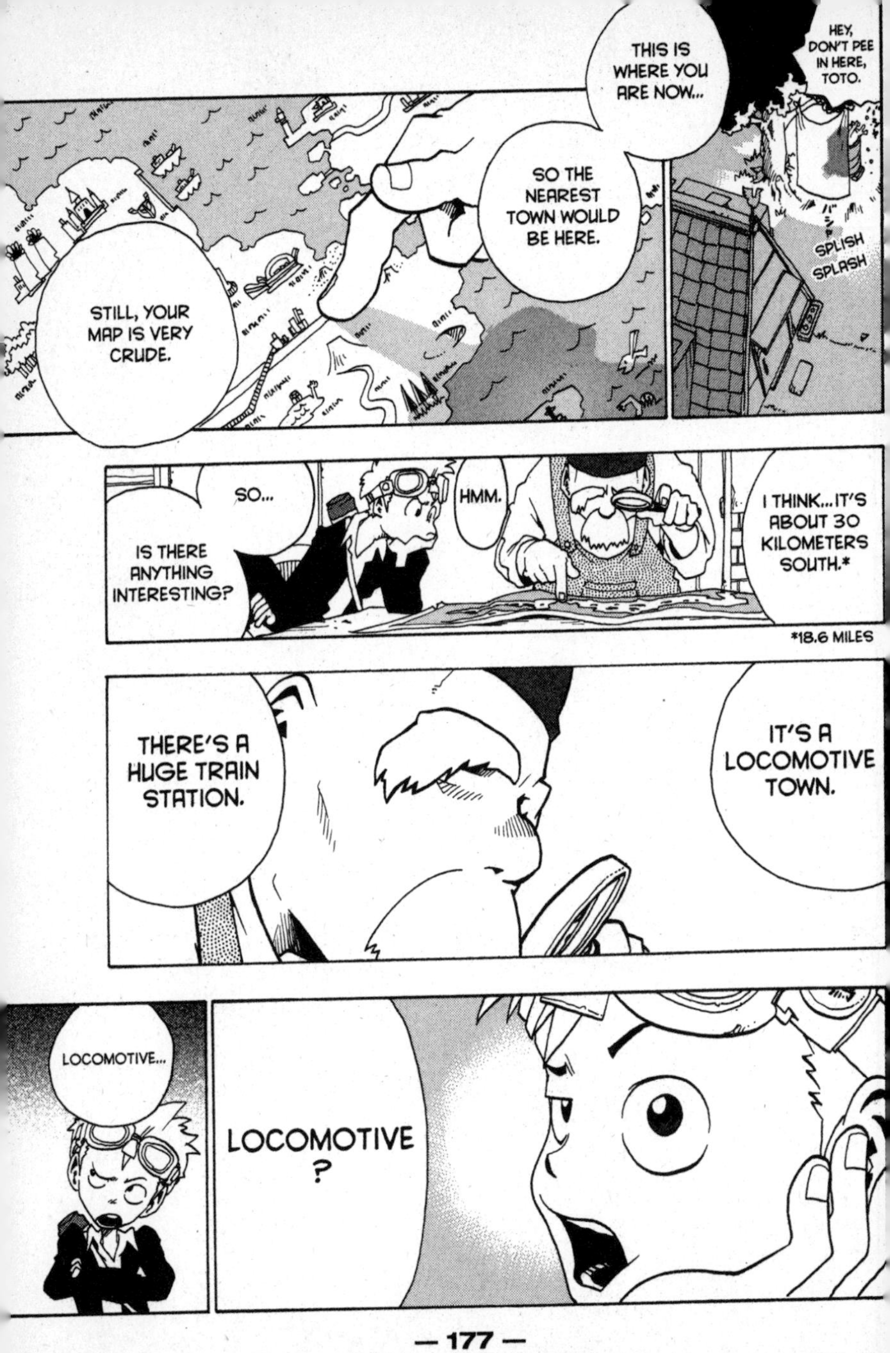
HEY, DON'T PEE IN HERE, TOTO.
SPLISH SPLASH
THIS IS WHERE YOU ARE NOW...
SO THE NEAREST TOWN WOULD BE HERE.
STILL, YOUR MAP IS VERY CRUDE.
I THINK...IT'S ABOUT 30 KILOMETERS SOUTH.*
HMM.
SO...
IS THERE ANYTHING INTERESTING?
*18.6 MILES
IT'S A LOCOMOTIVE TOWN.
THERE'S A HUGE TRAIN STATION.
LOCOMOTIVE?
LOCOMOTIVE...

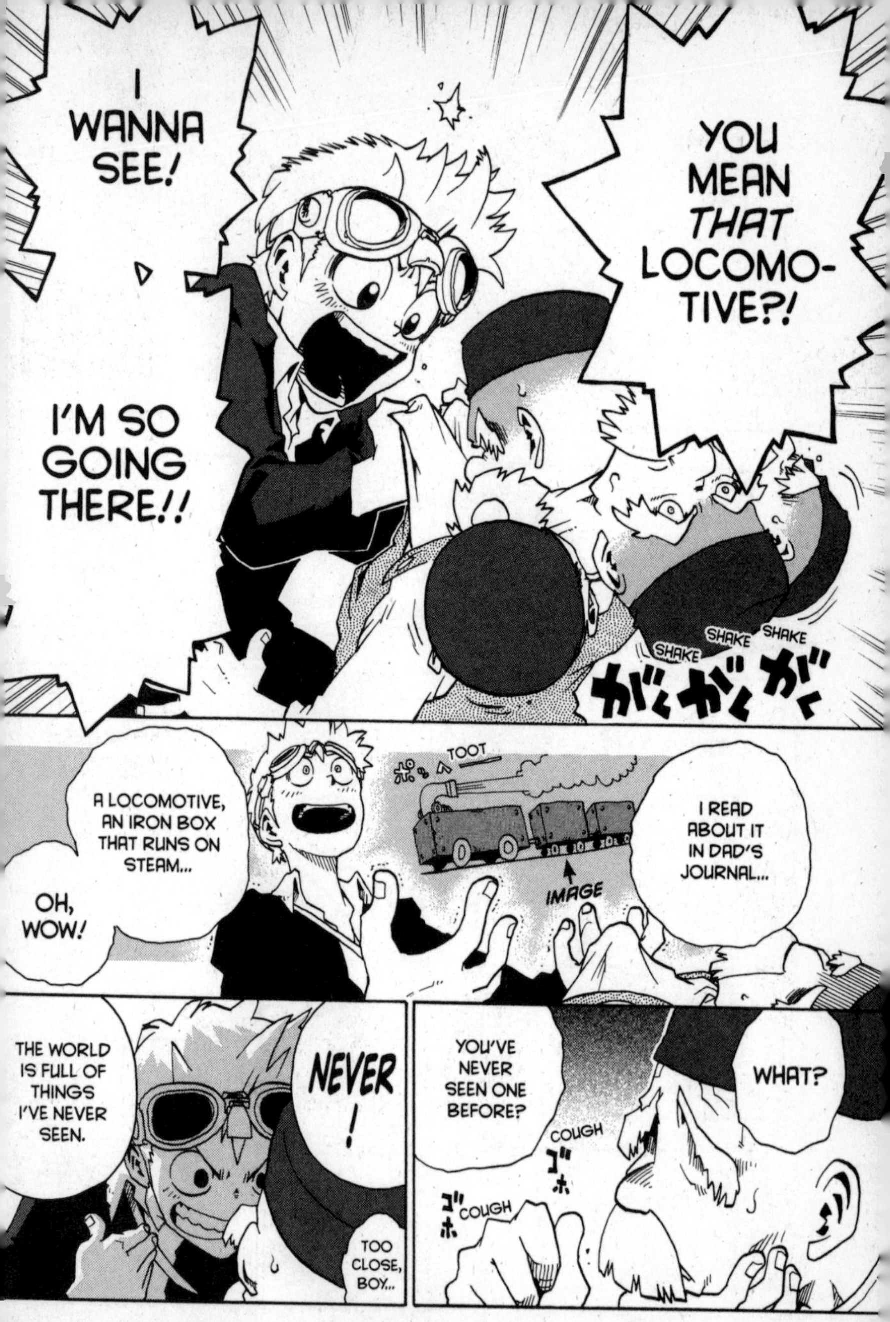
YOU MEAN THAT LOCOMOTIVE?!
I WANNA SEE!
I'M SO GOING THERE!!
SHAKE SHAKE SHAKE
がくがくがく
I READ ABOUT IT IN DAD'S JOURNAL...
TOOT
IMAGE
A LOCOMOTIVE, AN IRON BOX THAT RUNS ON STEAM...
OH, WOW!
WHAT?
YOU'VE NEVER SEEN ONE BEFORE?
COUGH
ゴホ
ゴホ
COUGH
NEVER!
THE WORLD IS FULL OF THINGS I'VE NEVER SEEN.
TOO CLOSE, BOY...

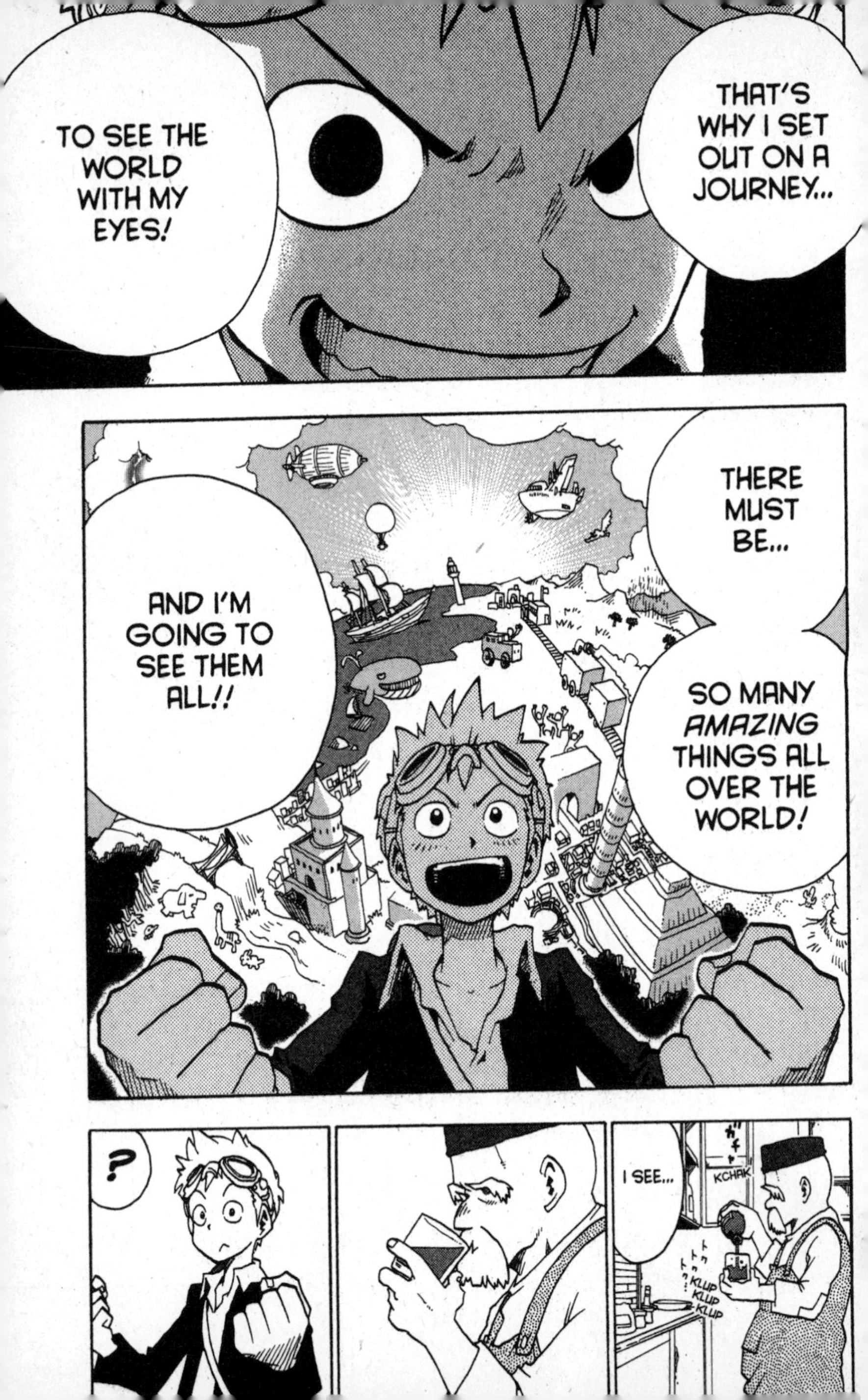
THAT'S WHY I SET OUT ON A JOURNEY...
TO SEE THE WORLD WITH MY EYES!
THERE MUST BE...
SO MANY *AMAZING* THINGS ALL OVER THE WORLD!
AND I'M GOING TO SEE THEM ALL!!
I SEE...
KCHAK
KLUP KLUP KLUP
?

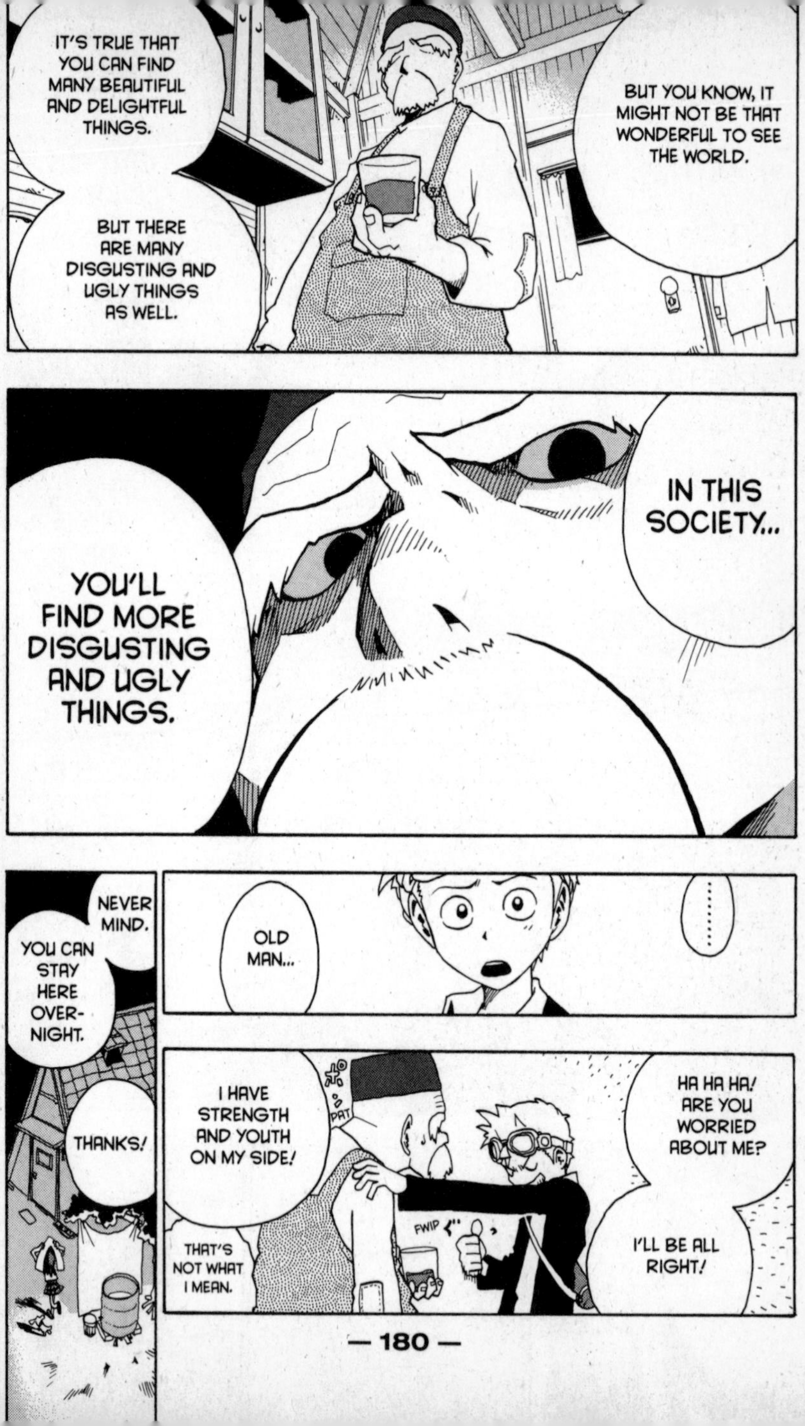
BUT YOU KNOW, IT MIGHT NOT BE THAT WONDERFUL TO SEE THE WORLD.
IT'S TRUE THAT YOU CAN FIND MANY BEAUTIFUL AND DELIGHTFUL THINGS.
BUT THERE ARE MANY DISGUSTING AND UGLY THINGS AS WELL.
IN THIS SOCIETY...
YOU'LL FIND MORE DISGUSTING AND UGLY THINGS.
......
OLD MAN...
HA HA HA! ARE YOU WORRIED ABOUT ME?
I'LL BE ALL RIGHT!
I HAVE STRENGTH AND YOUTH ON MY SIDE!
PAT
FWIP
THAT'S NOT WHAT I MEAN.
NEVER MIND.
YOU CAN STAY HERE OVER-NIGHT.
THANKS!

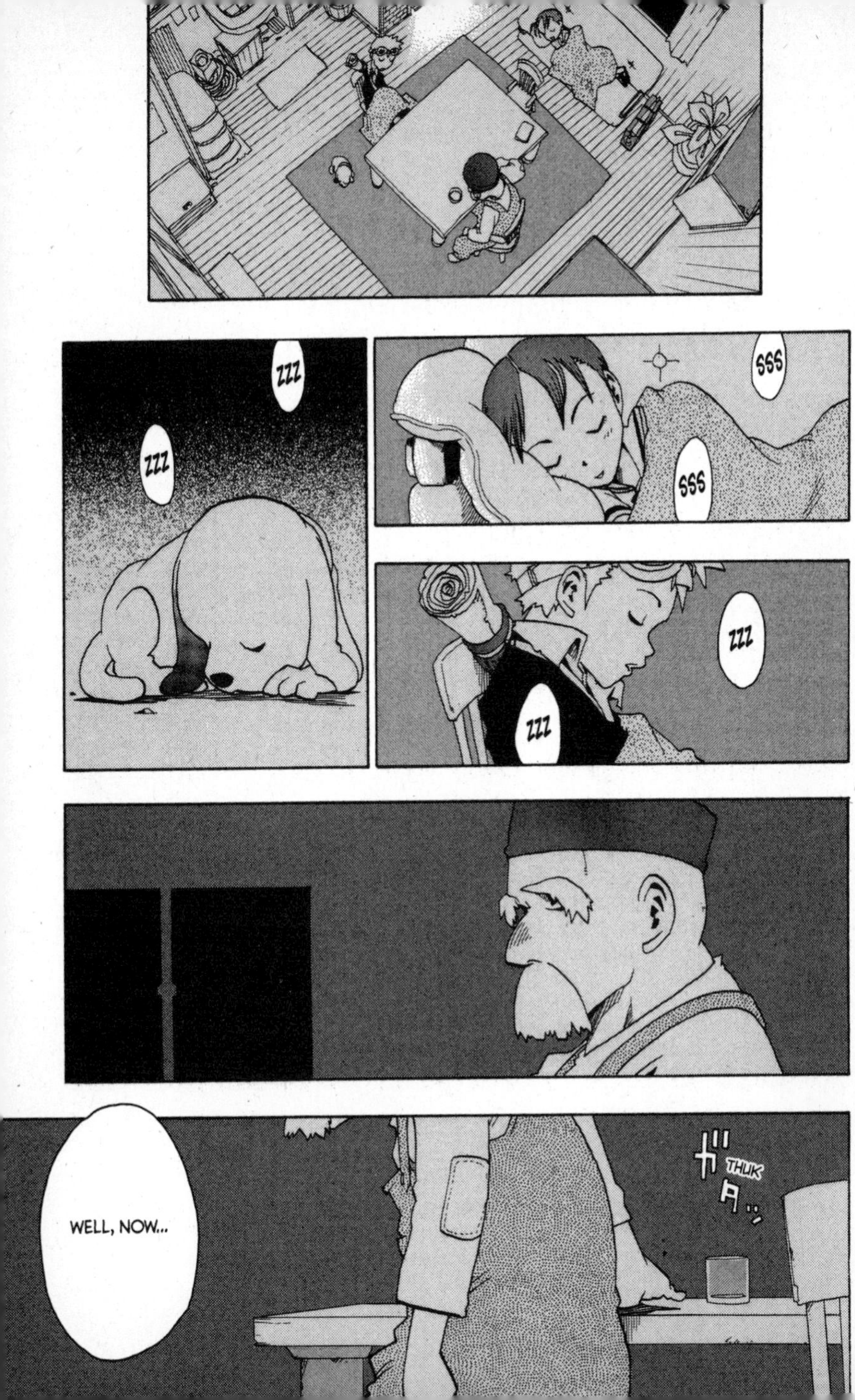
SSS
SSS
ZZZ
ZZZ
ZZZ
ZZZ
ガタッ
THUK
WELL, NOW...

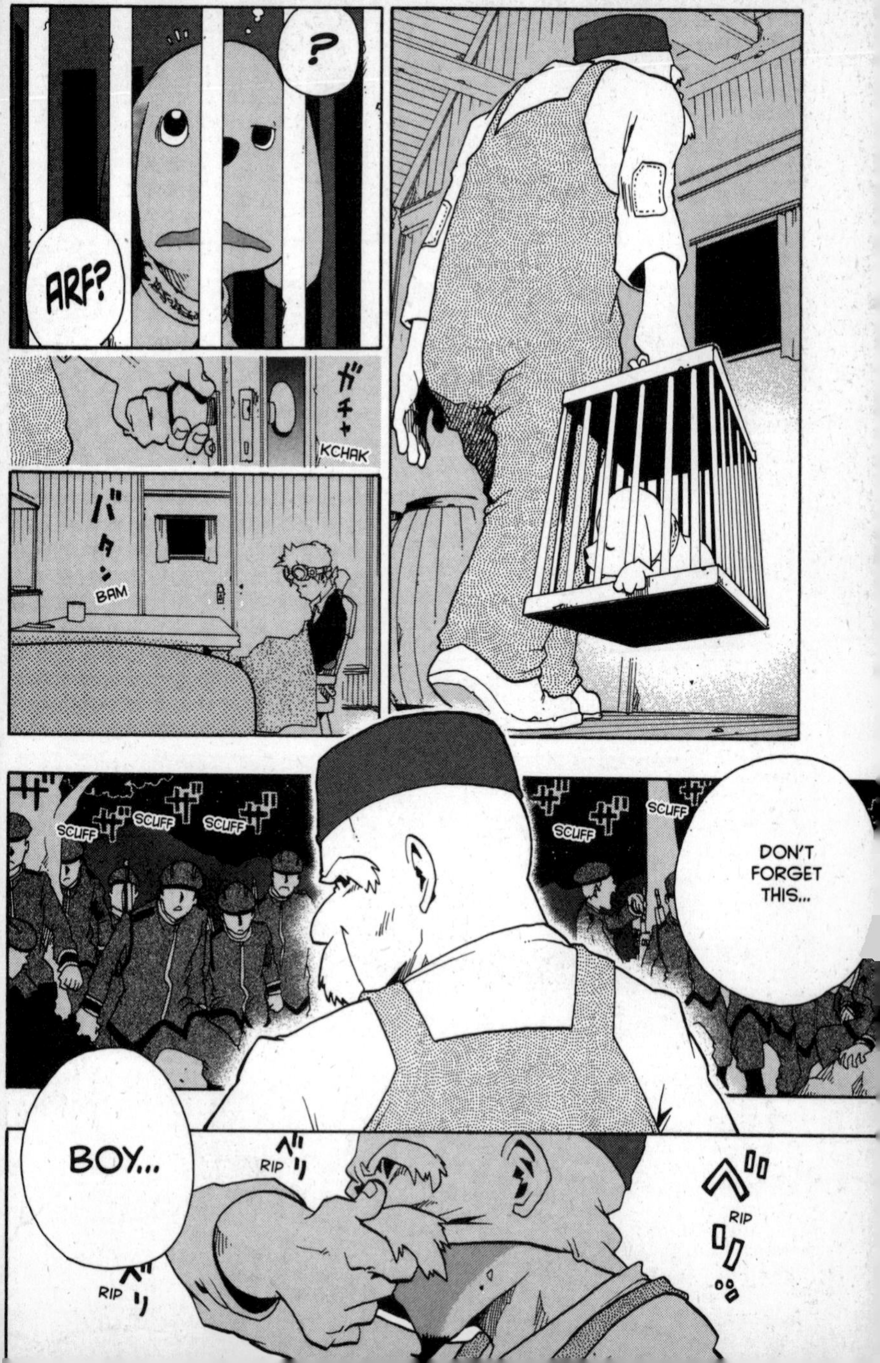

?
ARF?
ガチャ
KCHAK
バタン
BAM
SCUFF
SCUFF
DON'T FORGET THIS...
SCUFF
SCUFF
SCUFF
BOY...
ベリ
RIP
ベリ
RIP
ベリ
RIP

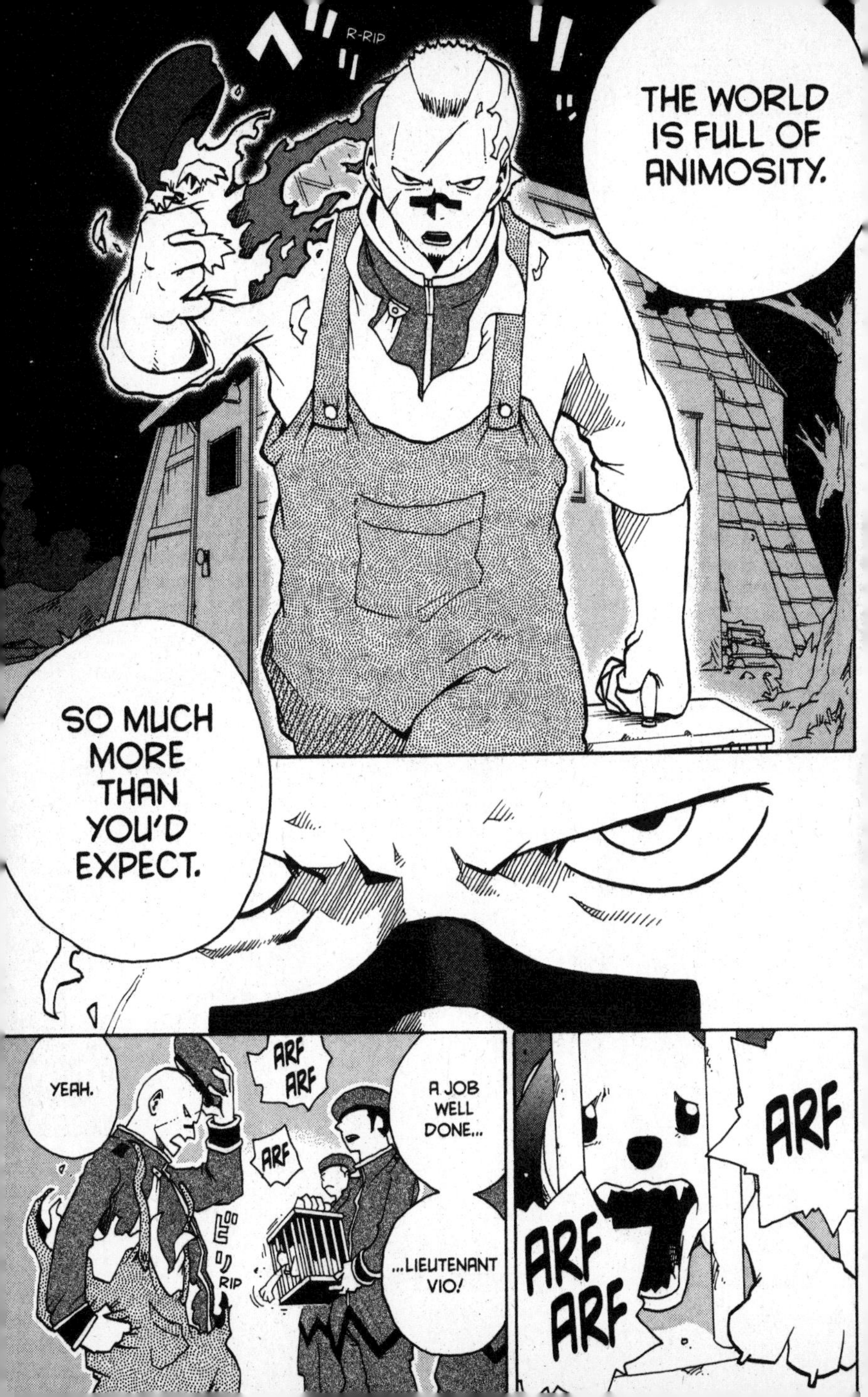
R-RIP
THE WORLD IS FULL OF ANIMOSITY.
SO MUCH MORE THAN YOU'D EXPECT.
ARF
ARF ARF ARF
A JOB WELL DONE...
...LIEUTENANT VIO!
ARF ARF
ARF
YEAH.
RIP

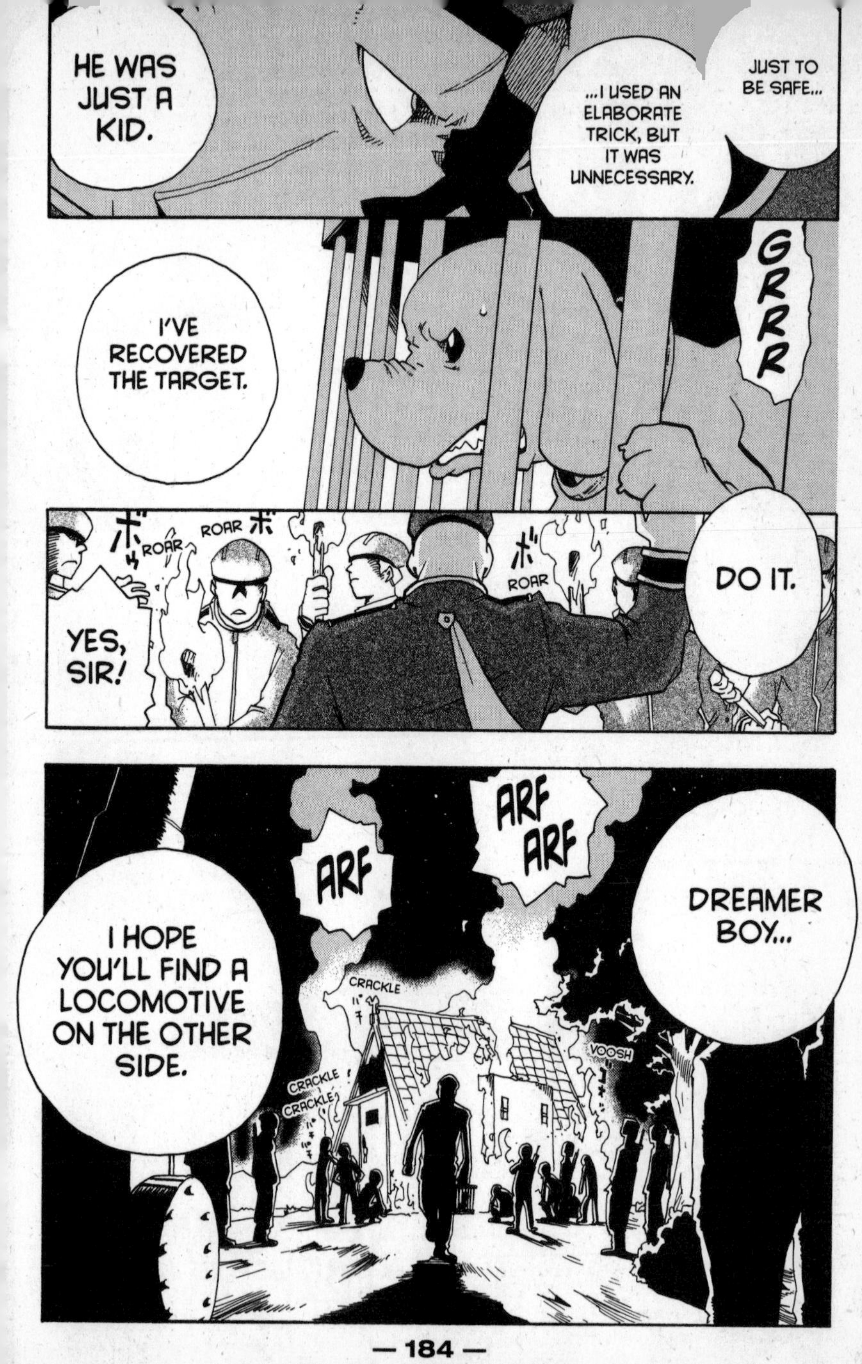
JUST TO BE SAFE...
...I USED AN ELABORATE TRICK, BUT IT WAS UNNECESSARY.
HE WAS JUST A KID.
GRRR
I'VE RECOVERED THE TARGET.
DO IT.
ROAR
ROAR
ROAR
YES, SIR!
DREAMER BOY...
ARF ARF
ARF
VOOSH
CRACKLE
CRACKLE CRACKLE
I HOPE YOU'LL FIND A LOCOMOTIVE ON THE OTHER SIDE.

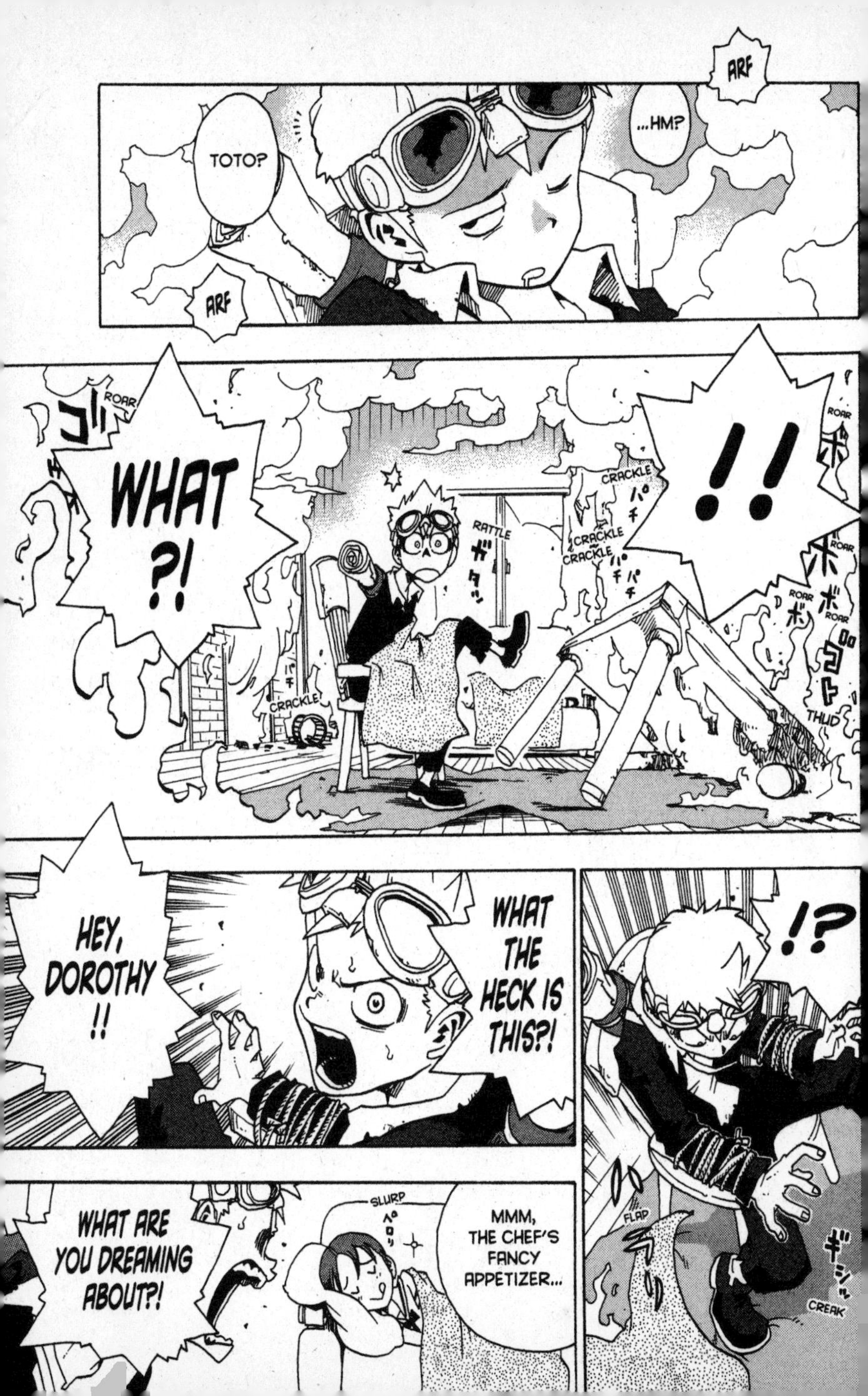
ARF
...HM?
TOTO?
ARF
!!
ROAR
ROAR
ROAR
ROAR
THUD
CRACKLE
CRACKLE
CRACKLE
RATTLE
WHAT ?!
ROAR
CRACKLE
!?
FLAP
CREAK
WHAT THE HECK IS THIS?!
HEY, DOROTHY !!
MMM, THE CHEF'S FANCY APPETIZER...
SLURP
WHAT ARE YOU DREAMING ABOUT?!

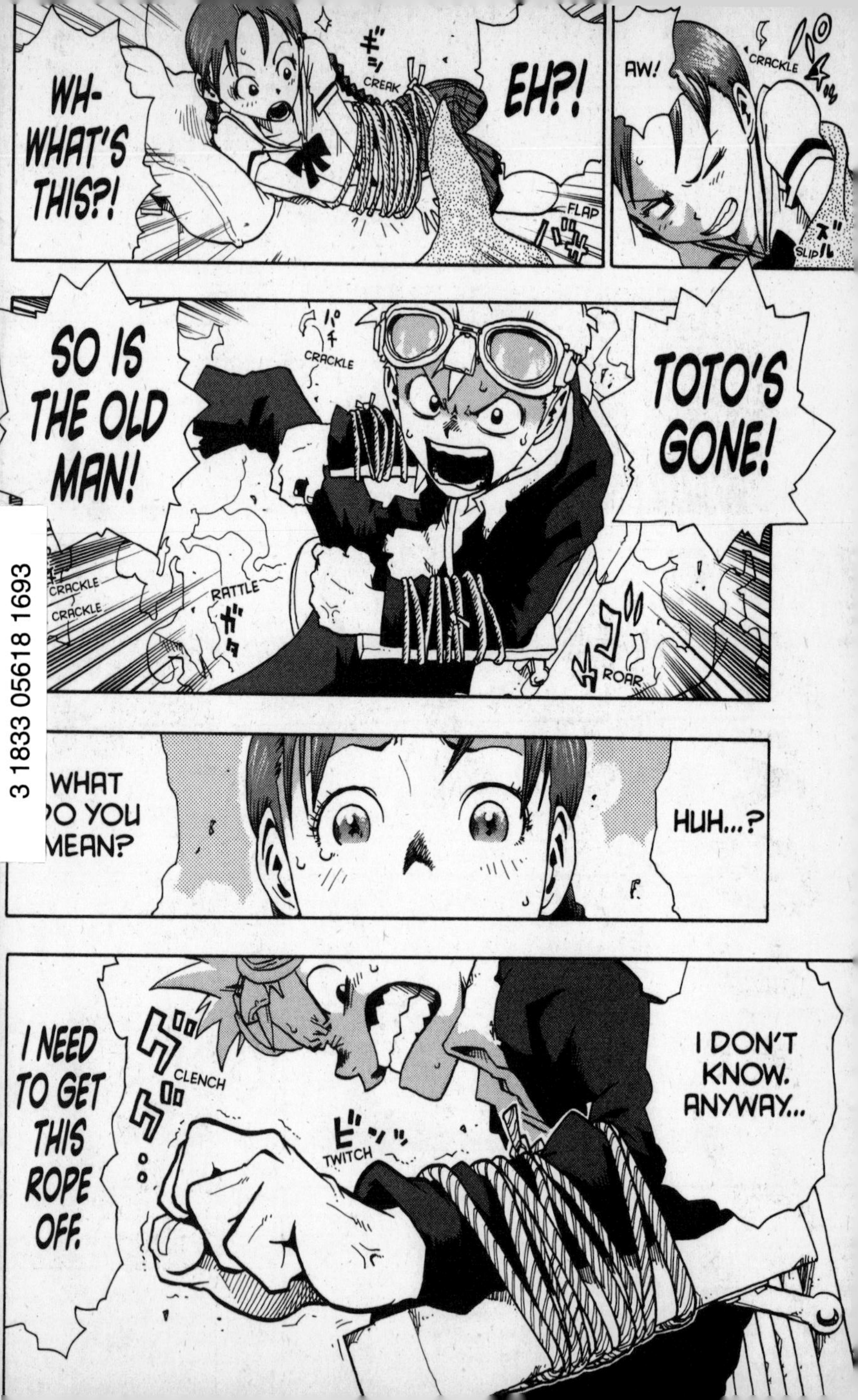
AW!
CRACKLE
SLIP
EH?!
CREAK
WH- WHAT'S THIS?!
FLAP
TOTO'S GONE!
ROAR
CRACKLE
SO IS THE OLD MAN!
RATTLE
CRACKLE
CRACKLE
HUH...?
WHAT DO YOU MEAN?
I DON'T KNOW. ANYWAY...
TWITCH
CLENCH
I NEED TO GET THIS ROPE OFF.

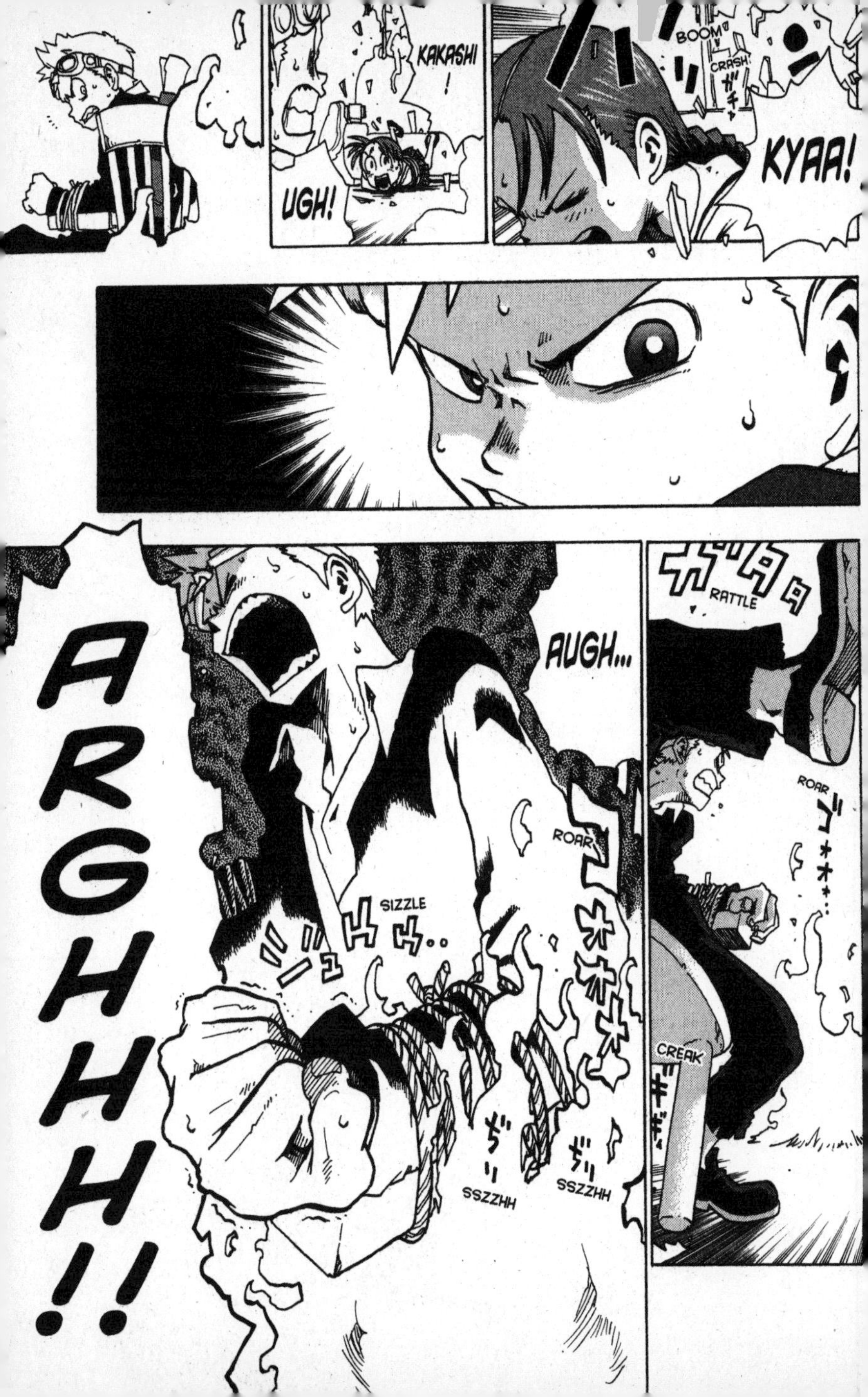

BOOM
CRASH
KYAA!
KAKASHI!
UGH!
RATTLE
ROAR
CREAK
AUGH...
ROAR
SIZZLE
SSZZHH
SSZZHH
ARGHHH!!

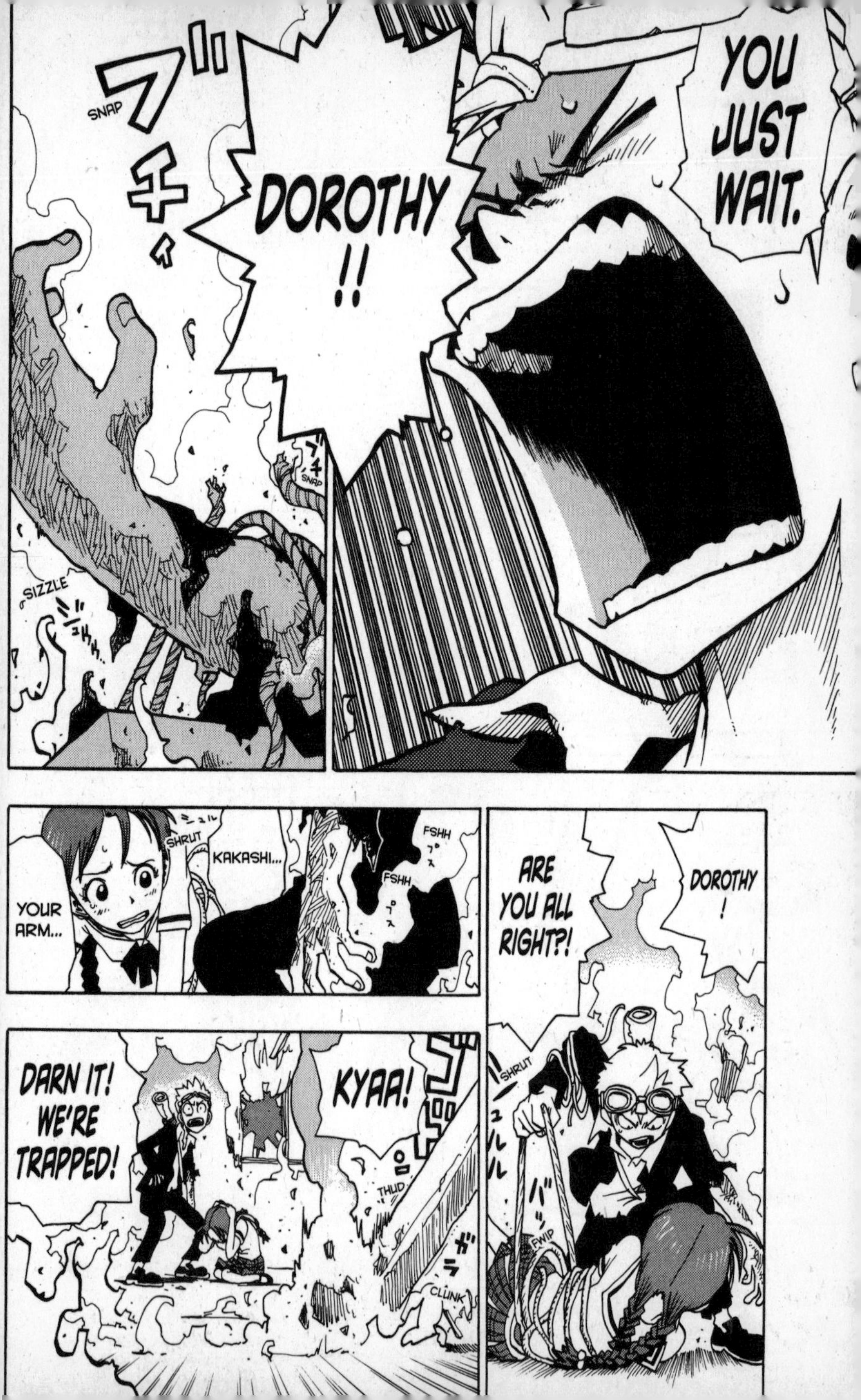
YOU JUST WAIT.
DOROTHY !!
SNAP
SNAP
SIZZLE
DOROTHY !
ARE YOU ALL RIGHT?!
SHRUT
FWIP
SHRUT
KAKASHI...
YOUR ARM...
FSHH
FSHH
KYAA!
DARN IT! WE'RE TRAPPED!
THUD
CLUNK

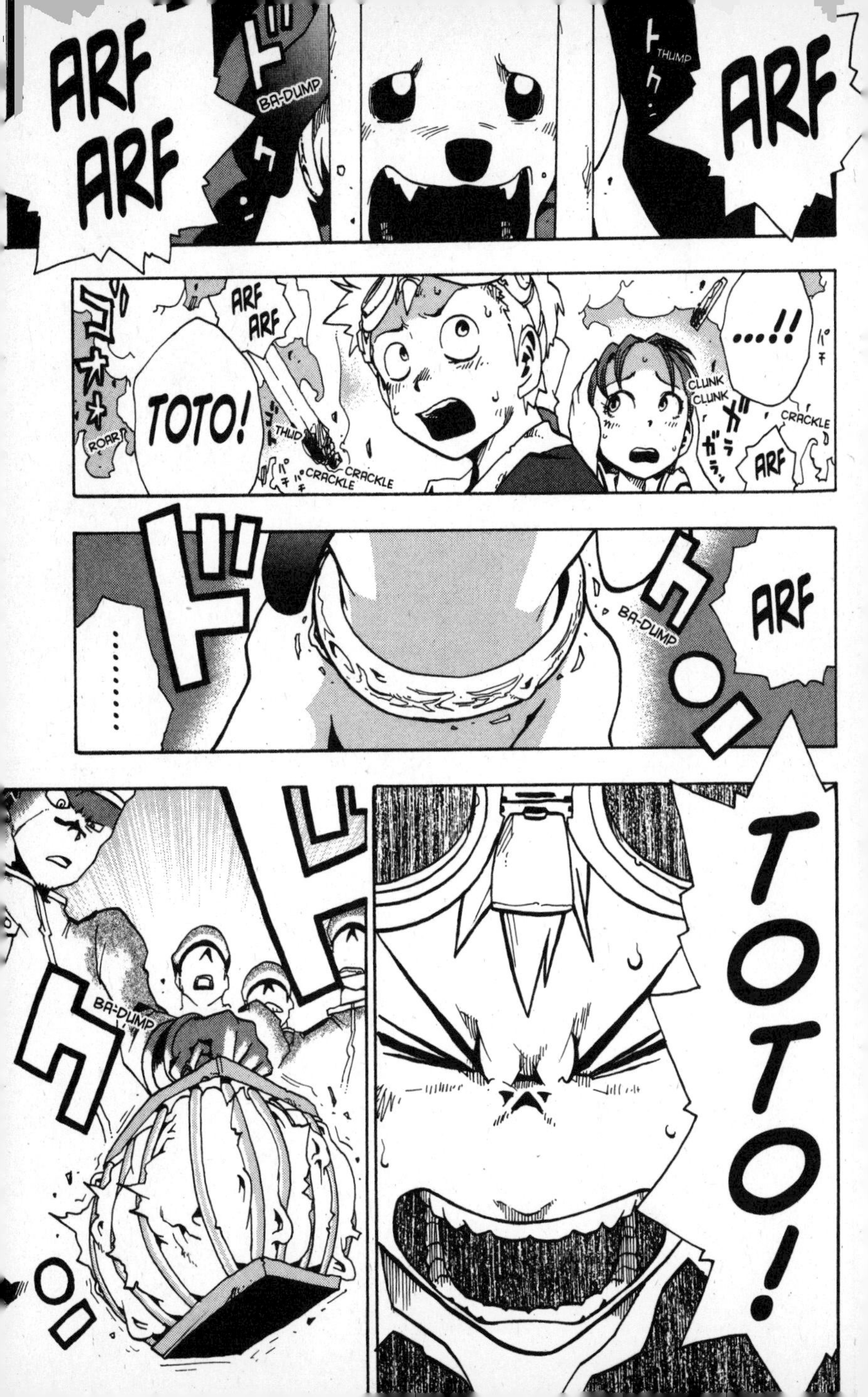
ARF
THUMP
BA-DUMP
ARF ARF
...!!
CLUNK CLUNK
CRACKLE
ARF
ARF ARF
TOTO!
ROAR
THUD
CRACKLE
CRACKLE
ARF
BA-DUMP
......
TOTO!
BA-DUMP

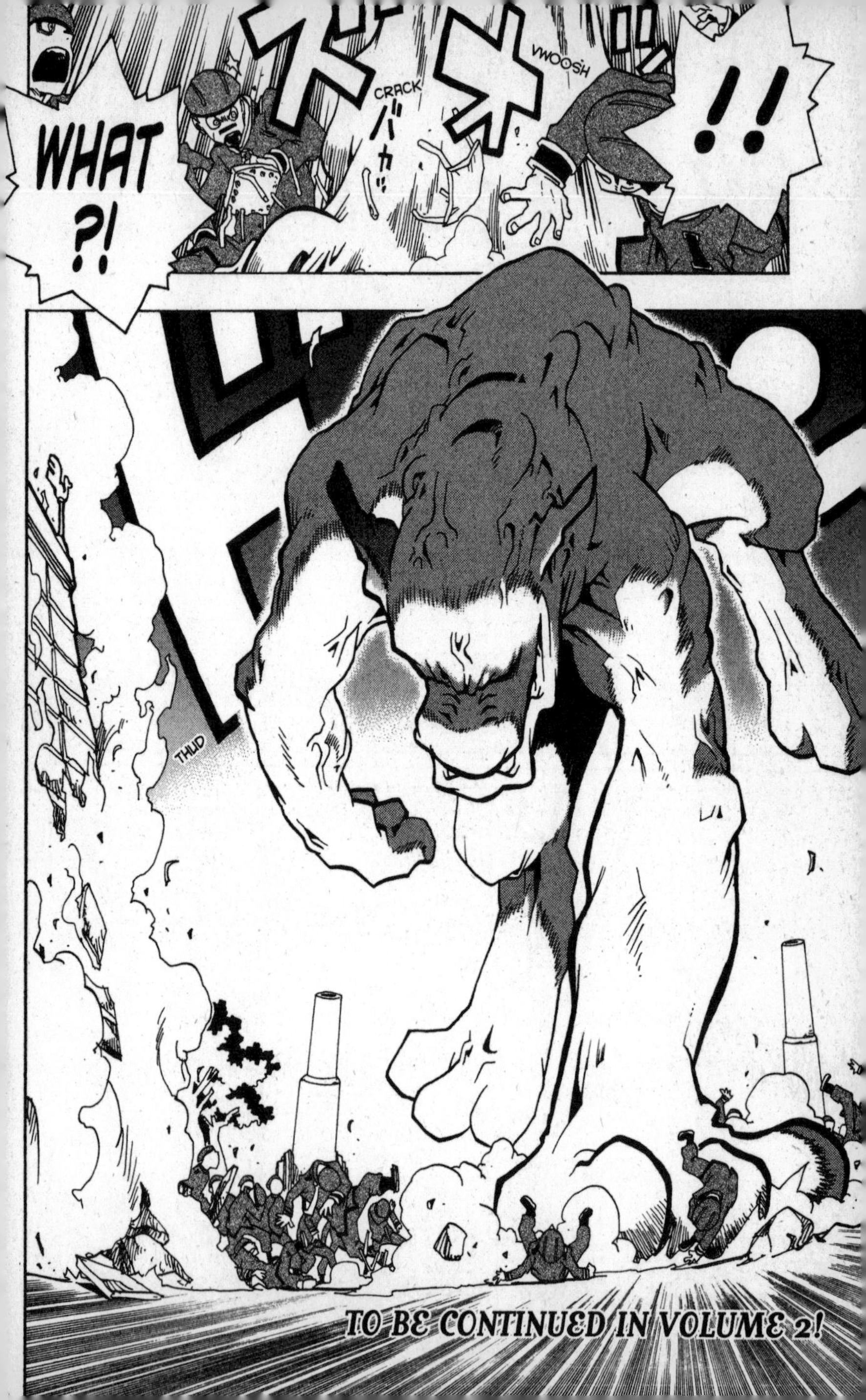
!!
VWOOSH
CRACK
バカッ
WHAT ?!
THUD
TO BE CONTINUED IN VOLUME 2!

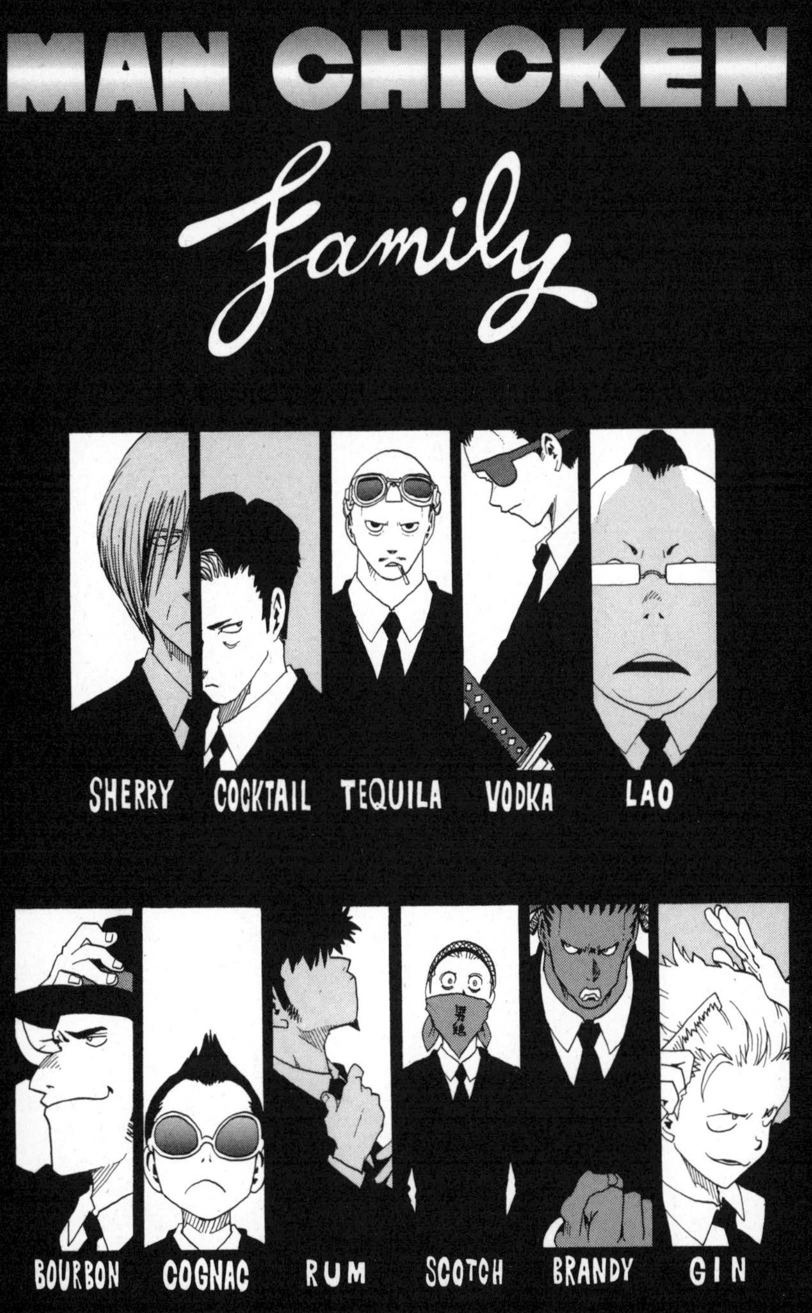
MAN CHICKEN
Family
SHERRY
COCKTAIL
TEQUILA
VODKA
LAO
BOURBON
COGNAC
RUM
SCOTCH
BRANDY
GIN

Translation Notes

Japanese is a tricky language for most Westerners, and translation is often more an art than a science. For your edification and reading pleasure, here are notes on some of the places where we could have gone in a different direction or where a Japanese cultural reference is used.

Kyaa

Kyaa is a girlish scream. It can be a lighthearted squeal of delight, but it can also indicate fear or surprise. From time to time, you'll hear Dorothy squealing, "*Kyaa!*"

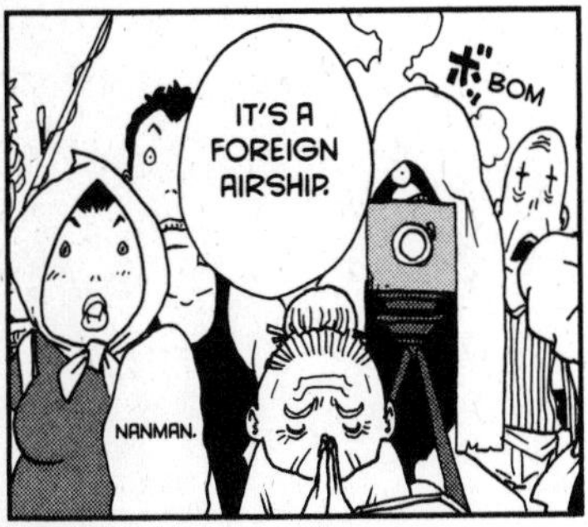
BOM
IT'S A FOREIGN AIRSHIP.
NANMAN.

Nanman, *page 26*

Nanman, short for *nanmanda* and an alternative translation for *namuamidabutsu*, is a Buddhist prayer whose meaning is similar to the Christian prayer "Lord have mercy on me."

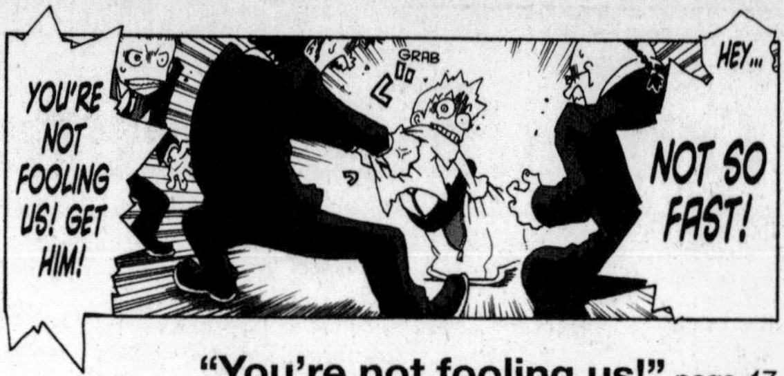
HEY...
NOT SO FAST!
GRAB
YOU'RE NOT FOOLING US! GET HIM!

"You're not fooling us!" *page 47*

Kakashi tried to find his way out of trouble by greeting the bandits with a nod before returning to the luggage.

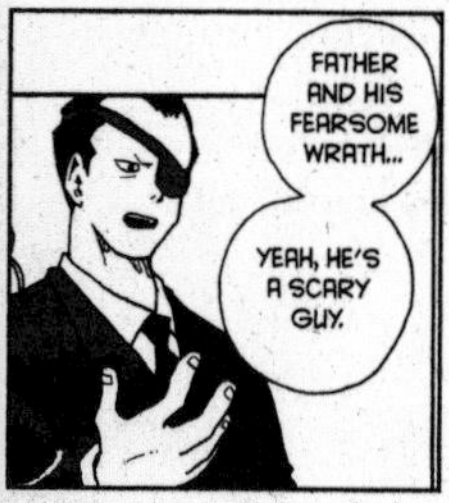
FATHER AND HIS FEARSOME WRATH...
YEAH, HE'S A SCARY GUY.

"Father and his fearsome wrath..." *page 93*

Vodka is actually saying, "Earthquake, lightning, fire, and father," a Japanese phrase that expresses a fear of great and awesome powers.

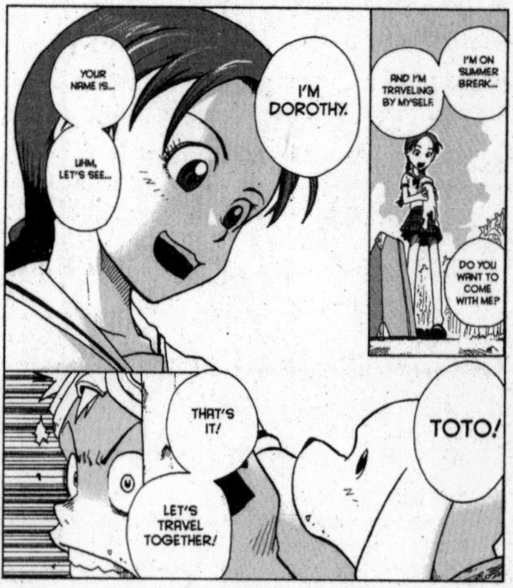
I'M ON SUMMER BREAK...
AND I'M TRAVELING BY MYSELF.
DO YOU WANT TO COME WITH ME?
YOUR NAME IS...
UHM, LET'S SEE...
I'M DOROTHY.
TOTO!
THAT'S IT!
LET'S TRAVEL TOGETHER!

Dorothy and Toto, *page 145*

Fans of classic Hollywood cinema or children's literature will probably get a little thrill of anticipation from this panel. Dorothy and Toto, of course, are characters from *The Wizard of Oz*, which was both a famous book and film. This is the first of many references to this story that you'll find in these pages.

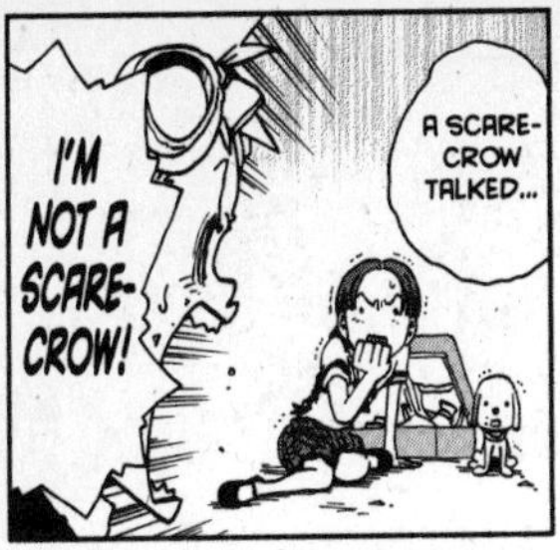
A SCARE-CROW TALKED...
I'M NOT A SCARE-CROW!

Named after a scarecrow, *page 147*

Kakashi is not just our intrepid hero's name; it also means "scarecrow" in Japanese. And allusion alert: The first companion that Dorothy meets on her journey in *The Wizard of Oz* is a magical talking scarecrow.

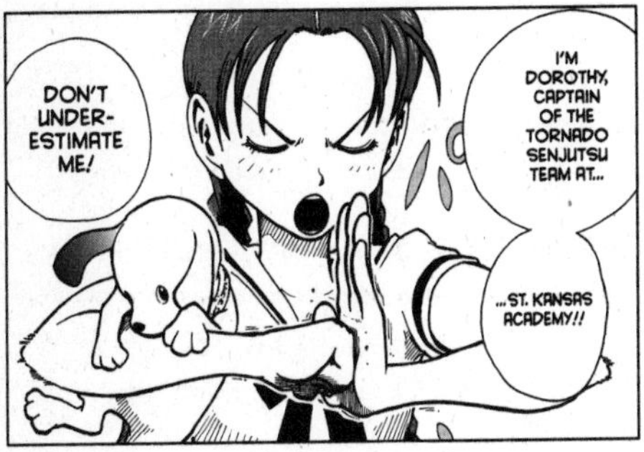
I'M DOROTHY, CAPTAIN OF THE TORNADO SENJUTSU TEAM AT...
...ST. KANSAS ACADEMY!!
DON'T UNDER-ESTIMATE ME!

Tornado *Senjutsu*, *page 158*

Tornado *senjutsu* is a martial art that relies on tornado-like spin techniques. This is really an appropriate school of martial arts for Dorothy as in *The Wizard of Oz* Dorothy is transported to the land of Oz by a tornado. So this Dorothy uses a martial art that employs tornado-like spin techniques.

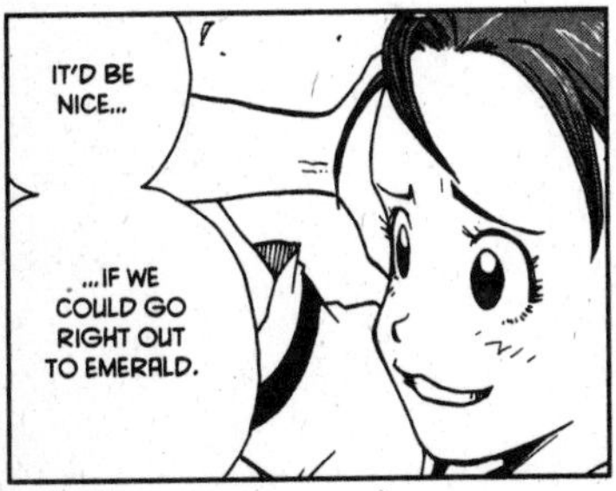
IT'D BE NICE...
...IF WE COULD GO RIGHT OUT TO EMERALD.

Emerald, *page 162*

Another *Wizard of Oz* reference: Getting to Emerald City was also Dorothy's goal in that story.

Preview of volume 2

We're pleased to present you with a preview of volume 2.
Please check our website (www.delreymanga.com) to see when this volume
will be available in English. For now you'll have to make do with Japanese!

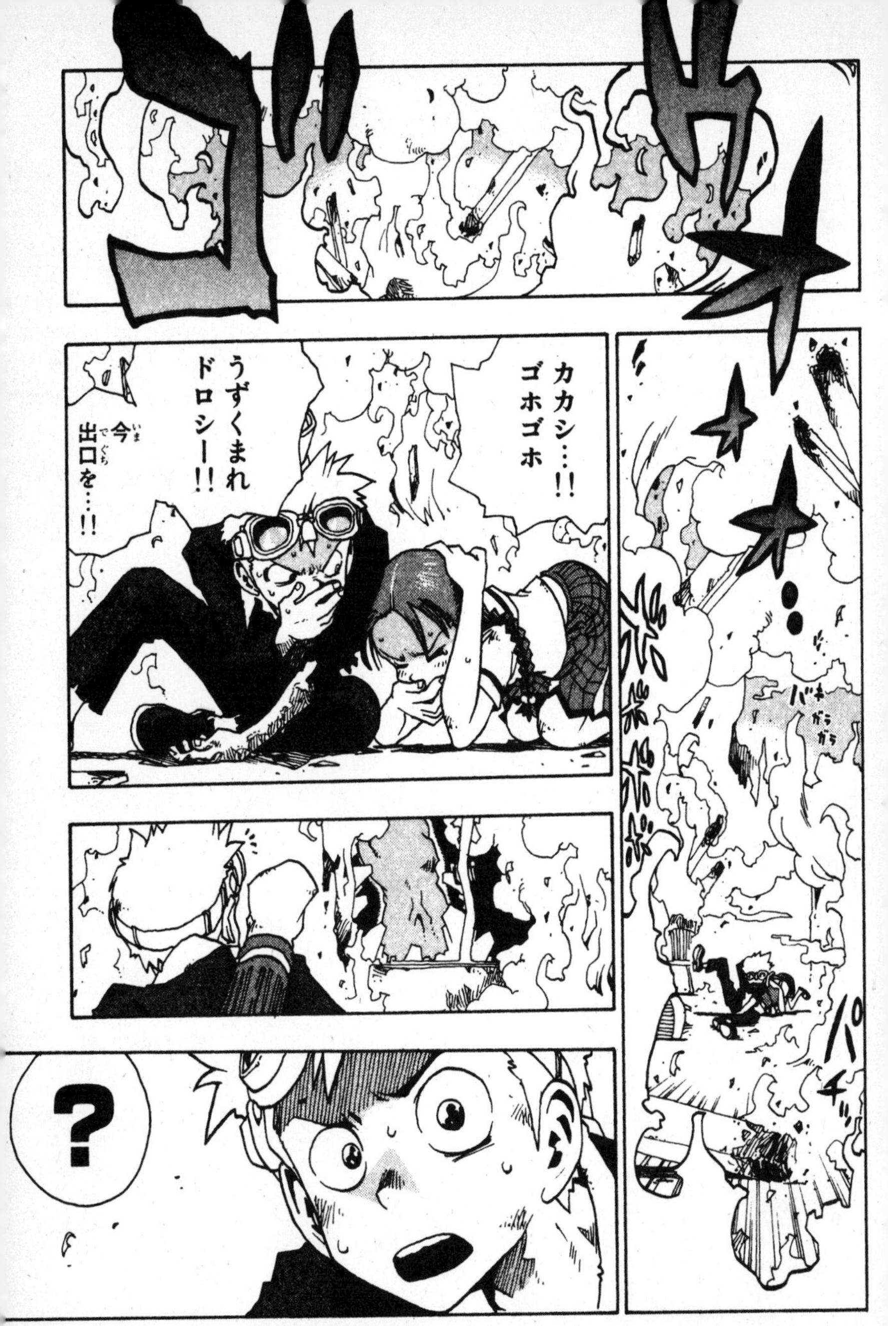
バキ
ガラ
ガラ
パチッ
カカシ…!!
ゴホゴホ
うずくまれ
ドロシー!!
今出口を…!!
?

第5話 魔犬の正体

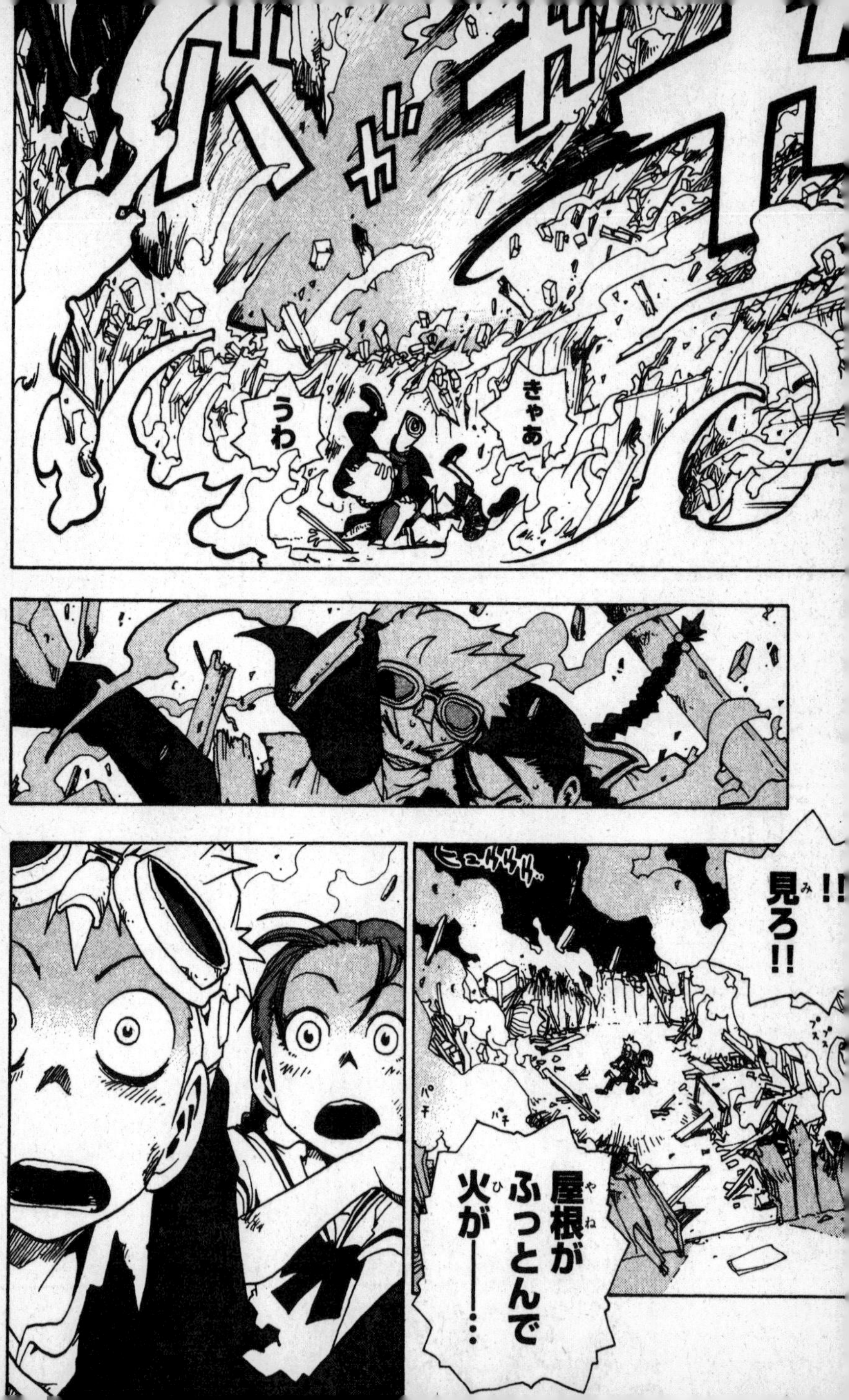
きゃあ
うわ
!!見ろ!!
屋根がふっとんで火が——…

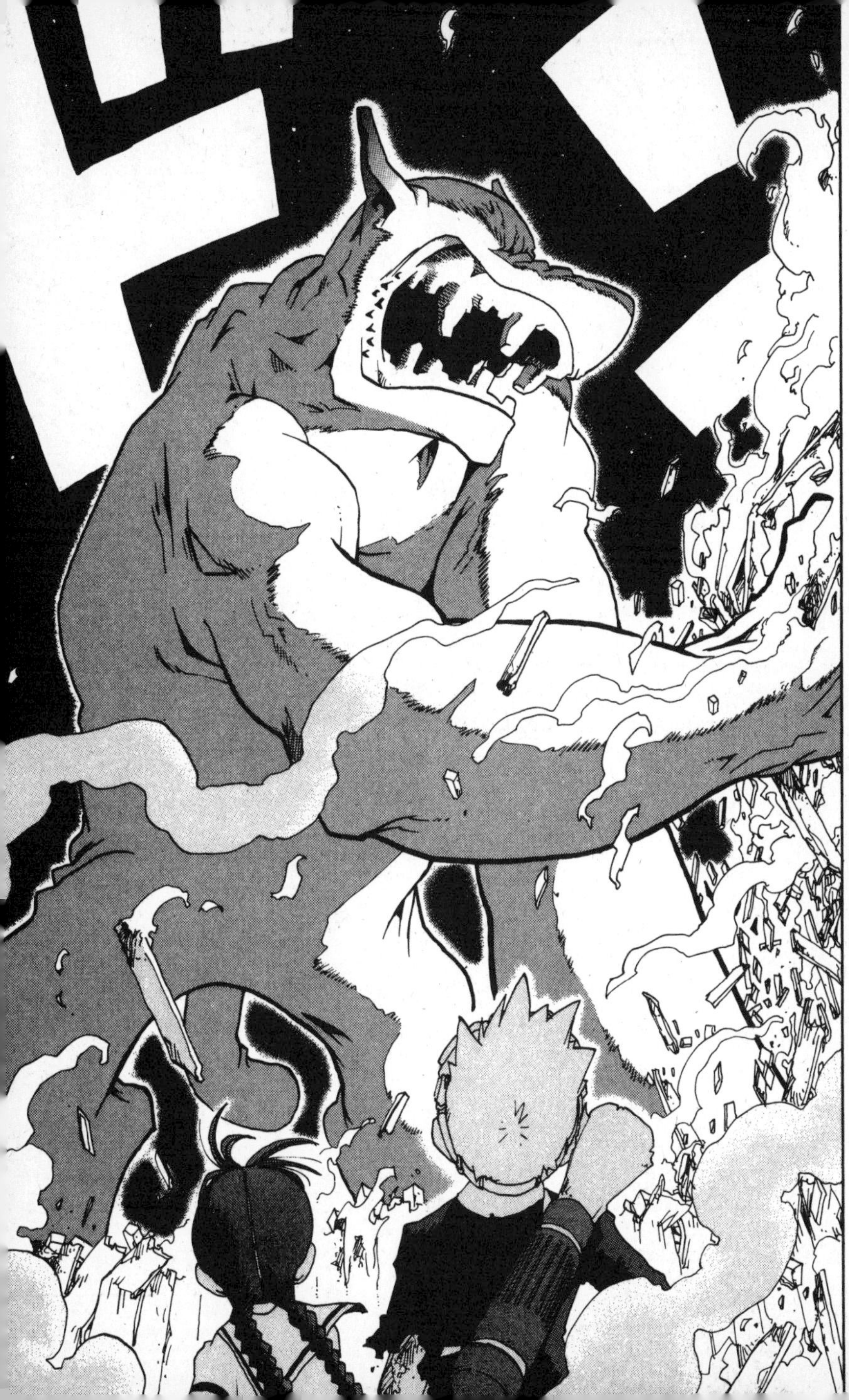

SHIKI TSUKAI

MANGA BY TORU ZEKU
ART BY YUNA TAKANAGI

DEFENDING THE NATURAL ORDER OF THE UNIVERSE!

The *shiki tsukai* are "Keepers of the Seasons"—magical warriors pledged to defend the planet's natural order against those who would threaten it.

When 14-year-old Akira Kizuki joins the *shiki tsukai*, he knows that it'll be a difficult life. But with his new friends and mentors, he's up to the challenge!

Special extras in each volume! Read them all!

VISIT WWW.DELREYMANGA.COM TO:
• Read sample pages
• View release date calendars for upcoming volumes
• Sign up for Del Rey's free manga e-newsletter
• Find out the latest about new Del Rey Manga series

RATING T AGES 13+

DEL REY MANGA
The Otaku's Choice.™

DRAGON EYE

BY KAIRI FUJIYAMA

HUMANITY'S SECRET WEAPON

Dracules—bloodthirsty, infectious monsters—have hunted human beings to the brink of extinction. Only the elite warriors of the VIUS Squad stand as humanity's last best hope.

Young Leila Mikami is one of the squad's most promising recruits, but she's not only training to battle the Dracules, she's determined to find the magical Dragon Eye, a weapon that will make her the most powerful warrior in the world.

Special extras in each volume! Read them all!

TOMARE!
STOP

You're going the wrong way!

MANGA IS A COMPLETELY DIFFERENT TYPE OF READING EXPERIENCE.

TO START AT THE *BEGINNING*, GO TO THE *END*!

That's right!

Authentic manga is read the traditional Japanese way—from right to left, exactly the opposite of how American books are read. It's easy to follow: Just go to the other end of the book, and read each page—and each panel—from right side to left side, starting at the top right. Now you're experiencing manga as it was meant to be!